FEDERAL

TAX RESEARCH

GUIDE TO

MATERIALS AND TECHNIQUES

By

GAIL LEVIN RICHMOND

Professor and Associate Dean
Nova Southeastern University Shepard Broad Law Center

SEVENTH EDITION

UNIVERSITY TEXTBOOK SERIES

New York, New York

FOUNDATION PRESS

2007

© 1990, 1997, 2002 FOUNDATION PRESS
© 2007 By FOUNDATION PRESS
  395 Hudson Street
  New York, NY 10014
  Phone Toll Free 1–877–888–1330
  Fax (212) 367–6799
  foundation–press.com

Printed in the United States of America

ISBN 978–1–59941–217–7

TEXT IS PRINTED ON 10% POST CONSUMER RECYCLED PAPER

To

Henry and Amy Richmond

PREFACE

In 1975 I first offered a Tax Practice Seminar involving current issues in taxation. Students selected issues and presented their findings as ruling requests, audit protest memoranda, and statements before congressional committees. After being deluged with requests for library tours, I consulted the standard legal research texts to compile readings describing the available materials. Much to my surprise, I discovered those texts devoted little, if any, space to materials commonly used for tax research. This text is an outgrowth of my 1975 library tours.

Research techniques are highly personalized. While the format of this text reflects my own preferences, it can be adapted to almost any variation the user may devise. Although I use it most frequently as an instructional guide for students, I know of many practitioners who have used it as an aid to finding materials.

The problems at the end of most chapters cover both historical materials and fairly recent items. Both types have value as teaching tools. Most problems involving recent law can be solved using electronic sources; those problems enhance or introduce online and CD/DVD research skills. Historical materials appear for a different reason. Because many electronic databases omit coverage of older materials, those problems force users to consult print or microform materials. Because electronic searches may involve usage fees, users who have access to print materials should be able to use them in situations where such use is cost effective.

Every new edition benefits from suggestions made by numerous tax professors, practitioners, and librarians. Library staff members at my own institution are particularly generous with their time and with their budget allocations. I could not describe so many items were they not committed to maintaining an excellent tax collection.

I wish to acknowledge the assistance of Lynda Harris and Jo Eterno, who deterred visitors to my office during this revision's final weeks. My research assistant, Paul Anderson, helped at various stages in this revision.

GAIL LEVIN RICHMOND

Fort Lauderdale, Florida
November 2006

SUMMARY OF CONTENTS

TABLE OF CONTENTS

FEDERAL

TAX RESEARCH

GUIDE TO

MATERIALS AND TECHNIQUES

SEVENTH EDITION

PART ONE

INTRODUCTION TO TAX RESEARCH

CHAPTER 1. OVERVIEW

SECTION A. INTRODUCTION

This text has four functions. First, it describes primary and secondary sources of federal tax law. Second, it presents information about services containing these sources. Third, it discusses evaluating and updating the results of your research. Fourth, and perhaps most important, it includes problems you can solve using these sources. In carrying out these functions, this text builds on material taught in a general legal research and writing, or lawyering skills, class.

Many attorneys believe tax research has nothing in common with traditional legal research, but that belief is erroneous. As is true in other areas of the law, tax research generally begins with a problem. To solve that problem, you must (1) determine the relevant law; (2) find that law; (3) update your findings and reconcile conflicting findings; and (4) communicate your conclusions. In other words, you can use techniques mastered in a basic legal research course. Likewise, you can often use traditional legal research sources in solving tax research problems.[1]

Even if you can use traditional methods and sources, you will probably prefer using materials that focus on taxation. Most library collections contain tax-oriented materials but differ in how they shelve them. Many libraries shelve them together in a "tax alcove." Other libraries group some tax-oriented materials (e.g., looseleaf services, treatises, and legislative histories) together and shelve others (e.g., tax-oriented periodicals) in the general collection. Even if dispersed throughout the collection, tax research sources are no more difficult to locate or use than are traditional research tools.

Electronic research follows a similar pattern. You can select from general services (e.g., Westlaw) that include tax libraries, or you can use services (e.g., Tax Research NetWork and Checkpoint) that focus on tax materials.

Because there are so many available materials, a library or database

---

[1] Because I assume users have some familiarity with traditional legal research tools, this text devotes relatively little space to such items. In some instances, particularly if a library lacks a tax-oriented tool, you may need to consult traditional materials.

may lack some materials discussed in this text or may contain materials omitted here. Fortunately, many alternative sources cover primary and secondary sources. Because it focuses on the types of materials available, this text should help you conduct successful tax research in virtually any law library or electronic resource.

SECTION B. EXTERNAL FACTORS AFFECTING RESEARCH

Three phenomena affect the research process: proliferation of sources; technological change; and publishing industry consolidation.

The number of primary and secondary authorities continually expands. Since this text's first edition, for example, the Internal Revenue Service began issuing additional types of guidance and stopped issuing other items. Litigation resulted in the release of other, previously unavailable, IRS items. In addition, the Tax Court began public release of Summary Opinions. Additional law reviews focusing on tax are being published.

Technology, particularly CD and DVD materials, web-based research sites, and even blogs, enhances the research process by covering numerous sources and allowing for easy database searching. Although some online sites require subscriptions, many others offer free access to materials. The federal government has been quite active in providing free online access to primary source materials and in making its sites more user-friendly.

Finally, the publishing industry continues to consolidate. Several once-independent companies are now commonly owned.[2] In addition, many services have been renamed, eliminated, or limited to electronic format. No one knows when this process will end. Because I focus on general tax research principles, you should be able to adapt your research strategy to the appearance of new materials and the disappearance of old ones.

SECTION C. FORMAT OF THIS TEXT

1. Listing and Describing Sources

Because several research tools contain more than one type of authority, I could discuss them in multiple sections of this text. In most instances, I

---

[2] Appendix E lists commonly owned publishers.

instead describe each tool once, generally in Parts Five and Six.[3] Parts Two through Four discuss the available primary sources, list research tools containing them, and cross-reference to descriptions in Parts Five and Six. This format avoids unnecessary repetition and allows you to gain familiarity with all the features of a particular tool in one place.

A caveat is in order. Neither my descriptions nor the illustrations can substitute for the information contained in a service's user's guide. This is particularly important for electronic services, which vary in their search command structures and continually change both coverage dates and sources included. Pathfinders and other library-prepared reference materials are also useful guides.

2. Problem Assignments

Most chapters include short problems. Locating the primary source materials you need for solving problems in Parts One through Four generally requires using materials described in Parts Five and Six. You should consult those descriptions on an as-needed basis. Although you can easily solve many of the problems using electronic sources, you may need to use print or microform materials when you search for older items.

3. Illustrations and Tables

Illustrations appear throughout this text. Because I obtained many of them through scanning or using a print screen function, the font or text size may differ slightly from a publisher's original version. The final product is close to the original and should not inconvenience or confuse researchers.

Illustrations are designed to show primary and secondary source material as it appears in the source from which it is excerpted. Tables compile useful information about particular topics.

Because I refer to some illustrations and tables in more than one chapter, I numbered them by chapter (e.g., Illustration 3-1; Table 5-3) to make them easier to locate.

4. Bold Face and Arrows

To emphasize terms discussed in this text, I put them in bold face type. Arrows (→) indicate discussion relating to an illustration or table.

---

[3] I describe a source in Parts Two through Four if it used for a single purpose. American Federal Tax Reports, for example, is discussed in Chapter 11.

5. Citation Format

Legal citation format is prescribed in a variety of sources, including TaxCite, The Bluebook, and the ALWD Citation Manual.[4] These sources differ in their treatment of various items, and their citation format often differs from that used by the material's original publisher.

Citation differences are particularly notable for IRS material. For example, TaxCite uses P.L.R. to cite private letter rulings (e.g., P.L.R. 2006-40-003). The Bluebook uses I.R.S. Priv. Ltr. Rul. (e.g., Priv. Ltr. Rul. 2006-40-003). The ALWD Manual uses either P.L.R. or Priv. Ltr. Rul. (e.g., P.L.R. 2006-40-003 or Priv. Ltr. Rul. 2006-40-003). Although all three hyphenate the ruling numbers, the IRS itself does not use hyphens and is likely to use PLR rather than the other identifiers. If you search for 200640003, you can easily find it online; if you search for 2006-40-003, you may be less successful. Thus, it is critical that you determine which format(s) the service you use recognize. In this regard, print services are likely to use a single format; some online services recognize more than one format.

Because citation manuals, law reviews, and courts use different citation formats, Appendix B includes several variations for selected primary sources. Before submitting your research, remember to format each citation in the style your recipient mandates.

Note that I do not italicize signals (such as "see" and "compare") or Latin terms (such as "i.e." and "e.g.") in text or footnotes. Unless they are part of a footnote citation, I also eliminated italicization for the names of primary and secondary source materials and other research tools (such as United States Code, OneDisc, and Westlaw). I made this decision primarily to enhance readability. It does not reflect a preference for a particular citation system.

6. Bibliography

This primary purpose of this text is to familiarize you with various types of authority and how to find them. If you are interested in

---

[4] TAXCITE: A FEDERAL TAX CITATION AND REFERENCE MANUAL (1995) (compiled by The Virginia Tax Review, Tax Law Review, and the ABA Section of Taxation; the ABA group was assisted by student editors of The Tax Lawyer); THE BLUEBOOK: A UNIFORM SYSTEM OF CITATION (18th ed. 2005) (compiled by the editors of the Columbia Law Review, Harvard Law Review, University of Pennsylvania Law Review, and The Yale Law Journal); ALWD CITATION MANUAL: A PROFESSIONAL SYSTEM OF CITATION app. 7 (3d ed. 2006) (compiled by the Association of Legal Writing Directors and Darby Dickerson).

particular topics addressed in the text (for example, deference), you may find the bibliography in Appendix D useful.

7. Appendixes

Part Seven contains five Appendixes:

- Appendix A   Commonly Used Abbreviations

- Appendix B   Alternate Citation Forms

- Appendix C   Potential Research Errors

- Appendix D   Bibliography

- Appendix E   Commonly Owned Publishers

CHAPTER 2. SOURCES OF LAW

SECTION A. INTRODUCTION

Because many factors influence the process, there is no "right" way to begin and end a tax research project. Your method of attack depends on the nature of the problem and your familiarity with the subject matter. While many research efforts begin with the relevant statutory provisions, others start with explanatory materials. The appropriate ending place depends on the type of problem and the number of sources you need to consult before resolving the issues raised.

At various points between the start and finish, most research efforts involve both primary and secondary authority. Primary authority carries more weight than does secondary authority. In addition, some primary authorities carry more weight than do others.

SECTION B. PRIMARY AND SECONDARY AUTHORITIES

Primary authority emanates from a branch of government: legislative; executive (including administrative); or judicial. It includes the Constitution, statutes, treaties, Treasury regulations, Internal Revenue Service (IRS) documents, and judicial decisions. If a problem has international aspects, authorities from multiple countries or from international organizations are likely to be relevant. **Secondary authorities**—including treatises, looseleaf services, and articles— explain (and sometimes criticize) primary authorities.

Primary authorities are discussed in Parts Two through Four; Parts Five and Six cover secondary authorities and collections of primary authority documents. The legislative histories discussed in Part Two have characteristics of both primary and secondary authority.[5]

---

[5] This text describes legislative histories in the materials on primary sources because (1) they emanate from a branch of government; (2) the IRS considers them authority for avoiding the substantial understatement penalty described later in this chapter; and (3) you would consult them immediately after reading statutory text in many research efforts. Nevertheless, many legislative history documents are considered secondary sources.

Section C. Hierarchy of Authority

Primary authorities carry more weight than do secondary authorities, and some primary authorities carry more weight than do others. An authority's value varies depending upon the body reviewing it and the purpose for which it is being submitted. The subsections below, covering precedential and substantial authority, illustrate these distinctions.

1. Precedential and Persuasive Authority

The Treasury Department and IRS recognize a hierarchy of sources. Courts also value some authorities more than others. Certain holdings constitute **binding precedent**, which must be followed. Others are considered merely **persuasive** and receive little, if any, deference. Secondary sources fall into the latter category, but so do many primary sources. For example, the IRS will follow a Supreme Court decision in its dealings with other taxpayers. It may, however, choose to ignore an adverse lower court opinion and continue litigating a particular issue. The telephone tax litigation is one example of the IRS continuing to litigate an issue.[6]

An authority is not precedential just because a particular court or administrative agency issued it. The form of issuance is also important. In some instances, for example, the IRS is not bound by its own pro- nouncements. Although it issues both officially published revenue rulings and privately published letter rulings, third parties with comparable facts may rely only on the revenue rulings. In like manner, a court may refuse to treat as precedential an opinion issued by another court. These limitations are discussed further in Parts Three and Four, which cover administrative and judicial sources.

2. Substantial Authority

An authority may have value even if the IRS rejects it. First, the Service might be incorrect. A court (perhaps even the Supreme Court) may rely on the particular authority in rendering its decision. Second, the item relied upon may shield the taxpayer from the Code section

---

[6] See Notice 2006-50, 2006-25 I.R.B. 1141, in which the IRS announced it would stop litigating this issue it had lost in five appellate courts. IRS an- nouncements concerning its litigation plans are discussed in Chapters 10 and 11.

6662(b)(2) penalty for substantial understatement of income tax liability.

Section 6662(d)(2)(B)(i) waives this 20 percent penalty if the taxpayer has **substantial authority** for a position. This determination requires that the taxpayer's position be backed by recognized authority and that the authority be substantial.[7]

Treasury regulations list the following items as authority:[8]

• applicable provisions of the Internal Revenue Code and other statutory provisions;

• proposed, temporary and final regulations construing such statutes;

• revenue rulings and revenue procedures;

• tax treaties and regulations thereunder, and Treasury Department and other official explanations of such treaties;

• court cases;

• congressional intent as reflected in committee reports, joint explanatory statements of managers included in conference committee reports, and floor statements made prior to enactment by one of a bill's managers;

• General Explanations of tax legislation prepared by the Joint Committee on Taxation (the Blue Book);

• private letter rulings and technical advice memoranda issued after October 31, 1976;

• actions on decisions and general counsel memoranda issued after March 12, 1981 (as well as general counsel memoranda published in pre-1955 volumes of the Cumulative Bulletin);

---

[7] The question of whether authority is substantial might arise in a tax ethics or tax practice and procedure course.

[8] Treas. Reg. § 1.6662-4(d)(3)(iii). Taxpayers can also avoid this penalty by adequately disclosing the relevant facts if there is a reasonable basis for the tax treatment claimed. I.R.C. § 6662(d)(2)(B)(ii). The section 6662 regulations also constitute authority for avoiding the penalty imposed on tax return preparers for taking a position that does not have a realistic possibility of being sustained on the merits. See I.R.C. § 6694(a); Treas. Reg. § 1.6694-2(b).

· Internal Revenue Service information or press releases; and

· notices, announcements and other administrative pronouncements published by the Service in the Internal Revenue Bulletin.

Conclusions reached in treatises or other legal periodicals and opinions rendered by tax professionals do not constitute authority for avoiding this penalty. In addition, the regulation provides rules by which overruled and reversed items lose their status as authority.

SECTION D. PROBLEMS

Indicate whether the taxpayer avoided the substantial understatement penalty in the holding below.

1. Xcel Energy, Inc. v. United States, 98 A.F.T.R.2d 2006-5770 (D. Minn. 2006), also available at 2006 U.S. Dist. LEXIS 55202

2. Roco v. Commissioner, 121 T.C. 160 (2003), available at http://www.ustaxcourt.gov/InOpHistoric/Roco.TC.WPD.pdf

3. Technical Advice Memorandum 8936001, available at 1989 PLR LEXIS 1813.

Items for which LexisNexis cites appear are also available on Westlaw and on tax-oriented online services.

CHAPTER 3. RESEARCH PROCESS

SECTION A. RESEARCH GOALS

Your goals will influence the course your research takes and the product you produce. Are you structuring a new transaction? Are you litigating the effects of a transaction your clients already completed? Are you testifying before Congress or the Treasury Department to advocate a statutory or administrative change?

In the first situation, future legislation and regulations may be as important as existing law. Because retroactive effective dates are a fact of life, you must be able to locate pending legislation and proposed regulations. In addition, you may consider requesting a letter ruling to provide comfort that the IRS agrees with your tax analysis.

After a transaction closes, future legislation is less important.[9] Your interest may shift to judicial opinions and to cases currently being litigated. If your client's substantive position fails, you may need to locate sufficient authority to avoid the substantial understatement penalty described in Chapter 2.[10] If the client prevails, you may look for authority to justify charging part of your legal fees to the government.[11]

In testifying at congressional or Treasury Department hearings, you may want to include detailed history supporting your position. You can find previous legislative and regulatory changes and their effects by tracing rules back to their inception and reading cases and commentary about prior versions.

The above list is not exclusive. You may be researching sources for an article, bibliography, CLE presentation, or class assignment. Your assignment may be narrow in scope (e.g., go to the Tax Court website and

---

[9] But technical corrections bills may affect transactions that took place several years earlier.

[10] I.R.C. § 6662(b). In addition, you may need to avoid I.R.C. § 6694(a) preparer penalties. See also Treas. Dept. Circular 230, § 10.34 (31 C.F.R. § 10.34).

[11] I.R.C. § 7430 provides for recovery of attorneys' fees if the government's position was not substantially justified and the taxpayer meets certain other requirements.

find all opinions authored by Judge Vasquez in 2006), or it may require you to consult a variety of primary and secondary sources (e.g., research and write an article arguing for the reinstatement of income averaging). No matter what your goal is, successful research requires an ability to locate relevant sources.

SECTION B. RESEARCH METHODOLOGY

As noted in Chapter 1, tax research has much in common with the legal research techniques covered in a basic research course. Using a set of facts presented, you determine the relevant issues and ascertain any additional facts that might be important. Because a project may be completed over a period of weeks or months, you must regularly update your research.

To resolve the issues you isolate, you must locate any governing statutory language. Legislative history or administrative pronouncements would be the next step if you desire guidance in interpreting the statute. You may then search for judicial decisions interpreting the statute or administrative provisions. In addition to interpreting statutes or regulations, judges may rule on their validity. Judicial decisions may cover constitutional challenges to statutes and regulations. In addition, courts may determine whether a regulation appropriately interprets a statute. [12] If your problem involves non-U.S. source income or citizens of other countries, the research expands to include applicable treaties.

If you are familiar with the subject matter involved, you might locate all of the above items without using any secondary materials other than a citator. When you lack such familiarity, you might start your project by consulting secondary materials. Secondary materials will help you determine which Code sections are involved and provide information about the underlying issues. Looseleaf services, treatises, and periodical articles will be particularly useful for this purpose.

Various factors influence the amount of time spent using explanatory material. Clearly written statutes require less explanation than do complex ones. Older statues are likely to have more explanatory materials than newer ones. If materials discussing a statutory amendment are limited, secondary materials criticizing the original provision

---

[12] Chapters 9 and 10 discuss the degree of deference courts must give administrative determinations.

may be useful guides to the change. If the change involves a completely new Code section, the explanatory material is initially limited to congressional reports and newsletter reports.

Chapter 4 includes a hypothetical fact pattern and isolates several issues for research. That problem should assist you in approaching the variety of research tools and levels of authority involved in a tax problem.

The problem appears in a separate chapter to facilitate using it as both an introduction to the research process and as a reference tool for subsequent material. Research problems in other chapters cover particular types of authority relevant to those chapters.

SECTION C. PRINT VERSUS ELECTRONIC RESEARCH

Given the large number of materials available in both print (bound and looseleaf), microform, and electronic (DVD, CD, and online) formats, how do you decide which format to select? Although that question has no single correct answer, factors discussed in the following paragraphs and in Chapters 19 and 20 will influence your choice.[13]

1. Availability of Materials

What is available in your library? Older materials, for example, may be available only in print or in microform.[14] This is particularly true for legislative history materials. In other situations, the library may not carry print subscriptions to materials available in electronic format. Decisions not to carry can be based on shelf space and filing costs,[15] availability of similar services from another publisher, or relative lack of use by library patrons.

If you subscribe to an electronic service, to which of its files do you have access? Many CD/DVD and subscription online services have pricing options that allow access to different databases.

---

[13] The discussion in this section largely ignores microforms. See Chapter 18 for a discussion of their advantages and disadvantages.

[14] The definition of "older" varies by source. As online services expand retrospective coverage, you are more likely to find one that includes the material you seek.

[15] For example, IRS letter ruling services require extensive shelf space.

2. Updating Frequency

How often is each source updated? Some print materials are updated weekly; others receive less-frequent supplementation. CD/DVD materials are not updated more frequently than monthly; some are updated even less frequently.[16] Online databases should be updated at least as often as print sources and often are updated more frequently. Primary source materials posted by the government body that produces them may be available immediately after being issued. This is particularly true for judicial opinions available at a court's website.

3. Type of Search

Is the research best conducted based on indexes or by searching for words or concepts? Research based on particular words or concepts is probably better served by electronic media than by print sources. Electronic searching is more efficient if, for example, you are searching for a "common law" or Code section phrase or for items associated with a particular judge or attorney. It may be more efficient if you are searching for articles by author or topic. It is always more efficient for updating recent judicial decisions or administrative rulings using citators.

Before you begin researching, do you need to familiarize yourself with the topic? If so, cost constraints may cause you to start with print materials, a topic discussed in Subsection 4.

a. Words and Concepts

Judicially declared concepts such as "step-transaction doctrine" and "form over substance" are not specifically covered in citators if they are neither case names nor Code sections. You can find materials relevant to these concepts using a print source's index; you can often find them more quickly by doing an electronic search.[17] The same is true for concepts that do appear in the Code (e.g., "effectively connected").

There are two risks associated with electronic searches for a particular word. First, if you (or the service itself) make a spelling error, you may not retrieve a document even though it exists. Words with variant spellings are particularly likely to cause problems. For example,

---

[16] Infrequent updating is less of a problem if the CD/DVD includes a link to online updates.

[17] Using a print index is advisable if you don't know all the relevant words or concepts.

"includible" and "excludible" might also be spelled "includable" and "excludable." If you know a word has variant spellings, you can use wild cards (discussed in Chapters 19 and 20) in your search. A second problem relates to specificity. For example, if you search for "car," you may miss sources that discuss automobile or motor vehicle. If an electronic service has a synonym option, using it reduces the risk of this type of error.

b. Cross-References

Electronic searches are more effective than print searches if you want to know which Code sections cite other sections. Their databases are updated more frequently than are print Code cross-reference tables. In addition, because you can search directly by Code section, you do not have to worry about editorial omissions. These omissions can occur in print sources. Finally, because electronic databases include hyperlinks, you can jump directly from one Code section to another.

c. Names of Judges or Attorneys

Searches involving particular judges or attorneys are at best difficult to accomplish using print materials. Finding every case in which Judge L. Paige Marvel appeared before the Tax Court when she was in practice or in which she authored an opinion after joining the court would require reading numerous volumes of regular and memorandum decisions.[18] As illustrated below, that search can be easily accomplished electronically.[19] Online searches can be restricted by judge name, attorney name, or date. If we wanted to know whether any of these cases involved a particular topic, such as compensation, we could add that to the search terms.

Illustrations 3-1 and 3-2 illustrate Westlaw and LexisNexis searches for these decisions. Illustration 3-3 illustrates a search in the Tax Court's website. My search on October 12, 2006, yielded 117 decisions in Westlaw and 116 in LexisNexis. The documents covered 1976 through 2006. The Tax Court website (www.ustaxcourt.gov) was not as promising. Its retrospective coverage extends back only to 1995. In addition, although I requested all opinions, the results included the following message: "Over 50 Opinions matched search criteria, only first 50 displayed."

---

[18] The search would be impossible to conduct using print sources if it included Summary Opinions, which are not compiled in bound volumes. CD/DVD services can be used for this type of search only if they include the attorneys' names.

[19] These searches assume that the Tax Court has had only one Judge Marvel, but that you aren't sure how many attorneys with that last name have appeared before the court. If you are also unsure how many Judge Marvels have served on the court, you could add the judge's first name in the first search segment.

Illustration 3-1. Search in Westlaw

Search

Selected Databases

Federal Taxation - Tax Court Cases (FTX-TCT) (i)

| **Terms and Connectors** | **Natural Language** |

Search: JU(MARVEL) & AT(PAIGE /2 MARVEL)   **Search Westlaw**

Thesaurus

Recent Searches & Locates

Dates: Unrestricted

Fields: Select an Option

→The database used was Federal Taxation – Tax Court Cases.

Illustration 3-2. Search in LexisNexis

Legal > Area of Law - By Topic > Taxation > Cases and Court Rules > Federal > US Tax Court Ca

Enter Search Terms

⊙ Terms and Connectors   ○ Natural Language   ○ Easy Search

WRITTENBY (MARVEL) or COUNSEL (PAIGE w/2
MARVEL)

Suggest Terms
for My Search   **Search**

Check Spelling

Restrict by Segment:

Select a segment, enter search terms for the segment, then click Add.

Select a Segment ▾   Add ↑

Note: Segment availability differs between sources. Segments may not be applied consistently across sources.

Restrict by Date:

⊙ No Date Restrictions ▾ ○ From   To   Date Formats...

→The database used was US Tax Court Cases, Memorandum Decs. & Board of Tax Appeals Decisions.

Illustration 3-3. Search in Tax Court Website

Opinions Search

Go to ▸ Today's Opinions

TC and Memorandum Opinions starting 09/25/95; Summary Opinions starting 01/01/01*	Help

Date Search:	[By Day: MM/DD/YY] [By Month MM/**/YY] [By Year **/**/YY]
Case Name Keyword:	(e.g., petitioner's last name)
Judge:	Marvel
Opinion Type:	All Types
Sort By:	Case Name
Text Search Opinion contains word(s):	Number of hits to display: All [Excluded Words List]

Search   Reset

d. Articles

Searches for articles on particular topics or by particular authors are also more conveniently done in electronic media. Print articles indexes are not cumulative. Each volume covers one or more years, necessitating a lengthy search. The process is further complicated because each index covers slightly different publications; at least one index imposes minimum page requirements for articles. Although their electronic versions have the same coverage limitations, you can search electronic databases far more quickly.

Two important limitations apply in selecting between print and electronic articles indexes. The first relates to availability; the second, to coverage dates. Neither Index to Federal Tax Articles, which has the most extensive retrospective coverage, nor Federal Tax Articles is currently available in any electronic format. Although both Index to Legal Periodicals and Current Law Index are available in electronic formats, pre-1980 materials are not currently included in the electronic data-bases.[20] Articles indexes are discussed further in Chapter 14.

e. Citators

There are at least two advantages to using a citator online. First, you can accomplish the search more quickly because you won't have to consult several volumes of print materials. Second, online citators provide easy access to the citing material. You can print out a list of citations or jump

---

[20] WilsonWeb does provide retrospective coverage for periodical articles covered by Index to Legal Periodicals.

to them directly using online hyperlinks. Citators are discussed further in Chapter 12.

Electronic services can also quickly perform citator-like searches. Even if, for example, a CD/DVD case service lacks a citator, you can use the initial case name as a search term and find all later cases or other material citing it.

4. Cost

Research tools are not free. Both your time and the cost of materials must be factored into a decision between competing sources. As noted in Subsection 1, your library may have limited your choice by deciding which materials it carries. Cost may determine which materials you select from those to which you have access.

You do not pay separately to use print and CD/DVD materials; the subscription price is a fixed cost. You pay nothing to use nonsubscription online materials, such as those available at government websites. Pricing for subscription services may be based on a fixed fee or may include time charges. You should consider both the time savings in speed (your "hourly rate" as a practitioner) and any incremental cost (fee for use) associated with subscription services.

If you are trying to familiarize yourself with a topic, print services may be preferable to electronic sources. The less you know about the topic, the more time you will spend reading explanatory material. Although you can reduce online time by downloading text, your lack of familiarity with the topic may result in your downloading too much or too little. If you have difficulty reading large amounts of text from a computer screen, you must factor in physical "costs" when deciding between print and electronic sources.

5. Need for Original Page Citations

If you must cite to the original volume and page numbers, the original print source obviously provides that information. Many online services also include original pagination; CD/DVD services are less likely to do so. If you need to cite more than one publication (e.g., official and unofficial citations), online services are more likely to include parallel citations than are print materials.

When using electronic sources, you take a slight risk that citations or pagination will be incorrect. Many websites, particularly those of government entities, avoid this problem by providing documents in PDF format. Westlaw also does this for the West reporter services. This format doesn't merely add pagination at appropriate breaks; it actually reproduces the original document. With the appropriate software, you can perform word searches in these PDF documents.

SECTION D. SUMMARY

Research generally involves using both primary and secondary sources. Various factors influence the order in which you consult them and the format in which you conduct your research. These factors include:

- how complicated the problem is in relation to your knowledge of the subject matter;

- the specific tools available in your library;

- the frequency with which services are updated;

- the cost-effectiveness of each service for the particular task;

- your need for correct page citations; and

- personal preferences you develop as you gain research expertise.

Remember that your research is not complete until you use appropriate updating tools to check your authorities.

CHAPTER 4. ILLUSTRATIVE PROBLEM

The following problem illustrates sources you can consult in doing tax research.

A. FACT PATTERN

Your clients recently refinanced their mortgage to take advantage of declining interest rates. When they purchased their home last year, interest rates were quite high. They made a down payment of $20,000 and borrowed $130,000 at 11.5 percent interest; their home was secured by a mortgage to Friendly Bank. The agreement with Friendly required them to refinance the loan or repay its full balance within five years.

Interest rates dropped to six percent last month. Generous Bank loaned your clients $129,500 and charged only one point ($1,295). They repaid Friendly the $129,500 principal remaining due on the original loan. They paid the point charged by Generous with funds in their checking account at Country Bank.

B. GOALS FOR RESEARCH

Your clients wonder how much of this year's interest they can deduct and how to handle the point, which represents prepaid interest.

Because they approached you after completing this transaction, your goals include assessing the tax consequences and advising on the appropriate tax return treatment. If they had approached you before refinancing, you might have advised them to pay a higher interest rate instead of paying the point. That advice would involve the interplay of tax consequences and their estimate of how long they plan to own the home.[21]

Note that I excluded some potential issues from consideration. For example, because I stated that the point is prepaid interest, you need not research the difference between deductible and nondeductible loan fees. And because the $1,295 was on deposit with a third bank and not added

---

[21] No matter how favorable the tax consequences are, a transaction must make sense financially. Tax consequences are but one factor to consider in judging the financial aspects. Intrafamily transactions must also meet clients' personal goals.

to the new loan, you can avoid researching when interest is actually paid.

C. INITIAL RESEARCH STRATEGY

Because federal tax rules are grounded in statutory provisions, locating relevant statutory text is critical. The method you use to locate that text is affected by your degree of familiarity with the subject matter.

If you were familiar with the Internal Revenue Code, you could go directly to Code section 163, which provides the rules for deducting interest, and section 461, which applies to prepayments. If you did not remember the section numbers, you could obtain that information from the subject index accompanying the Code.

If you had no knowledge of the area, you might consult one of the treatises or looseleaf services described in Chapter 13, using its topical index to locate discussions of interest and points paid as an interest substitute. Those discussions would refer you to sections 163 and 461.

Illustration 4-1. Excerpt from RIA Code Index

	Interest Current Code Topic Index
. .personal interest	
. . . disallowance of deductions	163
. .points, deduction	461
. .prepaid, taxable year of deduction	461
. .rates, undiscounted losses	846
. .real estate investment trusts	856
. .real estate mortgage investment conduits	860G

→Each publisher decides how extensive its index will be and how topics will be divided. The main difference between the online version shown here and the print version is that the latter uses two columns per page.

→RIA also publishes looseleaf services, which have their own topic indexes. Commerce Clearing House (CCH) also publishes both a Code and looseleaf services, each of which has a topical index.

1. Code Section 163

Your research indicates that Code section 163 is an appropriate place to begin your research.

Illustration 4-2. Excerpt from Code Section 163

SEC. 163. INTEREST

(a) General rule.—There shall be allowed as a deduction all interest paid or accrued within the taxable year on indebtedness.

....

(h) Disallowance of deduction for personal interest.—

(1) In general.—In the case of a taxpayer other than a corporation, no deduction shall be allowed under this chapter for personal interest paid or accrued during the taxable year.

(2) Personal interest.—For purposes of this subsection, the term "personal interest" means any interest allowable as a deduction under this chapter other than—

....

(D) any qualified residence interest (within the meaning of paragraph (3)), and

....

(3) Qualified residence interest.—For purposes of this subsection—

(A) In general.—The term "qualified residence interest" means any interest which is paid or accrued during the taxable year on—

(i) acquisition indebtedness with respect to any qualified residence of the taxpayer, or

....

(B) Acquisition indebtedness.—

(i) In general.—The term "acquisition indebtedness" means any indebtedness which—

(I) is incurred in acquiring, constructing, or substantially improving any qualified residence of the taxpayer, and

....

Such term also includes any indebtedness secured by such residence resulting from the refinancing of indebtedness meeting the requirements of the preceding sentence (or this sentence) ....

→Relevant provisions are found in several places in this section. That is a common characteristic of tax statutes. See Chapter 6 for a discussion of terminology used in discussing statutory material.

Illustration 4-2 reproduces relevant rules found in Code section 163(a) & (h). First, the general rule provides a deduction for interest paid or accrued during the taxable year. Second, "personal interest" is not deductible. Third, qualified residence interest is not considered personal interest, a conclusion that is not intuitively obvious. If you had ended your reading with section 163(h)(1), you would have given your clients erroneous advice.

Section 163 answers some of our questions. "Qualified residence interest" includes amounts paid to purchase or to substantially improve a qualified residence. Because amounts spent to refinance a loan also qualify, the new loan is considered an amount borrowed for the purchase of the residence.[22]

Section 163 does not answer all our questions. Further research is necessary because it does not specifically address points.

2. Code Section 461

The index shown in Illustration 4-1 indicates that Code section 461 applies to prepaid interest. Section 461(g) generally disallows a current deduction for prepaid interest. It allocates the interest to the period "with respect to which the interest represents a charge for the use or forbearance of money." In other words, your clients would prorate their deduction of the $1,295 over the life of the loan. However, they may qualify for a current deduction under section 461(g)(2), reproduced below.

Illustration 4-3. Code section 461(g)(2)

> This subsection shall not apply to points paid in respect of any indebtedness incurred **in connection with the purchase** or improvement of, and secured by, the principal residence of the taxpayer to the extent that, under regulations prescribed by the Secretary, such payment of points is an established business practice in the area in which such indebtedness is incurred, and the amount of such payment does not exceed the amount generally charged in such area.

Section 461 uses the term "in connection with the purchase" rather than the term "to purchase." It provides no rules for determining if points are paid in connection with a purchase. Because your clients' loan had onerous terms, including a five-year window for refinancing or paying in full, you want to argue that they meet the "in connection with" test.

D. FINDING ADDITIONAL AUTHORITY

If you research the "in connection with" issue, your initial question

---

[22] Section 163 may have other requirements that we are not researching here.

involves statutory interpretation. How does indebtedness incurred "in connection with" a purchase or improvement differ from indebtedness incurred "to" purchase or improve?

Normally, your first step would be taken in the Code itself. Many sections include definition provisions designed to limit the meaning of a particular word or phrase.[23] In other instances, definitions are provided elsewhere in the Code. For example, section 7701 includes an extensive list of definitions.

Neither Code section 461 nor section 7701 defines "in connection with" in this context. Because the Code contains no definition, you must focus your research on authorities interpreting the statutory language. For that step, you would consider what sources are available and which to consult first. You might start with congressional reports and progress to Treasury regulations, IRS rulings, and judicial opinions. You would consult treatises and other secondary sources as necessary throughout this process.[24] Illustrations 4-4 through 4-9 present selected materials relevant to our issue.

I locate IRS materials and judicial opinions using citators (Chapter 12) and reference materials that provide citations to particular Code sections, Treasury regulations, and IRS rulings. Looseleaf service supplement sections (Chapter 13) and newsletters (Chapter 16) are useful for locating recent changes. CD/DVD (Chapter 19) and online services (Chapter 20) are another means of locating relevant materials; online services are particularly useful for updating your research.

E. UPDATING YOUR RESEARCH

In a field that changes as rapidly as taxation, constant updating is critical. The relative frequency of supplementation will influence your choice between tools providing the same information. Remember to record the date each time you update your research. If you use a looseleaf service or other source that is updated periodically, be sure to record the

---

[23] See, e.g., I.R.C. § 71(a), which includes amounts received as alimony in gross income. Alimony is specifically defined in § 71(b). The recipient avoids being taxed on amounts received as "alimony" under the terms of a state court decree if those amounts fail to satisfy the § 71(b) requirements.

[24] Don't ignore dictionaries. Many courts use both general and law-related dictionaries in statutory interpretation. You can also consult a tax-oriented dictionary for explanations of terms you may encounter. See, e.g., RICHARD A. WESTIN, WG&L TAX DICTIONARY (2006).

date of the last release included in the service. You need not use that source for later material until the library receives a later release. In addition to updating, you must always check effective dates of new statutes and other material. Statutory changes that occurred this year, for example, may overrule or otherwise weaken the authority of regulations or rulings issued in an earlier year.

F. A NOTE ON PRINT VERSUS ELECTRONIC SOURCES

With the exception of the AOD in Illustration 4-9, I could easily complete this problem using print resources instead of electronic services.[25]

The Code and Treasury regulations are available through subscription-based print, CD/DVD, and online services and on government and other free websites. As explained in Chapter 9, the numbering system for most regulations is based on the underlying Code section. Once you know the Code section, you usually know which final, temporary, and proposed regulations you seek.

If I needed to familiarize myself with a topic before going to the primary sources, I could have read treatises or looseleaf services on CD/DVD or online. Using the print versions is likely to reduce both cost and potential eyestrain.

I probably could have located both Revenue Ruling 87-22 and the *Huntsman* decision more quickly using either a CD/DVD or an online service such as Westlaw or LexisNexis. I could have searched for rulings and cases using the relevant Code sections and various phrases, such as "in connection with," as search terms rather than using a Code-rulings table or print citator to find these materials. In later chapters, we will discuss specific methods for finding the materials illustrated here.

G. ILLUSTRATIONS

In my solution to this problem, I consulted a variety of sources. The most relevant are illustrated below. If I had not been familiar with interest and points, I would also have consulted a looseleaf service or treatise before reading primary sources.

---

[25] CCH carried AODs in its looseleaf IRS Positions service. Because of the sheer number, frequency, and variety of IRS releases each year (discussed in Chapter 10), electronic searching is clearly superior for finding these items.

Illustration 4-4. Excerpt from Temporary Treasury Regulation Section 1.163-10T

Section 1.163-10T Qualified residence interest (temporary).

(a) *Table of contents.* This paragraph (a) lists the major paragraphs that appear in this § 1.163-10T.

....

(j) *Determination of interest paid or accrued during the taxable year.*—(1) *In general.* For purposes of determining the amount of qualified residence interest with respect to a secured debt, the amount of interest paid or accrued during the taxable year includes only interest paid or accrued while the debt is secured by a qualified residence.

(2) *Special rules for cash-basis taxpayers.*—(i) *Points deductible in year paid under section 461(g)(2).* If points described in section 461(g)(2) (certain points paid in respect of debt incurred in connection with the purchase or improvement of a principal residence) are paid with respect to a debt, the amount of such points is qualified residence interest.

→The above provision fails to define the term "in connection with."

→This regulation was issued for Code section 163, but it focuses on Code section 461(g)(2). Interestingly, Code section 163 does not mention section 461 or cross-reference to it.

Illustration 4-5. Illustration 4-5. Excerpt from Mertens Code-Rulings Table

Code Sec.	Rev. Rul.
461(f)(3)	89–6
461(f)(4)	89–6
461(g)	83–84, 87–22
461(g)(1)	87–22
461(g)(2)	87–22

→Mertens provides references from Code sections to IRS revenue rulings and procedures. Citators (Chapter 12) also provide this information.

→You can also check Mertens to see if the IRS has revoked Revenue Ruling 87-22. As of November 1, 2006, the tables showed no IRS action.

Illustration 4-6. Excerpt from Rev. Rul. 87-22, 1987-1 C.B. 146

ISSUE

(1) If a taxpayer pays points on the refinancing of a mortgage loan secured by the principal residence of the taxpayer, is the payment deductible in full, under section 461(g)(2) of the Internal Revenue Code, for the taxable year in which the points are paid?

....

FACTS

Situation 1. In 1981, *A* obtained a 16-percent mortgage loan (old mortgage loan) exclusively for the purchase of a principal residence. On August 20, 1986, *A* refinanced the old mortgage loan, which had an outstanding principal balance of $100,000, with a $100,000, 30-year, 10-percent mortgage loan (new mortgage loan) from *L*, a lending institution. The new loan was secured by a mortgage on *A*'s principal residence. Principal and interest payments were due monthly, with the first payment due October 1, 1986, and the last payment due September 1, 2016. In order to refinance, *A* paid 3.6 points ($3,600) to *L* at the loan closing.

....

LAW AND ANALYSIS

....

An exception to the general rule of section 461(g)(1) of the Code is set forth in section 461(g)(2). Section 461(g)(2) provides that section 461(g)(1) shall not apply to points paid in respect of any indebtedness incurred in connection with the purchase or improvement of, and secured by, the principal residence of the taxpayer to the extent that such payment of points is an established business practice in the area in which such indebtedness is incurred and the amount of such payment does not exceed the amount generally charged in such area. Therefore, unlike the rule applicable to other instances of prepaid interest, if the requirements of section 461(g)(2) of the Code are satisfied, the taxpayer is not limited to deducting the points over the period of the indebtedness. *Schubel v. Commissioner,* 77 T.C. at 703-04.

In *Situation 1,* the proceeds of the new mortgage loan were used solely to repay an existing indebtedness. The legislative history of section 461(g)(2) of the Code states that a loan does "not qualify under [the] exception [in section 461(g)(2)] . . . if the loan proceeds are used for purposes other than purchasing or improving the taxpayer's principal residence. . . ." H.R. Rep. No. 94-658, 94th Cong., 1st Sess. 101 (1975), 1976-3 (Vol. 2) C.B. 695, 793. Although the indebtedness secured by the new mortgage was incurred in connection with *A*'s continued ownership of *A*'s principal residence, the loan proceeds were used for purposes other than purchasing or improving the residence, and thus the indebtedness was not "incurred in connection with the purchase or improvement of" that residence, as that language is used in section 461(g)(2). Accordingly, the points paid by *A* with respect to *A*'s new mortgage loan do not meet the requirements of section 461(g)(2) of the Code.

→This ruling is adverse to our clients' position.

Illustration 4-7. Excerpt from RIA Citator 2nd (vol. 2, 1978-89)

> Rev Rul 87-22, 1987-1 CB 146
>   s—IR-87-34, 1987 PH ¶ 54,743
>   k—Huntsman, James Richard and Zenith Annette, 91 TC
>   919, 91 PH TC 458
>   n—Huntsman, James Richard and Zenith Annette, 91 TC
>   922, 91 PH TC 459
>   e—Rev Proc 87-15, 1987-1 CB 625

→At the time *Huntsman* was decided, Prentice-Hall (PH; P-H)) published what is now the RIA Citator.

→Note that the illustration above does not include a citation to the appellate court opinion [Illustration 4-8]. Although the Tax Court cited Revenue Ruling 87-22, the appellate court did not. Using a citator to trace the Tax Court opinion, you would have found the appellate opinion.

Illustration 4-8. Excerpt from Huntsman v. Commissioner, 905 F.2d 1182, 1184 (8th Cir. 1990)

> Before LAY, Chief Judge, BEAM, Circuit Judge, and HANSON,* District Judge.
>
> LAY, Chief Judge. ....
> [2]   In determining the scope of section 461(g)(2), we first look to the language of the statute. *United States v. James*, 478 U.S. 597, 604 ... (1986) (citing *Blue Chip Stamps v. Manor Drug Stores*, 421 U.S. 723, 756 ... (1975) (Powell, J., concurring)). The statute merely requires a taxpayer's indebtedness to be "in connection with" the purchase or improvement of the taxpayer's residence. Thus, we find a fair reading of the statute requires that the indebtedness need only have an "association" or "relation" with the purchase of the taxpayer's residence.[5] The statute does not require all indebtedness to be "*directly related* to the actual acquisition of the principal residence." *Huntsman*, 91 T.C. at 921 (emphasis added).

→The Eighth Circuit Court of Appeals reversed the Tax Court. The Huntsmans' facts are not identical to your clients' (although they are close).

→In addition to checking for precedent in your particular jurisdiction (discussed in Chapter 11), you should check to see if the IRS accepted this result. [See Illustration 4-9.]

→You should also make sure that the relevant Code sections had the same language in 1990 as they do today.

Illustration 4-9. Excerpt from IRS Action on Decision 1991-02

The test that the Eighth Circuit has created requires examination of the facts of each case to determine if the refinancing is sufficiently connected with the purchase or improvement of the taxpayer's residence. The Service believes that Congress enacted section 461(g)(2) to eliminate the case-by-case approach to deductibility of points. Moreover, the legislative history indicates that Congress intended to limit the exception to points paid on indebtedness incurred to purchase or improve the taxpayer's principal residence. Accordingly, the Service maintains its position that points paid for a loan to refinance a mortgage on a taxpayer's principal residence are not deductible under I.R.C. § 461(g)(2). Thus it will not follow the court's holding with respect to this type of refinancing agreement outside of the Eighth Circuit. However, in the absence of an intercircuit conflict, the Service is of the opinion that the issue lacks sufficient demonstrable administrative importance to warrant a petition for certiorari.

RECOMMENDATION:

No certiorari

→In addition to using a citator to determine if other courts followed *Huntsman*, you should determine if the IRS plans to continue litigating this issue. AOD 1991-02 indicates that the IRS chief counsel's office did not recommend petitioning for certiorari in *Huntsman* but that the IRS would not follow *Huntsman* in other circuits. See Chapter 10 for information on researching IRS positions and for a less traditional AOD.

PART TWO

PRIMARY SOURCES: LEGISLATIVE

CHAPTER 5. CONSTITUTION

SECTION A. TAXING POWER

Congress's power to impose taxes emanates from the United States Constitution. That document includes several taxation provisions.

Table 5-1. Constitutional Provisions Regarding Taxation

Art. I, § 2, cl. 3: Representatives and direct Taxes shall be apportioned among the several States which may be included within this Union, according to their respective Numbers .... (Before amendment)

Art. I, § 7, cl. 1: All Bills for raising Revenue shall originate in the House of Representatives; but the Senate may propose or concur with Amendments as on other Bills.

Art. I, § 8, cl. 1: The Congress shall have Power To lay and collect Taxes, Duties, Imposts and Excises, to pay the Debts and provide for the common Defence and general Welfare of the United States; but all Duties, Imposts and Excises shall be uniform throughout the United States;

Art. I, § 9, cl. 4: No Capitation, or other direct, Tax shall be laid, unless in Proportion to the Census or Enumeration herein before directed to be taken.

Art. I, § 9, cl. 5: No Tax or Duty shall be laid on Articles exported from any State.

Art. I, § 10, cl. 2: No State shall, without the Consent of the Congress, lay any Imposts or Duties on Imports or Exports, except what may be absolutely necessary for executing it's inspection Laws: and the net Produce of all Duties and Imposts, laid by any State on Imports or Exports, shall be for the Use of the Treasury of the United States; and all such Laws shall be subject to the Revision and Controul of the Congress.

Amend. XVI: The Congress shall have power to lay and collect taxes on incomes, from whatever source derived, without apportionment among the several States, and without regard to any census or enumeration.

Because the income tax is specifically authorized by the Constitution's sixteenth amendment, it avoids an earlier holding that it was a direct tax subject to apportionment based on population.[26] The estate and gift taxes,

---

[26] Pollock v. Farmers' Loan & Trust Co., 158 U.S. 601 (1895); cf. Springer v.

on the other hand, are indirect taxes subject only to the requirement that they be uniform throughout the United States.

SECTION B. CONSTITUTIONAL LITIGATION

1. Items Challenged

Because several constitutional provisions explicitly mention taxation [Table 5-1], courts must occasionally determine whether a taxing statute or administrative interpretation complies with these rules. Examples appear in Table 5-2. Most cases raising constitutional claims involve provisions that do not mention taxation, such as those listed in. Table 5-3. Tax claims involving the Constitution do not generate a substantial body of important litigation in any year.

Table 5-2. Litigation Involving Tax Provisions

Mobley v. United States, 8 Cl. Ct. 767 (1985) (the apportionment clause–art. I, § 2, cl. 3)

Moore v. United States House of Representatives, 733 F.2d 946 (D.C. Cir. 1984) (the origination clause–art. I, § 7, cl. 1)

United States v. Ptasynski, 462 U.S. 74 (1983) (the uniformity clause–art. I, § 8, cl. 1)

United States v. International Business Machines Corp., 517 U.S. 843 (1996) (the export clause–art. I, § 9, cl. 5)

Murphy v. Internal Revenue Service, 460 F.3d 79 (D.C. Cir. 2006) (definition of income–amend. XVI)

2. Supreme Court Litigation Versus Constitutional Litigation

Keep two facts in mind. First, lower courts dismiss many constitutional claims; most of these claims never reach the United States Supreme Court. Second, most substantive tax litigation involves interpreting statutes or other rules rather than constitutional claims. If Congress

---

United States, 102 U.S. 586 (1881), concluding the Civil War income tax was indirect.

disagrees with a Supreme Court decision regarding interpretation, it can "overrule" the Court by amending the statute.

Table 5-3. Litigation Involving the Nontax Provisions

Demko v. United States, 216 F.3d 1049 (Fed. Cir. 2000) (nondelegation doctrine–judicially derived from art. I, § 1)

NationsBank of Texas, N.A. v. United States, 269 F.3d 1332 (Fed. Cir. 2001) (separation of powers doctrine–art. I, § 7, cl. 2)

Clinton v. City of New York, 524 U.S. 417 (1998) (the presentment clause–art. I, § 7, cl. 2)

United States v. Rosengarten, 857 F.2d 76 (2d Cir. 1988) (ex post facto laws–art. I, § 9, cl. 3)

Freytag v. Commissioner, 501 U.S. 868 (1991) (the appointments clause–art. II, § 2, cl. 2)

United States v. Hatter, 532 U.S. 557 (2001) (the compensation clause–art. III, § 1)

Hernandez v. Commissioner, 490 U.S. 680 (1989) (establishment of religion and free exercise of religion–amend. I)

Regan v. Taxation with Representation, 461 U.S. 540 (1983) (freedom of speech and association–amend. I; equal protection–amend. V)

United States v. Carlton, 512 U.S. 26 (1994) (retroactivity as a denial of due process–amend. V)

Manufacturers Hanover Trust Co. v. United States, 775 F.2d 459 (2d Cir. 1985) (equal protection/sex discrimination–amend. V)

Ianniello v. Commissioner, 98 T.C. 165 (1992) (double jeopardy–amend. V; excessive fines and cruel and unusual punishments–amend. VIII)

South Carolina v. Baker, 485 U.S. 505 (1988) (infringement on powers reserved to states–amend. X)

Shapiro v. Baker, 646 F. Supp. 1127 (D.N.J. 1986) (judicial doctrine of intergovernmental tax immunity)

SECTION C. RESEARCH PROCESS

If you want to know if a court has ruled on the constitutionality of a statute or administrative interpretation, you could use a citator and search on the particular statute or regulation. Electronic citators will be better for this purpose than print citators. First, they are updated more quickly. Second, many of the print Shepard's series did not cover IRS material or Tax Court Memorandum decisions. Third, the print CCH and RIA citators do not provide citations to the constitution or statutes.

Because substantive tax research rarely involves the Constitution, you may decide to perform your research using nontax materials.[27] You can also search electronic services for specific constitutional provisions or common terms (e.g., due process). Standard Federal Tax Reporter volume 1 includes materials on litigation involving constitutional claims.

SECTION D. PROBLEMS

1. Indicate which of the Constitution's tax provisions was involved in

   a. Thomson Multimedia Inc. v. United States, 219 F. Supp. 2d 1322 (CIT 2002)

   b. Union Elec. Co. v. United States, 363 F.3d 1292 (Fed. Cir. 2004)

   c. Consolidation Coal Co. v. United States, 64 Fed. Cl. 718 (2005)

   d. Flint v. Stone Tracy Co., 220 U.S. 107 (1911)

   e. Helvering v. Independent Life Ins. Co., 292 U.S. 371 (1934)

   f. Armstrong v. United States, 759 F.2d 1378 (9th Cir. 1985)

---

[27] The most useful materials are annotated Constitutions, such as those included in United States Code Annotated and United States Code Service, and digests. 1 BORIS I. BITTKER & LAWRENCE LOKKEN, FEDERAL TAXATION OF INCOME, ESTATES AND GIFTS ch. 1 (3d ed. 1999 & Cum. Supp.), discusses tax litigation involving constitutional claims.

2. Indicate which of the Constitution's nontax provisions was involved in

   a. Kane v. United States, 942 F. Supp. 233 (E.D. Pa. 1996)

   b. Stewart v. Commissioner, T.C. Memo. 2005-212 (2005)

   c. Durham v. Commissioner, T.C. Memo 2004-125

   d. Radnitz v. Commissioner, T.C. Summary Op. 2003-29

   e. Moritz v. Commissioner, 469 F.2d 466 (10th Cir. 1972)

3. Cite to the decision that involved the constitution and these facts.

   a. a 2003 Tax Court Summary opinion involving the taxation of disability income and taxpayers who are older than 65

   b. a 2000 Tax Court Memorandum opinion involving repeal of the "inhabitants rule"

   c. a 2002 Sixth Circuit opinion involving the retroactive amendment in 1998 of Rule 33 of the Federal Rules of Criminal Procedure

   d. a 2005 Second Circuit opinion involving a newspaper's claim that a retaliatory audit violated its First Amendment rights

   e. a 2006 Tax Court Memorandum opinion involving the limitation on the deduction for capital losses

   f. a 2002 Tax Court opinion involving including the gift tax paid on gifts made within three years of death in the decedent's gross estate

   g. a 2002 Court of International Trade opinion involving the deadline in 19 C.F.R. § 24.24(e)

4. What constitutional claim was rejected in these IRS documents?

   a. Technical Advice Memorandum 200629030

   b. Private Letter Ruling 8049030

   c. Technical Advice Memorandum 8011013

   d. Revenue Ruling 2005-19

Chapter 6. Statutes

Section A. Introduction

This chapter discusses statutes passed by Congress and authorized by the United States Constitution. It covers terminology used to describe statutes, lists sources in which you can locate current, repealed, and pending statutes, and introduces rules of interpretation.

In interpreting statutes, judges and administrative agencies may look to legislative history, a topic covered in Chapter 7. If a taxpayer has ties to another country, treaties may also be relevant. Treaties and their relationship to statutes are discussed in Chapter 8.

Your goals for Chapters 6 and 7 include locating all relevant documents, determining their relative importance, and updating your research to encompass pending items. In accomplishing these goals, you should become familiar with the process by which statutes are enacted and the terminology used to describe statutory and legislative history documents.

Section B. Functions of Statutes

The Constitution authorizes taxes, but it does not provide rules for measuring income, allowing deductions, or determining rates. That task is accomplished by Congress, which has enacted statutes imposing a variety of taxes.

Statutes define the tax base and penalties for noncompliance, provide effective dates, authorize administrative agencies to interpret the laws, and direct those same agencies to make reports to Congress. Your research may require you to locate statutes serving these purposes.

Section C. Statutory Scheme

1. Internal Revenue Code

Title 26 of the United States Code (U.S.C.) is more commonly referred to as the Internal Revenue Code of 1986. It contains the vast majority of statutes covering income, estate and gift, excise, and employment taxes.

The 1986 Code replaced the 1954 Code, which had replaced the 1939 Code. I refer to the 1986 statutory materials as the Code throughout this text. Any references I make to the two previous Codes–1939 and 1954– will include the Code year.[28]

a. Code Subdivisions

Because the Internal Revenue Code is a title of U.S.C., its first subdivisions are subtitles. The Code currently has 11 subtitles.

Table 6-1. Internal Revenue Code Subtitles

Subtitle	Subject
A	Income Taxes
B	Estate and Gift Taxes
C	Employment Taxes and Collection of Income Taxes
D	Miscellaneous Excise Taxes
E	Alcohol, Tobacco, and Certain Other Excise Taxes
F	Procedure and Administration
G	The Joint Committee on Taxation
H	Financing of Presidential Election Campaigns
I	Trust Fund Code
J	Coal Industry Health Benefits
K	Group Health Plan Requirements

Each subtitle is further subdivided into smaller units: chapter; subchapter; part; subpart; section; subsection; paragraph; subparagraph; clause; and subclause. [See Table 6-2.] Subdivisions may also be divided into sentences.

b. Code Subdivision Numbering System

Titles, chapters, parts, and sections are identified by number. Subtitles,

---

[28] Before 1939, tax statutes were reenacted in their entirety, or with necessary changes, on a regular basis. Because many current provisions can be traced back to the 1939 Code or even earlier—I.R.C. § 263, for example, contains language taken almost verbatim from § 117 of the 1864 Act—cross-references to these earlier materials are extremely useful. See Act of June 30, 1864, ch. 173, 13 Stat. 223, 281-82. Chapter 7 covers materials used to trace statutory language.

subchapters, and subparts are identified by letter. Subsections usually are identified by letter (e.g., subsection 163(d)), but a few are designated by number (e.g., subsection 212(1)). Successive subdivisions bear letters or numbers, as appropriate. The Code uses both upper and lower case letters and both Roman and Arabic numerals.

Table 6-2. Code Subdivisions: Section 45F(c)(1)(A)(i)(I)

Subdivision	Heading or Text
Title 26	Internal Revenue
Subtitle A	Income taxes
Chapter 1	Normal taxes and surtaxes
Subchapter A	Determination of tax liability
Part IV	Credits against tax
Subpart D	Business related credits
Section 45F	Employer-provided child care credits
Subsection (c)	Definitions. For purposes of this section—
Paragraph (1)	Qualified child care expenditures
Subparagraph (A)	In general. The term "qualified child care expenditure" means any amount paid or incurred—
Clause (i)	to acquire, construct, rehabilitate, or expand property—
Subclause (I)	which is to be used as part of a qualified child care facility of the taxpayer,

→Subdivisions may include only headings, only text, or both text and headings.

c. Unique and Repeated Code Subdivisions

Title, subtitle, chapter, and section numbers and letters are used only once. Other subdivision classifications are used multiple times. For example, there are several Subchapter As, but there is only one Chapter 1 (which appears in Subtitle A). The first chapter in Subtitle B is Chapter 11.

Although subchapter, part, and subpart classifications are used multiple times, subchapters are the most likely to cause a problem if you aren't careful. Practitioners frequently refer to four groups of sections in Subtitle A by their subchapter designation—Subchapter C, Subchapter J, Subchapter K, and Subchapter S.[29] If given an assignment to research a

---

[29] These subchapters cover, respectively, corporations, trusts and estates, partnerships, and "small business" corporations. Although Subtitle A has several Subpart Fs, international practitioners often refer to Subpart F as a shorthand

particular subchapter, be sure to ascertain the correct one before you begin.

d. Similar Subdivision Numbers

In using the Code's numbering system, be careful to note whether a letter is part of the section number or the subsection number. Code sections that include capital letters are most likely to cause problems. For example, section 2056(a) is not the same as section 2056A.

2. Other Statutes

Several tax-related provisions appear outside the Internal Revenue Code. These include provisions codified elsewhere and uncodified provisions. These provisions are discussed in Subsection D.4.

3. "Legislative" Pronouncements from the Executive Branch

The Treasury Department makes "legislative" pronouncements by issuing legislative regulations pursuant to an express statutory grant of authority. Regulations are discussed in Chapter 9.

The President also has limited "legislative" powers. See, for example, the highlighted language in Illustration 6-1.

Illustration 6-1. Code Section 1043(b)(2)

(2) Certificate of divestiture.
The term "certificate of divestiture" means any written determination—

(A) that states that divestiture of specific property is reasonably necessary to comply with any Federal conflict of interest statute, regulation, rule, or executive order (including section 208 of title 18, United States Code), or requested by a congressional committee as a condition of confirmation,

(B) **that has been issued by the President or the Director of the Office of Government Ethics,** and

(C) that identifies the specific property to be divested.

---

designation for the controlled foreign corporation Code sections in Chapter 1, Subchapter N, Part III.

Presidential declarations and executive orders can be found in government websites that cover the Weekly Compilation of Presidential Documents,[30] the Federal Register,[31] and the Internal Revenue Bulletin.[32] The presidential website also includes declarations and executive orders.[33] You will probably prefer searching across multiple years in commercial services such as Westlaw and LexisNexis.

SECTION D. TERMINOLOGY

The following paragraphs introduce terms used in discussing tax legislation. There is additional information in Chapter 7, Legislative Histories.

1. Bills and Acts

When proposed legislation is introduced in the Senate or House of Representatives, it is assigned a **bill** number. Each chamber numbers its bills separately in chronological order. A House bill is referred to as H.R. (e.g., H.R. 3838); a Senate bill is identified as S. Senators introduce bills involving taxation despite the constitutional requirement that bills for raising revenue originate in the House.[34]

Even though a bill may die because it passes neither chamber or only one chamber before Congress adjourns, don't be surprised to hear it referred to as an **act**.[35] Unfortunately, that term is not reserved for actual statutes. The bill's original name is likely to include the word Act. If you have access to the H.R. or S. number, you can find the bill in the Congressional Record whether or not it was enacted. Statutes at Large includes bill numbers for enacted legislation.

---

[30] See http://www.access.gpo.gov/nara/nara003.html.

[31] See http://www.gpoaccess.gov/fr/index.html.

[32] See http://www.irs.gov.

[33] See http://www.whitehouse.gov.

[34] If the House objects, it "blue-slips" the bill and returns it to the Senate.

[35] Unless a bill is enacted by the time a particular Congress ends, it dies. Its supporters must reintroduce it in a subsequent Congress and start the legislative process over. This rule does not apply to treaties (Chapter 8), which remain alive for action by a subsequent Congress.

2. Public Law Names and Acronyms

Although they carry Public Law numbers, acts are frequently referred to by a **popular name**. Congress often assigns different popular names to different titles of the same act.[36]

The act's text frequently includes its popular name. If that name includes a year, it is usually easy to locate the act's text in Statutes at Large or The Internal Revenue Acts of the United States (Chapter 17). In some situations, the year in the act's name is the year before the year of enactment. That is the case with one of the acts described in the next paragraph. If the year is not part of the name, use Shepard's Acts and Cases by Popular Names to obtain a citation. You can also obtain citations using an online service (Chapter 20) or in the Popular Names tables in Westlaw, U.S.C., U.S.C.A., or U.S.C.S.

Practitioners may refer to an act by the initials of its popular name rather than by the full name. For example, the Tax Increase Prevention and Reconciliation Act of 2005 is referred to as TIPRA.[37] Congress sometimes structures a popular name to provide a "catchy" acronym. For example, the short title for Public Law Number 109-227 is Heroes Earned Retirement Opportunities Act (HERO Act).[38]

3. Public Law Numbers

When a bill does become law, it receives a **public law number** (Pub. L. No.). These numbers are chronological by Congress.[39] They bear no relation to the original bill number and provide no information about the session of that Congress.[40]

---

[36] See, e.g., Pub. L. No. 109-135, 119 Stat. 2577. Section 1(a) provides a "short title" for the entire act: Gulf Opportunity Zone Act of 2005. Section 401 provides a separate short title for Subtitle A of Title IV: Tax Technical Corrections Act of 2005.

[37] Pub. L. No. 109-222, 120 Stat. 345 (2006).

[38] 120 Stat. 385 (2006).

[39] Statutes enacted before 1957 have chapter numbers instead of Pub. L. numbers.

[40] As indicated in note 38, the Tax Increase Prevention and Reconciliation Act of 2005 is Pub. L. No. 109-222. The Public Law number indicates that it was passed in the 109th Congress; it does not indicate in which of the two sessions. TIPRA was introduced in the 109th Congress as H.R. 4297.

4. Revenue Acts and Other Relevant Acts

Acts that have "Revenue" or "Tax" in their popular names clearly announce their relevance to taxation. Other acts that are likely to include substantive tax law include those with "Deficit Reduction," "Income," "Trade," or "Investment" in their titles.

Even if an act has a name, that name may contain no hint that it includes tax provisions. Other acts that include tax provisions may lack popular names altogether. For example, the Ricky Ray Hemophilia Relief Fund Act of 1998 treats certain payments as damages for purposes of Code section 104(a)(2).[41] Public Law Number 107-22, which changed the name of Education IRAs to Coverdell Education Savings Accounts, is an act that has no popular name.[42]

5. Codified and Uncodified Provisions

a. Codification in the I.R.C. and Elsewhere

Although most substantive tax provisions are included in the Internal Revenue Code, other titles of United States Code may include provisions relevant to your research. A provision may appear in another title of United States Code because an agency other than the Treasury Department has primary responsibility for the area of law involved. For example, many rules affecting retirement benefits appear in 29 U.S.C., the title that covers Labor.[43]

You can locate provisions in other titles using a subject matter index to U.S.C. The Related Statutes materials in Standard Federal Tax Reporter Code volume II include texts of many of these statutes. A CD/DVD (Chapter 19) version of U.S.C. or an online research tool (Chapter 20) is probably superior for this type of research.

b. Uncodified Provisions

Many revenue act provisions are uncodified; they are never added to

---

[41] Pub. L. No. 105-369, § 103(h), 112 Stat. 3368, 3371 (1998).

[42] 115 Stat. 196 (2001). Pub. L. No. 107-22 began as a Senate bill. S. 1190, 107th Cong., 1st. Sess. (2001). Although it amended the Code, it had no revenue implications and thus did not violate the origination clause. U.S. CONST. art. I, § 7, cl. 1.

[43] See also 37 U.S.C. § 558, providing tax deferments for military personnel while they are missing in action.

U.S.C. Most uncodified provisions involve effective dates for particular sections of the act. Others may direct the Treasury Department or IRS to do (or refrain from doing) something.[44] [See Illustration 6-2.] A third group involves substantive law provisions. [See Illustration 6-3.]

Because we expect statutes to have effective dates, it is second nature to look for them in the act itself or in a Code publication that includes effective date annotations. The other types of information are less common, however, and may well escape notice by someone who has not followed the progress of the particular legislation.

Uncodified substantive provisions are traps for the unwary. A very troublesome example involves so-called section 530 relief. Although you might assume that was its Code section number, you would be mistaken. Code section 530 involves Coverdell Education Savings Accounts. Section 530 relief has nothing to do with tax benefits for education. Instead, it is an act section involving guidance in the employee-independent contractor area.[45] It is not codified anywhere.

Illustration 6-2. Material Omitted from Code

> **SEC. 11144. TREASURY STUDY OF HIGHWAY FUELS USED BY TRUCKS FOR NON-TRANSPORTATION PURPOSES.**
> (a) STUDY.—The Secretary of the Treasury shall conduct a study regarding the use of highway motor fuel by trucks that is not used for the propulsion of the vehicle. As part of such study—
> (1) in the case of vehicles carrying equipment that is unrelated to the transportation function of the vehicle—
> (A) the Secretary of the Treasury, in consultation with the Secretary of Transportation, and with public notice and comment, shall determine the average annual amount of tax-paid fuel consumed per vehicle, by type of vehicle, used by the propulsion engine to provide the power to operate the equipment attached to the highway vehicle, and

→This excerpt is from is Pub. L. No. 109-59,[46] § 11144, 119 Stat. 1144, 1965 (2005). Studies such as this may lead to future legislation.

---

[44] Congress may ask for a report, impose a moratorium on Treasury regulations, or issue some other mandate to Treasury and IRS.

[45] Revenue Act of 1978, Pub. L. No. 95-600, § 530, 92 Stat. 2763, 2885, extended indefinitely by the Tax Equity and Fiscal Responsibility Act of 1982, Pub. L. No. 97-248, § 269(c), 96 Stat. 324, 552, and amended by the Small Business Job Protection Act of 1996, Pub. L. No. 104-188, § 1122, 110 Stat. 1755, 1766.

[46] In § 1(a), Congress gave this act two alternate popular names: Safe,

Illustration 6-3. Material Omitted from Code

SEC. 803. NO FEDERAL INCOME TAX ON RESTITUTION RECEIVED BY VICTIMS OF THE NAZI REGIME OR THEIR HEIRS OR ESTATES.

(a) IN GENERAL.—For purposes of the Internal Revenue Code of 1986, any excludable restitution payments received by an eligible individual (or the individual's heirs or estate) and any excludable interest—

(1) shall not be included in gross income; and

(2) shall not be taken into account for purposes of applying any provision of such Code which takes into account excludable income in computing adjusted gross income, including section 86 of such Code (relating to taxation of Social Security benefits).

For purposes of such Code, the basis of any property received by an eligible individual (or the individual's heirs or estate) as part of an excludable restitution payment shall be the fair market value of such property as of the time of the receipt.

→This excerpt is from the Economic Growth and Tax Relief Reconciliation Act of 2001, Pub. L. No. 107-16, § 803, 115 Stat. 38, 149 (2001). Although these provisions affect tax consequences, they are not codified.

6. Section Numbers

The Code, the Public Laws amending it or otherwise affecting taxation, and the bills that may become Public Laws all divide their provisions into sections. These section numbering systems bear no relationship to each other.[47] Take for example, Code section 1202(a)(1), which reads as follows:

> In general.—In the case of a taxpayer other than a corporation, gross income shall not include 50 percent of any gain from the sale or exchange of qualified small business stock held for more than 5 years.

Congress added the original version of that section to the Code in 1993, including it as section 13113(a) of the Revenue Reconciliation Act of 1993. The provision began as section 14113(a) of H.R. 2264, the Omnibus Budget Reconciliation Act of 1993, a subtitle of which was the Revenue Reconciliation Act of 1993.

The section is the basic unit used in finding the law. As discussed in

---

Accountable, Flexible, Efficient Transportation Equity Act: A Legacy for Users; and SAFETEA-LU. Several titles and subtitles have their own popular names. Title XI, which contains numerous amendments to the Code, did not receive a separate popular name.

[47] When researching an act or Code provision, remember to match the appropriate section number to the document being used.

Section C, the Code contains only one section 1, not one for each part, chapter, or other unit. Although sections are numbered sequentially, breaks in the sequence provide room for Congress to insert new sections as needed.

7. Enactment Date, Effective Date, and Sunset Date

These topics are critical aspects of tax research. Because pending legislation may add new legislation or amend or repeal existing law, it can totally change the outcome of a planned transaction.

a. Enactment and Effective Dates

Most acts have two relevant dates. The **enactment date** is the date the President signs the act (or allows it to become law without a signature) or Congress overrides a presidential veto. The **effective date**, on which the act's provisions apply to particular transactions, may coincide with, follow, or even precede the enactment date.

Tax legislation frequently involves several effective dates for individual sections of an act. It is risky to assume that the enactment date is the effective date or that the effective date of one section applies to all parts of a new act. Remember that effective dates rarely become part of the Code, but they do appear in the act itself.[48] The items listed in Subsection G.2. are useful for determining effective dates.

Illustration 6-4 illustrates separate effective dates in one act. Illustration 6-5 and Table 6-3 show the importance of effective dates.

Illustration 6-4. Effective Date Provisions in Economic Growth and Tax Relief Reconciliation Act of 2001, Section 303

(i) EFFECTIVE DATES.—
    (1) IN GENERAL.—Except as provided in paragraph (2), the amendments made by this section shall apply to taxable years beginning after December 31, 2001.
    (2) SUBSECTION (g).—The amendment made by subsection (g) shall take effect on January 1, 2004.

→The Economic Growth and Tax Relief Reconciliation Act of 2001 became law on June 7, 2001.

---

[48] Effective dates do appear in the Code for provisions that phase in over time or which apply in a different manner in different years. For example, the depreciation dollar limits in I.R.C. § 179(b)(1) vary based on the year the property is placed in service.

Illustration 6-5. Excerpt from Polone v. Commissioner[49]

Here, the Tax Court held that preamendment § 104 applied to Polone's May 1996 payment from UTA, but that postamendment § 104 applied to the November 1996, May 1997, and November 1998 payments because Polone received those payments after the amendment's effective date.

Table 6-3. Timeline in Polone v. Commissioner

Action	Date
Polone is fired by employer	April 21, 1996
Polone sues for defamation	April 24, 1996
Settlement of $4 million; Polone receives first $1 million	May 3, 1996
H.R. 3448 introduced in Congress	May 14,1996
I.R.C. § 104(a)(2) amended to include "physical" requirement	August 20, 1996 (effective date unless binding agreement, decree, or award in effect or issued before September 13, 1995)
Polone receives second installment	November 11, 1996
Polone receives third and fourth installments	May 5, 1997 & November 11, 1998

The exact language Congress uses is critical for determining an effective date. Table 6-4 indicates effective date formats with quite different meanings.

Table 6-4. Effective Date Formats

Effective for transactions occurring in taxable years beginning after December 31, 2006
Effective for transactions occurring after December 31, 2006
Effective for transactions occurring in taxable years ending after December 31, 2006

→If a taxpayer has a calendar year, the three effective dates above might yield the same results. If a taxpayer instead has a fiscal year that ends January 31, a transaction that occurs January 15, 2007, will be covered by the second and third effective dates but not by the first.

b. Sunset Date

As a general rule, Code provisions remain in effect until amended,

---

[49] 449 F.3d 1041, 1044 (9th Cir. 2006).

repealed, or declared unconstitutional. Congress may provide a specific **sunset date** for an individual Code provision. Unlike effective dates, sunset dates generally do appear in the Code.

Illustration 6-6. Sunset Date for Code Section 30

> (e) Termination.—
> This section shall not apply to any property placed in service after December 31, 2006.

→Note: sunset dates are frequently extended by subsequent legislation. The term **extenders** is commonly used for tax bill provisions postponing sunset dates. Section 30 has already been extended once.

Although sunset dates are generally calendar dates, specific events may also cause a provision to sunset. Code section 30B involves sunsets based on the earlier of a date or an event.

Illustration 6-7. Sunsets for Code Section 30B

> (f) LIMITATION ON NUMBER OF NEW QUALIFIED HYBRID AND ADVANCED LEAN-BURN TECHNOLOGY VEHICLES ELIGIBLE FOR CREDIT.
> (1) IN GENERAL. In the case of a qualified vehicle sold during the phaseout period, only the applicable percentage of the credit otherwise allowable under subsection (c) or (d) shall be allowed.
> (2) PHASEOUT PERIOD. For purposes of this subsection the phaseout period is the period beginning with the second calendar quarter following the calendar quarter which includes the first date on which the number of qualified vehicles manufactured by the manufacturer of the vehicle referred to in paragraph (1) sold for use in the United States after December 31, 2006, is at least 60,000
>
> ....
>
> (j) TERMINATION. This section shall not apply to any property purchased after—
>
> ....
>
> (2) in the case of a new advanced lean burn technology motor vehicle ... or a new qualified hybrid motor vehicle (as described in subsection (d)(2)(A), December 31, 2010, ...

SECTION E. RULES AFFECTING MULTIPLE SECTIONS

Some provisions apply to the entire Code; others affect only a particular subtitle or smaller unit. The latter groups indicate their scope by using language such as "for purposes of this paragraph." If you misread

the scope of a particular provision, you risk drawing erroneous conclusions. Illustration 6-8 shows varying scope limitations within a single
Code subsection.

Sections appearing in one subtitle or other subdivision of the Code may
apply to other subdivisions. Provisions affecting more than one type of tax
(separate subtitles) may appear in neither subtitle. Instead, they can be
found in Subtitle F, Chapter 80, Subchapter C (Code sections 7871-7873).

Although tax research requires access to rules found in varying parts of
the Code, the Code lacks a comprehensive cross-referencing system.[50]
Because they include textual discussion, looseleaf services and treatises
(Chapter 13) are useful in locating various provisions applicable to the
problem being researched.

Illustration 6-8. Scope Limits in Code Section 165(g)

(g) Worthless Securities.—
   (1) General rule.—If any security which is a capital asset becomes
worthless during the taxable year, the loss resulting therefrom shall,
for purposes of this subtitle, be treated as a loss from the sale or
exchange, on the last day of the taxable year, of a capital asset.
   (2) Security defined.—**For purposes of this subsection**, the term
"security" means—
       (A) a share of stock in a corporation; ....
   (3) Securities in affiliated corporation.—**For purposes of paragraph (1)**, any security in a corporation affiliated with a taxpayer
which is a domestic corporation shall not be treated as a capital asset.
For purposes of the preceding sentence, a corporation shall be
treated as affiliated with the taxpayer only if— ....

→The general rule applies for purposes of all income tax provisions ("this
subtitle"). Specific limitations and definitions have narrower application
("this subsection," "paragraph (1)," "the preceding sentence").

---

[50] Use of statutory language, including scope limitations and cross-references
between sections of one Code, is discussed in this chapter. Cross-referencing
section numbers from one Code to an earlier or later Code is discussed in Chapter
7, Legislative Histories.

SECTION F. DEFINITIONS

Many terms appear in the Code without definition. "Gross income" is one example. Others are defined in a section solely for purposes of that section. For example, section 1202(c) defines "qualified small business stock" for purposes of section 1202.

Some definitions apply to more than one Code section. Chapter 79 of the Code includes several definition provisions, most of which apply to the entire Code. If you cannot locate a definition in an individual section, be sure to check the definitions in Subtitle F, Chapter 79 (Code sections 7701-7704).

SECTION G. LOCATING CURRENT, REPEALED, AND PENDING LEGISLATION

In researching a tax problem, the time frame involved is quite important. If, for example, the research involves a proposed transaction, current law is certainly important. However, if that law is of recent vintage, the repealed statute it replaced may assist you in interpreting what the revised statute means. Moreover, if you ignore pending legislation, you do so at your peril. A bill changing the tax consequences of a proposed transaction could be enacted before your client negotiates a binding contract.[51]

If you are researching an existing Code section, you should read it in a codification rather than the most recent amending act. Codifications reflect the original statute as amended by all subsequent changes. Individual acts, on the other hand, reflect only amendments. As discussed earlier in this chapter, individual acts include information that might not appear in the Code, including effective dates and instructions to administrative agencies.

1. Current Code—Codifications

Several publishers produce annual versions of the Internal Revenue

---

[51] Effective dates for new legislation frequently precede the actual enactment date. Transactions subject to binding contracts on the effective date are often exempted. Notice 90-6, 1990-1 C.B. 304, provides guidance with respect to the existence of a binding contract for purposes of the Revenue Reconciliation Act of 1989. [See also Table 6-3.] Some acts include transition rules that benefit specific taxpayers. See, e.g., Pub. L. No. 99-514, § 204, 100 Stat. 2085, 2146 (1986).

Code.[52] Those publishing in a looseleaf format regularly integrate new material into the codication volumes. Publishers using bound volumes use supplements for new matter. CD/DVD (Chapter 19) and online services (Chapter 20) insert new material directly into the relevant database.[53]

Both United States Tax Reporter and Standard Federal Tax Reporter publish looseleaf Codes; these are discussed in Chapter 13. These Code volumes cover all types of taxes. [54]

Several publishers produce bound volumes of the Code. These are not updated as frequently as are the looseleaf services; in some cases, they are updated only annually. U.S. Code Congressional & Administrative News—Internal Revenue Code (discussed in Chapter 17), and Mertens, Internal Revenue Code are examples of bound volumes.

If you are unsure which Code section applies, use the publisher's topical index to assist you. [See Illustration 4-1.]

2. Individual Acts

Looseleaf services integrate the text of recent statutes into their codifications, but separate versions of an act are still valuable. These versions are available before the library receives pages to insert into a looseleaf codification. In addition, when the entire act is printed as a unit, it will include effective dates and congressional instructions to the IRS. [See Illustrations 6-2 and 6-4.] This information is omitted from the codifications or reproduced in relatively small print.

Acts are first published as slip laws and then bound in Public Law number order into the appropriate volume of United States Statutes at

---

[52] Codifications such as United States Code, United States Code Annotated, and United States Code Service include all titles of U.S.C., not merely the Internal Revenue Code.

[53] The GPO website offers online access to U.S.C. and its supplements.

[54] Although each service includes all federal taxes in its Code volumes, it covers only income and employment taxes in the compilation volumes discussed in Chapter 13. In addition to Standard Federal Tax Reporter, which focuses on income tax, CCH also publishes Federal Estate and Gift Tax Reporter and Federal Excise Tax Reporter. RIA's USTR service has three components, USTR—Income Taxes (income and employment taxes), USTR—Estate & Gift Taxes, and USTR—Excise Taxes. .Because the formats are similar, discussion in this text focuses on each publisher's income tax service.

Large.[55] The U.S. Government Printing Office website, GPO Access, provides text with Statutes at Large pagination beginning with laws enacted in the 104th Congress.[56] You can use GPO Access or THOMAS to find the text of statutes. Westlaw and LexisNexis also provide full text.

In addition to using nontax services,[57] you can find acts in two print services discussed in Chapter 17—Internal Revenue Bulletin (and the Cumulative Bulletin) and Internal Revenue Acts—Text and Legislative History. Mertens, Law of Federal Income Taxation—Code volumes (Chapter 13) included the text of new acts for the 1954 Code. It remains useful for 1954 Code historical research.

Illustration 6-9. Searching for a Statute on THOMAS

Search Multiple Congresses

__Search Bill Text__ | __Search Bill Summary, Status__ | Sea

Enter Word/Phrase to Search Bill Text

tax arrows

◌ Exact Match Only   ⦿ Include Variants (plurals, e·

Select Congress

| CHECK ALL | UNCHECK ALL |

☐ 109 ☑ 108 ☐ 107 ☐ 106 ☐ 105 ☐ 104 ☐

Which Bills?

◌ All

◌ Bills with Floor Action

⦿ Enrolled Bills Sent to the President

→If I knew that the 108th Congress passed an act relating to the taxation of arrows but didn't know the bill or act number, I would use this search screen and search for enrolled bills sent to the President.

---

[55] Statutes at Large is available online from Potomac Publishing Company; coverage begins in 1789. There are searchable PDF versions of each act.

[56] See Public and Private Laws at http://www.gpoaccess.gov/plaws/index.html. The site includes PDF and text versions.

[57] U.S. Code Congressional and Administrative News (USCCAN) and United States Code Service Advance are two such sources.

Illustration 6-10. Search Results on THOMAS

The LIBRARY *of* CONGRESS THOMAS

The Library of Congress > THOMAS Home > Bills, Resolutions > Search Results

THIS SEARCH	*THIS DOCUMENT*	*GO TO*
Next Hit	Forward	New Bills Search
Prev Hit	Back	HomePage
Hit List	Best Sections	Help
	Contents Display	

Limited To: Enrolled as Agreed to or Passed by Both House and Senate

57 Bills from the 108th Congress ranked by relevance on *"tax+arrows "*.
    1 bill containing your phrase (or variants of its words) **in the same order.**
    1 bill containing all your search words (or their variants) **near each other in any order**
    1 bill containing all your search words (or their variants) **but not near each other.**
    54 bills containing **one or more of your search words** (or variants).

→In addition to the results above, THOMAS provides a list of the bills in each category. The two most likely bills found were H.R. 5394 (same order) and H.R. 4520. THOMAS provides links to each.

Illustration 6-11. Options for Viewing H.R. 4520 on THOMAS

The LIBRARY *of* CONGRESS THOMAS

The Library of Congress > THOMAS Home > Bills, Resolutions > Search Results

THIS SEARCH	*THIS DOCUMENT*	*GO TO*
Next Hit	Forward	New Bills Search
Prev Hit	Back	HomePage
Hit List	Best Sections	Help
	Contents Display	

Bill 1 of 57
Final version (Enrolled Bill) as passed by both Houses. There are 3 other ver
GPO's PDF Display | Congressional Record References | Bill Summary & Status

→If I click on Bill Summary and Status, I learn that H.R. 4520 became Public Law 108-493. THOMAS lets me link to the PDF version of the act, which is available on the GPO website.

Illustration 6-12. Public Law 108-493 in Statutes at Large

118 STAT. 3984   PUBLIC LAW 108–493—DEC. 23, 2004

Public Law 108–493
108th Congress

An Act

Dec. 23, 2004   To amend the Internal Revenue Code of 1986 to modify the taxation of arrow
[H.R. 5394]   components.

        *Be it enacted by the Senate and House of Representatives of
the United States of America in Congress assembled,*

SECTION 1. EXCISE TAX ON ARROWS.

Applicability.   (a) REPEAL.—Subsection (b) of section 332 of the American
Ante, p. 1477.   Jobs Creation Act of 2004, and the amendments made by such

→The GPO version is a PDF of the Statutes at Large pages.

Illustration 6-13. Public Law Search on GPO Access

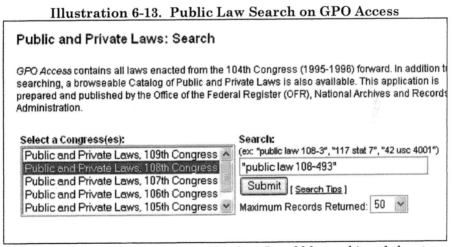

Public and Private Laws: Search

GPO Access contains all laws enacted from the 104th Congress (1995-1996) forward. In addition t
searching, a browseable Catalog of Public and Private Laws is also available. This application is
prepared and published by the Office of the Federal Register (OFR), National Archives and Records
Administration.

Select a Congress(es):

Public and Private Laws, 109th Congress
Public and Private Laws, 108th Congress
Public and Private Laws, 107th Congress
Public and Private Laws, 106th Congress
Public and Private Laws, 105th Congress

Search:
(ex: "public law 108-3", "117 stat 7", "42 usc 4001")

"public law 108-493"

Submit [Search Tips]

Maximum Records Returned: 50

→If I had known the Public Law Number, I could have skipped the steps
shown in Illustrations 6-9 through 6-11 and searched directly in GPO
Access to reach the result illustrated in Illustration 6-12.

3. Previous Law

The materials listed in subsection 1 contain the current law. Those
listed in subsection 2 are useful for finding a particular statute. Although

the materials listed here are similar to those in subsection 2, they allow a more comprehensive search. These materials provide the previous versions of amended sections and the text of legislation that has been repealed altogether. You can use them to trace a provision back through several revisions. Note that tracing is easier in the first four sources, which use fewer volumes.

The materials listed below cover different time periods, which are indicated in parentheses. With the exception of Mertens (Chapter 13), each is discussed in Chapter 17. Keep in mind that if a provision predates the 1954 Code, it has a different section number. You can locate the section numbers from earlier Codes by using the cross-reference tables discussed in Chapter 7, Legislative Histories.

- Cumulative Changes (covers 1939, 1954, and 1986 Codes)

- Barton's Federal Tax Laws Correlated (1913-52)

- Seidman's Legislative History of Federal Income and Excess Profits Tax Laws (1861-1953)

- Legislative History of the Internal Revenue Code (1954-65)

- Mertens, Law of Federal Income Taxation—Code (1954-85)

- Internal Revenue Acts—Text and Legislative History; U.S. Code Congressional & Administrative News—Internal Revenue Code (prior years' volumes; these two sets are best used together for this purpose) (1954 to date)

- Tax Management Primary Sources (1969 to 2003

- The Internal Revenue Acts of the United States: 1909-1950; 1950-1972; 1973-

If Seidman's is unavailable, you can use Eldridge, The United States Internal Revenue System. It provides annotated text for revenue acts prior to 1894 but does not give as much information as does Seidman's.

4. Pending Legislation

a. Print Services

You can use the weekly Congressional Index to locate and track pending items. It provides a brief digest of pending bills. It also indicates a bill's progress, listing hearings and other pertinent information. [See Illustrations 6-14 and 6-15.] Bills are indexed by subject matter as well as by author and bill number. Useful tables provide information about enactments by Public Law number; enactments by bill or resolution number; names of laws amended or enacted; and vetoes.[58]

Illustration 6-14. Excerpt from Congressional Index

H 2511—Energy—income tax—energy production, encouragement

By McCrery.

To amend the Internal Revenue Code of 1986 to provide tax incentives to encourage energy conservation, energy reliability, and energy production. (To Ways and Means.)

→Representative McCrery introduced H.R. 2511 in the 107th Congress, 1st Session.

Illustration 6-15. Excerpt from Congressional Index

2511

Introduced 7/17/01
Ref to H Ways & Means Com 7/17/01
Ordered reptd w/amdts by Ways & Means Com   7/18/01
Reptd w/amdts, H Rept 107-157, by Ways & Means Com   7/24/01

→No further action occurred with respect to this bill.

Although tax-oriented looseleaf services may cover pending legislation, only newsletters such as Tax Notes and Daily Tax Report list a significant number of bills introduced in the current Congress. Newsletter descriptions of most items are cursory.

b. Online Services

Online services (Chapter 20) are usually the best means for following pending bills. Online versions of newsletters such as Daily Tax Report track bills, but they are not the best tool for this purpose. If you want to follow a recently introduced bill through Congress, use the government's THOMAS site or use a commercial service such as LexisNexis or Westlaw. These tools are illustrated below for S. 1321, 109th Congress.

---

[58] Other useful tools include those published by Congressional Information Service (CIS), which follow a bill's progress through Congress, and the Weekly Compilation of Presidential Documents.

Illustration 6-16. Pending Legislation Information from THOMAS

S.1321
Title: A bill to amend the Internal Revenue Code of 1986 to repeal the excise tax on telephone and other communications.
Sponsor: Sen Santorum, Rick [PA] (introduced 6/28/2005)   Cosponsors (17)
Related Bills: H.R.1898, S.832
Latest Major Action: 9/15/2006 Placed on Senate Legislative Calendar under General Orders. Calendar No. 614.
Senate Reports: 109-336

ALL ACTIONS:

6/28/2005:
      Introductory remarks on measure. (CR S7526)
6/28/2005:
      Read twice and referred to the Committee on Finance.
      6/28/2006:
            Committee on Finance. Ordered to be reported with an amendment in the nature of a substitute favorably Subs
            of S.832.
9/15/2006:
      Committee on Finance. Reported by Senator Grassley with an amendment in the nature of a substitute and an amen
      109-336.
9/15/2006:
      Placed on Senate Legislative Calendar under General Orders. Calendar No. 614.

Illustration 6-17. Pending Legislation Excerpt from LexisNexis

Legislative Chronology:

1st Session Activity:

06/28/2005 ◆ 151 Cong Rec S 7520
      Referred to the Senate Committee on Finance.

06/28/2005 ◆ 151 Cong Rec S 7526
      Remarks by Sen. Santorum (R-PA)

2nd Session Activity:

06/28/2006 ◆ 152 Cong Rec D 718
      Order reported, as amended, by Senate Committee on Finance

09/15/2006 ◆ 152 Cong Rec S 9659
      Report filed, as amended, by the Senate Committee on Finance

→This excerpt is from LexisNexis Bill Tracking Report – Current Congress.

Illustration 6-18. Pending Legislation Information from Westlaw

AUTHOR: Sen Santorum, Rick

SUMMARY: A bill to amend the Internal Revenue Code of 1986 to repeal the excise tax on telephone an

STATUS:
06/28/2005 INTRODUCTORY REMARKS ON MEASURE. (CR S7526)
06/28/2005 READ TWICE AND REFERRED TO THE COMMITTEE ON FINANCE. 6/28/2006:COMMITTEE ON F
REPORTED WITH AN AMENDMENT IN THE NATURE OF A SUBSTITUTE FAVORABLY SUBSTITUTE AMENDME
TEXT OF S.832.
06/28/2006 COMMITTEE ON FINANCE. ORDERED TO BE REPORTED WITH AN AMENDMENT IN THE NATURE
FAVORABLY SUBSTITUTE AMENDMENT INCORPORATES THE TEXT OF S.832.
09/15/2006 COMMITTEE ON FINANCE. REPORTED BY SENATOR GRASSLEY WITH AN AMENDMENT IN THE
SUBSTITUTE AND AN AMENDMENT TO THE TITLE. WITH WRITTEN REPORT NO. 109-336.
09/15/2006 PLACED ON SENATE LEGISLATIVE CALENDAR UNDER GENERAL ORDERS. CALENDAR NO. 614.
2005 FD S.B. 1321 (NS)

→This excerpt concerning S. 1321 is from Westlaw US-BILLTRK.

5. Potential Legislation

Long before a bill is introduced, taxpayers may receive hints that legislation is likely. In presidential election years, for example, party platforms include potential legislative agendas. Presidential budget messages may also serve this function. Items of this nature appear in newsletters (Chapter 16) and in general interest newspapers. You can also find presidential documents at the President's website, http://www.whitehouse.gov. Political parties have their own sites.

Prior congressional action is another source of potential legislation. Treasury Department studies mandated in one act [Illustration 6-2] may lead to provisions enacted in a later year.[59] In addition, acts that die in one Congress are often reintroduced in a later Congress. Legislators frequently issue press releases announcing they are working on bills.

Although Treasury regulations usually follow (and interpret) statutes, there are occasional role reversals. Legislation may be enacted to codify positions taken in regulations.[60] Unpopular administrative positions or court decisions may also trigger legislative activity.[61]

---

[59] These and other government studies are discussed in Chapter 7. Reports issued by nongovernmental groups are discussed in Chapter 14.

[60] This occurred in 1996 for life insurance benefits paid before death during a terminal illness (I.R.C. § 101(g)), in 1984 for certain fringe benefits (I.R.C. § 132), and in 1971 for asset depreciation range (ADR) depreciation (1954 I.R.C. § 167(m)).

[61] See, e.g., I.R.C. § 108(d)(7)(A), a response to Gitlitz v. Commissioner, 531

Section H. Citators for Statutes

After Congress passes an act, litigation may ensue over the constitutionality or interpretation of individual Code sections. Constitutional litigation is discussed in Chapter 5, which includes examples of such claims. Litigation is more likely to involve disputes between the IRS and taxpayers over conflicting interpretations of statutory provisions.

Citators are an excellent tool for determining if a federal court has ruled on a statute's constitutionality. Because they are updated much more frequently, online citators are more useful search tools than are print citators. Online services also allow different types of searching. For example, if you use an electronic service, you may not even need its citator features. Instead, you can find constitutional challenges using a word search that includes the Code section and a variant of constitutional.

Not only do print citators lack the frequency and word search advantages, they may also have coverage issues. The Shepard's print citators did not cover Tax Court decisions as extensively as electronic citators do. These limitations even applied to the earliest volumes of Shepard's Federal Tax Citations. The CCH and RIA print citators did not cover statutes at all. Citators are discussed in greater detail in Chapter 12.

Section I. Interpreting Statutory Language

1. Sources for Interpreting Statutes

When litigation involves a statute's meaning, someone must interpret it. Although Congress has delegated the authority to issue interpretive rules to the Treasury Department (Chapter 9),[62] regulations rarely follow on the heels of a law's enactment.

In addition to administrative interpretations, or in their absence when none are available, courts may turn to legislative history documents (Chapter 7) as expressions of congressional intent. Legislative history materials take on particular significance if administrative rules are

---

U.S. 206 (2001).

[62] I.R.C. § 7805.

alleged to be unreasonable and the statute's "plain meaning" is in doubt.[63]

2. Using Statutory Language

As noted in Chapter 4, careful reading of Code provisions is a critical part of the research process. If the Code provides its own definition for a term, you must locate that definition. If a term is specifically defined for purposes of a particular Code subdivision (e.g., Code section 165(g)(2) in Illustration 6-8), you cannot automatically use that definition for another subdivision.

a. Intra-Code Cross-References

Because a single Code section rarely governs a transaction, your research must include a search for other operative sections. Congress frequently offers guidance in accomplishing this task by providing cross-references between Code sections that govern the same transaction.[64] Unfortunately, cross-references may appear in only one of the sections.[65] An intra-Code cross-reference table may provide the information you need.

Cross-reference tables showing Code sections citing to a particular section appear in Standard Federal Tax Reporter (Chapter 13). Although CD/DVD (Chapter 19) and online (Chapter 20) services lack tables, they may have other finding aids you can use to find cross-references. The OneDisc, for example, provides cross-references in the Background Notes for most Code sections. Services such as TaxExpert Online also include cross-references.

As Illustrations 6-19 and 6-20 indicate, different sources may yield different results. There is no substitute for reading the Code sections.

b. Limitations of Cross-Reference Tables and Similar Tools

These sources are worthless if Code sections interact but don't explicitly refer to each other.[66] Even if sections do refer to each other, an

---

[63] Supreme Court rulings on deference paid administrative interpretations are discussed in Chapters 9 and 10.

[64] I.R.C. §§ 267 and 707(b) specifically refer to each other.

[65] I.R.C. § 104 refers to I.R.C. § 213, but § 213 fails to mention § 104.

[66] Before its 1986 revision, I.R.C. § 336 failed to mention § 1245 and vice versa. Section 1245 clearly governed transactions affected by each section.

infrequently updated cross-reference table or other tool may not reflect the most recent statutory changes. Using a term search in a CD/DVD or online service presents much less risk that your source will not be current.

Reliance on these tools may induce a dangerous sense of security. If you are an experienced practitioner, you know which types of provisions affect others. In approaching a deductibility problem, for example, you would consider sections allowing the deduction as well as potential disallowance sections and timing provisions. You may locate these by glancing through the Code itself or by using a subject matter Code section index. [See Illustration 4-1.] Alternatively, you might use a subject-oriented looseleaf service (Chapter 13) to obtain this information. Less-experienced researchers should probably start with a looseleaf service.

Illustration 6-19. Excerpt from Standard Federal Tax Reporter Code Volume I Cross Reference Table III

IRC, 2006-CODE-VOL Cross-Reference Table III

Cross-Reference Table III

CROSS-REFERENCES WITHIN THE INTERNAL REVENUE CODE OF 1986

(As of January 19, 2004)

Section	Referred to in
1	Sections 2, 3, 15, 23, 24, 25A, 32, 41, 42, 55, 59, 63, 68, 132, 135, 137, 146, 162, 163, 179, 213, 219, 220, 221, 223, 301, 306, 453A, 460, 468B, 511, 512, 513, 584, 641, 646, 685, 691, 702, 774, 854, 857, 871, 876, 877, 891, 904, 911, 936, 962, 1022, 1260, 1291, 1301, 1398, 1446, 2032A, 2503, 2631, 3402, 3406, 4001, 4261, 6014, 6015, 6039F, 6103, 6242, 6323, 6334, 6428, 6601, 6652, 6655, 6867, 7430, 7518, 7519.

→The SFTR table covers only cross-references within the Internal Revenue Code.

→Other services include additional U.S.C. titles of United States Code. As of November 2006, this online version of the cross-reference table is two years old.

Illustration 6-20. Excerpt from TaxExpert Online

```
SECTION REFERRED TO IN OTHER SECTIONS

  This section is referred to in sections 2, 3, 15, 32, 41, 42, 59, 63
68, 135, 402, 453A, 460, 468B, 511, 513, 641, 691, 871, 876, 877, 891,
904, 962, 1291, 1398, 1446, 6014, 6103, 6652, 6655, 6867, 7518, 7519 of
this title; title 46 App. section 1177.
```

→TaxExpert includes provisions in other titles of United States Code.

c. Limitations on Cross-References as Interpretive Aids

While cross-references are useful in locating relevant statutory material, they lack independent interpretive significance. Code section 7806(a) provides that "[t]he cross references in this title to other portions of the title, or other provisions of law, where the word 'see' is used, are made only for convenience, and shall be given no legal effect."

3. Selected Maxims of Construction

Judges cite various rules of statutory construction in the course of interpreting statutes. The decisions listed below state or repeat several of these rules.[67] To appreciate their effect, you should read the opinions cited for each proposition. The weight given legislative history is discussed in Chapter 7; that given administrative interpretations is discussed in Chapters 9 and 10.

• The fundamental principle of statutory construction, *expressio unius est exclusio alterius*, applies. There is a firm presumption that everything in the I.R.C. was intentionally included for a reason and everything not in the code was likewise excluded for a reason—the expression of one thing is the exclusion of another. Speers v. United States, 38 Fed. Cl. 197, 202 (1997).

• "Under the principle of *ejusdem generis*, when a general term follows a specific one, the general term should be understood as a reference to subjects akin to the one with specific enumeration." .... In the usual instance, the doctrine of *ejusdem generis* applies where a "catch-all" term

---

[67] The Code also includes rules of construction: "No inference, implication, or presumption of legislative construction shall be drawn or made by reason of the location or grouping of any particular section or provision or portion of this title, nor shall any table of contents, table of cross references, or similar outline, analysis, or descriptive matter relating to the contents of this title be given any legal effect." I.R.C. § 7806(b).

precedes, or more often follows, an enumeration of specific terms in order to expand the list without identifying every situation covered by the statute. Host Marriott Corp. v. United States, 113 F. Supp.2d 790, 793 (D. Md. 2000).

• [T]he presumption is against interpreting a statute in a way which renders it ineffective or futile. Matut v. Commissioner, 86 T.C. 686, 690 (1986).

• [T]he courts have some leeway in interpreting a statute if the adoption of a literal or usual meaning of its words "would lead to absurd results *** or would thwart the obvious purpose of the statute." .... Or, to put it another way, we should not adopt a construction which would reflect a conclusion that Congress had "legislate[d] eccentrically." Edna Louise Dunn Trust v. Commissioner, 86 T.C. 745, 755 (1986).

• We should avoid an interpretation of a statute that renders any part of it superfluous and does not give effect to all of the words used by Congress. Beisler v. Commissioner, 814 F.2d 1304, 1307 (9th Cir. 1987).

• [T]he whole of [the section's] various subparts should be harmonized if possible. Water Quality Association Employees' Benefit Corp. v. United States, 795 F.2d 1303, 1307 (7th Cir. 1986).

• In terms of statutory construction, the *context* from which the meaning of a word is drawn must of necessity be the words of the statute itself. Strogoff v. United States, 10 Cl. Ct. 584, 588 (1986).

• [H]eadings and titles are not meant to take the place of the detailed provisions of the text. Nor are they necessarily designed to be a reference guide or a synopsis. Where the text is complicated and prolific, headings and titles can do no more than indicate the provisions in a most general manner;.... Factors of this type have led to the wise rule that the title of a statute and the heading of a section cannot limit the plain meaning of the text. Stanley Works v. Commissioner, 87 T.C. 389, 419 (1986).

• When a statute does not define a term, we generally interpret that term by employing the ordinary, contemporary, and common meaning of the words that Congress used. Merkel v. Commissioner, 192 F.3d 844, 848 (9th Cir. 1999).

• As a matter of statutory construction, identical words used in different parts of the Internal Revenue Code are normally given the same meaning. Disabled American Veterans v. Commissioner, 94 T.C. 60, 71 (1990).

· Stated another way, Congress must make a clear statement that a double benefit is intended before we will construe a provision to allow this result. Transco Exploration Co. v. Commissioner, 949 F.2d 837, 841 (5th Cir. 1992).

SECTION J. PROBLEMS

1. Indicate the subtitle, chapter, subchapter, part, and subpart for section

   a. 25A

   b. 465

   c. 991

   d. 1551

   e. 6330

   f. 7454

2. Indicate the presidential power or function referred to in Code section

   a. 274(h)(6)(C)(ii)(II)

   b. 896(c)

   c. 5064(b)(3)

   d. 6103(g)

   e. 7621(a)

   f. 7802(b)(5)

3. Give the bill number for Pub. L. No.

   a. 85-12

   b. 92-9

   c. 98-67

   d. 104-188

   e. 107-212

   f. 109-1

4. Indicate the popular name for

   a. Pub. L. No. 86-69

   b. Pub. L. No. 90-364

   c. Pub. L. No. 97-414

   d. Pub. L. No. 104-191

   e. Pub. L. No. 106-170

   f. Pub. L. No. 108-161

5. Indicate the full Statutes at Large citation, including Public Law or chapter number, for

   a. War Revenue Act of 1917

   b. Tax Adjustment Act of 1945

   c. Bank Holding Company Act of 1956

   d. Black Lung Benefits Revenue Act of 1977

   e. Social Security Domestic Employment Reform Act of 1994

   f. Installment Tax Correction Act of 2000

6. Indicate which tax provision appears in

   a. Puyallup Tribe of Indians Settlement Act of 1989, Pub. L. No. 101-41, § 10(d)

   b. South African Democratic Transition Support Act of 1993, Pub. L. No. 103-149, § 4(b)(8)

   c. Vision 100–Century of Aviation Reauthorization Act, Pub. L. No. 108-176, § 902(a)

   d. Energy Policy Act of 2005, Pub. L. No. 109-58, § 411(d)(1)

7. List the Treasury Department or other government entity study mandated in

   a. Omnibus Budget Reconciliation Act of 1990, § 11113

   b. Pub. L. No. 104-7, § 6

   c. American Jobs Creation Act of 2004, § 424

8. List the Code section added by

   a. Pub. L. No. 99-514, § 132(a)

   b. Pub. L. No. 103-66, § 13114(a)

   c. Pub. L. No. 97-34, § 121(a)

   d. Pub. L. No. 109-227, § 2(a)

9. Give the enactment date for

   a. Revenue Act of 1928

   b. Life Insurance Company Tax Act of 1955

   c. Revenue and Expenditure Control Act of 1968

   d. Anti-Drug Abuse Act of 1988

   e. Taxpayer Browsing Protection Act of 1997

   f. Clergy Housing Allowance Clarification Act of 2002

10. Indicate the effective dates of both the act and the specific act section listed below.

   a. Miscellaneous Trade and Technical Corrections Act of 1999, § 3001

   b. Job Creation and Worker Assistance Act of 2002, § 101

   c. Military Family Tax Relief Act of 2003, § 106

   d. Deficit Reduction Act of 2005, § 7301(d)

11. Give the sunset date for Code section as it read on November 1, 2006.

   a. 68

   b. 170(b)(1)(E)

   c. 512(b)(13)(E)

   d. 1014

12. Indicate the scope limitations (e.g., subtitle, section, clause) for Code section

   a. 291(a)

   b. 584(h)(3)(B)(ii)

   c. 643(a)

   d. 1271(a)

   e. 3306(a)

13. Indicate which Code section defines

   a. distilled spirits plant

   b. qualified agri-biodiesel production

   c. liquidity shortfall

   d. taxable vaccine

   e. rare disease or condition

14. Congress occasionally defines Code section terms by citing to other federal statutes. Find a Code provision that takes its definition from

   a. Public Utility Holding Company Act

   b. Stevenson-Wydler Technology Innovation Act of 1980

   c. Indian Gaming Regulatory Act

   d. Bank Holding Company Act of 1956

15. List all Code sections that refer to Code section. If possible, use more than one service in finding this information and list any differences between the services.

   a. 213

   b. 611

   c. 1442

   d. 6038

16. Do an online or CD/DVD search to find a more recent judicial decision citing a principle of interpretation listed in Section I. Your instructor may assign a particular principle for you to research.

17. Print out the tax planks from the Democratic and Republican platforms from the most recent presidential campaign.

18. Print out the tax proposals from the President's most recent State of the Union Address and Budget Message.

CHAPTER 7. LEGISLATIVE HISTORIES

SECTION A. INTRODUCTION

This chapter continues the discussion of statutes begun in Chapter 6 by describing legislative history materials and indicating where they can be found. In addition to hearings, reports by tax-writing committees, and congressional floor debate, it includes reports by other committees and by entities such as the Government Accountability Office. This chapter also explains the process for tracing current statutes back to earlier versions. Legislative history documents for treaties are covered in Chapter 8.

SECTION B. GROUPS INVOLVED IN LEGISLATION[68]

1. Congressional Committees

The **House Committee on Ways and Means** and the **Senate Committee on Finance** have primary jurisdiction over revenue bills. Other relevant committees include each chamber's **Budget Committee** and committees with jurisdiction over other areas with tax implications.[69] Each of these committees has subcommittees. If the House and Senate pass different versions of a bill, a **Conference Committee** meets to resolve these differences.

Five members each from Ways and Means and Finance sit on the **Joint Committee on Taxation** (JCT).[70] The JCT may issue proposals and reports, but it is not charged with drafting legislation. Its reports lack the interpretive significance of those issued by the tax-writing committees.

The JCT website lists reports for each year, beginning with 1981. Those

---

[68] Table 7-1 provides website information for entities described in this section. Table 7-2 indicates abbreviations by which many of these entities are known.

[69] E.g., the Subcommittee on Tax, Finance, and Exports of the House Small Business Committee.

[70] I.R.C. §§ 8001-8023. The JCT is charged with investigating the operation and effects of the tax system, its administration, and means of simplifying it. Id. § 8022. It also reviews tax refunds exceeding $2,000,000. Id. § 6405.

issued since 1992 are available on the JCT website. The JCT's General Explanation of legislation enacted by Congress (referred to as the Blue Book) can be used as authority if a taxpayer is disputing the substantial underpayment penalty discussed in Chapter 2.

The **Joint Economic Committee**, which is also staffed by members of each chamber, reviews the economy and recommends improvements in economic policy. Areas on which it issues reports include taxation.

2. Congressional Support Entities

Three entities are organized as nonpartisan support services. Each issues reports on various tax administration and policy issues. Two of them [Illustrations 7-7 and 7-8] make their reports available online.

The **Government Accountability Office** is the investigative arm of Congress. "It studies how the federal government spends taxpayer dollars. GAO advises Congress and the heads of executive agencies ... about ways to make government more effective and responsive. GAO evaluates federal programs, audits federal expenditures, and issues legal opinions."[71] The GAO issues numerous reports on tax administration and on substantive tax topics. It is headed by the Comptroller of the Currency.

The **Congressional Budget Office** "produces policy analyses, cost estimates of legislation, and budget and economic projections that serve as a basis for the Congress's decisions about spending and taxes."[72]

The **Congressional Research Service** (known as the Legislative Reference Service between 1914 and 1970) performs research on public policy matters for Congress. Its work is confidential, and the CRS website does not provide access to its reports.[73] The Westlaw FTX-CRS database carries CRS reports released since 1989. Tax Analysts includes CRS reports in Tax Notes Today, which is also available on LexisNexis.

3. The Executive Branch

The **President** may propose legislation, which a member of Congress

---

[71] GAO Website (http://www.gao.gov) The GAO was called the General Accounting Office until July 7, 2004.

[72] CBO Website (http://www.cbo.gov).

[73] CRS website (www.loc.gov/crsinfo).

will introduce, in messages to Congress (e.g., the State of the Union Address) or in other speeches. The **Office of Management and Budget** assists the President in formulating a budget and works with administrative agencies to ensure that their reports and testimony are consistent with the President's goals. The **Council of Economic Advisers** provides analysis and advice on developing and implementing economic policy.

Several other executive branch entities issue reports with respect to taxation. As discussed in Chapter 6, Congress often asks the **Treasury Department** and **Internal Revenue Service** to study and report on issues. The **IRS National Taxpayer Advocate** issues two reports to Congress each year. The first outlines objectives planned for the next year. The second discusses serious issues facing taxpayers and recommendations for solving them.[74] The National Taxpayer Advocate may also issue recommendations for legislation.

Table 7-1. Government Entities Involved in Legislation

Entity	Website
Congressional Budget Office	www.cbo.gov
Congressional Research Service	www.loc.gov/crsinfo
Council of Economic Advisers	www.whitehouse.gov/cea
Government Accountability Office	www.gao.gov
House of Representatives	www.house.gov
Budget Committee	www.budget.house.gov
Ways & Means Committee	waysandmeans.house.gov
Internal Revenue Service	www.irs.gov
IRS National Taxpayer Advocate	www.irs.gov/advocate
Joint Economic Committee	www.house.gov/jec
Joint Committee on Taxation	www.house.gov/jct
Office of Management and Budget	www.whitehouse.gov/omb
President	www.whitehouse.gov
Senate	www.senate.gov
Budget Committee	www.budget.senate.gov
Finance Committee	www.finance.senate.gov
Treasury Department	www.treas.gov
Inspector General for Tax Administration	www.treas.gov/tigta
Office of Tax Analysis	www.treas.gov/ota
Office of Tax Policy	www.treas.gov/offices/tax-policy

---

[74] See TAX NOTES TODAY, 2002 TNT 41-1 (Mar. 1, 2002) for a report on possible legislative initiatives in response to the Advocate's December 2001 report.

If you lack a web address, you can access government sites at FirstGov (www.firstgov.gov). It lists all branches of the federal government under Organizations. You can also use GPO Access (www.gpoaccess.gov) for this purpose.

Table 7-2. Abbreviations for Government Entities

Entity	Abbreviation
Congressional Budget Office	CBO
Congressional Research Service	CRS
Council of Economic Advisers	CEA
Government Accountability Office	GAO
Government Printing Office	GPO
Internal Revenue Service	IRS
Joint Economic Committee	JEC
Joint Committee on Taxation	JCT
Office of Management and Budget	OMB
Treasury Inspector General for Tax Administration	TIGTA
Treasury Office of Tax Analysis	OTA
Treasury Office of Tax Policy	OTP

4. Other Groups

Members of Congress regularly receive written input from constituents, professional societies, trade associations, and lobbyists. These groups also testify at hearings on proposed legislation. Several of these groups are listed in Chapter 14.

SECTION C. LEGISLATIVE PROCESS

The process for enacting tax legislation is virtually identical to that used for other federal laws. The major difference relates to the constitutional limitation discussed in Chapter 5: revenue-raising bills must originate in the House of Representatives.[75]

1. Introduction of Bill

The sponsoring legislator may present remarks for inclusion in the Congressional Record at the bill's introduction. If the administration is proposing an item, a presidential message may accompany the bill transmitted to Congress.

---

[75] See James V. Saturno, Blue-Slipping: The Origination Clause in the House of Representatives (Congressional Research Service Report, 2002), available on LexisNexis at 2002 TNT 114-16.

The bill receives a bill number when it is introduced. Similar bills may be introduced in the same chamber; each will have a separate bill number. The bill may be simultaneously introduced in each chamber and receive separate bill numbers in each. Bill numbers are sequential for each term of Congress (e.g., H.R. 1; S. 1); there is not a separate numbering system for each session within the two-year term.

2. Referral to Committee and Committee Action

After its introduction, the bill is referred to the appropriate committee, generally the House Ways and Means Committee or the Senate Finance Committee. The committee (or a subcommittee thereof) may hold hearings, which will be published. It usually issues a committee report to accompany the bill that is reported out of committee. These reports are numbered by Congress (e.g., H.R. Rep. No. 109-13, 109th Cong., 1st Sess. (2005)).

The version of the bill that the committee chair initially issues is referred to as the **chairman's mark**.[76] After committee deliberation, which may include input from committee, IRS, and Treasury staffs and from other groups described in Section B, the marked-up bill may differ significantly from its initial version.

The bill, or a similar version, may have been simultaneously considered in the other chamber or considered after being passed in the first chamber. The process in the second chamber, generally the Senate, is comparable to that described above.

3. House and Senate Floor Debate

A bill sent to the floor by committee can die in one chamber, pass intact, or pass with amendments. Each chamber separately deliberates on the bill before voting. Although Senate rules permit more extensive debate and floor amendments than do House procedures, each chamber can change the bill. A bill sent from one chamber to the other is called an **engrossed bill**.

Questions and answers and other statements made during floor debate can illuminate the meaning of legislation.[77] Be aware, however, that

---

[76] As of November 2006, all tax-writing committee chairs have been male.

[77] In Ashburn v. United States, 740 F.2d 843 (11th Cir. 1984), the court referred to committee reports and congressional debates as evidence of the meaning of a phrase in the Equal Access to Justice Act. See also Commissioner v.

statements can be made to an empty chamber or added as text but not spoken.

If both chambers pass the bill with identical terms, it can be sent to the President. If the versions differ, a Conference Committee is appointed.

4. Conference Committee Action

The Conference Committee meets to resolve House and Senate differences. It generates a third report, the **Conference Report**. That document is usually numbered as a House report. The Conference Report explains the resolution of House-Senate differences. [See Illustration 7-1.]

Illustration 7-1. Excerpt from H. Rep. No. 107-84, 107th Cong., 1st Sess. (2001), at 158

---

a skill required in a trade or business currently engaged in by the taxpayer, or (2) meets the express requirements of the taxpayer's employer, applicable law or regulations imposed as a condition of continued employment. However, education expenses are generally not deductible if they relate to certain minimum educational requirements or to education or training that enables a taxpayer to begin working in a new trade or business.[31]

HOUSE BILL

No provision.

SENATE AMENDMENT

The provision extends the exclusion for employer-provided educational assistance to graduate education and makes the exclusion (as applied to both undergraduate and graduate education) permanent.

Effective date.—The provision is effective with respect to courses beginning after December 31, 2001.

CONFERENCE AGREEMENT

The conference agreement follows the Senate Amendment.

→The conference report explains current law in addition to reporting on each chamber's proposals and resolution of House-Senate differences.

Engle, 464 U.S. 206 (1984), in which the Court's opinion on the meaning of I.R.C. § 613A cited to testimony at hearings, floor debate, and committee reports. Be aware that the Supreme Court has become less receptive to using legislative history materials in construing statutes.

5. Floor Action on Conference Report

Unlike the pre-conference bills, a bill that emerges from the Conference Committee cannot be further amended during floor debate. Each chamber must pass it or reject it as written. That "final" version (the **enrolled version**) is then prepared for submission to the President.

6. Correcting Drafting Errors

Unlike treaties, bills die when a Congress's second session ends.[78] Members work under extreme time pressure to pass pending legislation by that date. As a result, a conference report's version may contain errors, which Congress passes along with the rest of the bill. If both chambers agree, Congress can adopt a concurrent resolution making necessary changes before the act is enrolled for submission to the President. If they do not agree, or find the errors too late, a technical corrections bill is inevitable.[79]

7. Presidential Action

The President has four options. The bill becomes law if the President signs it within ten days of its presentment. It also becomes law if the President does nothing so long as Congress remains in session during that period. Alternatively, the President can veto the bill; Congress can override a veto only by a two-thirds vote in each chamber.[80] If the President does nothing and the congressional session ends during the ten-day period, the bill is "pocket-vetoed." The President may issue a statement when signing or vetoing a bill.

In 1996, Congress gave the President a different option, a so-called line-item veto over certain direct spending items and "limited tax benefits." The Supreme Court held that the line-item veto violated the Constitution's presentment clause.[81] Before Congress recessed for the

---

[78] Chapter 8 discusses other differences between statutes and treaties.

[79] See, e.g., H.R. Con. Res. 328, 98th Cong., 2d Sess. (1984), 98 Stat. 3454 (1984), making technical changes to the Tax Reform Act of 1984. Compare H.R. Con. Res. 395, 99th Cong., 2d Sess. (1986), which failed to pass, leaving flaws in the 1986 Act. When using the THOMAS website, search for these as H Res. rather than H.R. Res.

[80] For example, Congress overrode President Franklin Roosevelt's veto of the Revenue Act of 1943, ch. 63, 58 Stat. 21 (1944).

[81] Clinton v. City of New York, 524 U.S. 417 (1998).

2006 elections, its members were trying to write a line-item veto act that would not be unconstitutional.[82]

SECTION D. LOCATING LEGISLATIVE HISTORY DOCUMENTS: CITATIONS AND TEXT

The process used for locating legislative history documents varies depending on whether you are using print materials or electronic services. If you are using print materials, your research may involve two steps. First you must obtain citations for the documents needed. Then you must locate those documents.[83] When researching online or in a CD/DVD database, you may be able to skip the first step and find your documents using word and Code section searches or by searching on the act itself.

1. Statements on the Floor of Congress

The Congressional Record prints statements made when a bill is introduced and statements, questions, and answers made during floor debate. Make sure you check the Congressional Record pages for each chamber. Page numbers indicate H for House and S for Senate.

Congressional Record can be accessed through its indexes, but it is easier to search online. The service you use for this purpose will depend on the year involved.

The government's THOMAS website provides two methods of accessing the Congress Record back to 1989. First, you can use its Congressional Record page to search by key word, date, or speaker. In addition to statements relating to bills, this method will also recover statements made without respect to particular pending legislation. This search screen is shown in Illustration 7-2. Second, if you know the bill or Public Law Number, you can search its history as shown in Illustration 7-3.

The government also makes Congressional Record available online through GPO Access, beginning with 1994.[84] Beginning in 1995, the GPO Access version is available in PDF, making it easier to read than the THOMAS version. THOMAS often offers a link to GPO Access.

---

[82] See, e.g., H.R. 4890, 109th Cong., 2d Sess. (2006).

[83] Beginning in 1975, Statutes at Large includes citations to committee reports, Congressional Record items, and presidential messages immediately following the text of each act.

[84] See www.gpoaccess.gov/crecord/index.html.

Illustration 7-2. Congressional Record Section of THOMAS

Search the Congressional Record for the 109th Congress (2005-2006)

The Congressional Record is the official record of the proceedings and debates of the U.S. Congress. ● More about the Congressional Record

Search the Congressional Record | Latest Daily Digest | Browse Daily Issues

Browse the Keyword Index

Select Congress: 109 | 108 | 107 | 106 | 105 | 104 | 103 | 102 | 101

● Help

Enter Search

⬤ Exact Match Only   ◯ Include Variants (plurals, etc.)

Illustration 7-3. Congressional Record Link for H.R. 4520 (2004)

THIS SEARCH	*THIS DOCUMENT*	*GO TO*
Next Hit	Forward	New Bills Search
Prev Hit	Back	HomePage
Hit List	Best Sections	Help
	Contents Display	

Bill 20 of 2000
There are 5 other versions of this bill.

GPO's PDF Display References to this bill in the Congressional Record |

You can search Congressional Record online through commercial services such as Westlaw (CR database, beginning in 1985), LexisNexis

(Individual Congressional Record Materials, beginning in 1985), and LexisNexis Congressional. [See Illustration 7-4.] It is possible your library will offer access to LexisNexis Congressional that is separate from any subscription to the general LexisNexis service.

These services described in Chapter 17 print excerpts from Congressional Record: Tax Management Primary Sources (1969-2003); Internal Revenue Acts—Texts and Legislative History (since 1954); and Seidman's Legislative History of Federal Income and Excess Profits Tax Laws (1863-1953).[85] Barton's Federal Tax Laws Correlated, provides page citations for the period from 1953 through 1969.

The library's microform collection may be your best option for finding full text of older Congressional Record volumes.

Illustration 7-4. LexisNexis Congressional Search Page

Congressional Record & Rules

| Keyword Search | Get a Document | [?] |

Enter search terms

Search within: ⦿ Congressional Record ○ Rules of Congress

Restrict by speaker on the floor

Last Name :
Look up a Member

Restrict by
⦿ Date:
Previous 2 years ▾ Nov 12 2004 to Nov 12 2006

○ Congress:
Any Congress ▾ 99(1985-1986) to 109(2005-2006)

Clear form

2. Committee Hearings

Transcripts of hearings can be located in the library's government documents section or in its microform collection. Online versions are available through services as Westlaw, LexisNexis, and LexisNexis Congressional; coverage dates vary. For example, hearings since the late 1980s are included in the Tax Analysts database on LexisNexis. [See

---

[85] Seidman's is also available in the HeinOnline service discussed in Chapter 20 and illustrated in various chapters.

Illustration 7-5.]

Beginning with the 105th Congress, transcripts of hearings (including written submissions) can be found using the Government Printing Office website. Congressional websites also include some transcripts. The House Ways & Means Committee has a hearings link on its website.

Illustration 7-5. Excerpt from H.R. 2922 Hearing Transcript

Release date: 01 JUL 92
SUBCOMMITTEE ON SELECT REVENUE MEASURES
COMMITTEE ON WAYS AND MEANS
July 1, 1992

CHAIR RANGEL: The subcommittee will come to order.

Today, the Subcommittee on Select Revenue Measures will receive testimony on H.R.2922, the Lead-Based Paint Hazard Abatement Act, and the issue of taxing the lead industry to fund the cleanup of lead-based paint in our nation's homes.

H.R.2922 introduced by Congressmen Cardin, Stark, McDermott, Moody, Donnelly, Ford of Tennessee, Matsui, Guarini, myself and others, would establish a new lead abatement trust fund. The fund would be financed by an excise tax on lead produced in or imported into the United States.

Expenditures from the fund would be authorized for grants to state and local governments for the abatement of hazards associated with lead-based paint in low-income housing and day care centers.

Unfortunately, our nation's children all too often are innocent victims of lead poisoning. Poor children, in particular, cannot protect themselves from high-dose exposure in their homes and in day care centers. It is truly tragic to see our children — our nation's most valuable resource — needlessly suffer from this health risk.

Therefore, it is important for this subcommittee to examine whether there is a role for tax legislation in addressing this serious problem.

Today, we will hear more about the scope of the problem. Further, we will hear about whether or not it is appropriate to tax the lead industry to pay for the cleanup of paint in homes.

→The unofficial hearing transcript can be found at 92 TNT 141-54.

3. Tax-Writing Committee Reports

You can find committee reports in the library's government documents or microform collections if you have the appropriate citation. Reports are numbered sequentially by Congress, not by committee. The numbering does not restart when a term of Congress goes into its second session. Reports use initials to indicate which chamber issued them; the citation also indicates the number and session of Congress.[86]

a. Citations

Online sources provide immediate access to reports even if you lack citations. Unfortunately, they rarely cover pre-1954 Code material. If you need a citation to a report, several services provide that information.[87]

• Bulletin Index-Digest System (Chapter 17) (1954-1994)

• Barton's Federal Tax Laws Correlated (Chapter 17) (through 1969)

• Standard Federal Tax Reporter—Citator (Chapter 13) (Cumulative Bulletin rather than report number citations for amendments to 1954 and 1986 Codes; listed in Code section order)

• TaxCite (citations to reports printed in the Cumulative Bulletin for commonly cited statutes enacted between 1913 and 1993)

• Legislative History of the Internal Revenue Code of 1954 (Chapter 17) (1954 through 1969)

If you know the act number, title, or subject matter, you may also be able to obtain citations from a source such as LexisNexis Congressional, which covers a government legislative history compilation known as the Serial Set. Your library may also have the Serial Set in its microform collection.

b. Text in Print

Once you have a citation, you can find full or partial text of committee

---

[86] The House Budget Committee report for the Taxpayer Relief Act of 1997, Pub. L. No. 105-34, 111 Stat. 788, is H.R. REP. NO. 105-148, 105TH CONG., 1ST SESS. (1997). The Senate Finance report for the same act is S. REP. NO. 105-33, 105TH CONG., 1ST SESS. (1997). The Conference report is H.R. REP. NO. 105-220, 105TH CONG., 1ST SESS. (1997). Note that the House report did not emanate from the Ways and Means Committee.

[87] The government occasionally prepares citations to legislative history materials. See, e.g., Joint Committee on Taxation, Listing of Selected Federal Tax Legislation Reprinted in the IRS Cumulative Bulletin, 1913-1990 (JCS-19-91) (Dec. 19, 1991). This study appeared as a supplement to Daily Tax Report and can be accessed in the Tax Notes Today (TAXANA; TNT) file in LexisNexis at 91 TNT 258-17.

reports in several publications. Print sources include the following:

• Standard Federal Tax Reporter (Chapter 13) (limited coverage)

• United States Tax Reporter (Chapter 13) (limited coverage)

• Rabkin & Johnson, Federal Income, Gift and Estate Taxation (Chapter 13) (1954 Code only)

• Cumulative Bulletin (Chapter 17) (since 1913)[88]

• Internal Revenue Acts—Text and Legislative History (Chapter 17) (since 1954)

• Tax Management Primary Sources (Chapter 17) (1969-2003)

• Seidman's Legislative History of Federal Income and Excess Profits Tax Laws (Chapter 17) (1863-1953) (also available in HeinOnline)

• The Internal Revenue Acts of the United States: 1909-1950; 1950-1972; 1973- (Chapter 17)

Each service has limitations. These include providing only partial texts, printing only one committee report rather than all reports for an act, or omitting original pagination. Seidman's omits estate and gift taxes altogether.

The Internal Revenue Acts of the United States: 1909-1950 (and later series) provides full text with original pagination for all materials. Because it omits pre-1909 material, you should consult Seidman's, which includes partial texts, for earlier reports. [See Illustration 17-4.] The Internal Revenue Acts would be much easier to use if it had a comprehensive index.

c. Text in Electronic Format

If you need reports published in the last ten to fifteen years, online and CD/DVD services provide the most comprehensive coverage and are the easiest to search. The Westlaw Federal Tax Legislative History database (FTX-LH) begins in 1948 with selective coverage and provides full coverage since 1990. LexisNexis and LexisNexis Congressional also

---

[88] Committee reports for 1913 through 1938 appear in 1939-1 (pt. 2) C.B. With the exception of the 1954 Code, for which none are included, reports for most acts appeared in the Cumulative Bulletin. Post-1998 reports appear relatively slowly since the IRS adopted the current format.

include committee reports. RIA Checkpoint includes committee reports and JCT Blue Books since the 104th Congress (1995) [Illustration 7-6]. CCH Tax Research NetWork includes reports for major legislation beginning with the Tax Reform Act of 1986.

The government makes committee reports for the 104th and later Congresses available online through the Government Printing Office website. Those published in PDF format retain original pagination.

Illustration 7-6. Excerpt from Committee Report in Checkpoint

Committee Report for s104-281, pl104-188 , Senate

SMALL BUSINESS JOB PROTECTION ACT OF 1996

Click here for a PDF of Senate Report 104-281

TABLE OF CONTENTS

I.. Legislative Background

II.. Explanation of the Bill (Title I)

A.. Small Business Provisions

→Checkpoint offers both PDF and hyperlink reading options. The Tax Research NetWork version offers neither option; its reports run as straight text on the viewing screen.

4. Other Congressional Reports

One of the most important reports issued by the Joint Committee on Taxation's staff is the General Explanation ("Blue Book") of tax legislation.[89] That document can be used as authority if a taxpayer is disputing the substantial underpayment penalty discussed in Chapter 2.

Because the Joint Committee is not an official tax-writing committee, the Blue Book is not an official committee report and is not covered by many of the services that cover committee reports. The same is true for other Joint Committee staff reports and for reports of legislative

---

[89] The General Explanation issued by the Joint Committee staff is not the only "Blue Book." Other government entities also issue so-called Blue Books. See, e.g., Department of the Treasury, General Explanations of the Administration's Fiscal Year 2007 Revenue Proposals (Blue Book) (released in February 2006), available at the Office of Tax Policy website (http://www.treas.gov/offices/tax-policy/).

subcommittees.

The JCT website lists reports for each year, beginning with 1981. Those issued since 1992 are available as links on the JCT website. Reports from earlier years can be ordered in print versions until JCT exhausts its supply. These reports are carried in many other online services.

You may also want access to reports issued to Congress by supporting entities such as the Congressional Budget Office, Congressional Research Service, and Government Accountability Office.

You can find these items online, in microform collections (Chapter 18), and in library government documents collections. Government websites are particularly likely to include documents generated since 1993.[90] An important advantage of locating these documents online, whether through government websites or subscription services, is your ability to search for them based on concept rather than by document number. Illustrations 7-7 and 7-8 cover show the search features available on the GAO and CBO websites.

Illustration 7-7. Search Feature in GAO Website

Reports and Testimony
Browse by topic

Select one or more topics - OR - Search for words or phrases in titles, abstracts, and subjects

☐ All Topics	☐ Homeland Security
☐ Agriculture and Food	☐ Housing
☐ Budget and Spending	☐ Income Security
☐ Business, Industry, and Consumers	☐ Information Management
☐ Civil Rights	☐ International Affairs
☐ Economic Development	☐ Justice and Law Enforcement
☐ Education	☐ National Defense
☐ Employment	☐ Natural Resources
☐ Energy	☐ Science, Space, and Technology
☐ Environmental Protection	☐ Social Services
☐ Financial Institutions	☐ Special Publications
☐ Financial Management	☑ Tax Policy and Administration
☐ Government Operations	☐ Transportation
☐ Health	☐ Veterans Affairs

Select a date range:

From:

Month [November ▾] Year [Pre 1970 ▾]

→The GAO site allows you to search by topic or by agency. It uses the

---

[90] See Government Printing Office Electronic Information Access Enhancement Act of 1993, Pub. L. No. 103-40, 107 Stat. 112, codified at 44 U.S.C. § 4101.

Treasury Department and not the IRS in its agency search.

Illustration 7-8. Search Feature in CBO Website

→The CBO website covers reports issued since 2001. This site is searchable by topic rather than by agency.

As noted earlier, the CRS does not post its reports to its website. They are available online from Tax Analysts and are also carried in other services. For example, Tax Research NetWork has a CRS Reports and Other Studies that currently begins in 2003. The Westlaw FTX-CRS file contains selected reports issued since 1989.

5. Executive Branch Documents

Presidential messages appear in the Weekly Compilation of Presidential Documents, which can be located online at the Government Printing Office website through its GPO Access Executive page. You can also locate presidential documents at the White House website. Reports issued by the Office of Management and Budget, the Council of Economic Advisors, the Treasury Department, and the National Taxpayer Advocate can be found at their websites. Subscription-based online services also carry many of these documents.

SECTION E. UNENACTED BILLS

Services such as LexisNexis Congressional don't limit their coverage to enacted legislation. You can locate "legislative history" documents such as those described in Section D even for bills that do not become law. [See Illustration 7-9.] The GPO Access and THOMAS websites also cover unenacted legislation.

Illustration 7-9. Excerpt from Unenacted Bill-History in THOMAS

H.R.1340
Title: To amend the Internal Revenue Code of 1986 to allow taxpayers to designate that part or all of any income research conducted through the National Institutes of Health.
Sponsor: Rep Bilirakis, Michael [FL-9] (introduced 4/3/2001)   Cosponsors (34)
Latest Major Action: 7/11/2001 House committee/subcommittee actions. Status: Forwarded by Subcommittee t

ALL ACTIONS:

4/3/2001:
    Referred to the Committee on Ways and Means, and in addition to the Committee on Energy and Commerce
    the Speaker, in each case for consideration of such provisions as fall within the jurisdiction of the committee
4/3/2001:
    Referred to House Ways and Means
4/3/2001:
    Referred to House Energy and Commerce
    4/25/2001:
        Referred to the Subcommittee on Health, for a period to be subsequently determined by the Chairman
        7/11/2001:
            Subcommittee Consideration and Mark-up Session Held.
        7/11/2001:
            Forwarded by Subcommittee to Full Committee by Voice Vote.

SECTION F. USING LEGISLATIVE HISTORY IN STATUTORY INTERPRETATION

After a bill becomes law, the interpretive process begins. Whether you are researching to determine the best way to structure a transaction, or because litigation is already in process, you must locate authoritative interpretations of the law. In addition to locating legislative history materials issued for a current act, you may need to trace a Code section back to its original version.

1. In Lieu of Administrative Interpretations

Because Congress authorizes the Treasury Department to issue rules and regulations, you might start searching for interpretations in Treasury regulations (Chapter 9) or IRS documents (Chapter 10). These agencies cannot issue guidance as quickly as Congress enacts major legislation, and they invariably have a backlog of regulations and rulings projects.[91]

If no regulations are available, you can consult legislative history materials to ascertain congressional intent. Even after regulations appear, you can use legislative history to challenge their validity.[92] As discussed in Section G, courts vary in the degree of weight they grant legislative history.[93] Do not overlook this fact in doing your research.

2. Tracing Changes in Statutory Language

Legislative history necessarily includes the process by which a section evolved from its original version. Most 1986 Code provisions were continued from the 1954 Code using the same section numbering scheme. Although the 1939 Code's number system is quite different, you can easily trace current provisions to that Code or to earlier revenue acts.

Chapter 6 lists sources publishing the texts of prior laws. The materials below aid you in determining which sections of those laws are relevant.

a. 1986-1954-1939 Code Cross-Reference Tables

Code cross-reference tables provide cross-references between the 1939 and 1954 Codes. Although cross-references directly from the 1986 Code would also be helpful, the 1954 Code tables will suffice so long as the 1954 and 1986 section numbering systems remain substantially identical.

Certain limitations affect your use of cross-reference tables. First, Congress changed section numbers (adding new items and deleting or moving old ones) after enacting the 1954 Code and again in the 1986

---

[91] In a worst case scenario, regulations lag several years behind statutes. For example, Congress enacted I.R.C. § 385 in 1969; regulations adopted in 1980, and subsequently amended, were ultimately withdrawn. Regulations interpreting I.R.C. § 501(c)(9) were issued in 1980; Congress enacted that section's predecessor in 1928.

[92] See, e.g., United States v. Nesline, 590 F. Supp. 884 (D. Md. 1984), holding invalid a regulation that varied from the plain language of the statute and had no support in the committee reports; cf. Tutor-Saliba Corp. v. Commissioner, 115 T.C. 1 (2000), holding that a regulation comported with congressional intent.

[93] The Treasury Department and IRS cite to legislative history in administrative documents. See, e.g., T.D. 8810, 64 Fed. Reg. 3398 (1999) (conference report); Rev. Rul. 88-64, 1988-2 C.B. 10 (statement during floor debate).

Code. Cross-reference tables may not reflect these changes.[94] You must determine when each provision received its current section number. If the table has not been amended since then, use the previous section number in your tracing effort.

A second limitation is also worth noting. These tables reflect their compilers' opinions as to the appropriate cross-references. Different publishers' tables may yield different results. Illustrations 7-10 and 7-11 reflect this phenomenon for 1939 Code section 47.

These services provide tables cross-referencing the 1954 and 1939 Codes:

• United States Statutes at Large (Appendix in volume 68A following text of 1954 Code)

• Standard Federal Tax Reporter (Chapter 13) (Code volume I)

• Rabkin & Johnson, Federal Income, Gift and Estate Taxation (Chapter 13) (volume 7B)

• Mertens, Law of Federal Income Taxation—Code (Chapter 13) (1954-58 Code volume) (1954 to 1939 only)

• Cumulative Changes (Chapter 17) (1954 Code volume I)

• Barton's Federal Tax Laws Correlated (Chapter 17) (looseleaf volume)

• Seidman's Legislative History of Federal Income and Excess Profits Tax Laws (Chapter 17) (1953-1939 volume II)

• Legislative History of the Internal Revenue Code of 1954 (Chapter 17)

• Joint Committee on Taxation, Derivations of Code Sections of the Internal Revenue Codes of 1939 and 1954 (JCS-1-92) (Jan. 21, 1992), reprinted in Daily Tax Report, Jan. 23, 1992 (Special Supplement).

---

[94] For example, Code cross-reference tables list 1939 Code § 23(aa)(1) as the predecessor of 1954 Code § 141. However, 1986 Code § 141 deals with an entirely different topic. 1954 Code § 141 corresponds to 1986 Code § 63(c). The Westlaw FTX-IRC54 file contains the 1954 Code as it read immediately before the adoption of the 1986 Code. Westlaw has a comparable file, FTX-IRC39, for the 1939 Code. CCH Tax Research NetWork also has 1939 and 1954 Code files.

b. Tracing Pre-1939 Statutes

You can trace back provisions that predate the 1939 Code using the following tools.

• United States Statutes at Large (Appendix in volume 53 (pt. 1) following text of 1939 Code) (separate tables trace sections predating the Revised Statutes of 1875 back to their origin) [Illustration 7-12.]

• Barton's Federal Tax Laws Correlated (Chapter 17)

• Seidman's Legislative History of Federal Income and Excess Profits Tax Laws (Chapter 17)

• Joint Committee on Taxation, Derivations of Code Sections of the Internal Revenue Codes of 1939 and 1954 (JCS-1-92), Jan. 21, 1992, reprinted in Daily Tax Report, Jan. 23, 1992 (Special Supplement) (citations to Statutes at Large but no text)

Illustration 7-10. Excerpt from Seidman's Code Reference Table I

1954 CODE REFERENCES

[1953 Code section index precedes subject index]

TABLE I

1953 CODE SEC.	1954 CODE SEC.	1953 CODE SEC.	1954 CODE SEC.	1953 CODE SEC.	1954 CODE SEC.
13(a)	—	23(n)	167	44	453, 7101
15(a)	11	23(o)(1)-(5)	170	45	482
15(c)	1551	23(p)	404	46	442
21	63	23(q)(1)-(3)	170	47(b)-(c)	443, 6011(a)
22(a)	61	23(r)(1)	591	48	441, 7701

→Seidman's ceased publication when the 1954 Code was adopted. Its 1953-1954 table reflects the initial version of the 1954 Code. It does not reflect any section renumbered in a later year. Seidman's can be accessed in HeinOnline. This table is page 3005 of 1953-1939 volume II.

Illustration 7-11. Excerpt from CCH Cross Reference Table I

46	442
47(a)	443, 6011(a)
47(c)	443
47(e)	443
47(g)	443
48(a)	441, 7701(a)(23)

Illustration 7-12. Derivation of 1939 Code in 53 Statutes at Large

TABLE A.—*Derivation of Internal Revenue Code*

[*=Amending statute. †=Reenacting statute. ‡=Adding statute.]

I. R. C. section	Date	Volume	Page	Chapter	Section
1, page 4	1938, May 28	52	452	289	1.
2 ...do	...do	52	452	289	2.
3 ...do	...do	52	452	289	3.
4 ...do	...do	52	452	289	4.
11	...do	52	452	289	11.
12	...do	52	453	289	12.
13	...do	52	455	289	13.
14	...do	52	456	289	14.
15	...do	52	457	289	15.
21	...do	52	457	289	21.
22 (a)-(f)	...do	52	457	289	22.
22 (j)					
23	1938, May 28	52	460	289	23.
24	...do	52	464	289	24.
25	...do	52	466	289	25.
26	...do	52	467	289	26.
27	...do	52	468	289	27.
28	...do	52	470	289	28.
31	...do	52	472	289	31.
32	...do	52	472	289	32.
33	...do	52	473	289	33.
41	...do	52	473	289	41.
42	...do	52	473	289	42.
43	...do	52	473	289	43.
44	...do	52	473	289	44.
45	...do	52	474	289	45.
46	...do	52	474	289	46.
47	...do	52	475	289	47.
48	...do	52	475	289	48.
51	...do	52	476	289	51.
52 (a)	...do	52	476	289	52.
52 (b)					
53	1938, May 28	52	477	289	53.
54	...do	52	477	289	54.
55 (a) (1)	1926, Feb. 26	44	51	27	257 (a).
	1938, May 28	52	478	289	55 (a).
55 (a) (2)	1936, June 22	49	1671	690	55 (a).
	1938, May 28	52	478	289	55 (a).
55 (a) (3)	1926, Feb. 26	44	51	27	257 (a).

→This reproduction comes from HeinOnline. Its Statutes at Large Library goes from 1789 to 2004 as of November 2006.

SECTION G. JUDICIAL DEFERENCE

Although judicial opinions cite legislative history documents in deciding between conflicting statutory interpretations, many judges prefer to resolve cases based on the so-called "plain meaning" of the statute. Those judges may give more deference to Treasury regulations than to legislative history if the statute is deemed ambiguous.[95]

---

[95] Deference to administrative interpretations is discussed in Chapters 9 and 10. Even if not accorded deference for purposes of resolving an issue, committee reports, managers' statements in the conference report, pre-enactment floor statements by one of a bill's managers, and the Blue Book all constitute authority for purposes of avoiding the substantial understatement penalty discussed in

The following items illustrate judicial statements regarding the deference courts give legislative history. Several of these statements reiterate statements made in earlier cases.

• Delving into the legislative history is unnecessary because the statutes' language is unambiguous. United States v. Farley, 202 F.3d 198, 210 (3d Cir. 2000).

• While the court makes its holding under the plain meaning rule of statutory construction, the court's conclusion is supported by the predecessor to § 402(a) which was § 165(b) of the IRC of 1939 which had its beginnings in § 219(f) of the Internal Revenue Act of 1921. Shimota v. United States, 21 Cl. Ct. 510, 518 (1990).

• The language of the statute leaves us with uncertainty .... The Secretary has not issued any regulations under section 613(e)(3), that might have provided guidance. We look to the legislative history behind the statute for assistance. Newborn v. Commissioner, 94 T.C. 610, 627 (1990).

• Indications of congressional intent contained in a conference committee report deserve great deference by courts because "the conference report represents the final statement of terms agreed to by both houses, [and] next to the statute itself it is the most persuasive evidence of congressional intent." RJR Nabisco, Inc. v. United States, 955 F.2d 1457, 1462 (11th Cir. 1992).

• [The Bluebook] is not part of the legislative history although it is entitled to respect.... Where there is no corroboration in the actual legislative history, we shall not hesitate to disregard the General Explanation as far as congressional intent is concerned. Redlark v. Commissioner, 106 T.C. 31, 45 (1996).

• [The Blue Book] of course does not rise to the level of legislative history, because it was authored by Congressional staff and not by Congress. Nevertheless, such explanations are highly indicative of what Congress did, in fact, intend. Estate of Hutchinson v. Commissioner, 765 F.2d 665, 669-70 (7th Cir. 1985)

• Congress conveys its directions in the Statutes at Large, not in excerpts from the Congressional Record, much less in excerpts from the Congressional Record that do not clarify the text of any pending legislative proposal. Begier v. Internal Revenue Service, 496 U.S. 53, 68 (1990) (Scalia, J., concurring).

• While Congress's later view as to the meaning of pre-existing law does not seal the outcome when addressing a question of statutory interpretation, it should not be discounted when relevant. Sorrell v. Commissioner, 882 F.2d 484, 489 (11th Cir. 1989).

• While headings are not compelling evidence of meaning in themselves, the corresponding section of the Senate report clarifies and reinforces this analysis. That section is headed "Production, acquisition, and *carrying* costs" (emphasis added) and expresses the intent that "a single, comprehensive set of rules should govern the capitalization of costs of producing, acquiring, and *holding* property" (emphasis added). Reichel v. Commissioner, 112 T.C. 14, 18 (1999).

• Surrounding sentences are context for interpreting a sentence, but so is the history behind the sentence—where the sentence came from, what problem it was written to solve, who drafted it, who opposed its inclusion in the statute. Sundstrand Corp. v. Commissioner, 17 F.3d 965, 967 (7th Cir. 1994).

• We also find the Government's reading more faithful to the history of the statutory provision as well as the basic tax-related purpose that the history reveals. O'Gilvie v. United States, 519 U.S. 79, 84 (1996).

• Legislative history that is inconclusive, however, should not be relied upon to supply a provision not enacted by Congress. St. Laurent v. Commissioner, 71 T.C.M. (CCH) 2566, 2570 (1996).

Section H. Problems

1. Who introduced the following bill? What Code section would it add or amend?

    a. H.R. 5062, 107th Cong., 2d Sess.

    b. H.R.1419, 108th Cong., 1st Sess.

    c. S. 127, 108th Cong., 1st Sess.

    d. H.R. 5198, 109th Cong., 2d Sess.

2. Indicate the proposed popular name and all action for the bill described below.

    a. S. 763, 107th Cong., 1st Sess.

b. H.R. 7, 108th Cong., 1st Sess.

c. H.R. 4096, 109th Cong., 1st Sess.

3. What was the purpose of H.R. Con. Res. 528, 109th Cong.? Did it pass?

4. Who is the first person named on the witness list for the hearing described below?

a. Hearing on Member Proposals on Tax Issues Introduced in the 109th Congress, held by the House Ways & Means Subcommittee on Select Revenue Measures, Sept. 26, 2006

b. Hearing on Tax Simplification, held by the House Ways & Means Subcommittee on Oversight, June 15, 2004

c. Hearing on Corporate Inversions, held by the House Ways & Means Subcommittee on Select Revenue Measures, June 25, 2002

5. Provide House, Senate (and Conference, if one exists) report numbers for

a. Revenue Act of 1916

b. Foreign Investors Tax Act of 1966

c. Small Business Job Protection Act of 1996

6. Print the first page of the report requested.

a. Conference Committee report on the Revenue Act of 1934

b. Senate Finance Committee report for the Interest Equalization Tax Extension Act of 1973

c. House Ways & Means Committee report for the Small Business Job Protection Act of 1996

7. With respect to the document listed, provide the information requested by your instructor (author, month of issue, portion of text, etc.).

a. the most recent semiannual report of the National Taxpayer Advocate

b. the 2005 report of the President's Advisory Panel on Federal Tax

Reform

   c. a 2004 TIGTA report on the IRS and Freedom of Information Act requests

   d. a 2002 Treasury Department OTP report on capital gains taxes

   e. a 2006 JEC report on the estate tax

   f. a 2004 CBO report on effective tax rates between 1979 and 2001

   g. a 2006 GAO report on the capital gains tax gap

   h. a 2003 JCT report on the Enron investigation

8. Provide a Congressional Record citation for a

   a. Statement by Representative Osborne in October 2003: "Unfounded congressional comments impugning motives and denigrating character only give substance to the belief we have no national resolve or unity. Where there is unity of purpose, the whole exceeds the sum of its parts. And I saw that consistently in athletics. If people were committed to a common goal, they pulled together and the dissenting factors tended to fall away. But where there is a lack of unity, the whole is less than the sum of its parts. Sometimes I feel that that is what characterizes this body as we get fragmented, as we throw rocks at each other."

   b. Statement by Representative Gingrey in July 2005: "In the wake of the recent Supreme Court eminent domain decision, there is a rumbling across this great land. The American people know what this rumbling is. It is the sound of government bulldozers driven by IRS agents heading toward a condemned property near you."

   d. Statement by Representative Foxx in November 2005: "The Democrats' needle is stuck in a groove and it is playing the same song over and over: Tax and spend."

9. Provide both the corresponding 1954 Code section and the pre-1939 Code origin for the 1939 Code section listed.

   a. 63

   b. 811(c)

   c. 1503

Chapter 8. Treaties and Other International Material

Section A. Introduction

This chapter discusses treaties and other documents you can consult when researching the treatment of taxpayers with ties to both the United States and another country.

Treaties are agreements between two (bilateral) or more (multilateral) countries. Other relevant materials include statutes; congressional, State Department, and presidential documents; regulations; rulings; and judicial opinions. Documents issued by organizations to which the United States belongs, such as the World Trade Organization, may also be relevant.

Your goals include locating all relevant documents, determining their relative hierarchy and validity, and updating your research to encompass pending items. In accomplishing these goals, you should become familiar with the process by which treaties come into force and the terminology used to describe documents. You must also take into account changes in sovereignty. Newly independent or merged countries are not always covered by a treaty between the United States and the country with which they were formerly (or are currently) affiliated.

Section B. Functions of Treaties

Although United States citizens residing abroad pay United States income tax on both domestic and foreign-source income, they may also be taxed in the foreign country of residence. Similar problems may arise with regard to property and transfer taxes. Several statutory mechanisms exist to reduce the burden of taxation by more than one country. These include foreign income and death tax credits, an income tax deduction for foreign income and real property taxes, and an exclusion for certain foreign source income.[96] Treaties between the United States and others countries may also limit harsh tax consequences.

Treaties serve other tax-related purposes. These include promoting

---

[96] I.R.C. §§ 27, 164(a), 911, 912 & 2014.

trade by reducing tariffs and reducing tax evasion through exchanges of information with other countries. Although the United States may have separate income, estate, gift, and other treaties with a given country, in many instances the only tax treaty will be that covering income.

SECTION C. RELATIONSHIP OF TREATIES AND STATUTES

1. Authority for Treaties

Treaties are authorized by the Constitution. Article II, section 2, clause 2, provides that the President "shall have Power, by and with the Advice and Consent of the Senate, to make Treaties, provided two thirds of the Senators present concur ...." Article VI, clause 2, includes both statutes and treaties as the "supreme Law of the Land."

2. Conflict Between Treaties and Statutes

In determining which governs a transaction, neither a treaty nor a statute automatically receives preferential treatment by virtue of its status. As noted, the Constitution includes both statutes and treaties as the "supreme Law of the Land." While normally the "last in time" rule applies to reconcile conflicts between a treaty and a statute, that rule does not always apply.

In enacting Code sections, Congress can decide that treaty provisions will override statutory rules governing income earned (or property transferred) abroad by a United States citizen or resident or transactions undertaken in this country by a foreign national.[97] Congress can also provide that statutory rules will apply instead of treaty language. In addition, treaties can be overruled by a later statute, by a later treaty, or by treaty termination. Statutory repeal is an extraordinary step, taken in the 1986 Act for cases of treaty shopping.[98] Section J, Interpreting Treaties, includes several judicial decisions discussing the interplay

---

[97] See I.R.C. §§ 894(a) & 7852(d). Disclosure requirements apply to taxpayers who claim that a tax treaty overrules or modifies an internal revenue law. I.R.C. § 6114; Treas. Reg. § 301.6114-1; IRS Form 8833. See also I.R.C. § 7701(b); Treas. Reg. § 301.7701(b)-7.

[98] Pub. L. No. 99-514, § 1241(a), 100 Stat. 2085, 2576 (1986), modified for income tax treaties in 1988 by Pub. Law. No. 100-647, § 1012(q)(2)(A), 102 Stat. 3342, 3523. I.R.C. § 884(e)(1) currently reads: "No treaty between the United States and a foreign country shall exempt any foreign corporation from the tax imposed by subsection (a) . . . unless— (A) such treaty is an income tax treaty, and (B) such foreign corporation is a qualified resident of such foreign country."

between statutes and treaties.[99]

SECTION D. TREATY TERMINOLOGY

Treaties are often referred to as **conventions**. They are generally amended by documents called **protocols**. Because there may be a long delay before a signed treaty is actually ratified, a pending treaty may be amended several times before it goes into force. A treaty may also be amended after it enters into force. Congress may consider protocols along with the original treaty or at a later date.

The Senate can consent to the treaty as signed by the parties or it can express **reservations**. If the countries involved accept these reservations, the treaty process goes forward. If they do not, the treaty may be renegotiated or it may effectively die. A **ratified** treaty goes **into force** only after the governments exchange **instruments of ratification**.

Each treaty partner designates a **Competent Authority** to resolve disputes that may arise over which country has jurisdiction to tax an item. The competent authorities may enter into a **Memorandum of Understanding**. This document is not part of the treaty ratification process.

As was true for statutes, you must take note of **effective dates**. A treaty can become effective on the date it goes into force, at a later date, or even at an earlier date. Different treaty provisions may become effective at different dates. If a treaty is later amended by a protocol, the protocol is subject to the ratification process that applied to the original treaty and may have its own set of date limitations.

SECTION E. TREATY NUMBERING SYSTEMS

Treaties are numbered in a variety of ways, depending on which source is involved. Relevant numbering systems are those used by the State Department, the Senate, and the United Nations.

The State Department assigns each treaty a Treaties and Other International Acts Series (T.I.A.S.) number. T.I.A.S. began in 1945. The government previously published treaties in Treaty Series (T.S.) (1-994)

---

[99] See S. Rep. No. 100-445, 100th Cong., 2d Sess. 316 (1988), for a discussion of the relationship of statutes and treaties and the amendment of I.R.C. § 7852 by Pub. L. No. 100-647, § 1012(aa), 102 Stat. 3342, 3531 (1988).

and in Executive Agreement Series (E.A.S.) (1-506). T.I.A.S. numbering begins at 1501 to reflect that it continues the other series.

A treaty also receives a Senate Executive Document number or a Senate Treaty Document number. The Senate Executive Document system assigned each treaty a letter and a number based on the Congress that received the treaty for ratification. The Senate Treaty Document nomenclature began in the 97th Congress; this system gives each treaty a number and also indicates in which Congress the Senate Foreign Relations Committee published its recommendation to the full Senate.

The United Nations numbering system applies to treaties registered with that body (United Nations Treaty Series; UNTS). The United States is party to some, but not all, of these treaties.

You will rarely need to know the treaty numbers if your goal is limited to finding a treaty. The sources noted in Section G allow you to locate treaties by country. The T.I.A.S. number is important if you are using Shepard's Federal Statute Citations to find decisions interpreting treaties through 1995. The print Shepard's stopped covering treaties at that point.

Table 8-1. Treaty Numbers for the 1975 Income and Capital Tax Convention Between the United States and Iceland

Numbering System	Number
State Department	T.I.A.S. 8151
Senate	S. Exec. E, 94-1
United Nations	Reg. No. 14972, 1020 UNTS 211

Table 8-2. Treaty Numbers for the 1989 Income and Capital Tax Convention Between the United States and Germany

Numbering System	Number
State Department	T.I.A.S. not yet assigned
Senate	S. Treaty Doc. 101-10
United Nations	Reg. No. 29534, 1708 UNTS 3

→Treaties in Force (2005) lists no T.I.A.S. number for this treaty, which entered into force in 1991.

SECTION F. TREATY HISTORY DOCUMENTS

The treaty history discussed in this section is illustrated by excerpts from documents for the income tax treaty between the United States and Denmark. These documents were obtained from the Treasury Department, IRS, and GPO Access websites. Section G lists other sources for treaty documents.

Treaties, in common with statutes, involve both legislative and executive branches of government. However, the order in which each group acts is reversed. Treaties begin with the executive branch and are negotiated by representatives of each government. Unlike acts, pending treaties do not expire at the end of a Congress.

Although State Department representatives are consulted, the Treasury Office of Tax Policy has primary responsibility for tax treaty negotiations. The treaty signing process has two steps. After a treaty is **initialed**, it can still be changed; once it is **signed**, the Treasury Department releases it and sends it to the Senate for its consent. The House of Representatives is not involved in the treaty process.

The Treasury Department issues a press release alerting tax practitioners that a treaty has been signed and transmitted to the Senate. The Department release bears a number, in this case LS-64.

Illustration 8-1. Press Release Announcing Treaty Signing

PRESS ROOM

FROM THE OFFICE OF PUBLIC AFFAIRS

August 19, 1999
LS-64

UNITED STATES AND DENMARK SIGN NEW INCOME TAX TREATY

The Treasury Department announced Thursday that Assistant Secretary for Tax Policy Donald C. Lubick and Danish Chargé daffaires Lars Møller signed a new income tax Treaty between the United States and Denmark at the State Department in Washington. This tax Treaty, if ratified, will replace the current Treaty that entered into force on December 1, 1948, and will represent an important step toward achieving Treasurys goal of updating the United States existing tax treaty network.

In addition to the treaty text, the Senate Foreign Relations Committee receives the State Department's **letter of submittal** to the President and the President's **letter of transmittal** to the Senate. The Foreign Relations Committee issues a Senate Treaty Document, which contains these letters and the text of the treaty. [See Illustrations 8-2 and 8-3.]

The Treasury Department prepares a Technical Explanation for use by the Senate Foreign Relations Committee. The Joint Committee on Taxation also issues reports. The Foreign Relations Committee holds hearings. The Committee issues a Senate Executive Report transmitting the treaty to the full Senate for ratification. Debate by the full Senate appears in the Congressional Record. [See Illustrations 8-4 through 8–9.]

After the treaty is ratified by the appropriate government entities in each country, the countries exchange instruments of ratification and announce that the treaty has gone into effect. The Treasury Department issues a press release announcing this information.

Illustration 8-2. Excerpt from Letter of Submittal

LETTER OF SUBMITTAL

DEPARTMENT OF STATE
Washington, September 7, 1999

The PRESIDENT,
The White House.

THE PRESIDENT: I have the honor to submit to you, with a view to its transmission to the Senate for advice and consent to ratification, the Convention Between the United States of America and the Government of the Kingdom of Denmark for the Avoidance of Double Taxation and the Prevention of Fiscal Evasion with Respect to Taxes on Income, signed at Washington on August 19, 1999 ("the Convention"), together with a Protocol.

This Convention replaces the current convention between the United States of America and the Government of the Kingdom of Denmark signed at Washington on May 6, 1948. This proposed Convention generally follows the pattern of the U.S. Model Tax Treaty while incorporating some features of the OECD Model Tax Treaty and recent U.S. tax treaties with developed countries. The proposed Convention provides for maximum rates of tax to be applied to various types of income, protection from double taxation of income and exchange of information. It also contains rules making its benefits unavailable to persons that are engaged in treaty shopping....

The rules for the taxation of pension income under Article 18 of the proposed Convention vary from the rules found in the current treaty and the U.S. Model. The proposed Convention provides for taxation of private pensions only in the source State, subject to an exception for persons currently receiving pensions, who will continue to be taxed only in the country of residence.

Illustration 8-3. Excerpt from President's Letter of Transmittal

LETTER OF TRANSMITTAL

THE WHITE HOUSE, September 21, 1999.

To the Senate of the United States:

I transmit herewith for Senate advice and consent to ratification the Convention Between the Government of the United States of America and the Government of the Kingdom of Denmark for the Avoidance of Double Taxation and the Prevention of Fiscal Evasion with Respect to Taxes of Income, signed at Washington on August 19, 1999, together with a Protocol. Also transmitted for the information of the Senate is the report of the Department of State with respect to the Convention.

It is my desire that the Convention and Protocol transmitted herewith be considered in place of the Convention for the Avoidance of Double Taxation, signed at Washington on June 17, 1980, and the Protocol Amending the Convention, signed at Washington on August 23, 1983, which were transmitted to the Senate with messages dated September 4, 1980 (S. Ex. Q, 96th Cong., 2d Sess.) and November 16, 1983 (T. Doc. No. 98-12, 98th Cong., 1st Sess.), and which are pending in the Committee on Foreign Relations. I desire, therefore, to withdraw from the Senate the Convention and Protocol signed in 1980 and 1983.

→Note how long the prior proposed treaty was pending.

Illustration 8-4. Excerpt from Treasury Technical Explanation

INTRODUCTION

This is a Technical Explanation of the Convention and Protocol between the United States and Denmark signed at Washington on August 19, 1999 (the "Convention" and "Protocol"). References are made to the Convention between the United States and Denmark for the Avoidance of Double Taxation and the Prevention of Fiscal Evasion with Respect to Taxes on Income signed at Washington, D.C., on May 6, 1948 (the "prior Convention"). The Convention replaces the prior Convention.

Negotiations took into account the U.S. Treasury Department's current tax treaty policy, as reflected in the U.S. Treasury Department's Model Income Tax Convention of September 20, 1996 (the "U.S. Model") and its recently negotiated tax treaties, the Model Income Tax Convention on Income and on Capital, published by the OECD in 1992 and amended in 1994, 1995 and 1997 (the "OECD Model"), and recent tax treaties concluded by Denmark.

The Technical Explanation is an official guide to the Convention and Protocol. It reflects the policies behind particular Convention provisions, as well as understandings reached with respect to the application and interpretation of the Convention and Protocol. In the discussions of each Article in this explanation, the relevant portions of the Protocol are discussed. This Technical Explanation has been provided to Denmark. References in the Technical Explanation to "he" or "his" should be read to mean "he or she" and "his or her."

Illustration 8-5. Excerpt from Joint Committee on Taxation Explanation (JCS-8-99)

EXPLANATION OF PROPOSED INCOME TAX TREATY AND PROPOSED PROTOCOL BETWEEN THE UNITED STATES AND THE KINGDOM OF DENMARK

SCHEDULED FOR A HEARING
BEFORE THE
COMMITTEE ON FOREIGN RELATIONS
UNITED STATES SENATE
ON OCTOBER 13, 1999

PREPARED BY THE STAFF
OF THE
JOINT COMMITTEE ON TAXATION

OCTOBER 8, 1999

....

INTRODUCTION

This pamphlet, prepared by the staff of the Joint Committee on Taxation, describes the proposed income tax treaty, as supplemented by the proposed protocol, between the United States of America and the Kingdom of Denmark ("Denmark"). The proposed treaty and proposed protocol were both signed on August 19, 1999. The Senate Committee on Foreign Relations has scheduled a public hearing on the proposed treaty and proposed protocol on October 13, 1999.

Part I of the pamphlet provides a summary with respect to the proposed treaty and proposed protocol. Part II provides a brief overview of U.S. tax laws relating to international trade and investment and of U.S. income tax treaties in general. Part III contains an article-by-article explanation of the proposed treaty and proposed protocol. Part IV contains a discussion of issues with respect to the proposed treaty and proposed protocol.

I. SUMMARY

The principal purposes of the proposed income tax treaty between the United States and Denmark are to reduce or eliminate double taxation of income earned by residents of either country from sources within the other country and to prevent avoidance or evasion of the taxes of the two countries. The proposed treaty also is intended to promote close economic cooperation between the two countries and to eliminate possible barriers to trade and investment caused by overlapping taxing jurisdictions of the two countries.

→Note the reference to discussion of treaty issues in Part IV.

Illustration 8-6. Excerpt from Hearings (S. HRG. 106-356)

BILATERAL TAX TREATIES AND PROTOCOL: ESTONIA, TREATY DOC. 105-55; LATVIA, TREATY DOC. 105-57; VENE-ZUELA, TREATY DOC. 106-3; DENMARK, TREATY DOC. 106-12; LITHUANIA, TREATY DOC. 105-56; SLOVENIA, TREATY DOC. 106-9; ITALY, TREATY DOC. 106-11; GERMANY, TREATY DOC. 106-13

HEARING
BEFORE THE
COMMITTEE ON FOREIGN RELATIONS
UNITED STATES SENATE

ONE HUNDRED SIXTH CONGRESS
FIRST SESSION

OCTOBER 27, 1999

....

The committee met, pursuant to notice, at 3:05 p.m. in room SD-419, Dirksen Senate Office Building, Hon. Chuck Hagel presiding.

Present: Senators Hagel and Sarbanes.

Senator HAGEL. Good afternoon.

The committee meets today to consider bilateral income tax treaties between the United States and Estonia, Latvia, Lithuania, Venezuela, Denmark, Italy, and Slovenia as well as an estate tax protocol with Germany.
....
The treaties prevent international double taxation by setting down rules to determine what country will have the primary right to tax income and at what rates. These bilateral international tax treaties are important for America's economic growth.
....
The treaties with Denmark and Italy would modernize existing treaty relationships. These treaties generally track with the U.S. tax treaty model, although some deviate to various degrees from the U.S. model.
....
A variety of other issues has been raised by the Joint Committee on Taxation. I know our witnesses are fully aware of these issues and will be prepared to discuss them. As usual, the Joint Committee staff has prepared careful analysis of each of the treaties.

Illustration 8-7. Excerpt from Senate Foreign Relations Executive Report

---

TAX CONVENTION WITH DENMARK

NOVEMBER 3, 1999.—Ordered to be printed

Mr. HELMS, from the Committee on Foreign Relations,
submitted the following

R E P O R T

[To accompany Treaty Doc. 106-12]

The Committee on Foreign Relations, to which was referred the Convention between the Government of the United States of America and the Government of the Kingdom of Denmark for the Avoidance of Double Taxation and the Prevention of Fiscal Evasion with Respect to Taxes on Income, signed at Washington on August 19, 1999, together with a Protocol, having considered the same, reports favorably thereon, with one declaration and one proviso, and recommends that the Senate give its advice and consent to ratification thereof, as set forth in this report and the accompanying resolution of ratification....

VI. COMMITTEE COMMENTS

On balance, the Committee on Foreign Relations believes that the proposed treaty with Denmark is in the interest of the United States and urges that the Senate act promptly to give advice and consent to ratification. The Committee has taken note of certain issues raised by the proposed treaty, and believes that the following comments may be useful to the Treasury Department officials in providing guidance on these matters should they arise in the course of future treaty negotiations....

A. CREDITABILITY OF DANISH HYDROCARBON TAX.

....

The Congressional tax-writing committees and this Committee have made it clear in the past that treaties are not the appropriate vehicle for granting credits for taxes that might not otherwise be creditable under the Code or Treasury regulations. The Committee believes that it would be more appropriate for the United States to address unilaterally problems of the sort raised by special oil and gas taxes imposed by foreign countries. The Committee believes that treaties should not be used in the future to handle foreign tax credit issues which are more appropriately addressed either legislatively or administratively. Nevertheless, the Committee believes that given the circumstances surrounding the Danish hydrocarbon tax, it is justifiable to provide a credit for such tax in this case.

→Note the discussion in A. of using treaties to grant tax credits.

Illustration 8-8. Excerpt from Congressional Record

Mr. DOMENICI. Mr. President, I ask unanimous consent that the Senate proceed to consider the following treaties on today's Executive Calendar: Nos 4 through 14. I further ask unanimous consent that the treaties be considered as having passed through their various parliamentary stages, up to and including the presentation of the resolutions of ratification; all committee provisos, reservations, understandings, and declarations be considered agreed to; any statements be printed in the RECORD; and the Senate take one vote on the resolutions of ratification to be considered as separate votes. Further, that when the resolutions of ratification are voted upon, the motions to reconsider be laid upon the table, the President be notified of the Senate's action, and the Senate return to legislative session.

The PRESIDING OFFICER. Without objection, it is so ordered.

....

TAX CONVENTION WITH DENMARK

The resolution of ratification is as follows:

Resolved, (two-thirds of the Senators present concurring therein), That the Senate advise and consent to the ratification of the Convention between the Government of the United States of America and the Government of the Kingdom of Denmark for the Avoidance of Double Taxation and the Prevention of Fiscal Evasion with Respect to Taxes on Income, signed at Washington on August 19, 1999, together with a Protocol (Treaty Doc. 106-12), subject to the declaration of subsection (a) and the proviso of subsection (b).

(a) Declaration.—The Senate's advice and consent is subject to the following declaration, which shall be binding on the President:

(1) Treaty interpretation.—The Senate affirms the applicability to all treaties of the constitutionally based principles of treaty interpretation set forth in Condition (1) of the resolution of ratification of the INF Treaty, approved by the Senate on May 27, 1988, and Condition (8) of the resolution of ratification of the Document Agreed Among the States Parties to the Treaty on Conventional Armed Forces in Europe, approved by the Senate on May 14, 1997.

(b) Proviso.—The resolution of ratification is subject to the following proviso, which shall be binding on the President:

(1) Supremacy of constitution.—Nothing in the Convention requires or authorizes legislation or other action by the United States of America that is prohibited by the Constitution of the United States as interpreted by the United States.

→Note the limitations on the President in the Declaration and Proviso.

Illustration 8-9. Excerpt from Treaty

FROM THE OFFICE OF PUBLIC AFFAIRS

April 3, 2000
LS-521

TREASURY ANNOUNCES EFFECTIVE DATES OF NEW TAX AGREEMENT WITH DENMARK

The Treasury Department on Monday announced that a new income tax treaty with Denmark entered into force on March 31, 2000. The treaty, to which the U.S. Senate gave advice and consent to ratification in November, 1999, replaces the existing tax treaty between the United States and Denmark, which was signed in 1948.

On March 31, Denmark notified the United States that Denmark had complied with the constitutional requirements for entry into force of the bilateral income tax treaty between the two countries. The United States had previously provided reciprocal notification to the Denmark, and accordingly, the treaties entered into force on March 31. The treaties apply, with respect to taxes withheld at source, in respect of amounts paid or credited on or after May 1, 2000 and, with regard to other taxes, in respect of taxable years beginning on or after January 1, 2001.

Illustration 8-10. Press Release That Treaty Entered Into Force

FROM THE OFFICE OF PUBLIC AFFAIRS

April 3, 2000
LS-521

TREASURY ANNOUNCES EFFECTIVE DATES OF NEW TAX AGREEMENT WITH DENMARK

The Treasury Department on Monday announced that a new income tax treaty with Denmark entered into force on March 31, 2000. The treaty, to which the U.S. Senate gave advice and consent to ratification in November, 1999, replaces the existing tax treaty between the United States and Denmark, which was signed in 1948.

On March 31, Denmark notified the United States that Denmark had complied with the constitutional requirements for entry into force of the bilateral income tax treaty between the two countries. The United States had previously provided reciprocal notification to the Denmark, and accordingly, the treaties entered into force on March 31. The treaties apply, with respect to taxes withheld at source, in respect of amounts paid or credited on or after May 1, 2000 and, with regard to other taxes, in respect of taxable years beginning on or after January 1, 2001.

→Note the different effective dates.

→The LS in the press release number stands for the Secretary of the Treasury's initials (Lawrence Summers in this case).

Illustration 8-11. Press Release for Protocol to Treaty

May 3, 2006
JS-4231

United States and Denmark Sign Protocol to
Income Tax Treaty

Washington – Today the Treasury Department announced that U.S. Ambassador James P. Cain and Danish Tax Minister Kristian Jensen signed a new Protocol to amend the existing bilateral income tax treaty, concluded in 1999, between the two countries. The Protocol was signed Tuesday.

The agreement significantly reduces tax-related barriers to trade and investment flows between the United States and Denmark. It also modernizes the treaty to take account of changes in the laws and policies of both countries since the current treaty was signed. The Protocol brings the tax treaty relationship with Denmark into closer conformity with U.S. treaty policy.

The most important aspect of the Protocol deals with the taxation of cross-border dividend payments. The Protocol is one of a few recent U.S. tax agreements to provide for the elimination of the source-country withholding tax on dividends arising from certain direct investments and on dividends paid to pension funds. The Protocol also strengthens the treaty's provisions preventing so-called treaty shopping, which is the inappropriate use of a tax treaty by third-country residents.

Illustration 8-12. Exchange of Notes in Connection with Protocol

Copenhagen, May 2, 2006

Excellency:

I have the honor to refer to the Protocol signed today between the Government of the United States of America and the Government of the Kingdom of Denmark Amending the Convention for the Avoidance of Double Taxation and the Prevention of Fiscal Evasion with Respect to Taxes on Income, and to confirm, on behalf of the Government of the United States of America, the following understandings reached between our two Governments.

In reference to clause a) (iv) of paragraph 3 of Article 10 (Dividends) of the Convention, as amended by the Protocol, it is understood that the U.S. competent authority generally will exercise its discretion to grant benefits under such paragraph to a company that is a resident of Denmark if:

→Note the reference to how the competent authority will act.

SECTION G. LOCATING TREATIES AND THEIR HISTORIES

When a treaty goes into force, it is added to the State Department's Treaties and Other International Acts Series (T.I.A.S.). T.I.A.S. is the treaty equivalent of Statutes at Large; the treaty document equivalent of United States Code is United States Treaties and Other International Agreements (U.S.T.). Because official treaty publications are not updated nearly as quickly as their statutory counterparts, you should use other sources to obtain the text of recent treaties.

Tax treaties and their revising protocols are published in various places, several of which are limited to tax treaties. Many sources also provide access to at least some treaty history documents. Unfortunately, few sources provide access to all relevant information.

The sources below illustrate the formats in which you can locate treaties and other documents. Your library may also carry them in microform.

1. United States Government Sources

The Internal Revenue Service website includes PDF versions of treaty texts other than the most recently ratified treaties. The site also includes Treasury Technical Explanations for many of the treaties and Publication 901, which lists the most current treaties and provides information about how each treaty affects specific categories of taxpayers. It does not include congressional action, Joint Committee explanations, or press releases.

The Treasury Department Office of Tax Policy website provides access to proposed treaties, press releases, Joint Committee on Taxation explanations, and Treasury Technical Explanations. It does not include all these items for every treaty, and it does not include congressional action. In addition, it does not cover documents issued before October 1996. Many of its documents are available in both PDF and word processing formats.

GPO Access offers access to hearings, congressional debate, and committee reports for treaties.

The weekly Internal Revenue Bulletin contains the most recent material, which is reprinted in the Cumulative Bulletin at six month intervals.[100] Because of their arrangement, these publications are more useful for finding IRS material relating to treaties than for finding the treaties themselves. In addition to treaty texts, these services include the Senate Executive Reports and the Treasury Technical Explanations. The I.R.B. is available in print, online at the IRS website, and through subscription online services.[101]

2. Online Subscription Services

Tax treaties are available on LexisNexis and Westlaw. Oceana publishes Treaties and International Agreements Online; that service includes Oceana's Tax Treaties Online.

The publishers listed below make treaties available in the formats indicated.

3. Other Print and Electronic Sources

a. Tax Analysts Publications (DVD and online)

Tax Analysts covers treaty documents in its OneDisc Premium DVD and in an online Worldwide Tax Treaties service.[102]

Treaty documents include full texts of treaties and all documents comprising each treaty's legislative history. The Integrated Treaty Texts option shows treaties, as amended by subsequent protocols. Tax Analysts covers income, transfer tax, shipping and air transport, information

---

[100] These services are discussed in greater detail in Chapter 17. IRS Publication 901 contains selected information about treaties, including tax rates and exempt compensation.

[101] See Joint Committee on Taxation, Listing of Selected International Tax Conventions and Other Agreements Reprinted in the IRS Cumulative Bulletin, 1913-1990 (JCS-20-91), Dec. 31, 1991, for citations to both treaty documents and administrative guidance. This document is available in the Tax Notes Today file on LexisNexis at 92 TNT 2-8.

[102] Tax Analysts initially published an extensive microfiche database, which is useful for historical research. Coverage included bilateral, multilateral, and model tax treaties worldwide and United States tax-related treaties and agreements. Coverage for United States treaties included treaties currently in force, not yet in force, and superseded or terminated. A print index provided appropriate citations to the treaties and treaty documents covered. Treaty documents added before 1996 appeared in the Tax Notes International Microfiche Database; those added after 1995 appeared in the Tax Analysts Microfiche Database.

exchange, and social security treaties. It also includes model treaties, administrative documents (such as revenue rulings and field service advice), and judicial interpretations.

b. CCH Publications (looseleaf, CD-ROM, and Tax Research NetWork)

The CCH Tax Treaties service reproduces texts of United States income and estate tax treaties, exchange of information agreements, shipping and air transport treaties, and social security treaties. It reproduces selected treaty documents, including letters of submittal and transmittal, letters of understanding, and Treasury and congressional reports. CCH includes editorial comments and annotations, and it reproduces IRS publications providing withholding rate tables and Cumulative Bulletin citations for each treaty and protocol. It also includes texts of model treaties. Supplementation is monthly.

The CD-ROM and Tax Research NetWork services include hyperlinks to full text treaty history documents, administrative documents (such as revenue procedures and letter rulings), and judicial decisions.

c. RIA Publications (looseleaf, CD-ROM, and Checkpoint)

Chapter 20 of the Federal Tax Coordinator 2d[103] looseleaf service contains the text of United States income and estate and gift tax treaties. There is also explanatory material. Supplementation is weekly. RIA includes treaties in its monthly OnPoint CD-ROM and in its online Checkpoint service.

d. BNA Publications (looseleaf and TaxCore)

Tax Management Portfolios—Foreign Income[104] covers many countries but does not yet publish a Portfolio for each treaty country. The Detailed Analysis sections contain explanations, significant cases, and other annotations. The Working Papers sections print treaty texts as Worksheets. BNA includes treaties in its online TaxCore service.

e. Rhoades & Langer, U.S. International Taxation and Tax Treaties (looseleaf, CD-ROM, and online)

This treatise covers the treaty and non-treaty aspects of both inbound

---

[103] There is a comprehensive discussion of this service in Chapter 13

[104] A more extensive discussion of the Tax Management Portfolios appears in Chapter 13.

and outbound transactions. Following the topical discussion in the main text sections, Appendix A prints the text of current, proposed, and prior income tax treaties. It also prints estate and gift tax treaties, information exchange agreements, transportation agreements, social security totalization agreements, and other relevant agreements. Appendix B includes model treaties: OECD; United States; and United Nations. In addition to the print version, this treatise is available on LexisNexis CD-ROMs and online in LexisNexis.

In addition to its T.I.A.S. citation, a brief legislative history accompanies each treaty. If a treaty no longer applies, the service still covers that country and indicates when the treaty went out of force.

Cross-references to any pertinent regulations, revenue rulings and letter rulings follow each treaty article. Although the other treaties had annotations, estate and gift tax treaties did not appear to have annotations as of November 2006.

f. Legislative History of United States Tax Conventions (Roberts & Holland Collection) (looseleaf)

This looseleaf service, introduced in 1986, updates and expands a four-volume 1962 version prepared by the Joint Committee on Taxation staff. The sixteen volumes contain the full text of treaties and legislative history documents, including presidential messages, Senate Executive Reports, floor debate, Joint Committee staff explanations, and hearings. Official pagination is retained.

This service focuses on the history of the treaty rather than on subsequent judicial and administrative interpretations. Supplementation has tended to be relatively infrequent.

SECTION H. PENDING TREATIES

The government regularly announces the status of treaty negotiations. This information is carried in newsletters, looseleaf services, and on government websites.

If you want to determine if a tax treaty has been signed and is pending before the Senate, you can locate this information in the CCH Congressional Index, Senate volume (Treaties–Nominations tab). Looseleaf services such as those discussed in Section G are a good source of information about treaties that are being negotiated.

SECTION I. CITATORS FOR TREATIES

Two sources that formerly provided citations to judicial and administrative decisions regarding treaties are now of limited use for recent events. Shepard's Federal Statute Citations provides citations to court decisions involving treaties through 1995; you need the U.S.T. and T.I.A.S. citations to use this volume. Citations to IRS pronouncements (1954-1993/94) can be found in the Service's Bulletin Index-Digest System, discussed in Chapter 17.

In the absence of a formal citator, you can locate judicial and administrative rulings involving the application of a treaty in looseleaf, CD/DVD, and online services that focus on treaties or that have extensive treaty coverage.

SECTION J. INTERPRETING TREATIES

1. Administrative Interpretations

In many instances, the executive branch must issue regulations and other rulings to implement or interpret treaty provisions. For example, Title 26, Chapter I, Subchapter G of the Code of Federal Regulations provides regulations regarding tax treaties. These regulations do not follow the regulations numbering system described in Chapter 9, and they do not cover all treaty countries.[105]

The Internal Revenue Service issues revenue rulings and other guidance interpreting treaty provisions. You can locate these documents by using the treaty country as a search term instead of using a Code section. Chapter 10 discusses locating IRS documents.

2. Judicial Interpretations

Because treaties and statutes are both approved by Congress, many of the rules of interpretation applied to statutes apply to treaties. The list below illustrates interpretation rules applied to treaties and to situations involving a conflict between a treaty and a statute.

- [W]hen a treaty and an act of Congress conflict "the last expression

---

[105] See, e.g., Treas. Reg. § 513.2: "The fact that the payee of the dividend is not required to pay Irish tax on such dividend because of the application of reliefs or exemptions under Irish revenue laws does not prevent the application of the reduction in rate of United States tax with respect to such dividend."

of the sovereign will must control". Lindsey v. Commissioner, 98 T.C. 672, 676 (1992).

• Unless the treaty terms are unclear on their face, or unclear as applied to the situation that has arisen, it should rarely be necessary to rely on extrinsic evidence in order to construe a treaty, for it is rarely possible to reconstruct all of the considerations and compromises that led the signatories to the final document. However, extrinsic material is often helpful in understanding the treaty and its purposes, thus providing an enlightened framework for reviewing its terms. Xerox Corp. v. United States, 41 F.3d 647, 652 (Fed. Cir. 1994).

• Even where a provision of a treaty fairly admits of two constructions, one restricting, the other enlarging, rights which may be claimed under it, the more liberal interpretation is to be preferred. North West Life Assurance Co. of Canada v. Commissioner, 107 T.C. 363, 378 (1996).

• We construe a treaty like a contract. Amaral v. Commissioner, 90 T.C. 802, 813 (1988).

• It does appear, however, that in the case of treaties, courts have sometimes been more willing to resort to extra-textual, preparatory material to determine meaning, and also to allow for more liberal interpretation of the words of a treaty. In such instances the decision of the courts to resort to sources beyond the treaty language and/or to a more liberal interpretation of the written word often has occurred because the treaty language is not completely clear and requires further explanation. Snap-On Tools, Inc. v. United States, 26 Cl. Ct. 1045, 1065 (1992).

• Thus, to the extent that a treaty can reasonably be interpreted to avoid conflict with a subsequent enactment, such an interpretation is to be preferred. Norstar Bank of Upstate New York v. United States, 644 F. Supp. 1112, 1116 (N.D.N.Y. 1986).

SECTION K. OECD AND WTO

The United States belongs to several international organizations whose activities may affect U.S. tax legislation and administration. In addition to the United Nations, which has published a Model Tax Convention,[106]

---

[106] The UN model treaty focuses on relationships between developed and developing countries. The United States income tax treaties are based on the U.S. model treaty format or the OECD format.

the OECD and WTO are two of the most important.

1. OECD

The Organisation for Economic Co-operation and Development was formed in December 1960 as a continuation of the Organisation for European Economic Co-operation. The OECD issues "internationally agreed instruments, decisions and recommendations to promote rules of the game in areas where multilateral agreement is necessary for individual countries to make progress in a globalised economy."[107]

The United States is a signatory to the OECD Mutual Administrative Assistance in Tax Matters Convention, which entered into force in 1995. The OECD has published several model treaties, such as the OECD Model Tax Convention on Income and on Capital, which the United States takes into account in negotiating tax treaties.[108] Treaty explanations indicate variances from the OECD Model Treaty. [See Illustration 8-2.] A recent OECD project concerns harmful tax competition. That project led to a list of so-called Unco-operative Tax Havens.[109]

The OECD website has hyperlinks to a variety of reports and news releases related to taxation.

2. WTO

The World Trade Organization was formed in 1995 to deal with the global rules of trade between nations. It succeeded the General Agreement on Tariffs and Trade (GATT). Trade disputes resolved by WTO panels extend beyond such traditional measures as tariffs. Its 2002 holding, that U.S. tax provisions favoring foreign sales corporations were invalid export subsidies, led to several changes in the Internal Revenue Code.[110]

---

[107] OECD website (http://www.oecd.org). This site includes OECD Model Treaty information.

[108] The most recent OECD Model Treaty was issued in September 2005. The most recent U.S. Model Treaty was issued in November 2006.

[109] The OECD regularly reports on countries that have not made a commitment to transparency and effective exchange of information. The OECD site also discusses so-called Harmful Tax Practices and issues progress reports on that topic.

[110] World Trade Organization Appellate Body ruling (WT/DS108/AB/RW) (Jan. 14, 2002) on appeal from Panel Report, United States - Tax Treatment for "Foreign Sales Corporations" - Recourse to Article 21.5. of the DSU by the

Section L. Other International Material

1. General Information

If a transaction will take place in another country, you may need information about that country's tax laws and general business climate. Pamphlets published by major accounting firms and other organizations provide useful background information. Individual country websites are easy to access.[111] Background material appears in sources such as the Tax Management Portfolios (Chapter 13).

Although background materials provide an introduction, they cannot substitute for primary source materials. Many United States law libraries have collections of materials from other countries, particularly countries that use English as their primary language.

2. Material in Other Languages

Although not limited to international taxation, a practitioner may need access to materials in a language other than English. Treaties to which the United States is a signatory are published in both English and the official language of the other country. A limited number of United States tax forms are available from the IRS website in Spanish. The IRS also publishes Publication 850, an English-Spanish glossary of words and phrases.

3. Treaties with Native American Tribes

Treaties the United States entered into with Native Americans are beyond the scope of this text. You should be aware that tax rules applied to Native Americans may involve claims of treaty-based exemptions.[112]

European Communities (the "Panel Report"). The WTO Dispute Settlement Body adopted the Appellate Body ruling on January 29, 2002 (WT/DS/108/25). These and subsequent documents related to this dispute are available at the WTO website, http://www.wto.org. The WTO website can be searched by country and by type of dispute.

[111] See, e.g., http://www.hmrc.gov.uk/home.htm (United Kingdom Revenue & Customs); Being a business owner in Denmark, Business Lounge page, at http://www.denmark.dk.

[112] See, e.g., Cook v. United States, 86 F.3d 1095 (Fed. Cir. 1996).

Section M.　Problems

1. Which tax treaties are in force between the U.S. and the country listed?

   a. Australia

   b. Indonesia

   c. South Africa

   d. Thailand

2. When were the following U.S.-(Country Listed) treaties signed?

   a. Austria: social security totalization agreement

   b. Ghana: shipping and aircraft tax treaty

   c. Sri Lanka: protocol to income tax treaty

3. What is the T.I.A.S. number for the following U.S.-(Country Listed) treaties, and when did they enter into force?

   a. Belgium: shipping and aircraft tax treaty

   b. China: protocol interpreting the protocol to the income tax treaty

   c. Trinidad & Tobago: exchange of information agreement

4. Locate and provide citations for as many of the items illustrated as you can for the treaty selected by your instructor.

5. After completing Chapter 10, provide a citation for and holding of

   a. a 2006 IRS announcement concerning fiscally transparent entities and the U.S.-Mexico income tax treaty

   b. a 2005 IRS letter ruling regarding the base erosion test in the U.S.-Netherlands income tax treaty and the participation exemption

   c. a 2004 IRS revenue ruling regarding taxation of a nonresident partner and the U.S.-Germany income tax treaty

   d. a 2002 IRS chief counsel advice concerning students working as camp counselors and the U.S.-Czech Republic income tax treaty

e. a 1999 IRS technical advice memorandum discussing Code section 882(c) and the nondiscrimination provisions of the U.S.-Canada income tax treaty

f. a 2000 IRS field service advice concerning the standard deduction and the U.S.-Greece income tax treaty

6. After completing Chapter 11, locate and give the holding and any appeals action for

a. a Tax Court decision whether the U.S.-France income tax treaty prevented treating royalties as passive income

b. a D.C. Circuit decision involving the alternative minimum tax limitation on the foreign tax credit and the U.S.-Germany income tax treaty

c. a Court of Federal Claims decision involving the significance of being a grant recipient and the U.S.-Russian Federation income tax treaty

7. Print out tax information from a country-specific website.

PART THREE

PRIMARY SOURCES: ADMINISTRATIVE

Chapter 9. Treasury Regulations

Section A. Introduction

This chapter discusses regulations, which Congress authorizes in the Internal Revenue Code and in other statutes. It explains the different types of regulations—proposed, temporary, and final—and the difference between legislative and interpretive regulations. It also covers other terms used to describe regulations, judicial deference to administrative positions, and sources in which you can find relevant documents.

Your goals for this chapter include locating all relevant documents, determining their relative importance, and updating your research to include projects that may result in proposed regulations.

Section B. Administrative Guidance

As discussed in Chapters 6 and 7, Congress enacted the Internal Revenue Code and other statutes governing income, transfer, and excise taxes. Taxpayers interpret those statutes in determining their liability for these taxes. Courts become involved when there is a controversy between the government and a taxpayer. In interpreting statutes, both taxpayers and courts must consider administrative interpretations.[113]

The Treasury Department and Internal Revenue Service (IRS) interpret and enforce internal revenue laws. In some areas, such as employee benefits, they share their authority with other administrative agencies. This chapter focuses on one form of administrative guidance, regulations, primarily those issued as Treasury regulations. Chapter 10 focuses on IRS pronouncements.

Section C. Regulatory Scheme

1. Treasury Regulations

Title 26 of the Code of Federal Regulations (C.F.R.) is the Internal Revenue title of C.F.R. As such, it contains most of the regulations you

---

[113] Administrative interpretations are also relevant for treaties ratified by the Senate. Treaties are discussed in Chapter 8.

will need for resolving tax problems. Instead of citing these regulations as 26 C.F.R. sections, you can cite them as Treasury Regulations (Treas. Reg.).

Some Treasury-issued regulations appear elsewhere in C.F.R. Regulations in 31 C.F.R. (Money and Finance: Treasury) cover other Treasury Department functions, including Practice Before the Internal Revenue Service.[114]

2. Other Agency Regulations

If another agency has authority for provisions affecting tax law, its regulations are also relevant. For example, the Labor Department issues regulations in the employee benefit area. Those regulations appear in 29 C.F.R. Several Code sections defer to other agency interpretations.[115]

SECTION D. REGULATORY AUTHORITY

1. Entities Involved

The two most important entities involved in promulgating regulations are the Internal Revenue Service and the Treasury Department. Regulations are drafted by the Internal Revenue Service, but they are issued under the authority of the Secretary of the Treasury.

Code section 7805(a) authorizes the Secretary to "prescribe all needful rules and regulations for the enforcement" of the tax statutes. Other Code sections that refer to regulations also use the term "the Secretary." Code section 7701(a)(11)(B) defines that term to mean "the Secretary of the Treasury or his delegate." If the statute instead says "the Secretary of the Treasury," section 7701(a)(11)(A) prohibits delegation.

The Secretary of the Treasury has delegated the regulations drafting function to the Commissioner of Internal Revenue.[116] For that reason, this text generally refers to the IRS role in the regulations process. Nevertheless, you must refer to them as Treasury regulations, not IRS regulations.

---

[114] This group of sections begins at 31 C.F.R. § 10.0.

[115] See, e.g., I.R.C. § 4064(b)(1)(B): "The term 'automobile' does not include any vehicle which is treated as a nonpassenger automobile under the rules which were prescribed by the Secretary of Transportation ...."

[116] Treas. Reg. § 301.7805-1(a).

Section H describes the steps involved in issuing a regulation.

2. Limitations on Authority

Section 7805(a) authorizes issuing regulations, but it is not an absolute grant of authority. Several limitations apply to the IRS's authority to issue regulations. These relate to retroactivity and taxpayer burden. The government describes its compliance with these rules in the preambles that accompany regulations. [See Illustration 9-3.]

a. Code Section 7805(b) and Retroactivity

Code section 7805(b) imposes limits on issuing regulations with retroactive effect. Beginning with statutes enacted on July 30, 1996, a proposed, temporary, or final regulation cannot apply to any taxable period before the earliest of its filing with the Federal Register[117] or the date on which a notice substantially describing its expected contents is issued to the public. This rule does not apply to regulations filed or issued within 18 months of the statute's enactment, necessary to prevent abuse, or issued to correct procedural defects in previously issued regulations.[118]

b. Code Section 7805(f) and Small Business

Section 7805(f) requires the Treasury Department to submit proposed and temporary regulations to the Small Business Administration's Chief Counsel for Advocacy. The Chief Advocate is required to comment on the regulation's impact on small business. The preamble accompanying the final regulations must discuss these comments.[119]

c. Executive Order 12866

In 1993, President Clinton issued an order setting forth a statement of regulatory philosophy and principles and providing a regulatory planning and review process for proposed and existing regulations. The Office of

---

[117] A final regulation can be retroactive to the date its proposed or temporary version was filed. It might even relate back to an IRS notice, described in Chapter 10.

[118] Congress can legislatively waive Section 7805(b), and the IRS can authorize taxpayers to elect retroactive application.

[119] Comparable requirements apply to final regulations that are not based on proposed regulations, but the submission must occur before the regulation is filed.

Management and Budget is charged with ensuring that regulations follow the stated philosophy and principles. The order also requires that agencies submit their regulatory plans for the year for OMB review. In Executive Order 13258, President Bush made changes to Executive Order 12866 to reflect personnel changes.[120] You can search for agency submissions governed by Executive Order 12866 on the General Services Administration website. [Illustration 9-1.] You can also search directly in an online version of the Federal Register or in an online service covering Preambles to regulations.

d. Administrative Procedure Act

Agencies must publish notices of proposed rulemaking in the Federal Register.[121] These notices include information about the time and place for a public rulemaking procedure, indicate the agency's legal authority for promulgating the regulation, and indicate the terms or substance of the proposed rule. Publication generally must precede the effective date by at least 30 days. Although interpretative rules are exempt from these requirements, interpretive tax regulations generally follow the act's requirements.[122]

e. Regulatory Flexibility Act

Federal agencies that are required to publish notices of proposed rulemaking must prepare and publish for comment an initial regulatory flexibility analysis. This requirement also applies to notices of proposed rulemaking for interpretive rules involving the internal revenue laws that impose information collection requirements on small business.[123] The analysis includes information about the agency's objectives, the small entities affected, and the type of compliance requirements that will be involved. You can use the Advanced Search feature of the site shown in Illustration 9-1 to search for such items. [Illustration 9-2.] Alternatively, you can search in an online service covering the Federal Register or covering Preambles to Treasury Regulations.

---

[120] 67 Fed. Reg. 9385 (2002). Executive Order 12866 appears at 58 Fed. Reg. 51735 (1993).

[121] 5 U.S.C. § 553.

[122] The legislative-interpretive distinction is also important when a court is deciding how much deference the rule merits. Deference is discussed in Section K.

[123] See 5 U.S.C. § 603. A final regulatory flexibility analysis, including a description of public comments and the agency's response, accompanies the final regulation. Id. § 604.

Illustration 9-1. Search for EO 12866 Regulatory Reviews

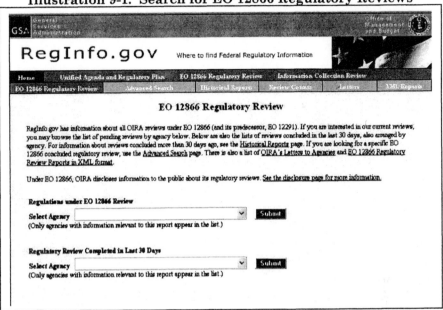

→Use the Historical Reports for older items.

Illustration 9-2. Regulatory Flexibility Analysis Search

Advanced Search

RIN*

Terms (Title and Abstract)*

Agency*

Department of Treasury

Sub Agency

Internal Revenue Service

Received Date Range   *(MM/DD/YYYY)*
From   To

Concluded Date Range   *(MM/DD/YYYY)*
From   To

☐ Were Economically Significant?

☐ Were Major?

☐ Imposed Unfunded Mandates?

☑ Required a Regulatory Flexibility Analysis?

☐ Small Entities Affected?

f. Paperwork Reduction Act of 1995

An agency that wants to require information submissions from the private sector must obtain OMB approval. Illustration 9-3 includes a section discussing information collections.

Illustration 9-3 Preamble Discussion of Regulatory Constraints

Paperwork Reduction Act

The collections of information in this final rule have been reviewed and, pending receipt and evaluation of public comments, approved by the Office of Management and Budget (OMB) under 44 U.S.C. 3507 and assigned control number 1545-1767. The collections of information in this regulation are in §1.472-8(e)(3)(iii)(B)(3) and (e)(3)(iv). To elect the IPIC method, a taxpayer must file Form 970, "Application to Use LIFO Inventory Method." This information is required to inform the Commissioner regarding the taxpayer's elections under the IPIC method. This information will be used to determine whether the taxpayer is properly accounting for its dollar-value pools under the IPIC method. The collections of information are required if the taxpayer wants to obtain the tax benefits of the LIFO method. The likely respondents are business or other for-profit institutions, and/or small businesses or organizations.

....

Special Analyses

It has been determined that this Treasury decision is not a significant regulatory action as defined in Executive Order 12866. Therefore, a regulatory assessment is not required. It also has been determined that section 553(b) of the Administrative Procedure Act (5 U.S.C. chapter 5) does not apply to these regulations. Pursuant to section 7805(f) of the Code, the proposed regulations preceding this Treasury decision was submitted to the Chief Counsel for Advocacy of the Small Business Administration for comment on their impact on small business. It is hereby certified that the collections of information in this Treasury decision will not have a significant economic impact on a substantial number of small entities. First, only taxpayers that adopt, or change to, the IPIC method will be affected by the collections of information. Second, relatively few small entities are expected to adopt, or change to, the IPIC method. Third, the burden of the collections of information is not significant. Therefore, a Regulatory Flexibility Analysis under the Regulatory Flexibility Act (5 U.S.C. chapter 6) is not required.

→The excerpts above appear in T.D. 8976, 67 Fed. Reg. 1075 (Jan. 9, 2002). The Paperwork Reduction Act begins at 44 U.S.C. § 3501.

SECTION E. REGULATIONS NUMBERING SYSTEM

1. Regulations Subdivisions

Title 26 C.F.R. has no subtitles and only one chapter (Chapter I – Internal Revenue Service, Department of the Treasury). Chapter I is divided into seven subchapters and numerous parts. [Table 9-1.]

There are subdivisions within each part, but they are not separately numbered and often lack formal titles (e.g., subpart). For example, one subdivision of Subchapter A, Part 1, is Normal Taxes and Surtaxes. Two of its subdivisions are Determination of Tax Liability and Computation of Taxable Income. Those units are themselves further subdivided. A partial list appears as Table 9-2.

The authority information (Code section 7805 or another section) appears immediately after a listing of sections in a particular group.

2. Regulations Numbering Scheme

Most regulations section numbers have two segments, which are separated by a decimal point, and a third segment, which follows a hyphen. The first segment, often called the prefix, indicates where the regulation appears; prefixes use the part numbers illustrated in Table 9-1.

The segment that follows the decimal point generally indicates the Code section being interpreted. Thus, Treas. Reg. § 1.106-1 interprets Code section 106. The third segment, which follows the hyphen, is similar to the subdivisions used for Code subsections and is discussed in Subsection 4.

Each regulations section is further subdivided into

- paragraphs (e.g., Treas. Reg. § 1.23-2(a));

- subparagraphs (e.g., Treas. Reg. § 1.23-2(e)(2)); and

- subdivisions (e.g., Treas. Reg. § 1.23-2(d)(4)(iv)).

The regulations do not uniformly follow the nomenclature above. For example, Treas. Reg. § 1.61-2(d)(1) contains the following language: "Except as provided in paragraph (d)(6)(i) of this section ...."

Smaller units exist but do not receive formal names. For example, Treas. Reg. § 1.274-2(b)(1)(iii)(a) says: "Except as otherwise provided in (b) or (c) of this subdivision ...." The subdivision referred to is (iii); (a), (b), and (c) are smaller units of (iii).

Regulations frequently contain examples. These may appear in a separate Examples subdivision (e.g., Treas. Reg. § 1.119-1(f)) or as part of a subdivision to which the example applies (e.g., Treas. Reg. § 1.162-5(b)(3)(ii)).

Table 9-1. List of Subchapters and Partial List of Parts

Subchapter A	Income Tax
Part 1	Income taxes
Part 2	Maritime construction reserve fund
Part 3	Capital construction fund
Part 4	Temporary income tax regulations under section 954 of the Internal Revenue Code
Part 5	Temporary income tax regulations under the Revenue Act of 1978
Subchapter B	Estate and Gift Taxes
Subchapter C	Employment Taxes and Collection of Income Tax at Source
Subchapter D	Miscellaneous Excise Taxes
Subchapter F	Procedure and Administration
Subchapter G	Regulations Under Tax Conventions
Subchapter H	Internal Revenue Practice
Part 601	Statement of procedural rules
Part 602	OMB control numbers under the Paperwork Reduction Act

→Subchapter E is currently Reserved.

3. Importance of Regulations Prefixes

The regulation prefix is critical for finding the correct regulation. First, regulations in different parts interpret the same Code section. For example, Treas. Reg. §§ 1.7520-1, 20.7520-1, and 25.7520-1 all interpret Code section 7520. Differences in their texts reflect their application to different taxes.

Second, regulations in some parts don't interpret a Code section but the number following the prefix is a Code section number. For example, Treas. Reg. § 1.1-1 is an income tax regulation for Code section 1. Treas. Reg. § 2.1-1 is a definition section dealing with the maritime construction reserve fund; it has nothing to do with Code section 1.[124] Although its

---

[124] Regulations in Part 601 follow this pattern. Treas. Reg. § 601.101, for

prefix (2) indicated it related to the maritime construction reserve fund [Table 9-1}, that information alone would not have told you that the regulation had nothing to do with Code section 1.

4. Relationship of Code and Regulations Subdivisions

The portion of the regulation that follows the hyphen does not indicate the Code subsection involved. In fact, there may be significantly more regulations sections than Code subsections. Table 9-2 illustrates the relationship of Code and regulations sections for Code section 61(a).[125]

Table 9-2. Relationship of Code and Regulations Subdivisions

Code Subsection	Regulations Section
61(a)	1.61-1, 1.61-14, 1.61-22
61(a)(1)	1.61-2, 1.61-15, 1.61-21
61(a)(2)	1.61-3, 1.61-4, 1.61-5
61(a)(3)	1.61-6
61(a)(4)	1.61-7
61(a)(5)	1.61-8
61(a)(6)	1.61-8
61(a)(7)	1.61-9
61(a)(8)	1.61-10
61(a)(9)	1.61-10
61(a)(10)	1.61-10
61(a)(11)	1.61-11
61(a)(12)	1.61-12
61(a)(13)	1.61-13
61(a)(14)	1.61-13
61(a)(15)	1.61-13

→Some Code subdivisions have more than one regulations section; others share a regulations section.

5. Letters Preceding Hyphen in Section Number

a. Formats

Most section numbers follow this format: Treas. Reg. § 1.61-1. Two other formats include a capital or lower case letter before the hyphen.

---

example, has nothing to do with I.R.C. § 101.

[125] The relationship between Treas. Reg. § 1.61-22, issued in 2003, and paragraphs in I.R.C. § 61(a) varies based on how the particular split-dollar life insurance arrangement is analyzed.

Capital letters must be used if the underlying Code section includes a capital letter. For example, Treas. Reg. § 1.263A-1 is a regulation for Code section 263A. Capital letters may also appear even though the Code section does not include a capital letter. Treas. Reg. § 1.170A-1 is an example of this situation. Section 170 regulations that lack the A (e.g., Treas. Reg. § 1.170-1) interpret the statute before its 1969 amendment.

Some regulations include lower case letters before the hyphen. Treas. Reg. § 1.672(a)-1 illustrates that format. The letter in parentheses may indicate the relevant Code subsection but does not necessarily do so.

b. Location in C.F.R.

If a section number includes a letter before the hyphen, it follows the regulations for the Code section that don't include a letter. If more than one letter is used, those regulations appear in alphabetical order. Temporary regulations always include a capital T, but it appears after the hyphen. Temporary regulations appear in the normal number order in C.F.R. [See Table 9-3.]

Illustrations 9-4 through 9-6 show the regulations order for Code section 142 in C.F.R, LexisNexis, and the 2006 Standard Federal Tax Reporter (SFTR). Each uses a different order.

6. Regulations Issued for Prior Internal Revenue Codes

Regulations issued for 1954 Code sections also apply to the 1986 Code to the extent Code sections remained unchanged. Regulations interpreting the 1939 Code followed a different numbering system. Unless I indicate otherwise, you can assume that references cover regulations interpreting the 1986 Code.

Illustration 9-4. Order of Section 142 Regulations in C.F.R.

1.142-0	Table of contents.
1.142-1	Exempt facility bonds.
1.142-2	Remedial actions.
1.142-4	Use of proceeds to provide a facility.
1.142(a)(5)-1	Exempt facility bonds: Sewage facilities.
1.142(f)(4)-1	Manner of making election to terminate tax-exempt bond financin

Illustration 9-5. Order of Section 142 Regulations in LexisNexis

□ § 1.142-0 Table of Contents.
□ § 1.142-1 Exempt facility bonds.
□ § 1.142(f)(4)-1 Manner of making election to terminate tax-exempt bond financing
□ § 1.142-2 Remedial actions.
□ § 1.142-3 Refunding issues. [Reserved]
□ § 1.142-4 Use of proceeds to provide a facility.
□ § 1.142(a)(5)-1 Exempt facility bonds: Sewage facilities.

Illustration 9-6. Order of Section 142 Regulations in SFTR

□   FINAL-REG, 2006FED ¶7740A, §1.142-0., Table of contents. --

□   FINAL-REG, 2006FED ¶7740B, §1.142-1., Exempt facility bonds

□   FINAL-REG, 2006FED ¶7740C, §1.142-2., Remedial actions

□   FINAL-REG, 2006FED ¶7740D, §1.142-3., Refunding issues. --

□   FINAL-REG, 2006FED ¶7740F, §1.142-4., Use of proceeds to pro

□   FINAL-REG, 2006FED ¶7741, §1.103-7., Industrial development

□   FINAL-REG, 2006FED ¶7742, §1.103-8., Interest on bonds to fin

□   PROP-REG-AMNDT, 2006FED ¶7743, §1.103-8., Interest on bon

□   PROP-REG-AMNDT, 2006FED ¶7744, §1.103-8., Interest on bon

□   TEMP-REG, 2006FED ¶7745, §17.1., Industrial development bo

□   FINAL-REG, 2006FED ¶7746, §1.103-9., Interest on bonds to fin

□   FINAL-REG, 2006FED ¶7747, §1.103-11., Bonds held by substan

□   FINAL-REG, 2006FED ¶7749, §5c.103-1., Leases and capital ex

□   TEMP-REG, 2006FED ¶7750, §5c.103-2., Leases and industrial

□   TEMP-REG, 2006FED ¶7751, §5f.103-2., Public approval of ind

□   FINAL-REG, 2006FED ¶7751B, §1.142(a)(5)-1., Exempt facility b

□   PROP-REG, 2006FED ¶7751D, §1.142(a)(6)-1., Exempt facility b

□   FINAL-REG, 2006FED ¶7751F, §1.142(f)(4)-1., Manner of making

→Standard Federal Tax Reporter includes final and temporary regulations, which are in C.F.R., and proposed regulations, which are not. Note the additional regulations, which are not strictly tied to section 142.

Table 9-3. Order of Section 25 Regulations in C.F.R.

Regulation	Regulation Topic
1.25-1T	Credit for interest paid on certain home mortgages
1.25-2T	Amount of credit
1.25-3	Qualified mortgage credit certificate
1.25-3T	Qualified mortgage credit certificate

SECTION F. TERMINOLOGY

This section introduces relevant terminology used for regulations and related documents.

1. Proposed, Temporary, and Final Regulations

You should expect to encounter regulations in three different stages. The citation format clearly indicates whether the item is a Proposed Regulation (e.g., Prop. Treas. Reg. § 1.801-4(g)); a Temporary Regulation (e.g., Temp. Treas. Reg. § 1.71-1T); or a Final Regulation (e.g., Treas. Reg. § 1.106-1). Assuming the citation is correct, a regulation that does not include either a "Prop." or a "T" is a final regulation. Each type can be cited as authority for avoiding the substantial understatement penalty discussed in Chapter 2.

a. Proposed Regulations

Proposed regulations offer guidance for taxpayers seeking to comply with statutory rules. Taxpayers receive an opportunity to submit written comments or testify at hearings before proposed regulations become final.

b. Temporary Regulations

The IRS can simultaneously issue a proposed regulation as a **temporary regulation**. Unlike a proposed regulation, a temporary regulation is effective when it is published in the Federal Register. It provides immediate, binding guidance, and receives more deference than a proposed regulation. It becomes operative without the benefit of public comment.

Code section 7805(e) mandates that temporary regulations issued after November 20, 1988, also be issued as proposed regulations; this ensures that there will be a notice and comment procedure.[126] Section 7805(e) also requires that temporary regulations expire no more than three years

---

[126] Proposed regulations need not be issued as temporary regulations.

after they are issued. This limitation does not apply to temporary regulations issued before that date, and several older temporary regulations are still in effect.

c. Final Regulations

Regulations issued after any necessary notice and comment period are referred to as **final regulations**. The final regulations may differ from the proposed or temporary regulations they replace for various reasons, including government response to taxpayer comments or judicial decisions. In addition to regulatory analysis information [Illustration 9-1], the preamble accompanying the Treasury Decision will indicate comments received and any changes made in response to comments.

2. Interpretive and Legislative Regulations

Regulations issued pursuant to the Code section 7805(a) general mandate are referred to as **interpretive** (or **interpretative**). These contrast to **legislative** regulations, issued for Code sections in which Congress included a specific grant of authority. The specific grant of authority allows IRS experts to write rules for technical areas.

The information accompanying each regulation indicates Treasury's authority for issuing the regulation, either a specific Code section (legislative), Code section 7805(a) (interpretive), or both. If the regulation is a final or temporary regulation, the authority information is added to the appropriate part of 26 C.F.R. As illustrated in Section K, courts give legislative regulations more deference than they accord interpretive regulations.

Understanding terminology is important. Interpretive and legislative relate to the authority for a particular regulation; proposed, temporary, and final relate to steps in the process for issuing regulations. For example, a regulation can be both final and interpretive.

3. Project Numbers and Notices of Proposed Rulemaking

a. Project Numbers

When the IRS opens a regulations project, it assigns it a **project number**. It then uses those project numbers for its proposed regulations. Although the project numbering system has changed several times, certain parts have remained constant.

Before a 1988 reorganization, most projects were drafted in the IRS

Legislation and Regulations Division and began with the letters LR. Employee benefits and exempt organization projects were designated EE; international projects, INTL. Projects begun under this system received new letter designations but not new numbers after 1988.

Between 1988 and August 1996, project numbers indicated the IRS division with responsibility for the project. [See Table 9-4.] The current numbering system began in August 1996. All project numbers now begin with REG, followed by a series of numbers, followed by the project's year. There is no indication of which IRS division has authority for the regulations project. A recent example of this numbering system is REG-105248-04, covering proposed regulations for Code section 853. The document appeared in the Federal Register in 2006. The -04 following the hyphen indicates it was a 2004 project.[127]

Although the numbering system no longer indicates which division produced the regulation,[128] that information does appear in the Drafting Information section included in the regulation's preamble.

Table 9-4. IRS Project Designations, 1988-1996

Designation	Division
CO	Corporate
EE	Employee Benefits and Exempt Organizations
FI	Financial Institutions and Products
GL	General Litigation
IA	Income Tax and Accounting
INTL	International
PS	Passthroughs and Special Industries

b. Notices of Proposed Rulemaking

The IRS publishes the text of a proposed regulation and its accompanying preamble as a **Notice of Proposed Rulemaking (NPRM)**. Notices include the project number and the **Regulation Identifier Number**

---

[127] 71 Fed. Reg. 54598 (2006).

[128] The IRS operating divisions that followed the Internal Revenue Service Restructuring and Reform Act of 1998, Pub. L. No. 105-206, 112 Stat. 685, don't replace the chief counsel units. The operating divisions (Wage & Investment; Small Business/Self-Employed; Large & Mid-Size Business; and Tax Exempt/Government Entities) are not part of the chief counsel's office. The chief counsel division for exempt organizations is now called tax exempt and government entities; general litigation has become part of procedure and administration.

(RIN) (discussed in Section I). Neither number reflects the underlying Code section number or the year the proposal is filed with the Federal Register.

The Service may publish an **Advance Notice of Proposed Rulemaking (ANPRM)**. Advance notices indicate rules the Service expects to propose and request public comment that may influence the resulting NPRM. The ANPRM also includes the project number and the RIN.

4. Treasury Decisions

Final and proposed regulations are issued as **Treasury Decisions (T.D.)**. Treasury Decisions are numbered sequentially; the current numbering system began in 1900. It does not indicate the year of issue or the Code section involved. After the regulation text is added to the C.F.R., the most important information in the T.D. is the preamble. [See Illustration 9-3]

5. Preambles and Texts of Regulations

Preambles to T.D.s and NPRMs discuss the regulation and provide other useful information, much of which is discussed elsewhere in this chapter.

Table 9-5. Preamble Segments

Paperwork Reduction Act
Background
Explanation of Provisions
Effective Date
Special Analyses
Comments and Public Hearing
Drafting Information
List of Subjects

Two items follow the preamble. The first is the amendment to the affected C.F.R. subdivision. This amendment indicates the Code section authorizing each regulation, a concept discussed in Subsection 2. The second item is the regulation's **text**. That language is added to the C.F.R. if it is a temporary or final regulation. If it is a proposed regulation, the text appears in the Federal Register but not the C.F.R.

6. Filing Date, Effective Date, and Sunset Date

Because they are not statutes, regulations are not enacted. Instead they are issued to the public by being filed with the Federal Register. The **filing date** generally precedes the publication date by a day or two. The

T.D. information following each temporary and final regulation includes the Federal Register date. That date is also listed before preambles to proposed, temporary, and final regulations. The date is important because of the rules concerning retroactivity discussed in Subsection D.2.

The preamble to the T.D. or NPRM includes the regulation's **effective date**, which can vary from its filing date and publication dates. The effective date for a proposed regulation is likely to read as follows: "These regulations are applicable to taxable years ending after the date final regulations are published in the Federal Register."

Final regulations generally continue in effect indefinitely. Temporary regulations issued after November 20, 1988, **sunset** no later than three years after they are issued. Although a final regulation continues in effect until it is withdrawn, its validity may be seriously compromised if the Code section it interprets is amended or if a judicial opinion rejects its reasoning. Use the T.D. date to determine when a regulation was promulgated or amended. If a regulation contradicts its Code section, it probably has not been amended to reflect the most recent statutory change.[129] If it varies from a judicial holding, the IRS may have decided to continue litigating its position rather than withdraw the regulation. Chapter 10 discusses administrative announcements regarding continuing litigation.

7. Semiannual Agenda and Priority Guidance Plan

Administrative agencies announce their regulatory plans twice a year in the **Semiannual Agenda of Regulations**. In addition, the Treasury and IRS issue an annual **Priority Guidance Plan (Business Plan)** for guidance they hope to issue during the next twelve months. These documents are discussed further in Section I.

SECTION G. RULES AFFECTING MULTIPLE PROVISIONS

As is the case for the Code, rules appearing in a regulation section may apply only to that section, or a subdivision thereof, or they may apply to several sections. See, for example, Treas. Reg. § 1.414(r)-3(c)(5)(iii)(A):

Solely for purposes of the separateness rules of this section and the assignment rules of section 1.414(r)-7, if an employee changes status as described in paragraph (c)(5)(iii)(B) of this section, an employer

---

[129] Looseleaf services that print regulations often indicate that a regulation does not reflect a statutory change.

may, for up to three consecutive testing years after the base year (within the meaning of paragraph (c)(5)(iii)(B)(1) or (2) of this section), treat the employee as providing the same level of service to its lines of business as the employee provided in the base year.

SECTION H. DEFINITIONS

As was true for the Code itself, the regulations frequently define terms within individual sections. In addition, several regulations sections enlarge upon definitions found in Internal Revenue Code Subtitle F, Chapter 79.[130]

SECTION I. REGULATORY PROCESS

1. IRS and Treasury

Regulations begin as projects assigned to drafters in the relevant division of the IRS chief counsel's office. The Semiannual Agenda of Regulations or Priority Guidance Plan will generally list these items. The Semiannual Agenda lists the Code section and Project Number and indicates a target date by which action, such as publishing the proposed regulations, will occur. The Priority Guidance Plan lists topics (e.g., Exempt Organizations, Financial Issues and Products) alphabetically. Within each topic, it lists both regulations and other guidance the Treasury Department and IRS hope to issue; Code sections are included for most items. For example, the 2006-2007 Plan includes as an item within the Subchapter S group "Proposed regulations under section 1361 providing guidance for S corporation banks."

Because the IRS may issue advance notices regarding its proposals,[131] researchers interested in future regulations must also check IRS documents discussed in Chapter 10.

After a notice and comment period, the IRS has several options. These include finalizing the proposed regulation without modifications, finalizing it with modifications, modifying it and asking for additional comments, or withdrawing it and starting the drafting process over again. Because proposed regulations, unlike temporary regulations, do not sunset after three years, the IRS can also retain the proposal in its

---

[130] See, e.g., Treas. Reg. § 301.7701-1.

[131] See, e.g., Notice 2006-60, 2006-29 I.R.B. 82.

original form without further action.

2. Congress

In March 1996, Congress added a congressional review procedure for agency rules. This procedure allows Congress to disapprove a "major" rule by a **joint resolution of disapproval**. A disapproved rule does not become effective unless the President vetoes the disapproval and Congress fails to override the veto. Major rules are suspended for up to 60 days for the congressional review and for additional time if needed for the override process.[132]

Congress may intervene by imposing a moratorium on regulations in a particular area, as it did for nonstatutory fringe benefits before the enactment of Code section 132. Congress could also reject a regulation by changing the statute to produce a different outcome. A current area of practitioner frustration relates to Code sections with no regulations despite statutory language saying the Secretary "shall" issue regulations.

Section J. Locating Regulations Documents

The first step in locating administrative documents is determining which items you need. The following paragraphs divide documents by type rather than by where you can find them.

1. Semiannual Agenda and Priority Guidance Plan

a. Semiannual Agenda

The Semiannual Agenda is issued twice a year and published in the Federal Register. It is required by the Regulatory Flexibility Act and Executive Order 12866. Preparation of the Unified Agenda covering federal agencies is coordinated by the Regulatory Information Service

---

[132] 5 U.S.C. §§ 801-808. A major rule is "any rule that the Administrator of the Office of Information and Regulatory Affairs of the Office of Management and Budget finds has resulted in or is likely to result in–(A) an annual effect on the economy of $100,000,000 or more; (B) a major increase in costs or prices for consumers, individual industries, Federal, State, or local government agencies, or geographic regions; or (C) significant adverse effects on competition, employment, investment, productivity, innovation, or on the ability of United States-based enterprises to compete with foreign-based enterprises in domestic and export markets." Id. § 804(2).

Center (RISC).[133] The Treasury Department and agencies within its umbrella are part of the Agenda.

The Treasury Department is responsible for several agencies in addition to the IRS. These include the Alcohol and Tobacco Tax and Trade Bureau, the Comptroller of the Currency, and the Office of Thrift Supervision. As a result, its Agenda is quite lengthy. Because it is not arranged in Code section order, it is difficult to search manually.

The Agenda is divided into two parts. Part I groups projects by agency. Within that grouping, it subdivides them into five categories: Prerule Stage; Proposed Rule Stage; Final Rule Stage; Long-Term Actions; and Completed Actions. The items in each category appear in **Sequence Number** order and also carry a **Regulation Identifier Number (RIN)**. The sequence number changes from one Agenda to another; the project's RIN never changes. If you know a project's RIN but not the actual project number, you can find it using an online search in the Agenda.

Neither the Sequence Number nor the RIN indicates the relevant Code section or the regulations Project Number.[134] Part II provides this information for each item in Part I. Part II is arranged by Sequence Number. [See Illustrations 9-9 and 9-10.]

Although the Agenda is issued semiannually, a Regulatory Plan is required only in the second Agenda of the year. That plan indicates the most important items that should be issued within the fiscal year.[135]

You can access the Agenda through the Government Printing Office site, GPO Access [Illustrations 9-7 and 9-8] and the General Services Administration site. As Illustration 9-8 indicates, there appears to be a 40-hit limit on the GPO site. You can do a Code search in the PFD files.

Several subscription services include the Agenda in their databases. For example, Tax Analysts includes it in the OneDisc. This version is arranged in Code section rather than Sequence Number order [Illustration 9-11]. Services covering the Federal Register, such as LexisNexis and

---

[133] The Regulatory Information Service Center is part of the General Services Administration (www.gsa.gov).

[134] The project illustrated in Illustrations 9-9 and 9-10 is RIN 1545-AM-97; its Project Number is REG-209006-89; it involves I.R.C. § 367. It includes a reference to its pre-1996 project number (INTL-089-89); see Table 9-4.

[135] The Agendas are scheduled for April and October but may appear later.

Westlaw, also cover the Agenda and are searchable by keywords.[136]

Illustration 9-7. Agenda Site in GPO Access

The Unified Agenda: Main Page

The Unified Agenda (also known as the Semiannual Regulatory Agenda), published twice a year (usually in April and October) in the Federal Register (FR), summarizes the rules and proposed rules that each Federal agency expects to issue during the next six months. It is published by the Office of the Federal Register National Archives and Records Administration (NARA). More.

Current Edition (2006) Only

- Quick Search: (ex: "page 30498", "21 cfr 107", "railroad retirement board" AND benefits)

  | treasury | Submit | [Search Tips]

- Browse the Table of Contents: April 2006 edition only

Previous Editions (1994 through 2005)

- Search (1994 forward)
- Browse (2002 forward)
- Search tips

→You can instead search on Internal Revenue Service.

Illustration 9-8. Agenda Search Results: Treasury

Search Database:

For: "TREASURY"

Total Hits: 40

[1]
ua24ap06 DEPARTMENT OF THE TREASURY (TREAS)
        Size: 97852 , Score: 1000 , TEXT , PDF , SUMMARY

[2]
ua24ap06 2499. UPDATE AND REVISION OF TREASURY REGULATION SECTIONS 1.381(C)(4)
        Size: 2097 , Score: 932 , TEXT , PDF , SUMMARY

[3]
ua24ap06 2337. CLAIMS ON ACCOUNT OF TREASURY CHECKS
        Size: 2402 , Score: 822 , TEXT , PDF , SUMMARY

[4]
ua24ap06 2537. REVISION OF TREASURY REGULATION SECTION 1.1561-
        Size: 2693 , Score: 733 , TEXT , PDF , SUMMARY

→This sites uses 40 as its default "hits" number.

---

[136] See, e.g., Department of the Treasury, Semiannual Agenda and Fiscal Year 2006 Regulatory Plan, 70 Fed. Reg. 65033 (2005). If you don't have a citation, you can find it by searching for either Semiannual Agenda or Unified Agenda.

Illustration 9-9. Excerpt from Semiannual Agenda Part I

Internal Revenue Service—Proposed Rule Stage		
Sequence Number	Title	Regulation Identifier Number
2438	Clarification of Treatment of Separate Limitation Losses	1545–AM11
2439	Outbound Transfers of Property to Foreign Corporations	1545–AM97
2440	Foreign Insurance Company—Domestic Election	1545–AO25
2441	Taxation of Global Trading	1545–AP01
2442	Information Reporting and Record Maintenance	1545–AP10
2443	Definition of "Highly Compensated Employee"	1545–AQ74

→This excerpt is from 71 Fed. Reg. 23056 (2006). Part I indicates Sequence Number, project title, and the RIN number.

Illustration 9-10. Excerpt from Semiannual Agenda Part II

CC:INTL

Agency Contact: Richard L. Chewning, Senior Counsel, Department of the Treasury, Internal Revenue Service, 1111 Constitution Avenue NW, Washington, DC 20224
Phone: 202 622–3850

RIN: 1545–AM11

2439. OUTBOUND TRANSFERS OF PROPERTY TO FOREIGN CORPORATIONS

Priority: Substantive, Nonsignificant

Legal Authority: 26 USC 7805; 26 USC 367

CFR Citation: 26 CFR 1

Legal Deadline: None

Abstract: The income tax regulations under section 367(a) will be amended to reflect the changes made to that section by the Technical and Miscellaneous Corrections Act of 1988. Section 367(a)(5) now provides that a transfer of assets to a foreign corporation in an exchange described in section 361 is subject to section 367(a)(1), unless certain ownership requirements and other conditions are met. The regulations will provide guidance regarding the application of this section. The change in the statute was necessitated by the repeal of "General Utilities."

Timetable:

Action	Date	FR Cite
NPRM	12/00/06	

Regulatory Flexibility Analysis Required: No

Small Entities Affected: No

Government Levels Affected: None

Additional Information: REG-209006-89 (INTL-089-89)

Drafting attorney: Milton Cahn (202) 622-3860

Reviewing attorney: Charles P. Besecky (202) 622-3860

CC:INTL

Agency Contact: Milton M. Cahn, Attorney–Advisor, Department of the Treasury, Internal Revenue Service, 1111 Constitution Avenue NW, Washington, DC 20224
Phone: 202 622–3860

RIN: 1545–AM97

2440. FOREIGN INSURANCE COMPANY—DOMESTIC ELECTION

Priority: Substantive, Nonsignificant

Legal Authority: 26 USC 7805; 26 USC 953

CFR Citation: 26 CFR 1

Legal Deadline: None

→Sequence Number 2439 from 71 Fed. Reg. 23105 (2006) indicates that a regulation for Code section 367 should be proposed by year-end.

Illustration 9-11. Regulatory Agenda Search in OneDisc

→OneDisc lets you search by Code section or key words. It also has a Code section table for projects.

b. Priority Guidance Plan

The Priority Guidance Plan, which has also been referred to as the Business Plan and the Guidance Priority Plan, includes both regulations and other forms of guidance that Treasury and IRS plan to issue during the year. Until 2002, the Plan covered a calendar year. Beginning with the plan issued in 2002, it covers a fiscal year ending June 30. It is covered by newsletters such as Daily Tax Report and Tax Notes and can be found online at the IRS and Treasury websites.

Illustration 9-12. Excerpt from 2006-2007 Priority Guidance Plan

B.	Executive Compensation, Health Care and Other Benefits, and Employment Taxes
1.	Guidance on accountable plans and per diem payments.
2	Guidance under section 83 on post-grant restrictions.
3.	Revenue ruling on taxable health benefits for beneficiaries.
4.	Proposed regulations on cafeteria plans under section 125 updating regulations for statutory changes and providing additional guidance.

→The Guidance Plan covers regulations, rulings, and other guidance.

2. Proposed Regulations

Proposed regulations are not included in C.F.R. They do appear in the Federal Register, which can be searched in print and electronically. Several services provide access to proposed regulations, which they arrange in order of their publication. If you are searching electronically in the Federal Register, you can search for proposed regulations by project number; Federal Register date; RIN number or the underlying Code section number. In addition to using a government site, you can search the Federal Register in LexisNexis and Westlaw.

Illustration 9-13. Search in OnPoint for Proposed Regulations

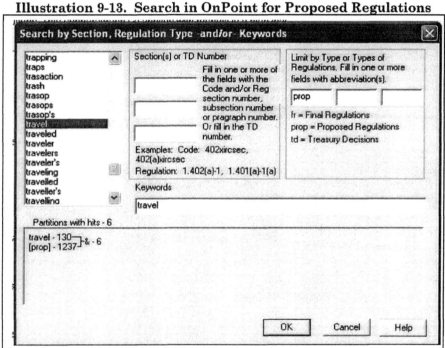

→The OnPoint CD-ROM search template lets you search by type of regulation, Code section number, regulations citation, or key words.

Illustration 9-14. Search Results in OnPoint

Proposed § 1.89(a)-1 Miscellaneous questions and answers relating to nondiscrimination rule..
Proposed § 1.117-6 Qualified scholarships.
Proposed § 1.482-9 Methods to determine taxable income in connection with a controlled servi...
Proposed § 48.4051-1 Heavy trucks and trailers; definition of highway vehicle.
Proposed § 10.71 Discovery.

→Based on the hit list above, I would probably refine my search and use both travel and expenses.

Looseleaf services frequently include proposed regulations in their compilation volumes along with temporary and final regulations. [See Illustration 9-6.] If a looseleaf prints proposed regulations in a separate volume, it may arrange them by Federal Register date. Those services generally include a table that cross-references from the underlying Code or regulations section to the appropriate page, paragraph, or section in the looseleaf service. They are unlikely to have tables cross-referencing project numbers.

3. Temporary and Final Regulations

a. C.F.R. and Federal Register

Temporary and final regulations are relatively easy to find. These items appear in both the Federal Register (as Treasury Decisions) and the C.F.R. (as "codified" regulations). Use the method for finding the Federal Register version that you would use to find a proposed regulation. Because the C.F.R. section numbers generally correspond to Code section numbers, it is easier to find temporary and final regulations in the C.F.R. than in the Federal Register.[137] You might choose to search in the Federal Register because it includes the preambles, and C.F.R. doesn't.

Keep one limitation in mind if you use the print version of the C.F.R. The government does not replace C.F.R. volumes every time an agency promulgates a new regulation. Instead it republishes C.F.R. titles on an annual basis; several titles are replaced each calendar quarter. The annual reissue of Title 26 includes regulations issued as of April 1. Searching C.F.R. print updates for later material is a tedious process.[138] It is easier to find regulations using a tax-oriented looseleaf service (print or electronic) or to search C.F.R. online.

b. Looseleaf Services

Standard Federal Tax Reporter and United States Tax Reporter incorporate temporary and final regulations into their compilation volumes, which are arranged in Code section order. Each is available in print and electronic versions.

---

[137] The method for issuing regulations in the Federal Register makes that publication analogous to Statutes at Large for revenue acts. Each T.D. is listed separately by publication date rather than by Code section. The Code of Federal Regulations, which is in section number order, is analogous to United States Code for statutes.

[138] That process is described in basic legal research texts.

Other tax-oriented services provide print versions of tax regulations. These include Mertens, Federal Tax Regulations, published in annual softbound volumes with updating throughout the year in a looseleaf Current Developments binder.

If you want the most recent items, don't use a print source such as U.S. Code Congressional & Administrative News—Federal Tax Regulations It is published annually and not updated during the year.

Looseleaf services are discussed further in Chapter 13. The USCCAN materials are described in Chapter 17.

c. Electronic Services

Several electronic sources print the text of regulations. Tax-oriented CD/DVD services include OneDisc, OnPoint, and Federal TaxExpert. These and other CD/DVD services are discussed further in Chapter 19. Depending on the subscription option you select, the CD/DVD may be updated monthly or less frequently. You can search for more recent regulations using a weekly print updating service or a newsletter. You are most likely to find the most recent changes by using an online service.

Online subscription sources for regulations include general services such as LexisNexis, Westlaw, and Loislaw. You can also search for regulations online in tax-oriented subscription services. These include Tax Research NetWork, Checkpoint, and TaxCore. Online services are discussed in Chapter 20.

You can also access regulations online at government sites. A search for a known citation appears as Illustration 9-15. A search by topic is illustrated in Illustration 9-16. If you use this site, you must update your research for Treasury regulations appearing after April 1. You can do so using the site's links to online versions of List of CFR Sections Affected (LSA). A search in a database such as LexisNexis or Westlaw is easier.

Illustration 9-15. Retrieving Regulation in GPO Access

Revision Year	Title	Part	Section	Subpart	File Type
2005 ∨	26	CFR 1	. 302-2	OR	Text ∨

Go Reset

→Use this screen if you know the citation. File Type options include PDF.

Illustration 9-16. Searching for Regulations in GPO Access

Select and search or browse available CFR Titles or volumes:

- All volumes for the selected Title(s) will be searched by default.
- Individual volumes can be searched by clicking the corresponding checkbox. To prevent duplicate search results, deselect the Title checkbox th|

Maximum Records Returned: |40 | Default is 40. Maximum is 200.

Search Terms: |redemptions |

[SUBMIT] [CLEAR]

Search Title	Search Volume	Chapter	Browse Parts	Regulatory Entity
☑ Title 26	☐ 1	I	1.1-1.60	Internal Revenue Service,
Internal Revenue	☐ 2		1.61-1.169	Department of the Treasury
Revised April 1, 2006	☐ 3		1.170-1.300	
	☐ 4		1.301-1.400	

→I conducted this search as if I did not know which Code sections concerned redemptions. Alternatively, I could have deselected Title 26 and searched only in Volume 4.

4. Earlier Versions of Regulations

a. 1954 and 1986 Codes

Prior language may be important if you are evaluating recent changes in a regulation or if your research involves a completed transaction. If you need the language of a 1954 or 1986 Code regulation, you can find that regulation's language in United States Code Congressional & Administrative News—Federal Tax Regulations (Chapter 17). This service has separate volumes for each year since 1954 and prints regulations in effect on January 1 of the particular year.

If you need a regulation that was both issued and withdrawn within a single calendar year and thus might be omitted from a USCCAN or GPO Access search for a single year, two other services may be of assistance. Cumulative Changes (Chapter 17) prints each version of a regulation. It has separate volumes for each Code. Until the mid-1990s, Mertens, Law of Federal Income Taxation (Chapter 13), published a Regulations series. That series published all income tax regulations issued or amended within a given time span (two or more years per volume).

If you lack access to the services listed above, make a list of T.D. numbers for the regulation you are tracing. Those numbers appear immediately after the particular regulation in C.F.R. and in most other versions of the regulations. The T.D.s are published in the Cumulative

Bulletins, which your library is likely to carry.[139] The Cumulative Bulletin is also available online.

Note one limitation in using T.D. numbers to find older versions of regulations. If a 1954 Code regulation was originally published before 1960, the IRS republished it that year in T.D. 6498, 6500, or 6516. The USCCAN service ignores the pre-1960 publication in its history notes; Cumulative Changes omits the 1960 T.D. numbers but includes the pre-1960 T.D.s. If you use any service to find T.D. numbers, be sure you know how that service treats those early items.

You have several options if you search for earlier regulations online. GPO Access allows you to search for regulations in effect on each April 1 from 1997 to the current year. [Illustration 9-17.] Commercial services also carry older regulations. The Westlaw file for older versions of the C.F.R. goes back to 1984. You can search in a single year, or you can search multiple years simultaneously. LexisNexis has C.F.R. archived files back to 1981. HeinOnline allows you to browse the C.F.R. back to its 1938 edition. [Illustrations 9-18 through 9-22.]

Illustration 9-17. GPO Access Regulations Search Gateway

26 Internal Revenue		Apr. 1, 2006	Apr. 1, 2005	Apr. 1, 2004	Apr. 1, 2003	Apr. 1, 2002	Apr. 1, 2001	Apr. 1, 2000	Apr. 1, 1999	Apr. 1, 1998	Apr. 1, 1997

→Select the year(s) you desire and then search as in Illustration 9-16. Each year appears separately on the search screen.

b. 1939 Code and Earlier

Early regulations don't follow the regulations format used elsewhere in this text. Initially they were issued with respect to individual revenue acts and were divided into articles rather than section numbers. The first named set of regulations was referred to as Regulations Number 33 and was issued in 1914.[140] The article numbers did not correspond to act section numbers.

---

[139] Finding Lists in the CCH and RIA citators indicate which volume of the Internal Revenue Bulletin or Cumulative Bulletin contains each T.D. For recent items, RIA is more likely to refer to the paragraph in United States Tax Reporter.

[140] See HENRY CAMPBELL BLACK, A TREATISE ON THE LAW OF INCOME TAXES (2d ed. 1915).

The Federal Register became available online in 1994 and in print in 1936. Thus, it is not a good source for finding early regulations. Even for years it covers, it is tedious to search in print. In many libraries, the best source for 1939 Code and earlier regulations will be the Cumulative Bulletin. It began publication in 1919; the first T.D. it includes is 2836.

The Government Printing Office published Treasury Decisions–Internal Revenue from 1899 until 1942. It covers 1898 through July 9, 1942. The current T.D. numbering system began in 1900 with the third volume. Many early T.D.s look less like regulations and more like "public" private letter rulings.[141] Letter rulings are discussed in Chapter 10.

If you have access to HeinOnline, you can browse the C.F.R. back to its 1938 edition to locate tax regulations. Illustrations 9-18 through 9-22 illustrate using HeinOnline for this purpose.

Illustration 9-18. Selecting a Search Option in HeinOnline

→If you know the year, use the options on the right-hand side of the screen. Otherwise, choose the Browse By Titles option on the left.

Illustration 9-19. Selecting a Title to Search in HeinOnline

Title Number	Title Name (Most Recent)
25	Indians
26	Internal Revenue
27	Alcohol, Tobacco Products and Firearms

→Select Title 26, Internal Revenue.

---

[141] "SIR: In reply to a letter of inquiry addressed to this office on the 29th ultimo by Frederick D. Howe, treasurer and manager of the Warren Specialty Company, Auburn, N.Y., will you please inform him that the beverage (liqueur) called creme de menthe being, as it is understood, a compound of distilled spirits with other materials, any person manufacturing it for sale must be required to pay special tax as a rectifier ...." T.D. 33, 3 Treasury Decisions–Internal Revenue 32 (1900).

Illustration 9-20. Selecting a Year to Search in HeinOnline

Code of Federal Regulations - Years for Title: 26 - Internal Revenue

Edition / Supplement Year

1938 - Edition
- 1939 - Supplement
- 1938 - Supplement
- 1940 - Supplement
- 1941 - Supplement
- 1943 - Supplement

Illustration 9-21. Selecting a Part for 1940 in HeinOnline

Code of Federal Regulations - Parts for Title: Internal Revenue Year: 1940 Sup.

Parts

Title: 26 Part: 3 - Income Tax under the Revenue Act of 1936
Title: 26 Part: 9 - Income Tax under the Revenue Act of 1938
Title: 26 Part: 19 - Income Tax under the Internal Revenue Code
Title: 26 Part: 21 - Excess-Profits Tax Imposed by Subchapter B of Chapter 2 of the Internal Revenue Code

Illustration 9-22. Excerpt from 1936 Material in HeinOnline

TITLE 26—INTERNAL REVENUE

CHAPTER I—BUREAU OF INTERNAL REVENUE

DEPARTMENT OF THE TREASURY

Subchapter A—Income and Excess-Profits Taxes

PART 3—INCOME TAX UNDER THE REVENUE ACT OF 1936

§ 3.22 (a)–3 *Compensation paid other than in cash.* * * * If a person receives as compensation for services rendered a salary and in addition thereto living quarters or meals, the value to such person of the quarters and meals so furnished constitutes income subject to tax. If, however, living quarters or meals are furnished to employees for the convenience of the employer, the value thereof need not be computed and added to the compensation otherwise received by the employees. * * * [As amended by T.D. 4965, Feb. 29, 1940; 5 F.R. 872]

place. If a taxpayer does not claim a deduction in its return for such a totally or partially worthless debt for the year in which such charge-off takes place, but claims such a deduction for a later year, then such charge-off in the prior year will be deemed to have been involuntary and the deduction shall be allowed for the year for which claimed, if the taxpayer produces sufficient evidence to show (1) that the amount claimed in such later year was ascertained to be worthless or recoverable only in part, as the case may be, in such year, and (2) that, to the extent that the deduction claimed in the later year was not involuntarily charged off in prior years, it was charged off in

→HeinOnline is most useful if you know the volume you want or have time to browse individual volumes.

5. Preambles

The Federal Register includes the preambles for each proposed, temporary, and final regulation with the regulation text. Excerpts or full text also appear in the Internal Revenue Bulletin and Cumulative Bulletin.[142]

Tax-oriented looseleaf services separate preambles from the regulations text. If they print the preambles, they do so in separate volumes.[143] Mertens, Federal Tax Regulations, publishes preambles for tax regulations in looseleaf volumes. Coverage begins in 1985. Standard Federal Tax Reporter (Chapter 13) prints preambles for proposed regulations in its U.S. Tax Cases Advance Sheets volume; it includes current year preambles for T.D.s in the Regulations Status Table in its New Matters volume. United States Tax Reporter (Chapter 13) prints preambles to proposed regulations in a separate volume for preambles; it prints current year preambles for T.D.s in the IRS Rulings section of its Recent Developments volume.

Tax Research NetWork includes the SFTR service, and Checkpoint includes USTR. If you use these looseleaf services online, simply use their Preamble option. Other electronic services may include preambles as a separate database (CD/DVD services) or in their Federal Register coverage. Illustration 9-3 shows part of a preamble.

6. Hearings Transcripts and Other Taxpayer Comments

Newsletters such as Daily Tax Report and Tax Notes report on testimony at hearings and taxpayer written comments. The Tax Notes Today file in LexisNexis includes texts of unofficial hearings transcripts and other taxpayer comments. You can also find these items online using services such as TaxCore. The preamble to final regulations summarizes taxpayer comments made in response to the NPRM.

SECTION K. CITATORS FOR REGULATIONS

Regulations rarely keep pace with new legislation activity. Whenever a Code section changes, researchers must review existing regulations. They may no longer be relevant. They may even be totally invalid. If a regulation appears to contradict statutory language, check the date of its

---

[142] Preambles for proposed regulations were added to the C.B. in 1981.

[143] If a regulation was issued in both proposed and temporary format, a looseleaf service may carry only the preamble to the temporary regulation.

most recent T.D. to see if it predates the statutory change.

When an existing regulation affects a transaction, that regulation's success or failure in litigation is certainly relevant. The government is bound nationally by adverse decisions in the Supreme Court. It is effectively bound within a particular circuit by an adverse circuit court decision because trial courts follow the law of their circuit. The IRS is not bound in its dealings with taxpayers in circuits that have not addressed the regulation. Because the Supreme Court hears relatively few tax cases, the government may decide not to withdraw a regulation merely because the Tax Court or a single circuit court invalidates it.[144]

A citator indicating judicial action on regulations is extremely useful for determining how courts ruled on challenges to particular regulations. Shepard's (LexisNexis) and KeyCite (Westlaw), each of which is described further in Chapter 12, serve that purpose. They allow you to check a particular regulation. The print and online citators provided by CCH and RIA are not as useful because they are based on T.D. number rather than regulation number. Because T.D.s often involve more than one regulations section, citators based on regulations section numbers are more likely to provide the desired information.

You can also search both CD/DVD and online services without using a citator by using the regulations section number and a variant of valid (or invalid) as your search terms. For example, I have two options for researching Treas. Reg. § 1.469-2 in Westlaw. I could enter the following in the Westlaw FTX-CS (Federal Taxation–Cases) database: 1.469-2 & valid invalid.[145] I could also go directly to the regulation and then use the KeyCite function. If I used a service that lacked a citator, my search would resemble the first option (modified to reflect that service's command structure).

SECTION L. JUDICIAL DEFERENCE

In determining the degree of deference they should give regulations, courts are guided by several Supreme Court decisions, the best-known of

---

[144] Compare Western Nat. Mut. Ins. Co. v. Commissioner, 65 F.3d 90 (8th Cir. 1995), invalidating Treas. Reg. § 1.846-3(c), with Atlantic Mut. Ins. Co. v. Commissioner, 111 F.3d 1056 (3d Cir. 1997), holding the regulation valid. The Supreme Court upheld the Third Circuit. See 523 U.S. 382 (1998).

[145] If I wanted to find decisions that used the term "validity," I could have refined my search by adding root expanders. Remember to check search terminology options when you use an electronic service.

which is *Chevron*.[146] The *Chevron* Court held[147]

> When a court reviews an agency's construction of the statute which it
> administers, it is confronted with two questions. First, always, is the
> question whether Congress has directly spoken to the precise ques-
> tion at issue. If the intent of Congress is clear, that is the end of the
> matter; for the court, as well as the agency, must give effect to the
> unambiguously expressed intent of Congress.[9] If, however, the court
> determines Congress has not directly addressed the precise question
> at issue, the court does not simply impose its own construction on the
> statute,[10] as would be necessary in the absence of an administrative
> interpretation. Rather, if the statute is silent or ambiguous with
> respect to the specific issue, the question for the court is whether the
> agency's answer is based on a permissible construction of the stat-
> ute.[11]

Although *Chevron* is not a tax decision, it is cited in many tax cases
and therefore appears if you enter *Chevron* into an electronic service.
There are also tax cases involving the same company. Examples in
Chapter 20 illustrate the risks of searching by case name alone in
electronic services.

The excerpts below illustrate judicial approaches to deference. Two
statements apply irrespective of the approach taken. First, the degree of
deference accorded legislative regulations is higher than that accorded
interpretive regulations. Second, proposed regulations receive much less
deference than do temporary or final regulations.

• To invoke these passages from our decisions for the general
proposition that regulations may not add rules not found in the statute
and not precluded by the statute is to misread them. Indeed, supplemen-

---

[146] Chevron U.S.A. Inc. v. Natural Resources Defense Council, Inc., 467 U.S.
837 (1984). Other decisions that courts may cite when discussing deference
include National Muffler Dealers Association v. United States, 440 U.S. 472
(1979), and National Cable & Telecommunications Association v. Brand X
Internet Services, 545 U.S. 967 (2005).

[147] Id. at 842-43 (footnotes omitted). The Court added: "If Congress has
explicitly left a gap for the agency to fill, there is an express delegation of
authority to the agency to elucidate a specific provision of the statute by
regulation. Such legislative regulations are given controlling weight unless they
are arbitrary, capricious, or manifestly contrary to the statute.[12] Sometimes the
legislative delegation to an agency on a particular question is implicit rather than
explicit. In such a case, a court may not substitute its own construction of a
statutory provision for a reasonable interpretation made by the administrator of
an agency.[13]" Id. at 843-44 (footnotes omitted).

tation of a statute is a necessary and proper part of the Secretary's role in the administration of our tax laws. Hachette USA, Inc. v. Commissioner, 105 T.C. 234, 251 (1995).

• Although the difference between these two approaches [*Chevron* and *National Muffler*] is negligible at best—any regulation which is "based upon a permissible construction" of an ambiguous statute will almost always "implement the congressional mandate in some reasonable manner" and vice versa, the Ninth Circuit is correct to rely upon the more narrowly tailored holding of *National Muffler*. Bell Federal Savings & Loan Association v. Commissioner, 40 F.3d 224, 227 (7th Cir. 1994).

• If the regulations constituted a reasonable interpretation of [the statute], we would be compelled to uphold them even if [the taxpayer's] interpretation were more reasonable. Estate of Bullard v. Commissioner, 87 T.C. 261, 281 (1986).

• The reasonableness of each possible interpretation of the statute can also be measured against the legislative process by which [it] was enacted. Commissioner v. Engle, 464 U.S. 206, 220 (1984).

• "[L]egislative" regulations ... are entitled to even greater weight than regulations issued pursuant to the general authority granted by Congress under section 7805(a). Fife v. Commissioner, 82 T.C. 1, 15 (1984).

• Where the Commissioner acts under specific authority, our primary inquiry is whether the interpretation or method is within the delegation of authority. Rowan Cos., Inc. v. United States, 452 U.S. 247, 253 (1981).

• A regulation may have particular force if it is a substantially contemporaneous construction of the statute by those presumed to have been aware of congressional intent.... Other relevant considerations are the length of time the regulation has been in effect, the reliance placed on it, the consistency of the Commissioner's interpretation, and the degree of scrutiny Congress has devoted to the regulation during subsequent re-enactments of the statute.[148] National Muffler Dealers Ass'n, Inc. v. United States, 440 U.S. 472, 477 (1979) (footnotes omitted).

• [Proposed regulations] carry no more weight than a position advanced on brief .... F.W. Woolworth Co. v. Commissioner, 54 T.C. 1233, 1265 (1970).

---

[148] At one time courts invoked a "re-enactment doctrine" if a regulation had been in effect through several revenue acts and Congress did not override it. Now that Congress amends specific provisions rather than re-enacting the entire Code, this doctrine is of questionable value.

Section M. Problems

1. What regulation was authorized by the listed Code section?

    a. 25A(i)

    b. 170(f)(11)(H)

    c. 411(a)(7)(B)

    d. 1296(e)

2. List all T.D.s issued for the regulation listed below.

    a. 1.132-1

    b. 1.164-1

    c. 1.351-1

    d. 1.904-1

3. Provide the List of Subjects from the T.D. listed below. (A single T.D. may involve multiple subjects and multiple Code sections.)

    a. 8425

    b. 8444

    c. 8798

    d. 9111

4. Who drafted the T.D. listed below? In which chief counsel division did that attorney work?

    a. 9180

    b. 8880

    c. 8580

    d. 8280

5. Who drafted the most recent version (original or amended) of Treasury regulation section

   a. 1.482-5

   b. 1.1031(a)-2

   c. 1.1368-3

   d. 1.1502-3

6. Who drafted the proposed regulations covered by Project Number

   a. REG-127819-06

   b. REG-133578-05

   c. REG-115054-01

   d. REG-113572-99

7. Your instructor will assign you a Code section that uses the term "the Secretary shall prescribe" regulations. Determine which status best describes those regulations.

   a. have been proposed

   b. have been issued as temporary or final regulations

   c. are in the most current version of the Priority Guidance Plan

   d. are not in any of the first three categories

8. List any items in the most recent Priority Guidance Plan relating to guidance for a topic selected by your instructor.

9. Go to the most recent Priority Guidance Plan. Your instructor will select a regulations project. Find that project in the most recent Semiannual Agenda and indicate all relevant dates for guidance.

10. Locate the court decision described and determine which regulation is involved. These decisions do not necessarily involve the regulation's validity.

   a. a 2003 Court of Appeals decision involving value-added payments from a farming cooperative

b. a 2002 Court of Appeals decision involving the lining of aluminum smelting machines

c. a 2005 District Court decision involving feuding brothers and funds allegedly transferred from Switzerland to Liechtenstein

d. a 2006 Tax Court decision involving taxpayers who operated a tree farm, a seamstress business, and a dog-breeding business.

11. Locate the court decision described below and indicate which regulation is involved. These decisions involve whether a regulation is valid.

a. a 2006 Tax Court decision and a generation skipping transfer tax regulation

b. a 2005 District Court decision and the check the box regulations

c. a 2004 Court of Appeals decision and Volvo trucks

d. a 2003 Supreme Court decision and a domestic international sales corporation

12. Draft comments on a proposed regulation selected by your instructor.

CHAPTER 10. INTERNAL REVENUE SERVICE DOCUMENTS

SECTION A. INTRODUCTION

This chapter discusses guidance, other than regulations, issued by the Internal Revenue Service. These documents can be issued more quickly than regulations, in part because they are not subject to notice and comment procedures. In addition to describing the different types of guidance, this chapter indicates which can be cited as precedential and which constitute "substantial authority," concepts discussed in Chapter 2. It also discusses sources in which you can find these documents, the role of the Freedom of Information Act and other statutes affecting the release of IRS documents, and judicial deference to various IRS pronouncements.

Your goals for this chapter include learning which documents are available and where they can be found, determining their relative importance, and locating IRS and judicial action with respect to items you've located.

SECTION B. TYPES OF IRS DOCUMENTS

There are several methods for categorizing IRS documents. Three such methods are their means of publication, their initial audience, and their status as precedent or as substantial authority.

1. Means of Publication

The IRS publishes several documents in the weekly Internal Revenue Bulletin. The most important of these are revenue rulings, revenue procedures, notices, and announcements. Items currently included in the I.R.B. are cumulated every six months and appear in the Cumulative Bulletin. Chapter 17 discusses changes in the C.B. format over time.

The IRS issues other types of guidance, such as private letter rulings and actions on decisions, that it does not publish in the I.R.B. Many of these items were released to the public following Freedom of Information Act (FOIA) litigation; others have been exempted from release by statute.

The materials in Sections C through E categorize IRS documents by their publication status: officially published in the I.R.B. or in other IRS publications; available because of FOIA litigation; or exempted from release by statute.[149]

2. Initial Audience

Documents published in the Internal Revenue Bulletin are directed to all taxpayers and their representatives. Private letter rulings, on the other hand, are directed to a specific taxpayer; the IRS makes them available to other readers after deleting identifying material. Still other documents are written for government personnel. Many of them, such as field service advice, are publicly available.

3. Status as Precedent or Substantial Authority

Items printed in the Internal Revenue Bulletin constitute authority for avoiding the substantial understatement penalty discussed in Chapter 2. These documents can be cited as precedent, and the IRS considers itself bound by them in its dealings with taxpayers whose facts are the same as those discussed in the documents. As discussed in Section I, the degree of deference they receive from courts is mixed.

Items that are not published in the I.R.B. fall into two categories. A few of them are not precedential but nevertheless constitute authority for avoiding the substantial understatement penalty. Others are neither precedential nor authority for avoiding the penalty. Even though these documents are not precedential, courts occasionally cite them.

SECTION C. OFFICIALLY PUBLISHED IRS DOCUMENTS

1. Revenue Rulings (Rev. Rul.)

a. Background

The IRS issues rulings designed to apply the law to particular factual situations. Unlike regulations, rulings do not first appear in proposed form for public comment.

Rulings fall into two categories—revenue rulings and letter rulings. If the IRS determines a ruling is of general interest, it publishes it in the Internal Revenue Bulletin as a **revenue ruling**.

---

[149] As new items come to light, they may initially be placed in a fourth category—subject to FOIA litigation.

Although a revenue ruling is not as authoritative as a Treasury regulation, any taxpayer whose circumstances are substantially the same as those described in the ruling can rely upon it.[150] Revenue rulings also constitute authority for avoiding the substantial understatement penalty. Subject to the limitations in Code section 7805(b), revenue rulings can apply retroactively unless their text indicates otherwise. [See Illustration 4-6 for an excerpt from a revenue ruling.]

Although the number varies from year to year, there have been relatively few revenue rulings issued in recent years.[151] Many of those actually issued represent regularly scheduled guidance rather than rulings on new topics.

b. Numbering System

The IRS numbers revenue rulings chronologically.[152] The ruling number has two segments separated by a hyphen; the first indicates the year and the second indicates the ruling number for that year.[153] The ruling number does not indicate which Code section is involved.

The IRS began issuing numbered revenue rulings in 1953 and adopted the current numbering system in 1954. Earlier rulings, with different names, appeared in pre-1953 Cumulative Bulletins. [See Table 10-1.]

c. Format

Revenue rulings begin by indicating the regulations section involved; the Code section number also appears.

Most recent revenue rulings contain five segments: Issue; Facts; Law; Analysis; and Holding. Other sections that may appear include Effect on Other Documents (for rulings that revoke, modify, obsolete, or otherwise affect a prior holding) and Effective Date. Rulings also indicate the IRS employee who drafted them or who can be contacted if the taxpayer has

---

[150] Although it happens rarely, the IRS has issued adverse rulings based on a set of facts encountered in an audit and then asserted the ruling as authority when the taxpayer litigated. See Rev. Rul. 79-427, 1979-2 C.B. 120, discussed in Niles v. United States, 710 F.2d 1391, 1393 (9th Cir. 1983).

[151] The IRS issued over 700 revenue rulings in 1955; it released 79 in 2005.

[152] The first ruling issued in 2007 is Rev. Rul. 2007-1. Each week's rulings are numbered sequentially, often in Code section order.

[153] The Service began using four digits for years in 2000. Before that it used two digits.

questions; Bulletins issued before 1998 omit drafting information.

Table 10-1. Pre-1953 Titles of Published Rulings

A.R.M.	Committee on Appeals and Review Memorandum
A.R.R.	Committee on Appeals and Review Recommendation
A.T.	Alcohol Tax Unit; Alcohol and Tobacco Tax Division
C.L.T.	Child-Labor Tax Division
C.S.T.	Capital-Stock Tax Division
C.T.	Carriers Taxing Act of 1937; Taxes on Employment by Carriers
D.C.	Treasury Department Circular
Dept. Cir.	Treasury Department Circular
E.P.C.	Excess Profits Tax Council Ruling or Memorandum
E.T.	Estate and Gift Tax Division or Ruling
Em.T.	Employment Taxes
G.C.M	Chief Counsel's Memorandum; General Counsel's Memorandum; Assistant General Counsel's Memorandum
I.T.	Income Tax Unit or Division
L.O.	Solicitor's Law Opinion
MS.	Miscellaneous Unit or Division or Branch
M.T.	Miscellaneous Division or Branch
Mim.	Mimeographed Letter; Mimeograph
Mim.	Solicitor's Law Opinion
O.	Office Decision
Op. A.G.	Opinion of Attorney General
P.T.	Processing Tax Decision or Division
S.	Solicitor's Memorandum
S.M.	Solicitor's Memorandum
S.R.	Solicitor's Recommendation
S.S.T.	Social Security Tax and Carriers' Tax; Social Security Tax; Taxes on Employment by Other than Carriers
S.T.	Sales Tax Unit or Division or Branch
Sil.	Silver Tax Division
Sol. Op.	Solicitor's Opinion
T.	Tobacco Division
T.B.M.	Advisory Tax Board Memorandum
T.B.R.	Advisory Tax Board Recommendation
Tob.	Tobacco Branch

2. Revenue Procedures (Rev. Proc.) and Procedural Rules

a. Background

Revenue procedures are published statements of IRS practices and procedures. These documents are published in the Internal Revenue

Bulletin and Cumulative Bulletin. Procedures of general applicability may also be added to the IRS Statement of Procedural Rules and published in the Code of Federal Regulations.

Several revenue procedures are issued each year to provide guidance on how to obtain rulings and other IRS advice. [See Table 10-2.] For example, the first procedure each year (e.g., Rev. Proc. 2007-1) provides procedures for obtaining rulings, determination letters, and closing agreements. It also includes a sample ruling request format and a schedule of user fees.

Revenue procedures constitute authority for avoiding the substantial understatement penalty.

b. Numbering System

Revenue procedures have been numbered chronologically since 1955. Beginning in 2000, the Service began using all four digits to indicate the year. The procedure number does not indicate the Code or regulations section involved.

Items included in the IRS Statement of Procedural Rules are part of 26 C.F.R. and are numbered as Treasury regulations (Chapter 9). Their prefix is 601.

c. Format

Revenue procedures include several subdivisions, the exact number of which are determined by the procedure's scope and complexity. The following subdivisions are commonly used: Purpose; Background; Scope; Effective Date; Effect on Other Documents; and Drafting Information. In appropriate cases, the procedure will also include sections such as Record Keeping, Request for Comments, and Paperwork Reduction Act.

3. Notices

The IRS issues **notices** to provide guidance before revenue rulings and regulations are available. As noted in Chapter 9, notices can describe future regulations in a manner that will pass muster under the Code section 7805(b) rules on retroactivity.[154]

---

[154] In some cases, the Service has used announcements to provide information and elicit comments about regulations it is drafting. See, e.g., Ann. 2002-9, 2002-7 I.R.B. 536 (deductibility and capitalization of costs associated with intangible assets).

Notices are numbered by year; the number does not indicate the Code or regulations section involved. Notices constitute authority for avoiding the substantial understatement penalty.

Notices may be subdivided into parts similar to those used for revenue rulings and procedures. Shorter notices have few if any formal subdivisions.

Table 10-2. Regularly Issued Revenue Procedures

Procedure	Subject
Year-1	Obtaining letter rulings, determination letters, and closing agreements; user fees
Year-2	Requesting technical advice
Year-3	Areas for which the IRS will not issue a ruling
Year-4	Obtaining rulings for exempt organizations and employee plans
Year-5	Technical advice for exempt organizations and employee plans
Year-6	Obtaining determination letters regarding the qualification of employee plans
Year-7	Areas for which the IRS will not issue a ruling (international)
Year-8	User fees for employee plans and exempt organization rulings

→These procedures, particularly the third item, may be updated during the year.

4. Announcements (Ann.)

Announcements alert taxpayers to a variety of information but are somewhat less formal than revenue rulings, revenue procedures, and notices. Information provided in announcements includes corrections to previously published regulations, lists of organizations classified as private foundations, and extensions of time to file forms.[155] They are numbered by year; the numbering does not indicate the underlying Code section. Announcements constitute authority for avoiding the substantial understatement penalty. These I.R.B. documents were added to the Cumulative Bulletin in 1998.

---

[155] For example, Ann. 2006-67, 2006-38 I.R.B. 509, announced corrections to temporary regulations.

Illustration 10-1. Excerpt from Notice 2006-11

Part III. Administrative, Procedural, and Miscellaneous

Relief From Certain Low-Income Housing Credit Requirements Due to Hurricane Rita

Notice 2006–11

The Internal Revenue Service is suspending certain requirements under § 42 of the Internal Revenue Code for low-income housing credit projects in the United States as a result of the devastation caused by Hurricane Rita. This relief is being granted pursuant to the Service's authority under § 42(n) and § 1.42–13(a) of the Income Tax Regulations.

BACKGROUND

On September 24, 2005, the President declared major disasters for the states of Louisiana and Texas as a result of Hurricane Rita. These declarations were made under the Robert T. Stafford Disaster Relief and Emergency Assistance Act, Title

agency of a state or a possession of the United States (state housing credit agency) may provide approval to project owners in their respective state or possession to provide temporary emergency housing for individuals displaced by Hurricane Rita (displaced individuals) in accordance with this notice.

I. SUSPENSION OF INCOME LIMITATIONS

The Service has determined that it is appropriate to temporarily suspend certain income limitation requirements under § 42 for certain qualified low-income projects. The suspension will apply to low-income housing projects approved by the state housing credit agency, in which vacant units are rented to displaced individuals. The state housing credit agency will determine the appropriate period of temporary housing for each project, not to extend beyond September 30, 2006 (temporary housing period).

displaced individual remains the same the unit's status before the displaced i dividual moves in. Displaced individua temporarily occupying vacant units w not be treated as low-income tenants u der § 42(i)(3)(A)(ii) (a low-income un that was vacant before the effective da of this notice will continue to be treat as a vacant low-income unit even if houses a displaced individual, a mark rate unit that was vacant before the effe tive date of this notice will continue to treated as a vacant market rate unit ev if it houses a displaced individual, and unit that was never previously occupi before the effective date of this notice w continue to be treated as a unit that h never been previously occupied even it houses a displaced individual). Thu the fact that a vacant unit becomes o cupied by a displaced individual will n affect the building's applicable fracti under § 42(c)(1)(B) for purposes of d termining the building's qualified bas nor will it affect the 20–50 test or 40–

5. Other Documents Published in the Internal Revenue Bulletin

The weekly Bulletins contain other information, much of which is issued by the IRS. Information from the IRS includes disbarment notices, delegation orders (Del. Order) announcing delegations of authority to various IRS offices, and **notices of acquiescence and nonacquiescence** (acq.; nonacq.).[156] The acquiescence notices are important because they indicate if the IRS will continue to litigate an issue it has lost in a judicial proceeding. IRS litigation plans are discussed further in Subsection D.6.

Non-IRS material includes Executive Orders issued by the President; Treasury regulations; new legislation and treaty documents; and Supreme Court decisions. These materials are discussed in other chapters.

6. Other IRS Documents

The IRS publishes numerous tax return forms, accompanying

---

[156] Most, but not all, I.R.B. items were cumulated every six months in the Cumulative Bulletin. Since 1998, the C.B. reprints all I.R.B. items. See Chapter 17 for a discussion of the C.B.

instructions, and explanatory booklets. These documents contain few, if any, citations to authority, and they do not indicate if the IRS position has been disputed. Even if they are misleading, taxpayers who rely on them cannot cite them as authority against a contrary IRS position.[157] These documents are not authority for avoiding the substantial understatement penalty.

The numbering system for tax return forms and explanatory booklets does not indicate the underlying Code section number. In addition, the numbering systems for forms and booklets are not coordinated. For example, Code section 280A provides the rules governing deductions for an office in the taxpayer's home. IRS Form 8829 is used for computing that deduction. Publication Number 587 explains the deduction rules to the public.

Section D. Publicly Released IRS Documents

The documents discussed in this section are useful for determining the IRS position on relevant issues. None of them can be cited as precedent,[158] but several constitute authority for avoiding the substantial underpayment penalty discussed in Chapter 2. Litigation resulted in their release and in the enactment of statutes requiring or restricting taxpayer access. You can find most of these documents on the IRS website.

1. Disclosure Legislation and Litigation

The lawsuit that first resulted in disclosure of unpublished documents involved private letter rulings and was brought under the Freedom of Information Act (FOIA).[159] That lawsuit resulted in the disclosure of rulings issued after October 31, 1976, and led to the enactment of Code section 6110, an IRS-specific disclosure statute.

---

[157] See Osborne v. Commissioner, 97-2 U.S.T.C. ¶ 50,524, 79 A.F.T.R.2d 97-3011 (6th Cir. 1997). See also TAM 8350008, involving an IRS refusal to allow a taxpayer to claim reliance on a portion of the Internal Revenue Manual or on the 1982 version of IRS Publication 544. But see Gehl Co. v. Commissioner, 795 F.2d 1324 (7th Cir. 1986); the decision not to seek certiorari is explained in AOD 1988-002.

[158] I.R.C. § 6110(k)(3).

[159] Tax Analysts and Advocates v. Internal Revenue Service, 405 F. Supp. 1065 (D.D.C. 1975) (brought under 5 U.S.C. § 552).

Section 6110, which has been amended several times since its 1976 enactment, requires the release of written determinations and of background file documents related to those written determinations. Written determinations are defined as rulings, determination letters, technical advice memoranda, and chief counsel advice.[160]

Chief counsel advice (CCA; C.C.A.) is "written advice or instruction prepared by any national office component of the Office is of Chief Counsel that is issued to counsel or service field or Service campus employees which interprets or sets forth policy with respect to a revenue provision."[161] Revenue provisions include statutes, regulations, revenue rulings and procedures, tax treaties, and other published or unpublished guidance.[162]

Section 6110 provides timetables for disclosure by the Service. The disclosure date is later than the document's actual issue date to allow time for notifying taxpayers that rulings they have requested are being made public and purging taxpayer-identifying information.

2. Numbering System

Unless a different system is indicated, the publicly released documents discussed in Section D use a common numbering system. The system is based on a multi-digit number (e.g., 84-37-084 or 200203010). Although citation manuals use the hyphens, the IRS does not use them for these documents on its website. Letters preceding the numbers indicate the type of document (e.g., private letter ruling, technical advice memorandum).

The hyphens are useful because they call attention to what the number means. The digits preceding the first hyphen reflect the year the document was released; the next two digits indicate the week of release;

---

[160] I.R.C. § 6110(a) & (b). Background file documents are "the request for that written determination, any written material submitted in support of the request, and any communication (written or otherwise) between the Internal Revenue Service and persons outside the Internal Revenue Service in connection with such written determination ... received before issuance of the written determination."

The IRS makes written determinations available in its FOIA Reading Room and on its website. It releases background documents only on written request; there are fees for finding these items, deleting confidential information, and duplicating them. Id. § 6110(e) & (k); Rev. Proc. 95-15, 1995-1 C.B. 523.

[161] IRM 37.1.1.1.1(4) (Aug. 11, 2004).

[162] I.R.C. § 6110(i).

the final digits are the document number for that week.

Although the document number does not reflect the underlying Code section, many documents also include Uniform Issue List (UIL) numbers. UIL numbers, which do reflect the underlying Code section, are discussed in Section G. The IRS website lets you sort documents by UIL number.

3. Private Letter Rulings (PLR; P.L.R.; Ltr. Rul.; Priv. Ltr. Rul.)

Private letter rulings are written in response to taxpayer requests for guidance as to a proposed transaction's tax consequence. In addition to the underlying facts, issues raised, and legal analysis, these rulings indicate which chief counsel's office division produced them.

Some private letter rulings are formally published as revenue rulings, but most are available to the public only through the section 6110 disclosure procedure. Although the IRS is not bound by them in its dealings with other taxpayers,[163] letter rulings issued after October 31, 1976, constitute authority for avoiding the substantial understatement penalty.

4. Determination Letters

Determination letters are similar to letter rulings but emanate from IRS district offices rather than the national office. District office personnel issue them only if they can be based on well-established rules that apply to the issues presented. Otherwise, the matter is appropriately handled by the national office.

5. Technical Advice Memoranda (TAM; T.A.M.; Tech. Adv. Mem.) and Technical Expedited Advice Memoranda (TEAM; T.E.A.M.)

Technical advice memoranda are issued by the national office in response to IRS requests arising out of tax return examinations. Unlike letter rulings, which focus on proposed transactions, technical advice memoranda cover completed transactions. In contrast to field service advice, discussed in Subsection 8, technical advice requests generally involve both the taxpayer and the IRS. Memoranda issued after October 31, 1976, constitute authority for avoiding the substantial understatement penalty.

---

[163] But see Ogiony v. Commissioner, 617 F.2d 14, 17-18 (2d Cir. 1980) (Oakes, J., concurring). Although commenting that they had no precedential force, the Supreme Court has cited private letter rulings as evidence of IRS inconsistent interpretation. See Rowan Cos., Inc. v. United States, 452 U.S. 247, 261 n.17 (1981).

In mid-2002, the IRS announced a pilot project for a new form of guidance. **Technical expedited advice memoranda**, which would initially be available only for matters under the jurisdiction of the associate chief counsel (Income Tax & Accounting), would result in a streamlined process for technical advice. Both the taxpayer and IRS would be involved in the process. The procedures for obtaining both TAMS and TEAMS are announced in the second revenue procedure each year.[164]

6. Actions on Decisions (AOD; A.O.D.; Action on Dec.; Action on Decision)

The IRS uses several means for announcing future litigation information. One mechanism is the notice of acquiescence or nonacquiescence in cases it has lost. Those notices appear in the Internal Revenue Bulletin. Until early 1993, the Service issued those notices only for Tax Court Regular decisions. It now issues them for all trial and circuit courts.[165]

An **action on decision** indicates *why* the Service recommends (1) appealing or not appealing an adverse decision and (2) acquiescing or not acquiescing in that decision. These are separate recommendations. The Service may recommend not acquiescing and continuing to litigate an issue even though it decides not to appeal the particular case it lost. For example, AOD 1984-022, reproduced as Illustration 10-2, involved a question of fact. The appellate court would be unlikely to reverse for this reason, but the IRS was not willing to concede the underlying issue in future litigation. [See Illustration 4-9 for a more traditional AOD.]

Unlike notices of acquiescence, AODs were never limited to Tax Court decisions. As is true for acquiescence notices, the IRS does not issue an AOD for every case it loses. Taxpayers can use AODs issued after March 12, 1981, as authority for avoiding the substantial understatement penalty.

AODs are numbered sequentially by year. The numbering system provides no information about the underlying case name or issue involved. In 2001 the IRS began including CC (Chief Counsel) in the AOD

---

[164] In CC-2006-013 (May 5, 2006), a Case Specific Advice Task Force recommended eliminating TEAMS.

[165] Although these notices should be the primary means of publishing this information in the Bulletin, the IRS occasionally uses other guidance for this purpose See, e.g., Rev. Rul. 94-47, 1994-2 C.B. 18; Notice 96-39, 1996-2 C.B. 309; Notice 95-57, 1995-2 C.B. 337. AODs are the primary non-I.R.B. method.

number (e.g., AOD CC-2002-02) on its website.[166] Although the IRS refers to these documents as AOD without periods, citation systems use other formats. For example, The Bluebook uses *action on dec.*; TaxCite uses *action on decision*.

7. General Counsel Memoranda (GCM; G.C.M.; Gen. Couns. Mem.)

Just as actions on decisions provide the reasoning behind litigation decisions, **general counsel memoranda** indicate the reasoning and authority used in revenue rulings, private letter rulings, and technical advice memoranda. IRS personnel used them in formulating positions.[167] Taxpayers can use GCMs issued after March 12, 1981, as authority for avoiding the substantial understatement penalty.

GCMs are numbered sequentially (e.g., GCM 39278). The numbering system does not indicate the year of issue, the Code section, or the document about which they supply information. The number of GCMs declined markedly during the 1990s; only one (39892, issued in 2002) has been issued since 1997.

8. Field Service Advice (FSA; F.S.A.); Strategic Advice Memoranda (SAM; S.A.M.)

IRS field attorneys, revenue agents, and appeals officers requested national office advice if a case presented a significant legal question of first impression and no guidance existed as to the chief counsel's legal position or policy.[168] The auditor could seek **field service advice** instead of a technical advice memorandum and could do so without the taxpayer's knowledge. Field service advice does not constitute authority for avoiding the substantial understatement penalty.

When the IRS initially announced the TEAM process, it planned to issue FSAs only for the purpose of providing field personnel with case-specific legal development strategies and assessment of litigation

---

[166] The website is not consistent in its use of digits. In some years, it has used three digits (e.g., -001) and in others two digits (e.g., -01) for the AOD number. Be prepared to search both ways for a document if you lack the case name.

[167] Do not confuse these GCMs with revenue rulings issued before 1953, many of which were also called general counsel memoranda. [See Table 10-1.]

[168] In CC-2006-013 (May 5, 2006), the Case Specific Advice Task Force noted that the IRM no longer provided procedures for FSAs. The Task Force noted that the IRM provides options other than TAMS for requesting advice from the national office. See IRM 33.1.2.2.3.2 (Aug. 11, 2004).

hazards. The change would have been accompanied by renaming these documents **strategic advice memoranda**.

9. Service Center Advice (SCA; S.C.A.)

The national office issued **service center advice** with regard to tax administration responsibilities. The Service began using the common numbering system for these documents in 1999. It used a separate numbering system in 1997 and 1998. SCAs do not constitute authority for avoiding the substantial understatement penalty.

10. IRS Legal Memoranda (ILM; I.L.M.)

Legal memoranda provide information about taxpayers to IRS field or service center personnel. These documents may respond to a field office query or they may provide information to the field (e.g., notice that a taxpayer's request to change accounting method has been denied). These documents do not constitute authority for avoiding the substantial understatement penalty. Although these documents use the common numbering system, different services call them by different names. Searching by number yields the same results irrespective of system; searching by title may not.[169]

11. Chief Counsel Bulletins
There are several types of chief counsel bulletins. These documents provide information to IRS employees about litigation in a variety of areas. None of them constitutes authority for avoiding the substantial understatement penalty.

Collection, Bankruptcy and Summonses Bulletins (CBS; C.B.S.) summarize recent court decisions. These documents were called General Litigation Bulletins through June 2000. Although numbered in a separate series, these bulletins also share the common numbering system. For example, Bulletin No. 490 is also CBS 200139029. The most recent bulletin posted on the IRS website in November 2006 was issued in January 2002 (Bulletin 496).

Criminal Tax Bulletins (CTB; C.T.B.) compile cases pertaining to criminal tax matters. They use the common numbering system.

Disclosure Litigation Bulletins (DLB; D.L.B.) discuss litigation and other developments concerning FOIA and related litigation. They do not use the common numbering system. Their numbering is by year. The

---

[169] Depending on the publisher, these documents may be referred to as chief counsel advice, chief counsel advisories, or IRS legal memoranda (ILM).

most recent bulletin posted on the IRS website in November 2006 was DLB 2000-3.

Tax Litigation Bulletins (TLB; T.L.B.) summarize recent court decisions and briefs. They also include recommendations for appellate action. These bulletins are numbered by year (e.g., TLB 96-5). These are no longer published on the IRS website. The **General Litigation Bulletin** has not been published since June 2000 (Bulletin 477).

12. Litigation Guideline Memoranda (LGM; L.G.M.)

Litigation guideline memoranda discuss variations on fact patterns and tactical approaches that IRS field personnel might use in litigation. In mid-1999, the Service released memoranda issued between January 1, 1986, and October 20, 1998. LGMs are now released using the timetable set forth in Section 6110. The numbering system initially reflected the IRS division involved (e.g., INTL-1 involved the foreign tax credit). Later items use the common numbering system (e.g., LGM 200018050).

13. Industry Specialization Program (ISP; I.S.P.); Market Segment Specialization Papers (MSSP; M.S.S.P.); Market Segment Understandings (MSU; M.S.U.)

These documents provide guidance to agents auditing returns in various types of businesses (**industry specialization program**); describe how the IRS reviews tax returns for various types of business (**market segment specialization papers**); and discuss employer/independent contractor issues in various industries (**market segment understandings**). They do not constitute authority for avoiding the substantial understatement penalty.

Examples of these documents include an ISP issued in 2000 that discussed the useful life of slot machines in the gaming industry; an MSSP issued in 2001 designed to assist IRS auditors in identifying and developing issues that are unique or frequent to business consultants (e.g., travel, employee/independent contractor, meals and entertainment, and claiming a not-for-profit activity as a business); and an MSU issued in 1998 for the moving industry.

These documents include numerous citations to authority. ISPs include UIL numbers. MSSPs include glossaries of terms a researcher can use to become familiar with a particular industry.[170]

---

[170] For example, a 1997 MSSP for artists and art galleries included brief explanations of painting styles (e.g., abstract, pop art, realism), painting techniques (e.g., oil, pastel) and print types (e.g., artist proof, lithograph,

These documents are identified by type, date, and industry; they do not carry separate numbers.

14. Chief Counsel Notices (CCN; C.C.N.)

IRS **chief counsel notices** notify personnel of policies, procedures, instructions, and delegations of authority. They do not constitute authority for avoiding the substantial understatement penalty.

Since fiscal 2001, these documents are numbered by year with CC as a prefix. Some include UIL numbers. For example, CC-2002-021 notified staff that the national office had changed its litigating position regarding capitalization of transaction costs related to the acquisition, creation, or enhancement of intangible assets or benefits. This document's cancellation date was set as the date on which the item announced was incorporated into the CCDM.[171] The UIL number this document related to was 263.00-00.

15. IRS Information Letters (IIL; I.I.L.)

The national office and key district directors issue **information letters** to taxpayers to call their attention to well-established principles of tax law. For example, IIL 200003007 was issued to a taxpayer who had requested a second extension of time to sell stock in a subsidiary. The letter discussed the applicable Code section 332 rules. These documents do not constitute authority for avoiding the substantial understatement penalty.

16. IRS Compliance Officer Memoranda (ICM; I.C.M.)

Compliance officer memoranda are issued to regional compliance and appeals personnel. They provide information on issues involving compliance and taxpayers' rights. They do not constitute authority for avoiding the substantial understatement penalty.

17. IRS Technical Assistance (ITA; I.T.A.)

The national office provides **technical assistance** to other IRS offices.

---

serigraph).

[171] CC-2002-021 was issued March 15, 2002. It noted that the Service had issued an Advance Notice of Proposed Rulemaking (ANPRM) regarding capitalization on January 24, 2002. The chief counsel notice did not provide a citation to that ANPRM (REG-125638-01). CCDM is the Chief Counsel Directives Manual, part of the IRM.

Technical assistance issued to district and regional offices, chief counsel field offices, and service centers is disclosable. These documents are not authority for avoiding the substantial understatement penalty.

These documents use the common numbering system (e.g., 200211042 dealt with whether the recipient of a transferable state remediation tax credit had gross income). Although Tax Analysts has indexed these documents as ITAs, LexisNexis, Westlaw, and the IRS website classify them as chief counsel advice or advisory.

18. Internal Revenue Manual (IRM; I.R.M.)

Your research may involve IRS operating policies. For example, you may want to determine IRS procedures for appeals or for dealing with rewards to informants. The **Internal Revenue Manual** is an excellent source of information about Service policies. It does not constitute authority for avoiding the substantial understatement penalty.

The Manual has numerous subdivisions; its numbering system is based on topics. For example, IRM 20.1.5 covers return related penalties; IRM 20.1.5.8 covers the substantial understatement penalty.[172] IRM Parts 30 through 39 constitutes the Chief Counsel Directives Manual. It is easier to search the IRM online using a commercial service than using the IRS website.

19. Legal Advice Issued by Attorneys in National Office or Field

The IRS website includes generic legal advice issued by attorneys in the national office and designed to provide guidance on industry-wide issues. They are numbered AM, followed by the year and the number (e.g., AM-2006-001). As of mid-November 2006, six such documents had been issued. It also issues advice from field attorneys, numbered by year and, week, with an F at the end (e.g., 20064602F).

20. Tax-Exemption Revocations and Denials

Since 2003, the IRS has been required to release redacted versions of revocations and denials of tax-exempt status.[173]

---

[172] IRM 20.1.5.8.1.1(3) (Oct. 1, 2005) covers items that constitute substantial authority. This IRM section does not add significantly to the information in Treas. Reg. § 1.6662-4(d)(3), but its arrangement makes it easier to read.

[173] Tax Analysts v. Internal Revenue Service, 350 F.3d 100 (D.C. Cir. 2003).

Illustration 10-2. AOD 1984-022

ACTION ON DECISION CC-1984-022

CC:TL
Br2:DCFegan

Re: Harold L. and Temple M. Jenkins v.
Commissioner
Venue: C.A. 6th
Dkt. No.: 3354-79
Dec. November 3, 1983
Opinion: T.C. Memo 1983-667

Issue: Whether Conway Twitty is allowed
a business expense deduction for payments to
reimburse the losses of investors in a defunct
restaurant known as Twitty Burger, Inc.
0162.01-17; 0162.29-00.

Discussion: The Tax Court summarized its
opinion in this case with the following "Ode to
Conway Twitty":

"Twitty Burger went belly up
But Conway remained true
He repaid his investors, one and all
It was the moral thing to do.

"His fans would not have liked it
It could have hurt his fame
Had any investors sued him
Like Merle Haggard or Sonny James.

"When it was time to file taxes
Conway thought what he would do
Was deduct those payments as a
business expense
Under section one-sixty-two.

"In order to allow these deductions
Goes the argument of the Commissioner
The payments must be ordinary and necessary
To a business of the petitioner.

"Had Conway not repaid the investors
His career would have been under cloud
Under the unique facts of this case
Held: The deductions are allowed."
Our reaction to the Court's opinion is
reflected in the following "Ode to
Conway Twitty: A Reprise":

Harold Jenkins and Conway Twitty
They are both the same
But one was born
The other achieved fame.

The man is talented
And has many a friend
They opened a restaurant
His name he did lend.

They are two different things
Making burgers and song
The business went sour
It didn't take long.

He repaid his friends
Why did he act
Was it business or friendship
Which is fact?

Business the court held
It's deductible they feel
We disagree with the answer
But let's not appeal.

Recommendation:
Nonacquiescence.

---

21. Other Documents[174]

Technical Memoranda (TM; T.M.; Tech. Mem.) provided background information on regulations. Much of their content is reflected in the

---

[174] In Tax Analysts v. Internal Revenue Service, 416 F. Supp. 2d 119 (D.D.C. 2006), the court held that advice prepared in less than two hours was disclosable.

preambles to T.D.s and NPRMs. Westlaw carries so-called Non Docketed Service Advice Reviews (NSAR; coverage from 1992 through 1999); these are memoranda to field personnel who raised questions regarding particular transactions (e.g., 1999 IRS NSAR 5242 concerned whether to let a taxpayer amend a return to reflect a subsequent year's purchase price reduction). Don't be surprised if you find a handful of documents in a new category. They may reflect no more than early responses to disclosure litigation. None of these documents constitutes authority for avoiding the substantial understatement penalty.

SECTION E. UNRELEASED DOCUMENTS

1. Advance Pricing Agreements (APA)

Advance pricing agreements are made between taxpayers and the IRS regarding income allocation between commonly-controlled entities. Companies that segment their operations between countries with different tax rates and structures can enter into APAs with both the United States and the other country if the two countries have a tax treaty. Code section 6110(b)(1)(B) exempts APAs from release to the public. The IRS does issue an annual report concerning APAs.[175]

2. Closing Agreements

Closing agreements memorialize the parties' agreement regarding specific taxpayer-IRS disputes. As a condition of the agreement, the IRS has occasionally forced publication of certain closing agreements with exempt organizations. Code section 6110(b)(1)(B) exempts closing agreements from release to the public.

SECTION F. LOCATING IRS DOCUMENTS

1. Documents Published in Internal Revenue Bulletin

a. Finding Lists

You can find citations to these documents using print or electronic sources. Print sources include Code-based looseleaf services, such as Standard Federal Tax Reporter and United States Tax Reporter. You can also use topic-based looseleaf services such as Federal Tax Coordinator 2d

---

[175] See, e.g., Ann. 2006-22, 2006-16 I.R.B. 779, for the report covering 2005. You can also find these reports on the IRS website.

and Rabkin & Johnson, Federal Income, Gift and Estate Taxation. Both types of looseleaf service are discussed in detail in Chapter 13. Another print source is the Service's own Bulletin Index-Digest System (Chapter 17), although it is useful only for 1954-1993/94 material.

Because revenue rulings and procedures, notices, and announcements carry numbers that don't correspond to Code or regulations sections, CD/DVD (Chapter 19) and online (Chapter 20) services are excellent tools for locating them. You can search many electronic databases by topic, Code or regulations section, or prior ruling. Use case citators to find acquiescences.

b. Digests

Unlike finding lists, digests provide descriptions that help you decide if a particular item is likely to be useful. Keep in mind that a digest's usefulness is a function of its compiler's expertise and its frequency of supplementation.

You can locate digests in a looseleaf service such as United States Tax Reporter (Chapter 13), in newsletters such as Tax Notes (Chapter 16), and in the Service's Bulletin Index-Digest System (Chapter 17; 1954-1993/94 material only).

c. Texts

Numerous services contain texts of Internal Revenue Bulletin items. Most of those listed below are available in both print and electronic formats.

Looseleaf services such as Standard Federal Tax Reporter and United States Tax Reporter include the text of current year rulings in their print services; electronic services may include older rulings or provide links to them on other databases. The Rulings volumes of Mertens, Law of Federal Income Taxation include full text of revenue rulings and procedures since 1954 but do not carry other Internal Revenue Bulletin documents. Looseleaf services are discussed further in Chapter 13.

Print versions of daily newsletters such as Daily Tax Report carry Internal Revenue Bulletin items as they are released; electronic versions include prior releases. They are discussed in detail in Chapter 16.

The print versions of the Internal Revenue Bulletin and Cumulative Bulletin (Chapter 17) include text of all items issued for a particular week (or six-month period); various online services include these documents but do not have full retrospective coverage. If you have a citation to a pre-1954 Code item, a print or microform Cumulative Bulletin may be the only place you can locate it.

d. A Note on Searching in Electronic and Print Sources

In using electronic sources, you must differentiate between those that allow searching by topic and those that include the relevant information but do not provide a means to find it using word or Code section searches. This distinction is particularly important for online services. If you can't find the item without knowing its citation, the source is less valuable than one that allows access based on Code sections or other search terms.

Illustrations 10-3 through 10-6 illustrate searching for a revenue ruling discussing whether expenses associated with quitting smoking qualify as medical expenses. I conducted this search in the IRS website, but I could have instead used a subscription service.

The IRS website includes a page that gives access to the Internal Revenue Bulletins. That page does not provide a mechanism to search for individual items if you don't know which Bulletin you want. Alternatively, you might try using the Advanced Search function, on another page of the IRS site, and search for the terms medical and smoking.

Illustrations 10-3 through 10-6 illustrate using the IRS Bulletin List and the IRS Advanced Search function. If you had a citation, you could use the Bulletin list to retrieve it. If you don't, try the Advanced Search.

Illustration 10-3. Internal Revenue Bulletin List on IRS Website

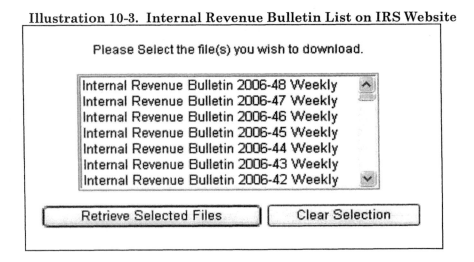

Illustration 10-4. Advanced Search Option on IRS Website

Advanced Search Options

SEARCH

Find Results

With all of the words:	medical smoking	in the body ∨
With the exact phrase:		in the body ∨
With any of the words:		in the body ∨
Without the words:		in the body ∨

Limit Search To

☐ Entire Site   ☐ Individuals   ☐ Internal Revenue Manual
☐ Forms and Instructions ☐ Businesses   ☐ Tax Statistics
☐ Publications   ☐ Charities & Non-Profits   ☐ e-file
☐ Notices   ☐ Government Entities   ☐ Español
☑ IR Bulletins   ☐ Tax Professionals   ☐ FAQs
                           (Includes Tax Regulations)

→The Advanced Search option also allows you to specify dates.

Illustration 10-5. Search Results on IRS Website

You Searched for: +medical +smoking   Summaries: Show | Hide

8 results found

Sort by: Relevance | Date   Results: 1-8

IRB 1999-25   56% ▮▮▮
... Rul. 99–28, page 6. Medical expenses; smoking- cessation programs. Un-   19 Dec 03
compensated amounts ... nicotine withdrawal are expenses for medical care that are   Highlight Term(s)
deductible under ... is not deductible as a medical expense. Rev. Rul. 79–162 ...
http://www.irs.gov/pub/irs-irbs/irb99-25.pdf - 155.4KB

IRB 2001-3.qxd   37% ▮▮▮
IRB 2001-3.qxd INCOME TAX Rev. Rul. 2001–3, page 319. Federal rates; adjusted   17 Jan 01
federal rates; adjusted feder-al long-term rate, and the long- term exempt rate. For   Highlight Term(s)
purposes of sections 1274, 1288, 382, and other ...
http://www.irs.gov/pub/irs-irbs/irb01-03.pdf - 586.3KB

IRB -2005-33 (Rev. August 15, 2005)   30% ▮▮▮
Internal Revenue Bulletin   11 Aug 05
... application. This ruling holds that a sub-account within a profit-sharing plan that   Highlight Term(s)
provides medical reimbursement expenses to each participant does not meet the
provisions of section 411 of ...
http://www.irs.gov/pub/irs-irbs/irb05-33.pdf - 474.9KB

→The first item appears promising. I should read each item because the results screen for most of them doesn't give adequate information. Note the Highlight Terms option, which I can use in each document.

Illustration 10-6. Excerpt from Revenue Ruling 99-28

Section 213.—Medical, Dental, Etc., Expenses

26 CFR 1.213–1: Medical, dental, etc., expenses. (Also section 262; 1.262–1.)

Medical expenses; smoking-cessation programs. Uncompensated amounts paid by taxpayers for participation in a smoking-cessation program and for prescribed drugs designed to alleviate nicotine withdrawal are expenses for medical care that are deductible under section 213 of the Code. The cost of nicotine gum and patches available without a prescription is not deductible as a medical expense. Rev. Rul. 79–162 is revoked.

Rev. Rul. 99–28

→This ruling appears promising. I need to use a citator to make sure it is still valid. See Chapter 12 and Section H of this chapter.

Instead of using the IRS website, I could have used LexisNexis, Westlaw, RIA Checkpoint, or CCH Tax Research NetWork with the same search terms. Chapter 20 illustrates searching in online services. I could also have searched in one of the CD/DVD services described in Chapter 19. Alternatively, I might have used one of the looseleaf services discussed in Chapter 13 to find annotations dealing with medical expenses for smoking cessation.

2. Other Officially Published Documents

You can also find IRS forms, instructions, and explanatory publications using the IRS website. You can use a word search similar to that shown in the preceding Illustrations if you don't know the name or number of the form or publication you seek. The IRS site includes these documents in full text. Other CD/DVD (Chapter 19) and online (Chapter 20) services also make these documents available.

Illustration 10-7. Search for Forms and Publications on IRS Website

Advanced Search Options

IRS Resources
- Compliance & Enforcement
- Contact My Local Office
- e-file
- Forms and Publications
- Frequently Asked Questions
- News
- Taxpayer Advocacy
- Where To File

SEARCH

Find Results

With all of the words:	medical smoking	in the body ▾
With the exact phrase:		in the body ▾
With any of the words:		in the body ▾
Without the words:		in the body ▾

Limit Search To

☐ Entire Site	☐ Individuals	☐ Internal Revenue Manual
☑ Forms and Instructions	☐ Businesses	☐ Tax Statistics
☑ Publications	☐ Charities & Non-Profits	☐ e-file
☐ Notices	☐ Government Entities	☐ Español
☐ IR Bulletins	☐ Tax Professionals (Includes Tax Regulations)	☐ FAQs

→If I already know the form or publication number, I can get them using the Forms and Publications option under IRS Resources.

Illustration 10-8. Results for IRS Forms and Publications Search

You Searched for: +medical +smoking   Summaries: Show | Hide

5 results found

Sort by: Relevance | Date   Results: 1-5

2006 Publication 502 🗎   59% ▬▬▬
Medical and Dental Expenses including the Health Coverage Tax Credit   17 Nov 06
... Cat. No. 15002Q What Are Medical Expenses? ...2 What Expenses Can ...   Highlight Term(s)
Expenses Can You Include This Medical and Year? ...2 How Much ... You Dental
Deduct? ...3 Whose Medical Expenses Can You Include? ...3 ...
http://www.irs.gov/pub/irs-pdf/p502.pdf - 187.7KB

2006 Instruction 1040 Schedule A & B 🗎   25% ▬▬▬
Instructions for Schedules A & B (Form 1040), Itemized Deductions and Interest   03 Nov 06
and Dividend Income   Highlight Term(s)
... deduct a part of your medical and dental expenses and un ... certain charitable
organizations if you Medical and Dental were at least ... of your vehicle to get medical
care is 18 tributions of ...
http://www.irs.gov/pub/irs-pdf/i1040sa.pdf - 85.8KB

2005 Publication 554 🗎   24% ▬▬▬
Older Americans' Tax Guide   02 Dec 05
2005 Publication 554 Contents Department of the Treasury Internal Revenue Service   Highlight Term(s)
What's New ...1 Reminders ...2 Publication 554 Introduction ...2 Cat. No. 15102R 1.
2005 Filing Requirements ...4 General Requirements ...
http://www.irs.gov/pub/irs-pdf/p554.pdf - 185.5KB

→I limited my search to PDF documents for the past two years.

3. Publicly Released Documents

Because the IRS issues so many of these documents, your library is more likely to provide access to them electronically than through a print service. If your library has a print service, you may prefer to find the item online and read it in print rather than trying to find it in print.

CCH and other publishers offer print versions of the Internal Revenue Manual. Because of the Manual's detailed structure, it is easier to find materials using an electronic version.

Illustration 10-9. Excerpt from Internal Revenue Manual Table of Contents

Part 30	Administrative
Part 31	Guiding Principles
Part 32	Published Guidance and Other Guidance to Taxpayers
Part 33	Legal Advice
Part 34	Litigation in District Court, Bankruptcy Court, Court of Federal Claims, and State Court
Part 35	Tax Court Litigation
Part 36	Appellate Litigation and Actions on Decision
Part 37	Disclosure
Part 38	Criminal Tax
Part 39	General Legal Services

→The IRM has detailed subdivisions, as shown in Illustration 10-10.

Texts of publicly released documents are included in numerous CD/DVD and online research sources. These include OneDisc, LexisNexis, Westlaw, Checkpoint, Tax Research NetWork, and TaxCore. You can search these services by Code section or by phrases describing the issue you are researching. Several examples are illustrated below.

Illustration 10-10. Excerpt from IRM Subdivisions on IRS Site

Part 32. Published Guidance and Other Guidance to Taxpayers

Chapter 3. Letter Rulings, Information Letters, and Closing Agreements

Section 1. Forms of Advice

32.3.1 Forms of Advice

- 32.3.1.1   Overview of Forms of Advice
- 32.3.1.2   Circumstances in Which the Associate Chief Counsel Issues Letter Rulings
- 32.3.1.3   Discretionary Authority to Issue Letter Rulings or Enter into Closing Agreements
- 32.3.1.4   Areas Where No Letter Rulings Will Be Issued
- 32.3.1.5   Referral of Matters to Other Offices
- 32.3.1.6   Letter Rulings
- 32.3.1.7   Determination Letters
- 32.3.1.8   Information Letters
- 32.3.1.9   Oral Advice to Taxpayers
- 32.3.1.10   Request for Expedited Treatment
- 32.3.1.11   Request to Send Response by Fax
- 32.3.1.12   Withdrawal of Requests and Notification to Field
- 32.3.1.13   Correction of Obvious Error
- 32.3.1.14   Requirements with Respect to Submission of Requests for Letter Rulings
- Exhibit 32.3.1-1   Sample Format for Recommendation of Application of Section 301.9100-1 Relief

→The IRM uses numerous decimals for subdivisions. This is a portion of Part 32 [Illustration 10-9]. The number after the first decimal (3) is the chapter. The next number is the section (1). Items 1 through 14 are the next level. There may be even more subdivisions (e.g., IRM 30.1.1.3.4.1). Illustration 10-11 covers searching IRM materials on OneDisc.

Although the IRS website provides free access to publicly released documents, its home page does not indicate where to find them. To find publicly available documents, click on Freedom of Information Act, which appears on the bottom of the home page. Then click on Electronic Reading Room. You will reach a screen that shows the types of documents currently available and can then search within categories. [Illustration 10-12.]

The IRS website first divides documents into major categories (Published Tax Guidance; Non-precedential Rulings & Advice; Admin Manuals & Instructions; Program Plans & Reports; and Training & Reference Manuals). Depending on your research topic, you may need to find documents in one or more of these areas. The link for IRS Written Determinations covers those documents discussed in Subsection D that follow a common numbering system. Documents such as AODs, that have their own numbering system, are listed separately and have their own search tools.

With one exception, electronic services operate the same way for publicly released documents as they do for documents published in the Internal Revenue Bulletin. That exception relates to the numbering system. As noted in Section D, commercial services may assign their own names to documents issued by the chief counsel's office. If you are not sure which name a particular service uses for chief counsel items, search across all possible databases rather than limiting yourself to a single database. Fortunately, all publishers use the same names for the most common items: letter rulings, technical advice memoranda, and actions on decisions.

Illustration 10-11. Search for IRM Information in OneDisc

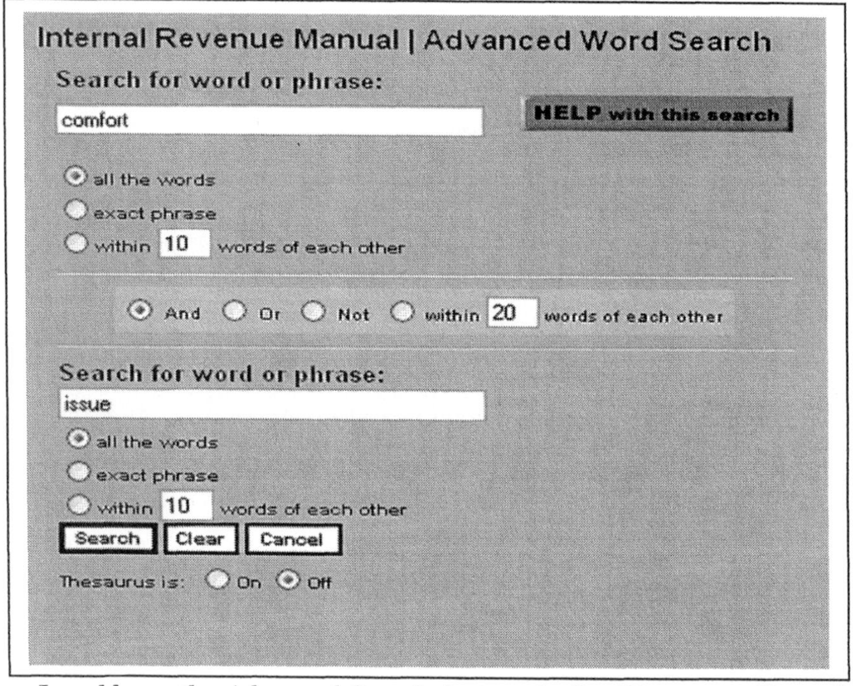

→I could use the Advanced Search feature in OneDisc to see if any IRM sections dealt with issuing so-called comfort rulings.

→I initially specified that "comfort" and "issue" had to be within 20 words of each other. This search gave me only eight hits, but one of them included IRM 32.3.1.4.10, which is what I wanted.

→I could have used "comfort rulings" as a search term.

Illustration 10-12. IRS Website Electronic Reading Room

Published Tax Guidance

- Advance Releases
  Early distribution of some IRB materials
  before they are published in the IRB.
- Applicable Federal Rate (AFR) revenue
  rulings
- Final or Temporary Regulations
  (Treasury Decisions) and Proposed
  Regulations
- IRS Publications & Notices
- *Internal Revenue Bulletins (IRB)*
  Weekly compilations of Revenue Rulings,
  Revenue Procedures, Announcements, and
  Notices.
  ...PDF format (1996 to present)
  ...HTML format (July 7, 2003 to present)

Admin Manuals & Instructions

- Appeals Coordinated Issues (ACI)
- Chief Counsel (CC) Notices
- Instructions to Staff
- Internal Revenue Manual (IRM)
- LMSB Coordinated Issues
- LMSB Industry Director Guidance

Program Plans & Reports

- Annual Performance Plan
- Art Appraisal Services Annual
  Summary Reports
- FOIA Annual Reports
- IRS Strategic Plan
- Priority Guidance Plan
- Privacy Impact Assessments
- Treasury Inspector General for Tax
  Admin. (TIGTA) Annual Audit Plans

Non-precedential Rulings & Advice

- Actions on Decisions (AOD)
- Appeals Settlement Guidelines
- Chief Counsel Bulletins
- Exempt Org. Field Memorandums
- General Counsel Memoranda
- Information Letters
- *IRS Written Determinations*
  Private Letter Rulings (PLR), Technical
  Advice Memorandum (TAM), & Chief Counsel
  Advice (CCA).
  ...By release number (starting in 1997)
  ...By UIL code (1.00-00 to 9999.99-00)
- Legal Advice Issued by Associate Chief
  Counsel
- Legal Advice Issued by Field Attorneys

Training & Reference Materials

- Advance Pricing Agreement (APA)
  Training Materials
- Chief Counsel Advice (CCA) Training
  Materials
- Disclosure Litigation Reference Book
- EO Tax Law Training Articles
- Market Segment Specialization
  Program (Audit Techniques Guides)
- Technical Training Program for
  Businesses

The two searches below compare finding items on the IRS website with finding them in commercial services. The first search involves AODs, which are issued in response to judicial decisions adverse to the government's position. [Illustrations 10-13 and 10-14.] The second search involves chief counsel advice. [Illustrations 10-15 and 10-16.] When using a commercial service, there are two important questions. First, does it have the most recent items? Second, does it include all types of chief counsel advice? For the former question, an online service is preferable to a CD/DVD service. For the latter, make sure you compare available items if you have access to more than one service.

Illustration 10-13. IRS Website AOD Finding List

Actions on Decisions (AOD)

NOTE: These documents do **NOT** contain proprietary ("Official Use Only") information.

AOD 2006-02: Pacific Gas and Electric Company v. U.S., 417 F...
AOD 2006-01: Erickson Post Acquisition, Inc. v. Comm., T.C. ...
AOD 2005-03: Montgomery v. Comm., 122 T.C. 1 (2004). This A...
AOD 2005-02: Sherwin-Williams v. Comm., 330 F.3rd 449 (6th C...
AOD 2005-01: Estate of Mitchell v. Comm., 250 F.3d 696 (9th...
AOD 2004-06: IRS v. Donald Snyder, 343 F.3d 1171 (9th Cir. 2...
AOD 2004-05: Diane Fernandez v. Comm., 114 T. C. 324 (2000) ...

[Retrieve Selected Files]   [Clear Selection]

→The IRS finding list sorts by AOD number, not by case name or issue, and covers only AODS issued since 1997. Files can be retrieved as PDF documents.

Illustration 10-14. Checkpoint Listing of AODS

− ☐ **Actions on Decisions (1967 to Present)**
  + ☐ **2006**
  + ☐ **2005**
  − ☐ **2004**
    📄 **AOD 2004-006, 10/19/2004**
    📄 **AOD 2004-005 -- IRC Sec(s). 6015, 09/01/2004**
    📄 **AOD 2004-004 -- IRC Sec(s). 6402; 6511; 6532; 7422, 09/01/2004**
    📄 **AOD 2004-003 -- IRC Sec(s). 7122, 8/3/2004**
    📄 **AOD 2004-002 -- IRC Sec(s). 6103; 6110, 7/1/2004**
    📄 **AOD 2004-001 -- IRC Sec(s). 301; 355, 1/22/2004**
  + ☐ **2003**
  + ☐ **2002**

→The Checkpoint Table of Contents indicates the Code sections for each AOD rather than listing them by taxpayer name. Instead of using the table of contents, I could have done key word, Code section, or taxpayer name searches in Checkpoint.

→Note that Checkpoint covers AODs issued since 1967.

SECTION G. UNIFORM ISSUE LIST (UIL)

The **Uniform Issue List** is a Code-section-based index of issues. The IRS assigns UIL numbers to documents released to the public pursuant to Code section 6110, which is discussed in Section D. This list is prepared by chief counsel office personnel.[176] AOD 1984-022 [Illustration 10-2] includes two UIL numbers, both involving Code section 162. The IRS publishes the list in Publication 1102; this publication is not revised annually.

The IRS varies in the terminology used for UIL numbers. The terms UIL, UILC, or Index may precede the actual UIL number in a document.

The IRS website lets you sort documents classified as written determinations based on document number or UIL number. As of November 2006, numbers are initially sorted by their digits (from left to right) rather than by their actual Code section number. As a result, documents based on Code section 1041 and 1042 follow those based on section 104; documents based on section 105 begin after those based on section 1042.

Illustration 10-15. IRS Website Written Determination Finding List

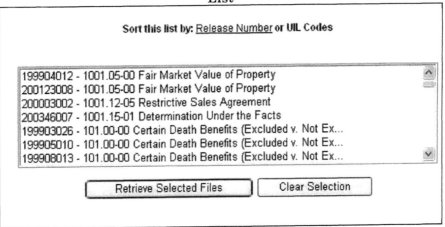

→The IRS website does not indicate whether the document is a letter ruling, technical advice memorandum, or other type of document.

→Note how UIL listings for Code section 1001 precede those for section 101 because the first three digits (100) in 1001 precede 101.

---

[176] IRM 30.7.1.5 (Oct. 5, 2005).

Illustration 10-16. IRS Document Search Options in LexisNexis

Taxation > Administrative Materials & Regulations > Federal > **Agency Decisions** (Remove "Taxation" tab)

Use checkboxes to select sources for searching across categories, pages, and tabs. Show Me...

☐	📄	IRS Bulletins, Letter Rulings & Memoranda Decisions, Combined	ⓘ ☐	📄	IRS General Counsel Memoranda
☐	📄	IRS General Counsel Memos, Actions on Decisions, & Technical Memos	ⓘ ☐	📄	IRS Private Letter Rulings and Technical Advice Memoranda
☐	📄	IRS Cumulative Bulletin, IRB, Letter Rulings, & Technical Advice Memos	ⓘ ☐	📄	IRS Service Center Advice
☐	📄	IRS Advance Releases	ⓘ ☐	📄	IRS Technical Memoranda
☐	📄	IRS Actions on Decisions	ⓘ ☐	📄	Litigation Guideline Memorandums
☐	📄	IRS Chief Counsel Advice	ⓘ ☐	📄	Department of Labor ERISA Opinion Letters
☐	📄	IRS Cumulative Bulletin and Internal Revenue Bulletin	ⓘ ☐	📄	Pension Benefit Guaranty Corporation Opinion Letters
☐	📄	IRS Field Service Advice Memorandums	ⓘ ☐	📄	TNT Applicable Federal Rates
☐	📄	IRS Chief Counsel Notices	ⓘ		

→LexisNexis offers the type of electronic search options available from non-government services. I can search one or more databases and can do so by Code section or key word.

SECTION H. CITATORS FOR IRS DOCUMENTS

The IRS reviews its pronouncements for continued relevance. In addition, some IRS rulings have been subjected to judicial scrutiny. The status of these items can be determined from CD/DVD (Chapter 19) and online (Chapter 20) services and from the citators illustrated in Chapter 12.[177] You can also use Mertens, Law of Federal Income Taxation—Rulings (Chapter 13) (since 1954), or the IRS Bulletin Index-Digest System (Chapter 17) (1954-1993/94 only).

Citators include judicial action and cover both I.R.B. documents and publicly available IRS determinations. [See Illustrations 12-4 and 12-8 through 12-10.] They are better-suited for determining continued relevance than are the Mertens and IRS services. The Mertens and IRS services have several limitations. First, they include only IRS action. Second, they cover only revenue rulings and procedures. Third, there is a risk that a revoked item was removed from the database. Because the

---

[177] Shepard's, KeyCite, RIA, and CCH citator services all cover IRS documents.

IRS service is no longer published, it should be considered an updating service of last resort and only for historical research.[178]

SECTION I. JUDICIAL DEFERENCE

The items discussed in this chapter receive less government and public review than do Treasury regulations. As indicated by the excerpts below, judges vary in the amount of deference paid these pronouncements. Although items released as a result of FOIA litigation are not precedential, many courts take note of their holdings.

Decisions giving deference to rulings and other IRS documents must be judged in light of the Supreme Court's *Mead* decision, which involved a Customs Service ruling letter. The Court held: "We agree that a tariff classification has no claim to judicial deference under *Chevron*, there being no indication that Congress intended such a ruling to carry the force of law, but we hold that under *Skidmore v. Swift & Co.*, 323 U.S. 134 (1944), the ruling is eligible to claim respect according to its persuasiveness."[179]

In addition to judicial deference issues, the IRS must also take its own published guidance into account. In Rauenhorst v. Commissioner, the Tax Court criticized the IRS for taking a litigating position that conflicted with a published revenue ruling.[180]

1. Officially Published Documents

• Revenue rulings are not binding precedent, but are entitled to some weight, as reflecting an interpretation of the law by the agency entrusted with its interpretation. Such rulings, however, do not require this court to apply a mistaken view of the law to a particular taxpayer. In particular, Supreme Court precedent makes clear that if a revenue ruling is found to

---

[178] The I.R.B. Current Actions on Previously Published Items is not cumulated over multiple years.

[179] United States v. Mead Corp., 533 U.S. 218, 221 (2001). See Chapter 9 for a brief discussion of *Chevron*. Another decision that you may see cited regarding deference is Bowles v. Seminole Rock & Sand Co., 325 U.S. 410 (1945). It relates to an agency's interpretation of its own rules.

[180] 119 T.C. 157 (2002). The IRS response is contained in a chief counsel notice, CC-2003-014, clarifying and superseding CC-2002-043. This document provides the rules that govern the requirement that IRS attorneys follow published guidance.

be unreasonable or contrary to law, it is binding neither on the Commissioner nor this court, based on the rationale that the Congress, and only the Congress, has the power to make law. Vons Companies, Inc. v. United States, 51 Fed. Cl. 1, 12 (2001).[181]

• We note that, in any event, revenue rulings are not entitled to any special deference. Bhatia v. Commissioner, 72 T.C.M. (CCH) 696, 699 n.5 (1996).

• Revenue rulings represent the official IRS position on application of tax law to specific facts. ... They relate to matters as to which the IRS is the "primary authority." ... Revenue rulings are accordingly entitled to precedential "weight." Salomon Inc. v. United States, 976 F.2d 837, 841 (2d Cir. 1992).

2. Other IRS Documents

• Nor are we persuaded by the preamble or technical advice memorandum upon which petitioners rely. In addition to the obvious fact that these documents also are not items of legislative history, these documents are afforded little weight in this Court. Allen v. Commissioner, 118 T.C. No. 1, n.12 (2002), 2002 WL 14007.

• The interpretation of Rev. Proc. 71-21 contained in the General Counsel Memorandum and the IRS decision under the Revenue Procedure is not reflected in a regulation adopted after notice and comment and probably would not be entitled to *Chevron* deference. *See Mead*, ... Here, however, as noted above, we are not dealing with an agency's interpretation of a statute and issues of *Chevron* deference, but with the IRS's interpretation of an ambiguous term in its own Revenue Procedure. In such circumstances, substantial deference is paid to an agency's interpretations reflected in informal rulings.... In the context of tax cases, the IRS's reasonable interpretations of its own regulations and procedures are entitled to particular deference. American Express Co. v. United States, 262 F.3d 1376, 1382-83 (Fed. Cir. 2001).

• Such private letter rulings "may not be used or cited as precedent," §

---

[181] The court later revised the first two sentences to read as follows: "Taxpayers generally may rely on a revenue ruling to support their interpretation of a provision of the Code, provided the ruling is unaffected by subsequent legislation, regulations, cases or other revenue rulings. Such rulings do not require this court to apply a mistaken view of the law to a particular taxpayer." (89 A.F.T.R.2d 2002-301 (2001)). The court also stated its view regarding letter rulings, technical advice memoranda, and general counsel memoranda.

6110(j)(3), and we do not do so. It does not follow that they are not relevant here. Transco Exploration Co. v. Commissioner, 949 F.2d 837, 840 (5th Cir. 1992).

• Although this ruling cannot be cited as precedent under 26 U.S.C. § 6110(J)(3) [sic], it highlights the confusion this section has engendered at the IRS. More importantly, the fact that the IRS has done an about face since 1986 makes us even more reluctant to adopt their interpretation of this statute without an understandable articulation of a tax policy supporting it. Estate of Spencer v. Commissioner, 43 F.3d 226, 234 (6th Cir. 1995).

• In *Herrmann*, the court would not rely on the GCM to interpret the plan involved because the GCM was fact specific to the plan for which it was written. The court, however, did rely on its interpretation of the Code section involved because it assumed the IRS would insist upon a uniform interpretation of the section. Here, where there is no case law in point, it is arguably permissible to use GCMs to *instruct* the court on how the IRS itself interprets § 501(c)(5), since they constitute the only real guidance as to what the IRS considers a labor organization for the purposes of a § 501(c)(5) exemption. Morganbesser v. United States, 984 F.2d 560, 563 (2d Cir. 1993).

• While recognizing that the IRM does not represent law and is in no way binding upon this court, the court believes that the manual reflects the more reasonable interpretation of the Revenue Code's mandate in this instance. Thus, the manual's agreement with the court's own independent reading of the statute bolsters the court's conclusion. Anderson v. United States, 71 A.F.T.R.2d 93-1589, 93-1591, 93-1 U.S.T.C. ¶ 50,249, at 87,958 (N.D. Cal. 1993), rev'd, 44 F.3d 795, 799 (9th Cir. 1995) ("But the IRS correctly concedes that its internal agents' manual does not have the force of law, *see Schweiker v. Hansen*, ..., and makes no *Chevron* argument for deference to this language from its manual, not promulgated as a regulation.")

3. IRS Litigating Positions

• We now hold that the IRS' position in the *amicus* brief was an informal agency policy pronouncement not entitled to *Chevron* deference. Matz v. Household International Tax Reduction Investment Plan, 265 F.3d 572, 574 (7th Cir. 2001).

Section J. Problems

1. Who drafted

    a. Rev. Rul. 99-6

    b. Rev. Rul. 2002-7

    c. Rev. Proc. 2004-15

    d. Rev. Proc. 2006-20

2. What is the most recent revenue ruling involving Code section

    a. 108

    b. 217

    c. 642

    d. 2056

3. What is the most recent revenue ruling referring to Treasury regulation section

    a. 1.106-1

    b. 1.355-1

    c. 1.421-1

    d. 1.1033-1

4. What is the status of the item listed? What later pronouncement effectuated the status change?

    a. Rev. Rul. 57-441

    b. Rev. Rul. 68-468

    c. Rev. Proc. 81-11

    d. Rev. Proc. 2004-73

5. List all current year revenue procedures indicating matters on which the IRS will not grant a ruling.

6. Find a current year notice announcing a regulations project.

7. What did the most recently issued IRS announcement involve?

8. What is the most recent revenue procedure providing information about

    a. determining the finality of adoptions for children born in a foreign country

    b. recognizing the income from annual credit card fees

    c. using both sections 121 and 1031 for the same property

    d. the safe harbor for qualified exchange accommodations and property owned by the taxpayer before its transfer to the agent

9. Which IRS publication is titled

    a. Tax Incentives for Empowerment Zones and Other Distressed Communities

    b. Fuel Tax Credits and Refunds

    c. Mutual Fund Distributions

    d. Passive Activity and At-Risk Rules

10. Who drafted or approved

    a. PLR 200614032

    b. PLR 200450005

    c. SCA 200236043

    d. FSA 200305028

11. Which Code sections are discussed in

    a. SCA 200231013

   b. TAM 200610017

   c. LTR 200327060

   d. GCM 35487

12. What is the most recent PLR or TAM involving Code section

   a. 106

   b. 118

   c. 304

13. What is the most recent PLR or TAM citing Treasury regulation section

   a. 1.83-7(a)

   b. 1.1374-4(a)

   c. 25.2511-2(b)

14. What is the status of the item listed? What later pronouncement effectuated the status change?

   a. TAM 9541005

   b. PLR 8946027

   c. TAM 200126008

15. Locate the document asked for below and indicate the Code section(s) involved:

   a. a 2003 PLR citing to Rev. Rul. 73-201

   b. a 2003 PLR citing to Rev. Proc. 2002-12

   c. a 2006 TAM citing to Rev. Rul. 67-221

   d. a 2004 FSA citing to Rev. Rul. 84-114

16. Which GCM was issued to explain the item listed or which cited to the item listed?

   a. Rev. Proc. 90-29

   b. Rev. Proc. 87-22

   c. Rev. Rul. 94-43

   d. Rev. Rul. 90-60

17. Which subsequent GCM changed the status of the GCM listed below, and what issue was involved?

   a. 39686

   b. 39197

   c. 37200

   d. 35904

18. Your instructor will assign an IRM segment. Prepare a full list of subdivisions for that segment.

19. Locate a PLR involving the following facts and indicate its holding.

   a. whether the Virgin Islands is part of the United States for purposes of like-kind exchanges

   b. the effect on a foundation's exemption of an ice arena

   c. the exchange of old-growth timberlands for reproduction timberlands

   d. an employer's health care plan that covers radial keratotomy

20. Locate a TAM involving the following facts and indicate its holding:

   a. whether therapeutic residential community qualified for section 530 relief

   b. whether payments allocated to emotional distress in an employment discrimination settlement were subject to FICA tax

   c. whether payments received for copyright infringement are eligible for section 1033 nonrecognition treatment

    d. whether a $35 gift coupon was a de minimis fringe benefit

21. Locate each AOD involving the following decision and indicate its holding:

    a. Olson v. Commissioner (1967 Tax Court)

    b. Intermet Corp. & Subs. v. Commissioner (2001 Tax Court)

    c. Royal Caribbean Cruises, Ltd.. v. United States (1997 Eleventh Circuit)

    d. Pacific Gas & Electric Co. v. United States (2005 Federal Circuit)

22. Provide a citation to the document described below indicating IRS acquiescence or nonacquiescence or other litigation plans based on the decision listed below. IRS action may be in an officially-published document or in some other document.

    a. Newberry v. Commissioner (1981 Tax Court); revenue ruling

    b. Fulton Gold Corp. v. Commissioner (1934 Board of Tax Appeals); revenue ruling

    c. Holdcroft Transportation Co. v. Commissioner (1946 Eighth Circuit); revenue ruling

    d. Glaze v. United States (1981 Fifth Circuit); chief counsel notice

    e. In re Mills (1999 Bankruptcy Court); chief counsel advice

23. Locate a non-I.R.B. document other than a letter ruling or technical advice memorandum involving the following facts. Provide the document type and citation and indicate its holding:

    a. whether the plaintiff is taxed on the portion of punitive damages payable to the state under a law giving the state fifty percent of the judgment

    b. after the employee died in prison, whether an employer could recover embezzled funds the employee was using to pay his tax liability

    c. payments in settlement of avigation rights

d. income splitting by domestic partners

e. whether an earned income credit claim can be disallowed because the taxpayer does not respond to the IRS's information requests

f. the relationship of IRS administrative summonses and the Family Educational Rights and Privacy Act

g. the deductibility of commissions that taxpayer selling weapons paid to procure military contracts

h. the withholding and employment tax rules regarding prisoners who worked under a Justice Department project

24. You have been assigned several clients for whom you expect to do tax controversy work. Locate and print out the first page of the following documents.

a. MSSP Audit Guide for grain farmers

b. MSSP Audit Guide for retail gift shops

c. MSSP Audit Guide for general livestock

d. MSSP Audit Guide for drywallers

25. Find the most recent judicial decision you can locate regarding deference to the IRS document listed. What did the court say?

a. revenue rulings

b. private letter rulings

c. field service advice

d. IRS publications

26. Congress occasionally rejects an IRS interpretation by amending the Code. Find the Code section that appears to reject the IRS ruling listed below.

a. CCA 200034029

b. CCA 200431012

27. Courts may be called on to decide cases in which the IRS had already issued a ruling or other disclosed advice. Locate the judicial decision that appears to involve the taxpayer who received (or was the subject of) the item listed. What was the outcome of the litigation?

   a. FSA 200245006

   b. PLR 200209053

   c. the FSA that appears at 1997 WL 33313757, IRS FSA

PART FOUR

PRIMARY SOURCES: JUDICIAL

Chapter 11. Judicial Reports

CHAPTER 11. JUDICIAL REPORTS

SECTION A. INTRODUCTION

This chapter discusses the courts that decide tax cases, both initially and on appeal, and the reporter services in which you can locate judicial opinions. It also lists name changes for several courts and indicates when each court began hearing tax cases.

Your goals for this chapter include locating pertinent decisions, judging their relevance in a particular jurisdiction, and updating your research to include cases that are working their way through the litigation and appeals processes. Because Congress can usually "overrule" a judicial decision it dislikes by amending the statute, remember to check recently passed and pending legislation before deciding that you can rely on a particular case as precedent. In addition, you must also check IRS litigating positions; the IRS may announce it will not follow an adverse lower court decision.

SECTION B. COURT ORGANIZATION

1. Trial Courts

Four courts serve as trial courts for most tax disputes: District Courts; the Court of Federal Claims; the Tax Court; and Bankruptcy Courts. Other bodies may also be relevant. The United States Court of International Trade hears cases involving tariffs and related tax matters.[182] In addition, as indicated in Chapter 8, disputes between governments may be heard by a World Trade Organization or other international tribunal. This chapter focuses on the four primary trial courts.

a. United States District Courts

Because District Courts are courts of general jurisdiction, their judges rarely develop as high a level of expertise on tax law questions as do judges of the Tax Court or even of the Court of Federal Claims. Taxpayers must pay the amount in dispute and sue for a refund as a condition to

---

[182] See, e.g., Princess Cruises, Inc. v. United States, 22 Ct. Int'l Trade 498 (1998). Many, but not all, CIT cases also appear in Federal Supplement. Appeals go to the Court of Appeals for the Federal Circuit.

litigating in District Court, the only tribunal where a jury trial is available.

A significant number of District Court decisions are not published in Federal Supplement but may be located in other reporter services.[183]

b. United States Court of Federal Claims

Although the Court of Federal Claims does not hear tax cases exclusively, the percentage of such cases it hears is likely to be greater than that heard in the average District Court. As in the District Court, a taxpayer must first pay the disputed amount before bringing suit.

Prior to October 1, 1982, this court was called the United States Court of Claims and the Court of Claims of the United States. Trials were conducted by a trial judge (formerly called a commissioner), whose decisions were reviewed by Court of Claims judges. Only the Supreme Court had jurisdiction over appeals from its decisions. Between October 1, 1982, and October 28, 1992, this court was called the United States Claims Court.

c. United States Tax Court

Because Tax Court judges hear only tax cases, their expertise is substantially greater than that of judges in the other trial courts. Tax Court cases are tried by one judge, who submits an opinion to the chief judge for consideration. The chief judge can allow the decision to stand or refer it to the full court for review.[184] The published decision indicates if it has been reviewed; dissenting opinions, if any, are included.

In some instances, special trial judges hear disputes and issue opinions.[185] When the amount in dispute exceeds $50,000, the special trial

---

[183] These include American Federal Tax Reports (A.F.T.R.) and U. S. Tax Cases (U.S.T.C.), discussed in Section C.5., CD/DVD materials (Chapter 19), and online services (Chapter 20). Freedom of Information Act litigation forced the Justice Department to make all District Court tax opinions available to the public. United States Department of Justice v. Tax Analysts, 492 U.S. 136 (1989).

[184] "Court review is directed if the report proposes to invalidate a regulation, overrule a published Tax Court case, or reconsider, in a circuit that has not addressed it, an issue on which we have been reversed by a court of appeals." Mary Ann Cohen, *How to Read Tax Court Opinions*, 1 Hous. Bus. & Tax L.J. 1, 5-6 (2001).

[185] The Supreme Court upheld this practice in Freytag v. Commissioner, 501 U.S. 868 (1991). The special trial judges were called commissioners until 1984.

judge does not issue the final opinion. The opinion is issued by a Tax Court judge. The judge writing the opinion indicated that he or she adopted the special trial judge's report. The Tax Court did not separately release the trial judge's report to taxpayers. In 2005, the United States Supreme Court held that withholding the trial judge's report violated the Tax Court's own rules.[186]

There are three types of Tax Court decisions, two of which can result in appeals. The government printing office publishes **Regular** (or **Reported**) **Opinions**; these present important legal issues. Other publishers print **Memorandum Opinions**, which involve well-established legal issues and are primarily fact-based.[187] The Tax Court also has a **Small Cases** division that taxpayers can elect to use for disputes of $50,000 or less. The **Summary Opinions** issued in those cases cannot be appealed or used as precedent. Until 2001, they were not published in any reporter service or on the Tax Court website.[188]

A taxpayer can sue in the Tax Court without paying the amount in dispute prior to litigating. Taxpayers also had this privilege in the Tax Court's predecessor, the Board of Tax Appeals.

Table 11-1. Names Used by Tax Court and Court of Federal Claims

Tax Court	Court of Federal Claims
United States Tax Court (since 1970)	United States Court of Federal Claims (since Oct. 29, 1992)
Tax Court of the United States (October 22, 1942-1969)	United States Claims Court (Oct. 1, 1982-Oct. 28, 1992)
Board of Tax Appeals (1924-October 21, 1942)	United States Court of Claims (1948-Sept. 30, 1982)
	Court of Claims of the United States (1863-1948)

---

[186] See Ballard v. Commissioner, 544 U.S. 40 (2005). The taxpayers sought access to the special trial judges' report because they had reason to believe it varied significantly from the Tax Court's published opinion. The Tax Court has since modified its Rule 183.

[187] Memorandum decisions have been appealed as far as the Supreme Court. See, e.g., Commissioner v. Duberstein, 363 U.S. 278 (1960).

[188] I.R.C. § 7463(b). The increase to $50,000 in 1998 is likely to increase the percentage of taxpayers using this litigation route. The previous limit was $10,000. A typical citation is Wheir v. Commissioner, T.C. Summ. Op. 2004-117.

d. United States Bankruptcy Courts[189]

In addition to deciding priority of liens and related matters, United States Bankruptcy Courts may issue substantive tax rulings. District Court judges, Bankruptcy Appellate Panels, or Courts of Appeals review Bankruptcy Court decisions.[190]

As a general rule, each circuit decides if it will use a Bankruptcy Appellate Panel (BAP) and whether the BAP will hear all cases. In 2005, Congress enacted the Bankruptcy Abuse Prevention and Consumer Protection Act of 2005.[191] That act provided circumstances under which Bankruptcy Court decisions can be appealed directly to the Court of Appeals.[192]

Bankruptcy cases often have two captions. One caption begins with "In re." The other follows the format used for most cases "Plaintiff v. Defendant." If you are looking for a particular bankruptcy case, note both the debtor and the trustee's names so that you can find the case no matter which case reporter or citator service you are using. Table 11-2 shows how a Bankruptcy Court case involving Guardian Trust Company (Henderson, Trustee) is captioned in three reporter services.

Table 11-2. Case Captions for Bankruptcy Court Decisions

Reporter Service	Caption
Bankruptcy Reporter	In re Guardian Trust Co., 242 B.R. 608 (Bankr. S.D. Miss. 1999)
U.S. Tax Cases	In re Guardian Trust Company, 99-2 U.S.T.C. ¶ 50,819 (Bankr. S.D. Miss. 1999)
American Federal Tax Reporter	Henderson v. United States, 84 A.F.T.R.2d 99-5940 (Bankr. S.D. Miss. 1999)

---

[189] These courts came into existence in 1979; bankruptcy trustees appointed by District Court judges previously administered these cases. See Pub. L. No. 95-598, § 201(a), 92 Stat. 2549, 2657 (1978). Bankruptcy judges are currently appointed by Court of Appeals judges. 28 U.S.C. § 152(a).

[190] See, e.g., In re Michaud, 199 B.R. 248 (Bankr. D.N.H. 1996), aff'd, Michaud v. United States, 206 B.R. 1 (D.N.H. 1997); In re Mosbrucker, 220 B.R. 656 (Bankr. D.N.D. 1998), aff'd, 227 B.R. 434 (B.A.P. 8th Cir. 1998), aff'd, 99-2 U.S.T.C. ¶ 50,883, 84 A.F.T.R.2d 99-6457 (8th Cir. 1999)(unpublished opinion).

[191] Pub. L. No. 109-8, 119 Stat. 23 (2005).

[192] Id. § 1233, amending 28 U.S.C. § 158(d)(2).

2. Courts of Appeals

When your research uncovers trial court decisions, you should trace them to the appellate court level. This is particularly important if decisions conflict with each other and none comes from your jurisdiction.

Decisions of District Courts and the Tax Court are appealed to the Court of Appeals for the taxpayer's geographical residence[193] and from there to the Supreme Court. Even if the Tax Court disagrees with a particular Circuit Court precedent, it will follow it if that court would hear the appeal.[194] After appellate reversal in several circuits, the Tax Court is likely to change its position for future litigation.[195]

Two Courts of Appeals are of relatively recent vintage. The Eleventh Circuit was carved out of the Fifth Circuit in 1981. If you represent a taxpayer who lives in the Eleventh Circuit, you should also consider Fifth Circuit decisions issued before October 1, 1981.[196]

The second recently established court is the Court of Appeals for the Federal Circuit, which was formed in 1982 to review decisions of what is now the Court of Federal Claims. Because the Supreme Court reviews so few Court of Appeals decisions, the Court of Federal Claims-Federal Circuit route offers a forum-shopping opportunity. Taxpayers can avoid adverse appellate court decisions from their "home" circuits by suing in the Court of Federal Claims.[197]

The Court of Appeals for the Federal Circuit also hears appeals from the United States Patent and Trade Office and from District Court

---

[193] From 1924 to 1926, appeals from the Board of Tax Appeals (the Tax Court's predecessor) were heard in District Court. Revenue Act of 1924, ch. 234, § 900(g), 43 Stat. 253, 336; Revenue Act of 1926, ch. 27, § 1001(a), 44 Stat. 9, 109.

[194] Golsen v. Commissioner, 54 T.C. 742 (1970).

[195] See, e.g., Fazi v. Commissioner, 102 T.C. 695 (1994).

[196] See, e.g., Estate of Kosow v. Commissioner, 45 F.3d 1524, 1529 (11th Cir. 1995), citing a 1972 Fifth Circuit decision. Because the Tenth Circuit was split from the Eighth Circuit in 1929, you are unlikely to find Eighth Circuit precedent relevant to research involving the Tenth Circuit. Splitting the Ninth Circuit into two or even three circuits has been proposed many times. See, e.g., H.R. No. 211, 109th Cong., 1st Sess. (2005).

[197] See Ginsburg v. United States, 184 Ct. Cl. 444, 396 F.2d 983 (1968), for a discussion of this phenomenon in the court's predecessor, the Court of Claims.

decisions involving patents. Because the USPTO approves business methods patents, including patents relevant to tax strategies, tax planning research may involve checking to see if a particular strategy is patented.[198]

In December 1989, the Federal Courts Study Committee recommended abolishing the present system for resolving tax controversies. The Committee recommended substituting a single trial court—the Tax Court—with appeals going to a specialized appellate court.[199] That suggestion, or variants using other courts, occasionally resurfaces.[200]

3. Supreme Court

As noted above, decisions from the Circuit Courts can be appealed to the United States Supreme Court. The Supreme Court hears cases involving both constitutional challenges and those involving statutory interpretation. The Court is unlikely to grant certiorari in a case involving only statutory interpretation unless there is a conflict between two or more circuits.

SECTION C. LOCATING DECISIONS

1. Finding Lists

If you need to find judicial decisions involving a particular statute, treaty, regulation, or ruling, you can compile a preliminary reading list using the annotated looseleaf services and treatises discussed in Chapter

---

[198] See http://www.uspto.gov/patft/class705_sub36t.html for lists of patents and applications involving tax strategies. See generally STAFF OF THE JOINT COMMITTEE ON TAXATION, BACKGROUND AND ISSUES RELATING TO THE PATENTING OF TAX ADVICE (JCX-31-06) (2006).

[199] FEDERAL COURTS STUDY COMM., TENTATIVE RECOMMENDATIONS FOR PUBLIC COMMENT (1989). Earlier in 1989, an ABA committee had proposed assigning trial court jurisdiction to the Tax Court. ABA STANDING COMMITTEE ON FEDERAL JUDICIAL IMPROVEMENTS, THE UNITED STATES COURT OF APPEALS: REEXAMINING STRUCTURE AND PROCESS AFTER A CENTURY OF GROWTH (1989).

[200] "If Congress decides to centralize tax appeals, the Federal Circuit provides a readily available forum for that purpose, one that already adjudicates appeals in tax cases coming to it from the Court of Federal Claims, and whose docket would be capable of absorbing appeals from the Tax Court or the district courts or both." COMMISSION ON STRUCTURAL ALTERNATIVES FOR THE FEDERAL COURTS OF APPEALS, TENTATIVE DRAFT REPORT (OCT. 1998), excerpted in Tax Notes today file on LexisNexis at 98 TNT 234-78.

13. You can also use one of the citators discussed in Chapter 12. Finally, you can simply run a CD/DVD or online search using the item as a search term.

2. Locating Citations

If you know the name of a case, but not its citation, how do you locate its text? Several sources will be useful in this type of search. CD/DVD (Chapter 19) and online (Chapter 20) services are particularly helpful because you can include facts and issues in your search request.[201] These services may include screens in which you can enter party names, judge names, or other information and retrieve a case. [See Illustrations 3-1, 3-2, 3-3, 11-1, and 11-2.]

If you lack access to an online service, there are print service options for locating case citations. If you know the taxpayer's first name and last names, you can use the RIA and CCH print citators (Chapter 12); both list taxpayers alphabetically. United States Tax Reporter (Chapter 13) also includes a Table of Cases. If you lack the taxpayer's first name, but do know the jurisdiction, you might instead consult the alphabetical list of parties in West's Federal Practice Digest 4th. That service does not include the Tax Court.[202]

If you know who the other party is, you can narrow your search among various tax reporter services. If, for example, the case is captioned "Taxpayer v. Commissioner," it arose in the Tax Court. Cases captioned "Taxpayer v. United States" arose in a District Court or the Court of Federal Claims.[203] Cases whose captions include "In re" often began in Bankruptcy Court, but reporter services differ in their captioning of

---

[201] CD/DVD services don't always include a citation to a case reporter service.

[202] These materials are particularly useful if CCH and RIA omit the case from their citators. Such omission is possible if nontax aspects of a case are more important than tax aspects. See, e.g., United States v. Rosengarten, 857 F.2d 76 (2d Cir. 1988), omitted from CCH, RIA, and Shepard's tax citators.

[203] Knowing where to start is particularly useful if you use print reporter services and lack access to the CCH and RIA citators and electronic services. If the case arose in the Tax Court, you can use the CCH Tax Court Reporter's Table of Decisions, including the Current and Latest Additions supplements to ascertain the CCH Decision Number. You can obtain a citation by cross-referencing those numbers to the official reports or the CCH Tax Court Memoranda service using cross-reference tables in Volume 2 of this service. You can locate cases originating in other trial courts, as well as all appeals court decisions, through A.F.T.R.'s Table of Cases, which is cumulated throughout each five-year period in the A.F.T.R. volumes.

bankruptcy cases. [See Table 11-2.]

Illustration 11-1. Using Get a Document in LexisNexis

Search	Research Tasks	Search Advisor	**Get a Document**	*Shepard's®*	Alerts

| Citation | Party Name | Docket Number |

Get by Party Name   ?

If you know one party,   `Fazi`   **v.**   `                `
use the first box.   Party   Party

Jurisdiction: Coverage Dates

○ Federal and State Courts: `All Federal & State Courts, Combined ▼`

⊙ Combined Federal Courts: `All Federal Courts                 ▼`

○ US Supreme Court

○ US Courts of Appeals: `All US Courts of Appeals ▼`

○ US District Courts: `All District Courts    ▼`

○ US Special Courts: `US Court of Federal Claims           ▼`

○ State Courts: `All State Courts, Combined ▼`

○ Canadian Cases: `All Canadian Cases   ▼`

Optional: Restrict by Date
⊙ `No Date Restrictions ▼`   ○ From `      ` To `      `

🔍 Search

→I knew only the taxpayer's name. If I had known the court, I could have searched only in the court. *Fazi* is a Tax Court decision. Because I ran this search as if I didn't have that information, I used the Combined Federal Courts search option. If I knew the citation or docket number, I could have used those features instead of searching by name.

→Bankruptcy Court, Court of Federal Claims, and Tax Court are options in the US Special Courts selection.

→Westlaw has a similar function (Find a Case by Party Name), but it does not include a date restriction option. It includes Bankruptcy Courts, Court of Federal Claims, and Tax Court in its Specialized Courts option.

Illustration 11-2. Using Find a Case by Citation in Checkpoint

Find a Case by Citation

Search All Federal Cases by Case Name
Example: Redlark

Case Name: [   ]   [Search]

American Federal Tax Reports
Example: 86 AFTR 2d 2000-7370

[   ] [USTC   ∨] [   ]   [Search]

Example: South Louisiana Bank

Case Name: [   ]   [Search]

→Checkpoint includes search by name and search by citation functions in one screen.

→Note that the box for searching American Federal Tax Reports offers a pull-down menu. You can search in A.F.T.R., in U.S.T.C., and in the West Reporters (Supreme Court Reports, Federal Reporter, and Federal Supplement). Neither Bankruptcy Reporter nor Federal Claims is a listed option, so you would need their parallel A.F.T.R. or U.S.T.C. citation.

→Checkpoint also has search boxes covering the three types of Tax Court decisions.

→Tax Research NetWork also has a decision search screen, but it is not as easy to use as those in LexisNexis, Westlaw, or Checkpoint.

3. Digests of Decisions

Digests are useful for locating decisions and for deciding which of those cases to read first. They may be less important if you are using online services that give an overview of each "hit" or if you search online services by Key Number.

Warren, Gorham & Lamont publishes several specialized digests. These include Corporate Tax Digest, Pass-Through Entity Tax Digest, Real Estate Tax Digest, and Tax Procedure Digest.

The IRS Bulletin Index-Digest System (Chapter 17) digests cases between 1954 and 1993/1994. Services such as Standard Federal Tax Reporter and United States Tax Reporter, both discussed in Chapter 13, digest cases in their compilation and updating volumes or in their newsletters. Newsletters such as Tax Notes and Daily Tax Report, both described in Chapter 16, also digest cases.

4. Texts of Decisions[204]

a. Other than Tax Court

With the exception of Tax Court decisions, you can locate federal court decisions involving taxation in the sets listed in Table 11-3. You can also locate these and Tax Court decisions (including Summary Opinions) online (Chapter 20), in microform (Chapter 18), and in CD/DVD format (Chapter 19). Online and CD/DVD services may have limited retrospective coverage; remember to check when each service began including a court's decisions. Retrospective coverage on individual court websites may be even more limited than it is on subscription-based electronic services.

Table 11-3. Print Reporter Services Other Than Tax Court

Court/ Service	Supreme Court	Court of Appeals	District Court	Bankr. Court	Federal Claims
U.S.	1796-				
S. Ct.	1882-				
L. Ed.	1796-				
A.F.T.R.	1796-	1880-	1882-	1979-	1876-
U.S.T.C.	1913-	1915-	1915-	1979-	1924-
F.		1880-	1882-1932		1929-1932 1960-1982
F. Supp.			1932-		1932-1960
Ct. Cl.					1863-1982
Cl. Ct.					1982-1992
Fed. Cl.					1992-
Bankr.				1979-	

→Several reporters are in second or third series (e.g., F., F.2d, F.3d).

→Only A.F.T.R. and U.S.T.C. print cases from all these courts.

→A.F.T.R. volumes 1-4 reprint cases by reporter service (e.g., Federal Reporter, United States Reports) and not in strict chronological order.

→Until 1912, so-called Circuit Courts decided cases; reports are found in Federal Cases and Federal Reporter.

---

[204] The Cumulative Bulletin (Chapter 17) has included Supreme Court decisions since 1920; it calls them Court Decisions (Ct. D.) Early Cumulative Bulletins included lower federal court decisions either as Ct. D.s or as Miscellaneous Rulings. Because the disparate labels make these items virtually impossible to locate, they are omitted from these lists.

b. Tax Court

Coverage of Tax Court decisions varies.[205] The government published Regular decisions by the Tax Court's predecessor, the Board of Tax Appeals in the Board of Tax Appeals Reports (B.T.A.). The government did not publish B.T.A. Memorandum decisions. Prentice-Hall printed both Regular and Memorandum decisions.

The government also publishes Tax Court Regular decisions in Tax Court of the United States Reports and United States Tax Court Reports; both are cited as T.C. It does not officially publish Tax Court Memorandum decisions. The Tax Court website includes Regular and Memorandum decisions since 1995 and Summary Opinions since 2001.

Both Commerce Clearing House and Research Institute of America (which acquired the Prentice-Hall service) publish Tax Court decisions in a variety of formats. Their reporter services are discussed in Subsection 5.

5. Tax-Oriented Case Reporter Services

Most of the sets listed above are published by the Government Printing Office or by West and are used the same way for tax research as for nontax research. The sets published by Research Institute of America and Commerce Clearing House differ enough from the others to warrant further discussion. These sets are available in print and as part of their respective publishers' online services: RIA Checkpoint and CCH Tax Research NetWork. Those services are illustrated in Chapter 20.

a. American Federal Tax Reports and U.S. Tax Cases

The use of these sets can be coordinated with the use of each publisher's looseleaf reporting service, A.F.T.R. with RIA United States Tax Reporter and U.S.T.C.[206] with CCH Standard Federal Tax Reporter. Each service publishes decisions from all courts except the Tax Court, and each includes "unpublished" decisions omitted from Federal Supplement and

---

[205] Table 11-1 lists relevant dates and court names for the Tax Court and Board of Tax Appeals. Although the Board began in 1924, it did not issue Memorandum decisions until 1928.

[206] The earliest volumes of this service print all Supreme Court decisions and those lower court decisions of "genuine precedent value ...." *Foreword* to 1 U.S.T.C. (1938). When CCH began issuing two volumes per year, it expanded coverage.

Federal Reporter.[207]

Each service first includes decisions in an Advance Sheets volume of the related looseleaf reporting service. This initial publication in conjunction with the looseleaf services results in recent decisions being available in print on a weekly basis. While both services are supplemented weekly, each occasionally prints decisions before the other does.

These cases also appear in the listings of new material in the services' update volumes (Recent Developments for United States Tax Reporter; New Matters for Standard Federal Tax Reporter). The listings appear in Code section order and are cross-referenced to discussions in the services' compilation volumes. As a result, you can locate a recent case when you know the Code section involved but not the taxpayer's name, and you can immediately find a discussion of the topic in the compilation volumes. The daily newsletters (Chapter 16), which are probably the only more current print source of these cases, often print only partial texts or digests and don't provide full-year cumulative indexes.

The reference method is important if you use these services. CCH cites decisions in the U.S.T.C. advance sheets and bound volumes by paragraph number (e.g., 88-1 U.S.T.C. ¶ 9390). RIA cites to decisions in A.F.T.R. by page number (e.g., 62 A.F.T.R.2d 88-5228).

The bound volumes include all types of tax cases—income, estate and gift, and excise; the individual Advance Sheets volumes do not. The different types of cases appear in Advance Sheets sections accompanying each publisher's looseleaf service for the particular area of tax law.

b. Tax Court Reports

Both CCH and RIA publish Tax Court reporters. RIA publishes bound volumes of the Tax Court Memorandum Decisions. A Tax Court Reported & Memorandum CD-ROM covers both Tax Court and Board of Tax Appeals Regular and Memorandum decisions.

The CCH Tax Court Reporter has three looseleaf volumes. Volume 1 contains Memorandum decisions and Volume 2 contains Regular decisions. Volume 3, which is discussed in Section D, contains information about pending litigation. Volume 1 has an alphabetical Table of Decisions, while Volume 2 provides cross-references to CCH case numbers.

---

[207] See, e.g., Alexander v. United States, 88-1 U.S.T.C. ¶ 9390, 62 A.F.T.R.2d 88-5228 (N.D. Ga. 1988); Estate of McLendon v. Commissioner, 96-1 U.S.T.C. ¶ 60,220, 77 A.F.T.R.2d 96-666 (5th Cir. 1995) (unpublished opinion).

c. Citation Format for CCH and RIA Reporter Services

Citation formats for the services published by CCH and RIA vary depending upon whether you follow the guidelines established by The Bluebook, ALWD, or TaxCite.[208] Depending on the format adopted, you are likely to encounter any of the Table 11-4 citation formats.

Table 11-4. Citation Formats for CCH and RIA Reporters

Reporter Service	Possible Citation Formats
American Federal Tax Reports	AFTR; A.F.T.R.; A.F.T.R. (P-H); A.F.T.R. (RIA); AFTR2d; A.F.T.R.2d; A.F.T.R.2d (RIA)
U.S. Tax Cases	USTC para.; U.S.T.C. ¶; U.S. Tax Cas. (CCH)
Tax Court Reports	T.C.R. (CCH) Dec.; T.C.R. Dec. (P-H) ¶; T.C.R. Dec. (RIA) ¶; Tax Ct. Rep. (CCH); Tax Ct. Rep. Dec. (P-H); Tax Ct. Rep. Dec. (RIA)
Tax Court Memorandum Decisions	T.C. Memo; TCM; para. #, P-H memo T.C.; T.C.M. (CCH); T.C.M. (P-H) ¶; T.C.M. (RIA) ¶; T.C.M. (P-H); T.C.M. (RIA)
Board of Tax Appeals Memorandum Decisions	B.T.A. Mem. Dec. (P-H) ¶; B.T.A.M. (P-H)

6. Appeals

You can determine if a trial court decision has been affirmed or reversed by using a citator. Alternatively, if you found the decision in an online service, you can simply click to find the decision's subsequent history. Illustration 11-3 shows this ability in Westlaw.

Illustration 11-3. Case Status and Other Options in Westlaw

Because the IRS often indicates its recommendation about appealing adverse decisions in actions on decisions and notices of acquiescence (Chapter 10), you should also research these documents before deciding if appeals are likely in cases of interest.

---

[208] Although the ABA Section of Taxation is one of TaxCite's participants, ABA publications often use formats other than those listed in TaxCite.

7. Parallel Citations

Online and CD/DVD services make cases accessible without regard to reporter service. Online services are more likely to include citations than are CD/DVD services.

If you use bound volumes for your research, you may find that the volume for which you have a citation is not on the library shelf. Because so many case reporters cover each court level, you may be able to find that case in another set. All you need is the correct citation for the other reporter service.

Because general reporter services print nontax as well as tax decisions, numerous volumes cover each year's cases. Looking up the case name in several volumes is a tedious method of finding another printing. You can accomplish this task more quickly by locating the case citation in a citator (Chapter 12) and obtaining a parallel citation to the same decision in another reporter.

8. Briefs

Briefs are relevant in determining which arguments the taxpayers and government have raised for court consideration. Westlaw's FTX-BRIEF file covers selected briefs filed with the Supreme Court, Circuit Courts, and the Tax Court. Many cases available on Westlaw include a link to the relevant briefs. Lexis has a U.S. Supreme Court Briefs file, a Selected Federal Briefs and Motions file, and a Tax Analysts Tax Court Filings file. The Tax Analysts file covers briefs and petitions included in the Tax Analysts database. It is unlikely that these services will provide a brief for every trial court action.

SECTION D. CITATORS FOR DECISIONS AND HEADNOTES

There are four commonly used citators for judging the relative authority of any tax decision, and many libraries own or have online access to all of them. The four are Shepard's, KeyCite, RIA Citator, and CCH Citator. KeyCite is only available online. The others are available in print and online (but the RIA Citator has more retrospective coverage in its print version). All four are discussed and illustrated in Chapter 12.

IRS action with regard to cases it has lost can be located in the Bulletin Index-Digest System (1954-1993/94) (Chapter 17) or in a service covering IRS documents (Chapter 10).

There is one caveat regarding using different reporter services. That relates to headnotes or syllabus numbers. These numbers are relevant when you use a citator to check for later treatment of a judicial decision. As discussed in Chapter 12, each reporter service makes its own decision regarding the headnotes or syllabus numbers it assigns a case. If you read a case in one service and are interested in a particular syllabus issue, make sure the citator you use is keyed to that service. Table 11-5 indicates how many headnotes or syllabus numbers appear in various reporter services for Estate of Mitchell as decided by the Ninth Circuit in 2001.

Table 11-5. Headnotes/Syllabus Numbers in Estate of Mitchell

Service	Citation	Headnotes
Federal Reporter	250 F.3d 696	10
LexisNexis	2001 U.S. App. Lexis 7990	9
A.F.T.R.	87 A.F.T.R. 2d 2001-2043	2
U.S.T.C.	2001-1 U.S.T.C. ¶ 60,403	0

SECTION E. EVALUATING DECISIONS

1. In General

Courts must determine how much weight to give opinions in cases cited by the taxpayer or government. An individual court, whether Tax Court, District Court, or Court of Federal Claims, will give its own decisions far more deference than it will give decisions of the other trial courts.

If a Court of Appeals has ruled, that opinion will be binding precedent for District Court, Bankruptcy Court, and Tax Court cases that will be appealed in that circuit. Otherwise, the opinion will be persuasive precedent. Supreme Court decisions are binding precedent for all courts.

If a court ruled against the government position, and the IRS issues a notice of acquiescence, an action on decision, or other document explaining why it won't appeal, the precedential value of the decision is further enhanced. Instead of acquiescing, the IRS announcement may indicate it will continue litigating. [See, e.g., Illustration 4-9.] These IRS documents are discussed in Chapter 10.

2. Unpublished Opinions

There is a difference between an **unpublished opinion** and an opinion to which you cannot get access. Many services include decisions issued under no-publication rules. You may want to find these decisions, as they shed light on the court's thinking. In the past, some circuits allowed citations to those opinions; other circuits barred the citations. On April 12, 2006, the Supreme Court approved proposed Federal Rule of Appellate Procedure 32.1, allowing citation to those opinions in all circuits. Note that the Court's ruling relates to citing the opinions; it does not mandate whether a court must treat them as precedent.[209]

3. Officially Published Opinions

There is also a difference, as noted earlier in this chapter, between an officially published opinion and one available through other reporter services. Unless designated by court or statute as not precedential, both sets of opinions can be cited as precedential or persuasive authority.

Unofficial reporters may include official pagination, but they do not have to do so. If you need to cite official pagination, you must use reporters that provide that information. If courts abandon the requirement of citing to print page numbers, and more decisions are posted online, the distinction between official and other publication sources will diminish for items other than headnotes, as illustrated in Table 11-5.

4. Statements Regarding Deference

If no appeals have been taken, you may be tempted to accord greater weight to a Tax Court decision than to a decision of another trial court. Although the Tax Court judges have specialized knowledge, the degree of deference their decisions receive is not necessarily greater than that given decisions from other trial courts.

The items below illustrate statements regarding deference to decisions.

• We review the Tax Court's construction of the tax code de novo.... Although we presume that the Tax Court correctly applied the law, we give no special deference to the Tax Court's decisions. Best Life Assur. Co. of Calif. v. Commissioner, 281 F.3d 828, 830 (9th Cir. 2002).

• The Commissioner also argues that a sufficient explanation had been provided, relying upon an older body of case law that purports to grant great deference to the Tax Court.... In these cases, however, the Tax Court provided some justification for its conclusions in a manner that allowed us to understand and reconstruct the Tax Court's rationale. In the case at hand, the Tax Court merely announced the discount it applied

---

[209] This rule would go into effect unless Congress voted not to accept it. See http://www.supremecourtus.gov/orders/courtorders/frap06p.pdf for the Court's transmittal of the proposed rule.

to the Estate's stock without any explanation. Estate of Mitchell v. Commissioner, 250 F.3d 696, 703 n.6 (9th Cir. 2001).

• A finding is clearly erroneous when, although there is evidence to support it, a review of the entire record leaves the reviewing court with the definite and firm conviction that a mistake has been made.... This standard of review requires that we accord great deference to the values established by the tax court, but it does not render us a mere rubber stamp. Gross v. Commissioner, 272 F.3d 333, 343 (6th Cir. 2001).

• For the following reasons, pursuant to 28 U.S.C. § 1334(c)(1), we voluntarily ABSTAIN: (1) This adversary proceeding involves a classic two-party dispute, the outcome of which will have little or no effect on the estate;[3] (2) there is litigation currently pending before the United States Tax Court, Docket # 4516-88; (3) the litigation requires the resolution of complex issues of tax law, some of which are unsettled or are questions of first impression; (4) there is a specialized forum for hearing this kind of dispute (i.e., the United States Tax Court); and (5) resolution of the issues would require this Court to interpret decisions of the United States Tax Court.[4] .... In the circumstances, and in deference to its expertise in the subject matter of the litigation, this adversary proceeding is transferred to the United States Tax Court for hearing and adjudication. In re Williams, 209 B.R. 584, 585 (Bankr. D.R.I. 1997) (footnotes omitted).

SECTION F. PROBLEMS

1. Indicate the names of the parties, court involved, and year, for the decision listed below. If the case appears in U.S.T.C., A.F.T.R., and either a West or an official reporter, indicate how many headnotes or syllabus numbers appear in each version.

   a. 2001-44 I.R.B. 379

   b. 2003-1 U.S.T.C. ¶ 50,248

   c. 2003 WL 21177682

   d. 69 A.F.T.R.2d 92-731

2. Give the preferred citation for the decision involving the taxpayer listed below. Use a citation to LexisNexis or Westlaw only if you cannot locate a citation to a reporter service. Limit yourself to the lowest court that has issued an opinion.

a. Milton Hildebran

b. James Pavlosky

c. Donald Wiechens

d. Timothy Dexter

3. Was the lower court affirmed or reversed on appeal?

a. 341 F. Supp. 2d 1308

b. 109 T.C. 416

c. 93 T.C. 572

d. 308 F. Supp. 2d 1360

4. In which case does the following language appear?

a. "This case will demonstrate how, under the Louisiana Law Civil, the past is not dead; how the past will not die; and how, indeed, the past is not even past."

b. "Notwithstanding the replacement of quills and little men wearing green eyeshades by modern accounting machines, taxes are not literally 'self-assessing'."

c. "This case is an example of how the best laid plans of mice and men can often go awry."

d. "If these weren't clear enough, there are also seven columns of single-spaced regulations. Secs. 1.304-1 through 1.304-5, Income Tax Regs. The result is a rococo fugue of tax law."

e. "Because one half of the pair in this case cannot operate independently, the better analogy is to 'bread and butter,' 'pancakes and syrup,' 'chips and dip,' or less abstemiously, to 'Corona and lime,' or least appetizingly, to 'tequila and worm.'"

5. Locate judicial decisions involving the following issues.

a. a 2001 Tax Court decision involving whether the taxpayer could rely on IRS telephone advice

b. a 2002 Tax Court decision regarding Social Security benefits and married taxpayers who had separate bedrooms when they shared an abode

c. a 2005 District Court decision in which the court refused to follow a 1982 decision of a different District Court

d. a 2005 Tax Court decision involving a theft loss deduction for a house that had structural defects

e. a 2006 Tax Court decision involving whether coal mines subject to supply contracts were of like kind to unencumbered gold mines

f. a 2003 Circuit Court decision involving whether unpaid lottery winnings had to be valued using IRS tables

g. a 2005 Circuit Court decision involving whether issuing a 30-day letter constituted taking a position

h. a 1984 Eleventh Circuit decision treating a Fifth Circuit decision as binding precedent

i. a 2003 Bankruptcy Court decision regarding a home office deduction

6. In each case below, the Tax Court overruled its prior holding on an issue. Provide the citation for the case you find and the earlier case.

a. a 1991 decision regarding the existence of a small S corporation exception to the unified S corporation audit provisions

b. a 2002 decision regarding the validity of Treas. Reg. § 1.163-9T

c. a 2006 decision regarding equitable innocent spouse relief in a nondeficiency case

d. a 2006 decision regarding the timely mailing is timely filing rule

7. Provide the citation for the facts involved in the following judicial decisions, including both trial court and any appeals.

a. a taxpayer who answered the door carrying a can of mace

b. an IRS levy and a 48 cents tax debt

c. glaring IRS agents at a jury trial

d. the cost of driving to meet with IRS personnel auditing the tax-payer's return

e. the habitat of the Mexican spotted owl

f. theft of family memories

g. symbolic marriage in Fiji

h. a plastic surgeon and two cabana boys

i. the value of four-day-old bread

8. Provide the citation for judicial decisions, including both trial court and any appeals, involving the tax consequences of the following celebrities or individuals who interacted with them.

a. a cameraman kicked by Dennis Rodman

b. advance season ticket deposits received by a Florida baseball team

c. the company for which Warren Buffett is best known

d. royalties received by Enrico Caruso

e. value of art owned by the widow of photographer Alfred Stieglitz

f. the marital status of a member of the first team to fly around the world without stopping or refueling

PART FIVE

SECONDARY SOURCES

Chapter 12. Citators

Section A. Introduction

You can use citator services to determine if a particular statute, treaty, regulation, ruling, or judicial decision has been criticized, approved, or otherwise commented upon in a more recent proceeding. As shown in Illustrations 14-3 through 14-6, Shepard's lets you determine if a judicial opinion has cited a particular periodical article or if an article has cited a particular decision. KeyCite also offers this ability.

Goals for this chapter include determining coverage and format differences for each citator and citator-like service. You should also feel comfortable using word searches in electronic services instead of using print or electronic citators.

Section B. Terminology

This chapter discusses services that are called **citators** and services that perform citator-like functions. I refer to the latter as **updating services** or as **citator-like services**. In their print versions, citators and updating services group statutes, judicial decisions, or other documents in a particular format (for example, by year of decision, alphabetically, or by type of tax). Each item is followed by a list of later items that cite to it.

A later item may merely cite the earlier item as authority or it may discuss the earlier item and indicate agreement or disagreement with its holding. The discussion may center on the earlier item as a whole or on a particular issue involved in that item.

In this chapter, the earlier material is referred to as the **cited** item; any later material that refers to it is a **citing** item. Subdivisions such as **headnote** or **syllabus** numbers, which refer to issues, are referred to by either term throughout this text.

Section C. Citator Format and Coverage Overview

This section provides a brief overview of differences in citator format and coverage. Detailed descriptions of each citator appear in Sections D through G.[210] Section I provides information about citator-like services.

Three of the four citators described below are available in both print and electronic formats; the fourth is electronic only. Electronic versions are generally superior to print for five reasons: (1) ease of use; (2) updating frequency; (3) the ability to search the equivalent of multiple print citator volumes; (4) citations to secondary authority; and (5) hyperlinks.

Illustrations of citator results for a revenue ruling appear in Chapter 10. Illustrations in Section H of this chapter cover a judicial decision. Both focus primarily on electronic citators.

1. Arrangement

a. Cited Items in Print Citators

The manner in which cited items are arranged is relevant only if you use a print citator and need to locate the correct citator volume. Arrangement is irrelevant for an electronic citator.

Print citators follow a variety of format conventions. The major distinction is between citators that arrange cited cases by reporter service citation and those that arrange them alphabetically. A second distinction relates to the overall arrangement of multivolume services.

Shepard's divides its print service by the type of cited item. Thus, Supreme Court decisions are in different volumes than Courts of Appeals decisions. [See Table 12-1.] Softbound volumes cover citations issued since the bound volumes were published. Within each set, it arranges cited cases by numerical reporter citation. When using Shepard's, make sure you have an accurate citation for the case you are checking.

Research Institute of America (RIA) divides its print citators by time period but not by type of court. Like Shepard's, RIA issues supplementary volumes for later material. Within each volume, RIA arranges cited decisions in alphabetical order.

Commerce Clearing House (CCH) has three looseleaf citators, to correspond with its separate looseleaf services for income, estate and gift, and excise taxes. Within each service, it arranges decisions in alphabeti-

---

[210] Because each citator has a different scope and format, the separate discussions in Sections D through G treat each cited primary authority in the same order.

cal order. CCH updates its citators with supplementary pages.

When using CCH and RIA,, knowing the taxpayer's first name makes searching easier, particularly if the taxpayer has a common surname. Note that alphabetization rules may vary, particularly for names that begin with numbers (e.g., 21 West Lancaster precedes Twenty Mile Joint Venture in RIA but not in CCH).

b. Citing Items

The arrangement for citing items is important no matter what type of citator you use. When listing citing items, RIA subdivides citing cases by syllabus number, then by rank of citing court, and by date order within each group. Shepard's print service arranges citing items by circuit, and then by rank of court, and then by date order in each group. The electronic Shepard's follows this arrangement but lists the most recent items first. West's KeyCite arranges citing judicial decisions by treatment category (e.g., positive, cited, mentioned); within each category, it lists them by court and lists the most recent items first. CCH subdivides the cited case by each court that heard it and separately provides citations to each decision. It lists appellate courts before lower courts within each group.

2. Syllabus Number and Judicial Commentary

Shepard's, KeyCite, and RIA use syllabus numbers to indicate issues and words or letter symbols to indicate judicial commentary (e.g., distinguished, explained); CCH does neither. Remember that you risk erroneous results if you rely solely on an editor's judgment.

3. Miscellaneous Differences

CCH uses fewer citing cases than do the others; it limits its coverage to citing cases that affect the cited case's "effectiveness as precedent." The online Shepard's and KeyCite include numerous secondary sources as citing items. All services are more likely than the general Shepard's print service to include Tax Court (particularly Memorandum decisions) and IRS material as citing items.

SECTION D. SHEPARD'S CITATIONS

Shepard's publishes a general version that is useful for traditional legal research, including tax research, and a special Shepard's Federal Tax Citator version. Shepard's is also available online in LexisNexis. This discussion focuses on the online version.

Because of its long history, Shepard's is the best-known citator. The print Shepard's volumes include some secondary materials, such as citations to A.L.R. and to Lawyers' Edition annotations, and the Shepard's Federal Tax Citator includes citations to articles in specialized tax periodicals.[211] The online Shepard's service includes far more secondary source material than does either print service. Unlike the general Shepard's print volumes, the electronic version cites to IRS material.

The online Shepard's uses the codes shown in Illustration 12-1 to alert you to how the citing item treated the cited item.

Illustration 12-1. Shepard's Online Citing Reference Codes

* Signal Legend:
  ● - Warning: Negative treatment is indicated
  [Q] - Questioned: Validity questioned by citing refs
  ▲ - Caution: Possible negative treatment
  ◆ - Positive treatment is indicated
  (A) - Citing Refs. With Analysis Available
  (I) - Citation information available

Shepard's citing items appear in this order: legislative history; cases; IRS material; and secondary materials. Supreme Court decisions appear before Courts of Appeals. Within each circuit, Circuit Court opinions come first, followed by District Court (or Court of Federal Claims) and then by Bankruptcy Court opinions. Tax Court opinions (Regular and Memorandum) are the last federal judicial decisions; they are followed by state decisions. Items appear in reverse chronological order.

You can choose to find all citing references (Full option) or those for which Shepard's provides analytical notations (QWIC option). Shepard's provides both hyperlinks and pinpoint citations to the exact page.

1. Constitution, Statutes, and Treaties

If a constitutional provision has been cited by a federal or state court, or by the IRS, Shepard's includes it in a list of citing references. [Illustration 12-2.] Shepard's also includes citations in law reviews.

---

[211] Shepard's initially cited to Tax Law Review; the most recent volumes include citations to Journal of Taxation and to TAXES—The Tax Magazine.

Shepard's accords the same treatment to statutes and also indicates if the statute's validity has been passed upon. [Illustration 12-3.] Shepard's also indicates any subsequent congressional amendments or repeal of statutory material.

The print Shepard's stopped covering treaties in 1995. The online Shepard's does not currently include a "Shepardize" tab with its treaties.

Illustration 12-2. Citations to Constitution in Shepard's

View: Cite | KWIC | Full
Display Options ▸

PREV 951 - 1000 of 1452 Total Cites NEXT
Save As Shepard's Alert® | Unrestricted | All Neg | All Pos | FOCUS™- Restrict B
Shepard's® U.S. Const. amend. 16, U.S. Const. amend. 16

985. **Cited by:**
Niedringhaus v. Commissioner, 99 T.C. 202, 1992 U.S. Tax Ct. LEXIS 63, 99 T.C. No. 11 (1992)

99 T.C. 202 p.219

IRS AGENCY MATERIALS

986. **Cited by:**
Notice 2006-31, 2006 IRB LEXIS 127, 2006-15 I.R.B. 751, Notice 2006-31 (I.R.S. 2006)

2006 IRB LEXIS 127
Notice 2006-31

987. **Cited by:**
TAM 200629030, PLR No. 200629030, 2006 PLR LEXIS 1034 (I.R.S. 2006)

PLR No. 200629030

988. **Cited by:**
Rev. Proc. 2006-2, 2006 IRB LEXIS 27, 2006-1 I.R.B. 89, Rev. Proc. 2006-2 (I.R.S. 2006)

→Shepard's included 1,452 citing references to the sixteenth amendment.

Illustration 12-3. Citations to I.R.C. Section 104(a)(2) in Shepard's

33. **Decision for Government at:**
Pagan-Valez v. United States, 1997 U.S. Dist. LEXIS 14992, 80 A.F.T.R.2d (RIA) 6631, 97-2 U.S. Tax Cas.

80 A.F.T.R.2d (RIA) 6631 p.6631, (edition 1994)
97-2 U.S. Tax Cas. (CCH) P50720, (edition 1994)

D.C. CIRCUIT - COURT OF APPEALS

34. **Unconstitutional in part by, Cited by:**
Murphy v. IRS, 460 F.3d 79, 2006 U.S. App. LEXIS 21401 (D.C. Cir. 2006)

Unconstitutional in part by:
460 F.3d 79 p.92

D.C. CIRCUIT - U.S. DISTRICT COURT

35. **Constitutional by, Interpreted or construed by, Cited by:**
Murphy v. IRS, 362 F. Supp. 2d 206, 2005 U.S. Dist. LEXIS 4309, 95 A.F.T.R.2d (RIA) 1505 (D.D.C. 2005)

→There were 135 citations in the KWIC option; 819 in the Full option.

2. Regulations and IRS Documents

The online Shepard's lets you Shepardize both regulations sections and IRS documents. Illustration 12-4 shows the results from Shepardizing Revenue Ruling 87-22, discussed and illustrated in Chapter 4.

Illustration 12-4. Citations to Revenue Ruling 87-22 in Shepard's

View: KWIC | **Full**   ◀◀◀ 1 - 29 of 29 Total Cites ▶▶▶   **FAST Print** Print | Download
Display Options ▶   Save As *Shepard's* Alert® | Unrestricted | All Neg | All Pos | FOCUS™- Restrict By
                                                         Shepard's® ❶ Rev. Rul. 87-22, Rev. Rul. 87-22

U.S. TAX COURT

✔ Select for Delivery
☐   1. **Cited by:**
         Huntsman v. Commissioner, 91 T.C. 917, 1988 U.S. Tax Ct. LEXIS 141, 91 T.C. No. 57 (1988)●

IRS AGENCY MATERIALS

☐   2. **Cited by:**
         Field Serv. Adv. Mem., 1997 FSA LEXIS 479 (I.R.S. 1997)

         1997 FSA LEXIS 479

☐   3. **Cited by:**
         Action on Dec. CC-1991-02, AOD 1991-02, 1991 AOD LEXIS 4 (I.R.S. 1991)❶

         AOD 1991-02
         1991 AOD LEXIS 4

☐   4. **Cited by:**
         Rev. Proc. 87-15, 1987-1 C.B. 624, 1987 IRB LEXIS 322, 1987-14 I.R.B. 47, Rev. Proc. 87-15 (I.R.S. 1987)❶

→Compare these results to those in Illustration 4-7. Shepard's 29 citations included law review articles and treatises.

3. Judicial Decisions

The electronic version indicates both the first page of the citing decision and the page where the citation to the earlier item appears. Although print Shepard's indicates the syllabus numbers; instead of West's Key Numbers, the online version uses LexisNexis headnotes.

The Shepard's citations to judicial decisions are illustrated in Section H.

4. Other Materials

As noted in the preceding paragraphs, Shepard's lists law review articles that cite to primary source authorities. In addition, you can use Shepard's to obtain citations to law review articles. Illustration 12-5 shows the citing references to one of the articles that cited Revenue Ruling 87-22. Illustration 14-7 shows judicial citations to a law review article.

Illustration 12-5. Citations to 7 Va. Tax Rev. in Shepard's

> ► (CITATION YOU ENTERED):
> ARTICLE: WHERE HAS ALL THE INCOME GONE? THE MYSTERIOUS RELOCATION OF INTEREST AND PRINCIPAL IN COUPC
> STRIPPING AND RELATED TRANSACTIONS, 7 Va. Tax Rev. 303 (1987)
>
> LAW REVIEWS AND PERIODICALS (11 Citing References)
>
> ✔ Select for Delivery
> ☐   1. ARTICLE: The Virtual Reality of Eliminating Tax Deferral, 12 Am. J. Tax Pol'y 449 (1995)
>
> ☐   2. ARTICLE: Tax Aspects of REMIC Residual Interests, 2 Fla. Tax Rev. 149 (1994)

Table 12-1. General Shepard's Volumes Covering Taxation

Cited Item	Shepard's Volumes
Constitution	Federal Statute Citations
Statutes	Federal Statute Citations
Treaties	Federal Statute Citations (until 1995)
Regulations	Code of Federal Regulations Citations
Revenue Rulings	Not Covered
District Court	Federal Citations
Federal Claims	Federal Citations
Bankruptcy Court	Bankruptcy Citations
Court of Appeals	Federal Citations
Supreme Court	United States Citations

SECTION E. RIA CITATOR

The RIA Citator began as the Prentice-Hall print citator. It is still available in print and is also carried online in both RIA Checkpoint and in Westlaw. The earlier volumes are available only in the print version. The online services limit themselves to RIA Citator 2d. Unless you need earlier material, the online version will be easier to use than the print version because you will not have to use multiple volumes.[212] If you do need earlier materials, and the choice is between the RIA and CCH print citators, RIA is likely to provide more extensive results.

The discussion below covers the online RIA Citator.

1. Constitution, Statutes, and Treaties

The RIA Citator does not cover the Constitution, statutes, or treaties.

---

[212] The first series covers federal tax cases from 1796 to 1954.

2. Regulations and IRS Documents

RIA covers both regulations and IRS documents, but it is not the best source for finding to citations to regulations. It lists cited regulations in T.D. (rather than regulations section) number order; this is not the best method for finding regulations, as a single T.D. may cover several sections. Illustrations 12-6 through 12-8 illustrate RIA Citator citations to Revenue Ruling 87-22 in both Checkpoint and Westlaw.

Illustration 12-6. Searching in RIA Checkpoint

| Annot | ▶ FTC | ▶ Citator |

Rev. Rul. 87-22, 1987-1 CB 146, IRC Sec(s). 461

Headnote:

Rev. Rul. 87-22, 1987-1 CB 146 -- IRC Sec. 461 [1](Also Section ▢_163; ▢ 1.163-1.)

Reference(s): Code Sec. 461; Reg § 1.461-1

Points paid in connection with the refinancing of a mortgage.

Points paid as a result of the refinancing of a mortgage secured by the principal residence of a taxpayer are not deductible in full for the taxable year paid under ▢ section 461(g)(2) of the Code.

→RIA Checkpoint includes a Citator link with primary source items.

Illustration 12-7. Results in RIA Checkpoint

Filter this Document by Court: ALL ⌄

Rev Rul 87-22, 1987-1 CB 146, ,

Judicial History

Same case or ruling : IR- 87-34 , 1987 PH ¶54,743 , ,

Cited In

Cases reconciled : Huntsman, James Richard & Zenith Annette, 91 TC 919 , 91 PH TC 458 *(11/17/1988)*

Cited in dissent : Huntsman, James Richard & Zenith Annette, 91 TC 922 , 91 PH TC 459 *(11/17/1988)*

Cited favorably : Rev Proc 87-15 , 1987-1 CB 625 , ,

Illustration 12-8. RIA Checkpoint Results in Westlaw

> Rev Rul 87-22
> 1987-1 CB 146
>
> Same case or ruling
> IR 87-34, 1987 PH 54,743, ¶ 54,743
>
> Cases reconciled
> Huntsman, James Richard & Zenith Annette, 91 TC 917, 919, 91 PH TC 458
>
> Cited in dissent
> Huntsman, James Richard & Zenith Annette, 91 TC 917, 922, 91 PH TC 459
>
> Cited favorably
> Rev Proc 87-15, 1987-1 CB 624, 625

3. Judicial Decisions

RIA arranges citing cases according to the pertinent RIA syllabus number of the cited case. Within syllabus groupings, RIA lists cases by rank of the citing court, starting with the Supreme Court. Within each group of courts, the earliest cases generally appear first. Geographical jurisdiction is indicated for cited and citing decisions, but District Court subdivisions are not indicated.

Citations are given for both the first page and the citing page. Case citations are given to the RIA case reporters as well as to the official and West services.[213]

RIA also includes citations to IRS action with respect to the cited decision. Citations for revenue rulings and procedures are given to the appropriate volume and page of the Internal Revenue Bulletin or Cumulative Bulletin or to United States Tax Reporter; letter rulings and T.D.s are cited by number, followed by a reference to United States Tax Reporter.

RIA citations to judicial decisions are illustrated in Section H.

4. Other Materials

RIA does not cover law review articles in its citator.

---

[213] The print RIA uses letters to indicate whether or not subsequent decisions follow the cited decision. Citations to subsequent decisions indicate the page where the cited case is mentioned, not the first page of the citing material.

SECTION F. CCH STANDARD FEDERAL TAX REPORTER— CITATOR[214]

The CCH print citator service is actually three separate services. Standard Federal Tax Reporter—Citator is a two-volume service that covers the income tax. The CCH Federal Estate and Gift Tax Reporter and Federal Excise Tax Reporter have their own citator sections, which cover those taxes.[215] The three services combined have fewer volumes than does the full RIA Citator service.[216] If you access the CCH Citator online through CCH Tax Research NetWork, you avoid having to use separate citator services. This discussion focuses on the online service.

1. Constitution, Statutes, and Treaties

The CCH Citator does not cover the Constitution, statutes, or treaties.

2. Regulations and IRS Documents

CCH covers both regulations and IRS documents, but it is not the best source for finding to citations to regulations. It lists cited regulations in T.D. (rather than regulations section) number order; this is not the best method for finding regulations, as a single T.D. may cover several sections.

Case citations for decisions discussing these items include citations to the CCH case reporter services; many citations include the official and West publications. CCH Decision numbers are given for Tax Court materials. The editors provide no indication as to how non-IRS citing material dealt with the cited material.

Cited rulings and procedures have their location in the Cumulative Bulletin or Internal Revenue Bulletin indicated. CCH lists citing items issued by the IRS only by number.

---

[214] SFTR's non-citator features are described in Chapter 13.

[215] Although the SFTR citator volumes list non-Tax Court cases involving estate and gift taxes and excise taxes, actual citations to those cases appear only in the Citator sections of Federal Estate and Gift Tax Reporter and Federal Excise Tax Reporter.

[216] While its compactness makes it the easiest print citator to use, the CCH citator has the fewest useful features and omits, through editorial selection, many citing cases. It does provide paragraph cross-references to discussion in the SFTR compilation volumes.

Illustration 12-9 shows the results obtained using CCH Citator for citations to Revenue Ruling 87-22 in Tax Research NetWork. This search was the least productive of those I ran in the various citators.

Illustration 12-9. Tax Research NetWork Results

CCH-CITATOR, 2006FED, Main Finding Lists, Rev. Rul. 87-22

Rev. Rul. 87-22 , 1987-1 CB 146

ANNOTATED AT ... 2006FED ¶9402.043; ¶9402.60

　　　　1987 CCH ¶6422

Illustration 12-10. Tax Research NetWork Results

Rev. Rul. 84-108 , 1984-2 CB 32

ANNOTATED AT ... 2006FED ¶6662.986

　　　　1984 CCH ¶6601

　　　　Cited in:

O'Gilvie, SCt, 96-2 USTC ¶50,664, 519 US 79, 117 SCt 452

Schmitz, CA, 94-2 USTC ¶50,455

Reese, CA, 94-1 USTC ¶50,232

Miller, CA-4, 90-2 USTC ¶50,511, 914 F2d 586

Rice, DC-Calif, 93-2 USTC ¶50,488, 834 FSupp 1241

O'Gilvie, DC-KS, 92-2 USTC ¶50,344

A.P. Burford, DC, 86-2 USTC ¶9724, 642 FSupp 635

Let. Rul. 200243021

Rev. Rul. 85-98

→Unlike the search in Illustration 12-9, the search for citations to Revenue Ruling 84-108 yielded both judicial decisions and IRS rulings.

3. Judicial Decisions

CCH limits itself to cases commented on or cited in SFTR. It does not indicate which syllabus number is involved in the citing case; likewise, it does not indicate whether the citing material follows or distinguishes the cited decision. Its case citations refer to the CCH case reporters and to the official and West services. Citations to subsequent decisions in services other than U.S.T.C. indicate the first page of the citing case, not the page where reference is made to the cited material.[217]

CCH includes numerical citations to revenue rulings, letter rulings, and revenue procedures discussing the cited decision. It indicates IRS acquiescence or nonacquiescence in adverse judicial decisions.

CCH citations to judicial decisions are illustrated in Section H.

4. Other Material

CCH does not cover law review articles in its citator.

SECTION G. WEST'S KEYCITE

When LexisNexis acquired full ownership of Shepard's, Westlaw substituted its KeyCite system for Shepard's citators. Unlike the systems discussed in Sections D through F, KeyCite is available only online. After you locate a primary source on Westlaw, you click the KeyCite icon to obtain citations to later materials included in the Westlaw database. Alternatively, if you already have a citation, you can go directly to KeyCite and enter that citation.

You can use KeyCite, to obtain all references (neutral, positive, and negative along with secondary materials) to the cited item, or you can limit yourself to negative references. KeyCite provides hyperlinks to the citing material.

Citing material is arranged by category (e.g., Discussed, Cited, Mentioned). Within categories, judicial decisions are arranged by level of court. Within each level, the most recent material is listed first. KeyCite indicates both the first page and the citing page for later material. If the number of citing sources is large enough, categories may be subdivided into topics.

---

[217] Citations to U.S.T.C. are to the paragraph number assigned the case, not to the U.S.T.C. page number.

Illustration 12-11. KeyCite Citing Reference Codes

▶ In cases and administrative decisions, a **red flag** warns that the case or administrative decision is no longer good law for at least one of the points of law it contains. In statutes and regulations, a **red flag** warns that the statute or regulation has been amended by a recent session law or rule, repealed, superseded, or held unconstitutional or preempted in whole or in part.

▷ In cases and administrative decisions, a **yellow flag** warns that the case or administrative decision has some negative treatment, but has not been reversed or overruled. In statutes and regulations, a **yellow flag** warns that a statute has been renumbered or transferred by a recent session law; that an uncodified session law or proposed legislation affecting the statute is available (statutes merely referenced, i.e., mentioned, are marked with a green C); that the regulation has been reinstated, corrected or confirmed; or that the statute or regulation was limited on constitutional or preemption grounds or its validity was otherwise called into doubt, or that a prior version of the statute or regulation received negative treatment from a court.

H In cases and administrative decisions, a **blue H** indicates that there is direct history but it is not known to be negative.

C A **green C** indicates that the case/administrative decision has citing references but no direct history or negative citing references. It also indicates that a statute/regulation has citing references, but no updating documents.

★★★★ **Depth of treatment stars** indicate how extensively a cited case or administrative decision has been discussed by the citing case.

" **Quotation marks** indicate that the citing case or administrative decision directly quotes the cited case.

1. Constitution, Statutes and Treaties

KeyCite provides citations to cases that have interpreted constitutional provisions. It also lists articles and other secondary source materials. KeyCite also provides citations to cases and IRS materials that have interpreted statutes and to cases that have discussed the constitutionality of statutes. Cases are arranged by issue.[218].

KeyCite alerts you to pending legislation and provides information

---

[218] The service includes pre-1954 Code cases, but with some erroneous results. For example, KeyCiting 26 USC 213 (medical expenses) yielded decisions citing section 213 of pre-Code revenue acts.

about prior amendments to the statute. KeyCite does not cover treaties.

Illustration 12-12. Citing References to Constitution in KeyCite

Citing References: limited to C.B., selected document types
(Showing 38 of 1369 documents)

SELECT TO PRINT, EMAIL, ETC.

☐ ▷ 1 Ivan Allen Co. v. U. S., 95 S.Ct. 2501, 2501, 422 U.S. 617, 617, 45 L.Ed.2d 435, 435, 36 A.F.T.R.2d 75-5200, 75-
5200, 75-2 USTC P 9557, 9557, 1975-2 C.B. 228, 228 (U.S.Ga. Jun 26, 1975) (NO. 74-22)

Administrative Decisions (U.S.A.)

IRS Revenue Rulings

☐ C 2 Rev. Rul. 2005-19, 2005-14 I.R.B. 819, 2005 WL 583383, 2005-1 C.B. 819,(IRS RRU Mar 14, 2005)

Administrative Codes (U.S.A.)

☐ C 3 26 CFR s 1.1-1; s 1.1-1 Income tax on individuals.

☐ C 4 26 CFR s 1.61-1; s 1.61-1 Gross income.

→After running a search for references to the sixteenth amendment, I limited citing references to the 38 that appear in the Cumulative Bulletin.

Illustration 12-13. Citing References to I.R.C. section 104 in KeyCite

Citing References
(Showing 5236 documents)

SELECT TO PRINT, EMAIL, ETC.

Held Unconstitutional by

☐ H 1 Murphy v. I.R.S., 460 F.3d 79, 80+, 373 U.S.App.D.C. 126, 126+, 98 A.F.T.R.2d 2006-6088, 2006-6088+, 2006-2 USTC
P 50,476, 50476+ (D.C.Cir. Aug 22, 2006) (NO. 05-5139)

Citations From U.S.C.A. (U.S.A.)

1/2. Constitutionality

☐ H 2 Polone v. C.I.R., 449 F.3d 1041, 1042+, 97 A.F.T.R.2d 2006-2780, 2006-2780+, 2006-1 USTC P 50,367, 50367+, 06
Cal. Daily Op. Serv. 4706, 4706+, 2006 Daily Journal D.A.R. 6955, 6955+ (9th Cir. Jun 05, 2006) (NO. 04-72672)

☐ ▷ 3 Murphy v. I.R.S., 362 F.Supp.2d 206, 207+, 95 A.F.T.R.2d 2005-1505, 2005-1505+, 2005-1 USTC P 50,237, 50237+
(D.D.C. Mar 22, 2005) (NO. CIV.A. 03-02414RCL)

☐ C 4 Allum v. C.I.R., 2005 WL 1692488, *1692488+, T.C. Memo. 2005-177, 2005-177+, 90 T.C.M. (CCH) 74, 74+, T.C.M.
(RIA) 2005-177, 2005-177+ (U.S.Tax Ct. Jul 20, 2005) (NO. 2424-03)

☐ H 5 Polone v. C.I.R., 2003 WL 22953162, *22953162+, T.C. Memo. 2003-339, 2003-339+, 86 T.C.M. (CCH) 698, 698+,
T.C.M. (RIA) 2003-339, 2003-339+ (U.S.Tax Ct. Dec 16, 2003) (NO. 12665-00)

KeyCite also provides graphical presentations of a statute's history. [See Illustration 12-14 for a partial history of Code section 104.]

2. Regulations and IRS Documents

KeyCite provides citations to judicial decisions, officially published and publicly available IRS documents, and secondary sources interpreting regulations and IRS documents. KeyCite provides T.D. numbers and dates for regulations. It provides dates and Cumulative Bulletin cites (if any) for IRS documents.

3. Judicial Decisions

In addition to hyperlinks, KeyCite indicates both the first page of the citing decision and the page where the citation to the earlier item appears. KeyCite citations to judicial decisions are illustrated in Section H.

Illustration 12-14. Partial KeyCite History for I.R.C. section 104

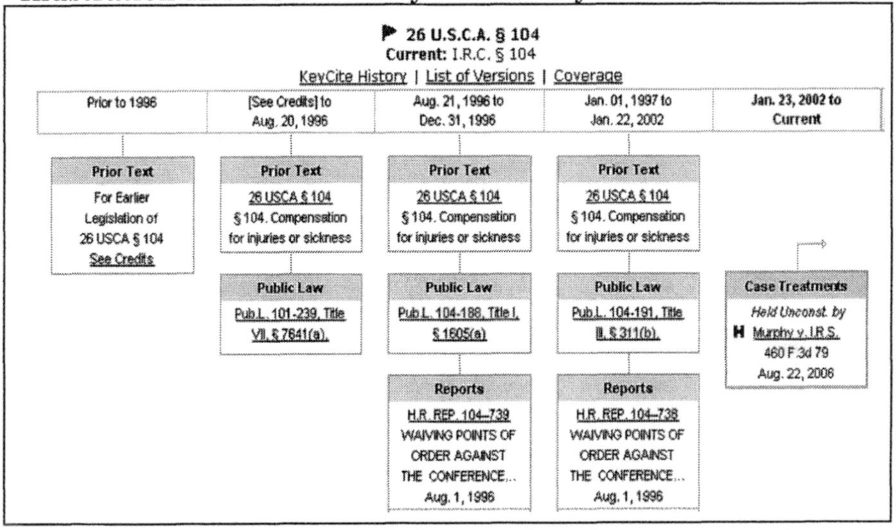

→This KeyCite feature also includes presidential messages, testimony at congressional hearings, and material in Congressional Record.

4. Other Materials

As was true for Shepard's, KeyCite indicates if a judicial decision has cited an article and if an article has mentioned a judicial decision.

SECTION H. ILLUSTRATIONS

The illustrations below indicate the results obtained using *Fox v. Commissioner* as the cited case in the citators discussed in Sections D through G.

The citing case of *Oelze v. Commissioner* will be used to indicate different results reached by different citators. *Oelze* begins this section as Illustration 12-15. Relevant citator differences are covered in the notes accompanying the illustrations.

• Shepard's Federal Citations (print) [Illustration 12-16]

- Shepard's Citations (online) [Illustration 12-17]

- RIA Citator 2nd (print) [Illustration 12-18]

- RIA Citator 2nd on Westlaw [Illustration 12-19]

- RIA Citator 2nd on Checkpoint [Illustration 12-20]

- CCH Citator on Tax Research NetWork [Illustration 12-21]

- Westlaw KeyCite [Illustration 12-22]

Illustration 12-15. Text of Oelze v. Commissioner

53 A.F.T.R. 2d 84-912 (726 F.2d 165)

PER CURIAM:

The petition for rehearing is denied.

In this petition for rehearing, the taxpayer, Richard E. Oelze, urges this court to follow the holding of the United States Court of Appeals for the Seventh Circuit in Fox v. Commissioner, 718 F.2d 251 [52 AFTR 2d 83-6083] (7th Cir.1983) and hold that the Tax Court may not dismiss a taxpayer's petition for redetermination of tax liability for failure to comply with discovery orders unless the court first finds that the taxpayer's failure to comply is willful and in bad faith, and that the taxpayer totally failed to respond to the discovery orders.

[1] In Eisele v. Commissioner, 580 F.2d 805 [42 AFTR 2d 78-5886] (5th Cir.1978), this court, in a half-page per curiam opinion, affirmed dismissal by the Tax Court pursuant to Rule 104, noting simply that the dismissal is "explicitly authorized" by the rules. **In the case before us here, it is unnecessary to decide whether this circuit should follow the Seventh Circuit in imposing stricter standards for dismissals for failure to comply with discovery orders, pursuant to Eisele. This is true because even under the** **analysis of Fox, the Tax Court's dismissal is justified in this case.** The taxpayer's continued failure to cooperate with the Commissioner, the necessity for four orders to comply with the Commissioner's discovery requests, the taxpayer's continuous reliance on a baseless fifth amendment claim, and the taxpayer's last-minute attempt to comply with the discovery order all demonstrate that Oelze acted wilfully. Additionally, the Tax Court issued four separate discovery orders, some explicitly warning the taxpayer that failure to comply would result in dismissal of the case. Though the taxpayer finally did partially comply with one of the orders, he did so only after repeated and total failure to supply the Commissioner with the information he requested. Such partial compliance under these circumstances cannot serve to exonerate the taxpayer from willful failure to comply with the orders of the court.

Oelze's petition for rehearing is Denied

→The *Oelze* decision appears in three case reporter services. This version is from A.F.T.R.; it also appears in F.2d and U.S.T.C. Note the **[1]**. A.F.T.R. assigned one syllabus number to both *Fox* and *Oelze*. West gave *Fox* seven numbers; LexisNexis gave it five.

Illustration 12-16. Excerpt from Shepard's Federal Citations

—251—
Fox v Internal
Revenue
1983

s 60TCt 1058
s60TCt 1123
125FRD321
125FRD339
Cir. 4
916F2d⁴174
Cir. 5
f 726F2d⁵165
Cir. 7
852F2d²283
995F2d²1381
830FS²1230
e 110FRD²267
Cir. DC
777F2d44
c 82TCt 601

→The print Shepard's materials are in several volumes of the Federal Citations set that covers the Federal Reporter. This illustration reproduces part of the citations from 1995 volume 12. *Oelze* is marked in bold. The f indicates that *Oelze* followed *Fox*.

Illustration 12-17. Excerpt from Shepard's on LexisNexis

CITING DECISIONS (28 citing decisions)

4TH CIRCUIT - COURT OF APPEALS

✔ Select for Delivery
☐   1.   **Cited by:**
          Hillig v. Comm'r, 916 F.2d 171, 1990 U.S. App. LEXIS 18188, 66 A.F.T.R.2d (RIA) 5
          1990) ⚠LexisNexis Headnotes HN5

          916 F.2d 171 p.174

5TH CIRCUIT - COURT OF APPEALS

☐   2.   **Followed by:**
          Oelze v. Commissioner, 726 F.2d 165, 1983 U.S. App. LEXIS 14118, 53 A.F.T.R.2d

          726 F.2d 165 p.165

6TH CIRCUIT - COURT OF APPEALS

☐   3.   **Cited by:**
          McFerren v. Commissioner, 1995 U.S. App. LEXIS 4732, 75 A.F.T.R.2d (RIA) 1498,
          Headnotes HN2, HN5

→LexisNexis cited *Oelze* with respect to its fifth headnote in *Fox*.

Illustration 12-18. Excerpt from RIA Citator 2nd (print)

FOX, GEORGE J. v COMM., 52 AFTR2d 83-6083, 718
F2d 251 (USCA 7, 10-6-83)
k—Vermouth, Jon W., 88 TC 1499, 88 PH TC 763 [See
52 AFTR2d 83-6086, 718 F2d 254]
e—Figura, Donald W., 1984 P-H TC Memo 84-2304 [See
52 AFTR2d 83-6086]
q-1—Oelze, Richard E. v Comm., 53 AFTR2d 84-913,
726 F2d 165 (USCA 5)
e-1—Aruba Bonaire Curacao Trust Co., Ltd., Trustee v
Comm., 56 AFTR2d 85-6469, 777 F2d 44 (CADC)
q-1—Dusha, Edward P., 82 TC 601, 605, 82 PH TC 303,
315
e-1—Douglas, Floyd E., 1983 PH TC Memo 83-3288
f-1—Kuhn, Cynthia J., 1984 PH TC Memo 840-2600
f-1—Baranski, Richard R. & Geraldine A., 1984 PH TC
Memo 84-2603
e-1—Williamson, Lucas F., Jr., 1985 PH TC Memo
85-390

→Because *Fox* was decided after 1977, I could ignore the earliest volumes
of this citator. The results above are from volume 2 (1978-1989). Note the
reference to q-1. RIA uses this notation to indicate that *Oelze* questioned
the result in the first (only) AFTR syllabus number in *Fox*.

Illustration 12-19. Excerpt from RIA Citator 2nd on Westlaw

FOX, GEORGE J. v COMM.
52 AFTR 2d 83-6083, 718 F2d 251, 83-2 USTC ¶ 9622
CA7
10/6/1983

Cited favorably
Hillig, Bernard J. v Comm., 66 AFTR 2d 90-5721, 90-5723, 916 F2d 171, 174 (CA4) [See 52 AFT

Cited favorably
Shepherd, Charles E. v. Com., 81 AFTR 2d 98-2466, 98-2468, 147 F3d 633, 635 (CA7) [See 52

Cases reconciled
Vermouth, Jon W., 88 TC 1488, 1499, 88 PH TC 763 [See 52 AFTR 2d 83- 6086, 718 F2d 254]

Cited favorably
Figura, Donald W., 1984 PH TC Memo 84,567, 84-2304 [See 52 AFTR 2d 83- 6086]

Cited favorably
Allnutt, Fred, 2002 RIA TC Memo 2002-311, 2002-1867 [See 52 AFTR 2d 83- 6086]

Decision questioned (1)
Oelze, Richard E. v Com., 53 AFTR 2d 84-912, 84-913, 726 F2d 165, 165 (CA5)

→Illustration 12-19 lists cases that do not appear in Illustration 12-18.
The online citator lists additional cases, because it covers all the volumes
in RIA Citator 2d. You would get the same results using the print service,
but you would have to consult several citator volumes. The online version
also provides hyperlinks to the citing material.

Illustration 12-20. Excerpt from RIA Citator 2nd on Checkpoint

FOX, GEORGE J. v COMM., 52 AFTR 2d 83-6083, 718 F2d 251, 83-2 USTC ¶9622, (CA7, 10/6/1983)
Citator 2nd (RIA)

Cited favorably : Hillig, Bernard J. v Comm., 66 AFTR 2d 90-5723 , 916 F2d 174 *(CA4, 10/16/1990) [9 2d 83-6085, 718 F2d 255]*

Cited favorably : Shepherd, Charles E. v. Com., 81 AFTR 2d 98-2468 , 147 F3d 635 *(CA7, 6/25/1998) AFTR 2d 83-6085, 718 F2d 255]*

Cases reconciled : Vermouth, Jon W., 88 TC 1499 , 88 PH TC 763 *(6/17/1987) [See 52 AFTR 2d 83-608 254]*

Cited favorably : Figura, Donald W., 1984 PH TC Memo 84-2304 *[See 52 AFTR 2d 83-6086]*

Cited favorably : Allnutt, Fred, 2002 RIA TC Memo 2002-1867 *[See 52 AFTR 2d 83-6086]*

Decision questioned1 : Oelze, Richard E. v Com., 53 AFTR 2d 84-913 , 726 F2d 165 *(CA5, 12/28/1983*

→There is one difference between Illustration 12-19 and Illustration 12-20. RIA provides hyperlinks to *Allnutt* in Checkpoint but not in Westlaw.

Illustration 12-21. Excerpt from CCH Citator on Tax Research NetWork

, 2006FED, Main Citator Table, Fox, George

CA-7--(aff'g an unreported TC), 83-2 USTC ¶9622; 718 F2d 251

Shepherd, CA-7 , 98-2 USTC ¶50,511 , 147 F3d 633

McFerren, CA-6, 95-1 USTC ¶50,227

Oelze, CA-5, 84-1 USTC ¶9274 , 726 F2d 165

Harper, TC, Dec. 48,610, 99 TC 533

Geodesco, Inc., TC, Dec. 47,039(M), 60 TCM 1452, TC Memo. 1990-637

Dusha, TC, Dec. 41,123, 82 TC 592

Douglas, TC, Dec. 40,715(M), 47 TCM 791, TC Memo. 1983-786

→The online and print versions include the same items. Neither indicates how the citing item treated the original case.

Illustration 12-22. Excerpt from Westlaw KeyCite

▷   **Fox v. C.I.R.**
                                          718 F.2d 251
                                          C.A.7,1983.
                                          Oct 06, 1983

                                   Negative Cases (U.S.A.)

SELECT TO PRINT, EMAIL, ETC.

Disagreed With by

☐ **C** 1 Dusha v. Commissioner of Internal Revenue, 82 T.C. 592, 601+, 82 T.C. No. 47, 47+, Tax Ct. Rep.
      41123+ (U.S.Tax Ct. Apr 09, 1984) (NO. 23713-82) ★ ★ ★ ★ **HN: 2,5,7 (F.2d)**

Disagreement Recognized by

☐ **C** 2 Vermouth (Jon W.) v. Commissioner of Internal Revenue, 88 T.C. 1488, 1499+, 88 T.C. No. 84, 84
      (CCH) 43,984, 43984+ (U.S.Tax Ct. Jun 17, 1987) (NO. 28158-85) ★ ★ **HN: 2,5 (F.2d)**

                                   Positive Cases (U.S.A.)
                                   ★ ★ ★ **Discussed**

☐ **H** 3 In re Thomas Consolidated Industries, Inc., 456 F.3d 719, 725+, 46 Bankr.Ct.Dec. 233, 233+, Ban
      (7th Cir.(Ill.) Jul 31, 2006) (NO. 05-2729) **HN: 2,5,6 (F.2d)**

☐ **C** 4 Geodesco, Inc. v. C. I. R., 1990 WL 205212, *205212+, T.C. Memo. 1990-637, 1990-637+, 60 T.(
      1452+, T.C.M. (P-H) P 90,637, 90637+ (U.S.Tax Ct. Dec 18, 1990) (NO. 43972-86, 36394-87) ★ |

                                   ★ ★ **Cited**

☐ **H** 5 Roger J. Spott, D.D.S., P.A. v. C.I.R., 875 F.2d 316, 316+ (4th Cir. May 22, 1989) (Table, text in
      2926, 88-2927) **HN: 2,5 (F.2d)**

☐ **H** 6 Oelze v. C.I.R., 726 F.2d 165, 165+, 53 A.F.T.R.2d 84-912, 84-912+, 84-1 USTC P 9274, 9274+ (.
      1983) (NO. 83-4084) **HN: 6 (F.2d)**

→KeyCite indicates that *Oelze* cited *Fox* and involved the sixth headnote
assigned in F.2d.

SECTION I. UPDATING SERVICES IN LIEU OF CITATORS

The citator services discussed above cover most types of primary
authority. You can also determine continued validity for revenue rulings
and procedures using two services discussed in greater detail in Chapters
13 and 17. However, these services have an inherent limitation. They use
only IRS material as citing material and ignore judicial decisions citing to
rulings. In addition, as the dates below indicate, the IRS service is useful
only for research periods ending by 1994.

If you are interested in finding only IRS material or if you need a print
service that uses a Code section format, these are available:

• Mertens, Law of Federal Income Taxation—Rulings (Chapter 13)

• IRS Bulletin Index-Digest System (Chapter 17) (1954-1993/94)

There are several differences between these services. The IRS service
has separate volumes for each tax—income, estate and gift, and excise. It

subdivides cited material by Code section and, when relevant, by regulations section. Mertens subdivides cited material by Code section, often using smaller subdivisions such as subsections and paragraphs.

The IRS service provides digests of citing items elsewhere in the service. Mertens subscribers have access to the full text of the revenue rulings and procedures used as cited and citing items.

SECTION J. PROBLEMS

1. Your instructor will assign you a primary source item to check in as many citators as are available to you. Make a list of differences in citing documents and a list of any differences in treatment. If you find differences in treatment, go to the actual citing material to determine which citators were correct.

2. Several of the problems in other chapters are easily completed with a citator. If you initially completed a problem using a particular citator, redo it using a different publisher's service and compare your results.

Chapter 13. Looseleaf Services, Encyclopedias, and Treatises

You may wish to consult explanatory materials early in the research effort, perhaps even before you read the relevant statutes.[219] If so, you are likely to use a looseleaf service, encyclopedia, or treatise. Those texts will provide insight into the problem being researched. In addition, you can draw upon their liberal use of citations for a preliminary reading list of cases and administrative pronouncements. Each is updated at frequent intervals, and most have at least one related newsletter.

While general research texts would list some of these materials as looseleaf services and others as legal encyclopedias or treatises, those classifications are less significant in this context than are classifications based upon their formats. Most of them take a subject matter approach, but two of the best-known services are arranged in Code section order.

Section A. Code Section Arrangement

The Commerce Clearing House[220] and Research Institute of America[221] looseleaf services take essentially the same approach. Each service's **compilation volumes** print the full texts of Code sections and Treasury regulations along with editorial explanations. An annotation section listing cases and rulings follows each section. Users wanting ready access to the text of the law alongside explanatory material will appreciate this format.

Because of the arrangement described above, problems involving multiple Code sections do not receive comprehensive discussion. Although the publishers supplement their looseleaf materials with newsletters and other aids, Code-based services are not as suited as are subject-based services for learning about issues involving multiple Code sections.

---

[219] In appropriate cases you can use these textual materials to ascertain which statutes are involved. In addition, you should consult these materials whenever you desire additional textual information.

[220] Standard Federal Tax Reporter (income tax); Federal Estate and Gift Tax Reporter; Federal Excise Tax Reporter.

[221] United States Tax Reporter—Income Taxes; United States Tax Reporter—Estate & Gift Taxes; United States Tax Reporter—Excise Taxes. RIA also publishes subject matter format services (e.g., Federal Tax Coordinator 2d).

Although each service is arranged in Code section order, all materials are assigned paragraph numbers. A "paragraph" can be the size of a traditional paragraph, but it might be several pages long. Unless noted otherwise, each service cross-references between paragraph numbers, not between page numbers.

These services have subject matter indexes; their format makes Code section indexes unnecessary. New material arrives weekly for insertion in the compilation volumes or in a separate updating volume. These new developments are indexed according to the paragraph in the main compilation to which they relate, i.e., in Code section order.

Libraries often carry both services,[222] and users eventually develop a preference for one or the other. As each service's annotations are editorially selected, using both can reduce the risk that you will miss a valuable annotation. Using both may substantially increase research time, and the extra material obtained rarely justifies the additional time involved.

The two services are discussed individually below.

1. Standard Federal Tax Reporter

The discussion of this CCH looseleaf service follows the format in which it is arranged. Several volumes, such as the Citator, are discussed in greater detail elsewhere in this text; appropriate cross-references to those discussions appear here. A Taxes on Parade newsletter provides cross-references to SFTR.

The online Code and compilation volumes follow the same format and include the helpful tables described below. Illustrations of SFTR are taken from the online version, which is available on the CCH Tax Research NetWork. Additional illustrations of the CCH service appear in Chapters 6, 7, and 12. If you are using the online version, you do not need to know volume numbers. Online links help you navigate between materials.

a. Code Volumes. These volumes print, in Code section order, all provisions involving income, gift and estate, employment, and excise taxes as well as procedural provisions. A brief explanation of amendments since 1954 (including the Public Law number and section and effective dates) follows each Code provision. These explanations include information about prior statutory language. These volumes are updated

---

[222] The library may carry the looseleaf or online version.

at intervals following Code amendments.

Volume I's Source Notes and Finding Lists section covers a variety of useful legislative history information.[223] Tables I and II provide cross-references between the 1939 and 1954 Codes. Table III indicates sections of the 1986 Code that refer to other sections [Illustration 6-19]. Because the Code itself is not fully cross-referenced, this table is valuable for researching an unfamiliar area. Table III does have limitations. First, as shown in Illustration 6-19, it is not revised as frequently as statutes are enacted. Second, it does not include references in other titles of United States Code. Finally, because related Code sections may not refer to each other at all, it will not cover many "relationships." Fortunately, you can use the annotated materials discussed in this chapter to familiarize yourself with interrelated Code sections.

A Legislative History Locator Table lists the committee reports and dates for acts that affected the Code since 1954. This Table includes the act name and number, bill number, report numbers, and Cumulative Bulletin cite (if any). Another set of lists, which begins with 1971 legislation, covers Acts Supplementing the 1954 and the 1986 Codes. These lists provide the Public Law number, bill number, date, and Statutes at Large citation for each act; they include popular names for several acts. These lists are in Public Law number order. Each act is arranged in act section order; the list indicates every Code section affected by an act section.[224] These lists do not indicate how the particular Code sections were affected.

Volume I also includes a Public Laws Amending the Internal Revenue Code section. It lists Public Law number and Congress, popular name, and enactment date. These materials begin in mid-1954 and are in Public Law number order.

Volume I includes both a Topical Index and a Table of Contents listing all Code sections in order.

Volume II prints the text of non-Code statutory provisions affecting federal taxes in the Related Statutes section that begins in 1939. Volume II also includes subject matter and Code section lists of 1954-1966 amendments to the 1939 Code. The Code section list includes Public Law

---

[223] You should be aware that the Volume I listings are not as up to date as other parts of the service. In October-2006, some of the lists described here were current only through 2004 while others did reflect 2006 developments.

[224] Some libraries may have retained a special 1971 SFTR publication covering earlier acts.

number and Congress, act section, and SFTR paragraph number.

b. Index Volume and Compilation Volume 1. Both volumes provide useful tables and other reference material. Because it covers the annotations in addition to the Code, the topical index in the Index volume is far more detailed than the index in Code volume I. The Index volume also includes:

- Tax calendars
- IRS Service Center addresses
- Exemption and Standard Deduction Amounts
- Tax rates since 1909
- Withholding tables
- Depreciation tables—class life ADR; MACRS
- Annuity tables, including valuation for life estates and remainders
- Savings bond redemption tables
- Interest rate tables
  applicable federal rates since 1984
  uniform tables and procedures for compounding interest
  interest on overpayments/underpayments
- Low income housing credit rates and recapture information
- Per diem rates
- Checklists
  for completing tax returns
  income and deductions
  medical expenses—summary of rulings and cases
  real property tax dates by state
  tax elections
  information return filing
  disaster areas declared in current and preceding year
- Tax terms—explanatory definitions of commonly used jargon

Compilation volume 1 includes the following reference material:

- Tax planning by topic—e.g., impact of divorce; retirement
- Inflation adjustments for several years—by topic and Code section
- Return preparer information
- Who Is the Taxpayer?—discussion and annotations
- Constitutional and tax protest materials, including annotations

c. Compilation Volumes. Volumes 1-18 contain, in Code section order, the full text of the Code, proposed, temporary, and final regulations, and digest-annotations to revenue rulings and revenue procedures, letter rulings and other publicly available IRS documents, and judicial decisions. [Illustrations 13-2 through 13-6.] An alphabetical index is provided if the annotations section is lengthy. CCH provides an editorial explanation, including citations to the annotations, for each Code provision.

Immediately after each Code section, the editors indicate which Public Laws have amended it and print text of, or citations to, committee reports; a brief T.D. history also follows regulations sections. The pre-amendment text is omitted in the historical notes for both Code and regulations sections.

Regulations follow the Code section material. If a regulation does not reflect Code amendments, SFTR indicates that fact at the top of each regulations page. Because regulations are printed in Code section order, regulations from different parts of 26 C.F.R. (or even from other titles of C.F.R.) appear together. [See Illustration 13-1.] Because regulations from other C.F.R. titles follow their own prefix system, it is critical that your citation indicate Treas. Reg. (or 26 C.F.R.) for Treasury regulations and the other C.F.R. title for other regulations. See, e.g., 40 C.F.R. § 20.1, which appears in SFTR with Code section 169. If this were a Treasury regulation, the prefix 20 would indicate an estate tax regulation and the 1 following it would indicate Code section 1 (which covers income tax rates).

Illustration 13-1. SFTR Grouping of Regulations for Section 169

Pollution control facilities --Sec. 169— Select All ☐
☐   IRC, 2006FED ¶11,502, Sec. 169., AMORTIZATION OF POLLUTION CONTROL FACILITIES
☐   Legislative History [6]
☐   FINAL-REG, 2006FED ¶11,503, §1.169-1., Amortization of pollution control facilities
☐   FINAL-REG, 2006FED ¶11,504, §1.169-2., Definitions
☐   FINAL-REG, 2006FED ¶11,505, §1.169-3., Amortizable basis
☐   FINAL-REG, 2006FED ¶11,506, §1.169-4., Time and manner of making elections
☐   FINAL-REG, 2006FED ¶11,507, §20.1., Applicability. --
☐   FINAL-REG, 2006FED ¶11,508, §20.2., Definitions. --

→The regulations list does not indicate that §§20.1 and 20.2 are from 40 C.F.R. That information does appear if you click on each regulation's hyperlink.

The compilation volume covering taxation of foreign income also includes summaries of United States tax treaties.

Repealed tax provisions may be re-enacted in whole or part. Volume 18 includes annotations arising under expired laws, such as excess profits taxes. These will be useful for historical research as well as in the event of re-enactment.

Volume 18 also lists IRS and Tax Court forms (numerically and alphabetically), IRS publications (numerically), Treasury and IRS personnel, and IRS procedural rules.

Illustration 13-2. Excerpt from SFTR Compilation Online

Federal Tax - CCH Explanations and Analysis - Standard Federal Income Tax Reporter - Income --Secs. 61-90 -

Property exchanged for services --Sec. 83— Select All ☐

☐   IRC, 2006FED ¶6380, Sec. 83., PROPERTY TRANSFERRED IN CONNECTION WITH PERFORMANCE OF SERVICES

☐   Legislative History [5]

☐   FINAL-REG, 2006FED ¶6381, §1.83-1., Property transferred in connection with the performance of services

☐   FINAL-REG, 2006FED ¶6382, §1.83-2., Election to include in gross income in year of transfer

☐   FINAL-REG, 2006FED ¶6383, §1.83-3., Meaning and use of certain terms

☐   PROP-REG-AMNDT, 2006FED ¶6383F, §1.83-3., Meaning and use of certain terms, REG-105346-03, 5/24/2005.

☐   FINAL-REG, 2006FED ¶6384, §1.83-4., Special rules

☐   FINAL-REG, 2006FED ¶6385, §1.83-5., Restrictions that will never lapse

☐   FINAL-REG, 2006FED ¶6386, §1.83-6., Deduction by employer

☐   PROP-REG-AMNDT, 2006FED ¶6387, §1.83-6., Deduction by employer, REG-105346-03, 5/24/2005.

☐   FINAL-REG, 2006FED ¶6388, §1.83-7., Taxation of nonqualified stock options

☐   FINAL-REG, 2006FED ¶6389, §1.83-8., Applicability of section and transitional rules

☐   CCH-EXP, Restricted Property [20]

☐   CCH-ANNO, Restricted Property [28]

☐   Current Developments [13]

Illustration 13-3. Excerpt from SFTR Explanation

CCH-EXP, 2006FED ¶6390.01, Restricted Property: Synopsis - restricted property

Restricted Property: Synopsis - restricted property

Code Sec. 83 provides rules for the taxation of stock or other property that is transferred to an employee or independent contractor in connection with the performance of services and that is subject to restrictions that affect its value (see ¶6390.021 et seq.). The service provider is generally taxed on the fair market value of such property over any amount paid for it at the time of its receipt (see ¶6390.03 et seq.). However, a recipient whose interest in the property is subject to a substantial risk of forfeiture will not be taxed on the value of the property until the risk of forfeiture is removed. The restrictions on the property are not taken into account in determining its value except in cases where the restriction by its terms will never lapse (see ¶6390.04)

→Online looseleaf services provide hyperlinks to primary sources and to other documents.

Illustration 13-4. Excerpt from SFTR Annotation List Online

CCH-EXP, STANDARD FEDERAL TAX Annotations related to §83

FEDERAL INCOME TAX

Restricted Property

Advance rulings. -- ... 2006FED ¶6390.11

Constitutionality. -- ... 2006FED ¶6390.13

Effective date. -- ... 2006FED ¶6390.22

Performance of services. -- ... 2006FED ¶6390.25

Restrictions. -- ... 2006FED ¶6390.30

→Each annotation has a link to its compilation paragraph.

Illustration 13-5. Excerpt from SFTR Annotation Online

CCH-ANNO, 2006FED ¶6390.11 Restricted Property: Advance rulings

Restricted Property: Advance rulings

The IRS will not issue determination letters or rulings with respect to whether a restriction constitutes a substantial risk of forfeiture if the employee is a controlling shareholder or whether a transfer has occurred if the amount paid for the property involves a nonrecourse obligation. In addition, determination letters or rulings will not be issued as to which corporation is entitled to a deduction under Code Sec. 83(h) in cases where a corporation undergoes a corporate division if the facts are not similar to those described in Rev. Rul. 2002-1, 2002-1 CB 268. Rulings or determination letters will not ordinarily be issued with respect to when compensation is realized by a person who, in connection with the performance of services, is granted a nonstatutory option without a readily ascertainable fair market value to purchase stock at a price that is less than the fair market value of the stock on the date the option is granted. The procedure is effective January 3, 2006.

Rev. Proc. 2006-3, I.R.B. 2006-1, 122

→The online version provides hyperlinks to the Code sections, to the original SFTR paragraphs, and to any Current Developments. If we were using the print version, we would have gone to the New Matters volume and looked for updating material for ¶6390.11.

d. New Matters Volume. The compilation volumes' annotations receive little updating during the year involved. Instead, recent material is indexed in the New Matters volume (volume 19). Because the Cumulative Index (including a Latest Additions supplement) is based on the paragraph numbers used in the compilation volumes, it is easy to use the New Matters volume to find recent developments. [Illustrations 13-2 and 13-3.]

SFTR reproduces updating material as follows:

• New Matters volume—texts of revenue rulings and procedures; digests of Tax Court Regular and Memorandum Opinions

• U.S.T.C. Advance Sheets volume—texts of decisions rendered by all other courts

• Compilation volumes—Code and regulations.

The New Matters volume has several other helpful features. In addition to a Topical Index of current year developments, there are sections devoted to highlights of important new developments (CCH Comments and CCH Tax Focus and Features). These items, which are covered in the Topical Index, also contain cross-references to the compilation volumes.

The New Matters volume digests a limited number of publicly available IRS documents. It also includes preambles for current year Treasury Decisions and indicates where final and temporary regulations appear in the SFTR service.

A Case Table (including a supplement for Latest Additions) lists each year's decisions alphabetically. It indicates (1) which trial court is involved and where the decision appears in the U.S.T.C. Advance Sheets or SFTR New Matters volumes;[225] (2) appeals by either side and IRS acquiescence or nonacquiescence in unfavorable decisions; and (3) outcome at the appellate level.

A Supreme Court Docket, which also lists cases alphabetically, includes a brief digest of the issues involved and their disposition. This table includes cases in which the Court denies certiorari.

A Finding List of Rulings cross-references current year IRS documents to the appropriate paragraphs in volume 19. Consult this list in addition to the Finding Lists in the SFTR Citator when checking the status of IRS items.

e. U.S. Tax Cases (U.S.T.C.) Advance Sheets Volume. This volume contains the preambles to proposed income tax regulations. Lists of

---

[225] It does not indicate the state for District Court and lists only decisions covered in SFTR. Bankruptcy Court cases are listed as BC-DC (Bankruptcy Court-District Court).

proposed income tax regulations appear in both topical and Code section formats; the topical format is arranged chronologically rather than alphabetically.

This volume also contains the texts of income tax decisions rendered by courts other than the Tax Court.[226] You can locate these items using the Cumulative Index in the New Matters volume. Decisions appear in the order in which they are received rather than in Code section order. These decisions will later be issued in hardbound volumes as part of the U.S.T.C. reporter service discussed in Chapter 11.

f. Citator.[227] You can use these volumes, which list decisions alphabetically, to determine if subsequent decisions have affected earlier items. The Citator also covers revenue rulings, revenue procedures, other IRS items, and Treasury Decisions. The Citator provides cross-references to discussions of cases and rulings in the compilation volumes. The Citator is discussed in Chapter 12.

The final item in the second volume is a list of Cumulative Bulletin citations to committee reports for sections amending the 1986 Code. These materials are in Code section order. Because Cumulative Bulletins covering legislation are produced relatively slowly, these lists are unlikely to reflect recent legislation.

Illustration 13-6. Current Developments for ¶ 6390.11

Related Information
2 documents.

---

1. REV-PROC, 2006FED ¶46,476. Restricted property transfers; Compensation; Election: Consent to revoke. –, Rev. Proc, 2006-31 (June 13, 2006) – [IRC]
   Rev. Proc. 2006-31, I.R.B. 2006-27, June 13, 2006.
   [Code Sec. 83

2. REV-PROC, 2006FED ¶46,238. Internal Revenue Service: Advanced rulings; Areas of nonissuance. –, Rev. Proc, 2006-3 (January 3, 2006) – [IRC]
   Rev. Proc. 2006-3, I.R.B. 2006-1, 122, January

→As of mid-November 2006, two additional revenue procedures had been issued.

---

[226] Preambles and recent court decisions involving estate and gift taxes or excise taxes appear in the CCH services covering those topics. Court decisions involving all taxes appear in the U.S.T.C. hardbound volumes.

[227] The Citator is discussed in more detail in Chapter 12.

2. United States Tax Reporter—Income Taxes

Prentice-Hall revamped its Federal Taxes service in 1990, improving the layout to make the materials easier to locate and read. Research Institute of America continued the new format when it acquired and renamed this service.

The discussion of USTR follows the format in which it is arranged. Several of its volumes, and the RIA Citator, are discussed in greater detail elsewhere in this text; this section includes appropriate cross-references to those discussions. Illustrations of USTR are taken from the online version, which is available on RIA Checkpoint. An additional illustration of the RIA service appears in Chapters 4. If you are using the online version, you do not need to know volume numbers. Online links help you navigate between materials.

a. Code Volumes. The two Code volumes print, in Code section order, all provisions involving income, gift and estate, employment, and excise taxes as well as procedural provisions.[228] Historical information follows Code provisions that have been amended. Historical material includes the Public Law number, the Public Law section number, and the effective date of any amendments. Prior statutory language is provided for several sections; this material can also be obtained from Cumulative Changes, discussed in Chapter 17.

Volume I contains a Topic Index to the Code [Illustration 4-1] and a listing of all Code sections. Volume I also contains an Amending Acts section. This section includes Public Law number, date, act title or subject, and Cumulative Bulletin or Statutes at Large citation for acts since 1954. This section is not separately indexed and does not list the Code sections amended.

b. Index Volume. Volume 1 contains an extensive index (main and supplementary sections), using paragraph numbers, to the material in the compilation volumes discussed below. This index uses different typefaces to denote Code section numbers and locations, location of topical discussions, and location of regulations text. Volume 1 also includes a Glossary, which provides succinct definitions of terms (both words and phrases) used by tax practitioners.

c. Tables Volume. Volume 2 contains main, supplementary, and current Tables of Cases and main and supplementary Tables of Rulings. These tables cross-reference cases and rulings to the appropriate discussions in the compilation volumes or in the Weekly Alert newslet-

---

[228] Repealed Code sections are included in the Code and compilation volumes.

ter.[229] RIA provides case citations to several different reporter services in addition to A.F.T.R. Special notations indicate paragraph numbers for decisions printed in RIA's Tax Court Memorandum Decisions service. A Supreme Court docket listing indicates petitions filed and granted.

The case tables are not citator supplements. The main table merely lists cases discussed in USTR. The supplementary and current tables indicate appeals action and IRS acquiescences for cases previously reported in the main table. The rulings tables, which cover both Internal Revenue Bulletin and other documents, do indicate prior or subsequent IRS action; they do not indicate judicial action.

d. Compilation Volumes. Volumes 3-15A contain, in Code section order, the full text of the Code; final, temporary and proposed regulations; and digest-annotations to revenue rulings, letter rulings and other IRS releases, and judicial decisions. Texts of committee reports (or Cumulative Bulletin citations) are also included. Paragraph numbers assigned to these materials correspond to the Code section involved.

Italicized material indicates changes in Code sections. If a regulation has not been updated to reflect a Code amendment, that information appears at the beginning of the regulation. There is an extensive editorial explanation, and citations to the annotations, for each Code provision.

e. Recent Developments Volume. The Recent Developments Volume (volume 16) contains a Cross Reference Table that cross-references from USTR paragraphs to updating material. Use this table to determine if a recent ruling or decision has been issued in any area of interest.

USTR reproduces the updating material in the Recent Developments volume (IRS rulings and procedures), in the A.F.T.R.2d Decisions Advance Sheets volume (texts of decisions rendered by courts other than the Tax Court), or in the Weekly Alert newsletter (digests of Tax Court decisions).

The Recent Developments volume provides Public Law number, title or subject, and introduction and signing dates for acts since 1987.

f. A.F.T.R.2d Decisions Advance Sheets Volume. Volumes 17 and 17A contain the texts of recent income tax decisions from all courts except the Tax Court.[230] You can locate these items by Code section using the

---

[229] The Weekly Alert provides cross-references to both Federal Tax Coordinator and United States Tax Reporter.

[230] Recent court decisions involving estate and gift taxes or excise taxes appear

Cross Reference Tables in the Recent Developments volume. Decisions appear in the order they were received rather than in Code section order. Decisions printed in this volume will later be issued in hardbound volumes as part of the A.F.T.R. reporter service discussed in Chapter 11.

g. Federal Tax Regulations Volume. Volume 18 prints the preambles to proposed regulations. Coverage is chronological. A Finding List is in Code section order. Regulations whose numbers do not correspond to a Code section appear before traditionally numbered regulations. This list indicates Federal Register publication date.

h. Citator. The RIA Citator is not part of USTR and does not cross-reference to it. You can use this citator with any looseleaf service to determine the status of both judicial decisions and IRS items. A full discussion of the RIA Citator appears in Chapter 12.

Illustration 13-7. Excerpt from USTR Compilation Online

Checkpoint Contents
 Federal Library
  Federal Editorial Materials
   United States Tax Reporter
    Income (USTR)
     Computation of Taxable Income §§61-291
      Items Specifically Included in Gross Income §§71-90
       ☐ Currently in: **§83 Property transferred in connection with performance of services**

☐ ◈ **§83 Property transferred in connection with performance of services.**
 ✚ ☐ **Committee Reports for Code Sec. 83**
 ✚ ☐ **Regulations for Code Sec. 83**
 ✚ ☐ **Explanations for Code Sec. 83**
 ✚ ☐ **Advance Annotations for Code Sec. 83**
 ✚ ☐ **Annotations for Code Sec. 83**

Illustration 13-8. Excerpt from USTR Explanation

▶ Annot | ▶ IRC | ▶ Regs | ▶ Com Rpts | ▶ Hist | ▶ AdvAnnot | ♁ Compare It

EXP ¶834 Restricted property.

An employer may choose to compensate an employee for his services by giving him stock or other property that is subject to restrictions, such as restrictions on sale or a requirement that the property be returned if the employee leaves his job. An employee who receives restricted property as compensation must report it as income in the year of receipt, *unless* the property is substantially nonvested. Code Sec. 83(a) .

⚓ CAUTION: Code Sec. 83 rules apply to all transfers in connection with the performance of services. Thus, transfers to independent contractors, such as attorneys, are also included.

in the RIA services covering these topics. Court decisions for all taxes appear in the A.F.T.R. hardbound volumes.

Illustration 13-9. Excerpt from USTR Annotation List Online

📄 <u>ANN ¶615.030(5) Contract to buy stock.</u>

📄 <u>ANN ¶615.031(75) Split-dollar insurance.</u>

📄 <u>ANN ¶835.01(1) Constitutionality.</u>

📄 <u>ANN ¶835.01(5) Advance rulings.</u>

📄 <u>ANN ¶835.01(10) Employer's educational benefit trust.</u>

📄 <u>ANN ¶835.01(15) Independent contractors.</u>

📄 <u>ANN ¶835.01(20) Waiver of transfer restrictions.</u>

📄 <u>ANN ¶835.01(40) Transfers by shareholders.</u>

📄 <u>ANN ¶835.01(50) Treatment on return.</u>

📄 <u>ANN ¶835.01(55) Nonexempt trusts.</u>

📄 <u>ANN ¶835.01(60) Stock options.</u>

Illustration 13-10. Excerpt from USTR Annotation Online

▶ Expl ▶ IRC ▶ Regs ▶ Com Rpts ▶ Hist ▶ AdvAnnot

Ann ¶ 835.01(60). Stock options.

Additional tax on corporate officer's exercise of stock option imposed. FMV was value when stock was sold without regard to section 16(b), SEC Act of 1934, requiring realized profits from sale of corporate stock exercised within 6 months of option to be recoverable by corp.

Edward J. Phillippe (1982) <u>TC Memo 1982-30</u> , *PH TCM ¶82,030* .

Taxpayer didn't have income from option to purchase stock because sellback provision subjected stock to substantial risk of forfeiture. Tax Court's finding that stock was transferable before sellback provision lapsed was error. Sellback provision required taxpayer to sell shares back to corp. at original cost if he wanted to sell them in less than one year from day he exercised option.

Robinson, et al. v Comm. (1986, CA1) <u>58 AFTR 2d 86-6181</u> , *805 F2d 38* , *86-2 USTC ¶9790* , *rev'g (1984)* <u>82 TC 444</u> , *Related proceedings: (1984)* <u>82 TC 467</u> .

→Click the AdvAnnot tab (indicated by an arrow) to reach the most current items for this annotation.

Illustration 13-11. Excerpt from USTR AdvAnnot Online

Ann ¶ 835.01(60). Stock options.

IRS properly determined that engineer/MBA/Chilean immigrant misreported income from same-day exercise and sale of employer-provided stock options: taxpayer's argument that options qualified for capital treatment as ISOs was belied by evidence, including computation worksheets, Forms W-2, and fact that employer made withholdings, all of which indicated options were NQSOs rather than ISOs. And in any event, taxpayer's same-day exercise and sale precluded ISO treatment since same-day transaction violated Code Sec. 422 's 1-year holding period requirement. Taxpayer's reading of statute and reliance on Publication 525 as providing alternative holding period choices was erroneous.

Jorge O. Svoboda, Et Ux., (2006) *TC Memo 2006-235 , RIA TC Memo ¶2006-235 .*

Former employee/sales assistant was denied CDP-related claims to recalculate AMTI and invalidate his Code Sec. 83(b) election to recognize income on ISO exercise of nonvested stock that was subject to substantial risk of forfeiture. Operative documents clearly showed that transfer and taxpayer's acquisition of beneficial interest in nonvested stock occurred for Reg § 1.83-3(a)(1) purposes on exercise, when taxpayer gained stockholder rights and entitlement to all regular dividends. Also, mere existence of employment termination-related condition/lapse restriction didn't change result since that restriction was only lapse and condition wasn't *certain* to occur. So, because stock transfer and taxpayer's ensuing Code Sec. 83(b) election were legally valid, he was obligated to recognize AMTI to extent shares' exercise-date FMV exceeded option price.

Anthony J. Kadillak, (2006) *127 TC No. 13 .*

Section B. Subject Arrangement: Multiple Topics

The second group of materials is quite varied; many libraries lack at least one of them or carry others not discussed here. Each covers a wide range of topics using a subject matter arrangement.

If you use several services, you will get quicker access to relevant items in the second (or later) service by using tables for cases and other primary sources. Once you have obtained these items from one service, you can use them to locate relevant discussion in the other service. If the second service lacks these tables,[231] you can enter it from its topical or Code section index.

1. Federal Tax Coordinator 2d

This weekly service contains excellent discussions of all areas of taxation, with minimal coverage of employment taxes. Federal Tax Coordinator identifies most items by paragraph number. It identifies the text of Code, regulations, and treaties by page number. The Weekly Alert newsletter provides cross-references to both Federal Tax Coordinator and United States Tax Reporter.

Material in each volume is discussed in the following paragraphs.

---

[231] For example, Tax Management Portfolios lack case and rulings tables. They have excellent Code and topical indexes.

a. Topic–Index Volume. This volume contains an extensive Topic Index, which you can use to locate appropriate discussion in the text volumes. There are main and current sections.

b. Finding Tables Volumes. Volume 1 includes several Finding Tables that indicate where items are discussed in the text volumes. These tables cover the Internal Revenue Code, Public Laws since 1991, other United States Code titles, temporary and final regulations, Treasury Decisions for the past six months, Labor regulations, and proposed regulations. There is also a table of Code sections that is not tied to discussion in the service.

Volume 1 also includes a Law-Regulations Table. It provides a list of Code sections for which the regulations do not reflect the most recent Code amendment. This table is in Code section order and includes the relevant acts amending that Code section.

Volume 2 contains a Rulings and Releases Table giving cross-references to discussions in the text volumes. The table arranges each type of IRS document chronologically. Letter rulings are included.

Volume 2 also includes an alphabetical list of cases with cross-references to discussions in the text volumes. This list includes citations to various case reporter services, often including both A.F.T.R. and U.S.T.C. in addition to reporters such as Federal Reporter.

A Supreme Court Docket and a Court of Appeals Docket indicate where discussion of pending cases appears in the text volumes. The Supreme Court materials classify cases as recently decided, petition granted, petition denied, and petition filed.

c. Practice Aids Volume. Volume 3 includes sample letters to clients on a wide variety of topics. [See Illustration 15-2.] It also includes planning checklists, tax tables, a tax calendar, interest and annuity tables, and tables showing where tax return forms are discussed in the text. Other reference items, such as applicable federal rates and per diem amounts, appear in the text volumes. A Current Legislation Table lists acts since 1993 by Public Law number, subject, committee reports, and relevant dates.

d. Text Volumes. The text volumes (4-26, including some additional volumes such as 10A and 14A) are arranged by chapters using a subject matter approach. Discussions in each chapter include liberal use of citations and analysis of as yet unresolved matters.

Each chapter has the following arrangement: a Detailed Reference Table for topics included; cross-references to topics of potential relevance discussed in other chapters; discussion of each topic, including extensive footnote references; and text of Code and regulations sections applicable to the chapters being discussed. Chapters are subdivided into topics, and then into paragraphs. [See Illustration 13-12.]

Volume 20 contains the texts of United States income, estate, and gift tax treaties and textual material dealing with the treaties. United States and OECD model treaties are also included. Although this service prints only treaties currently in effect, it does include a list of treaties awaiting ratification or exchange of instruments of ratification.

Illustration 13-12. Excerpt from Federal Tax Coordinator Text

¶H-2500 Introduction—Property Received in Connection with the Performance of Services.

An employee or independent contractor is taxable on property received "in connection with the performance of services" when the property is substantially vested, that is, when the property is either not subject to a substantial risk of forfeiture, or is transferable to a third party free of this risk. The service provider who receives transferred property may instead elect to include the income from the transfer in gross income for the year in which the property is received, i.e., before the property becomes substantially vested. If property received in a transfer is disposed of before it becomes substantially vested, income is realized with the disposition.

The rules that apply to the transfer of property "in connection with the performance of services" (under Code Sec. 83) apply even if property is transferred other than as *compensation* for the services provided, see ¶H-2503.

> **RIA observation:** A disadvantage of using restricted stock or other property as compensation (without sufficient other compensation) is that it can put an employee or independent contractor in an economic bind by requiring the payment of tax on a substantial amount of compensation income without permitting the recipient to effectively obtain funds from the stock or other property with which to pay the tax.

→Federal Tax Coordinator uses paragraphs for most cross-references.

→The online version provides hyperlinks to other paragraphs and to the relevant primary source material. Full text is provided for judicial decisions in the online version. The print version does not include the text of decisions.

e. Proposed Regulations. Volumes 27 and 27A contain proposed regulations reproduced in the order in which they were issued, along with preambles and Federal Register citations. A cross-reference table lists the proposed regulations in Code section order. Proposed regulations issued as temporary regulations are reproduced in the Text Volumes instead of the Proposed Regulations Volumes.

f. Internal Revenue Bulletin. Volume 28 contains reprints of the weekly Internal Revenue Bulletin. Because the material in volume 28 is not indexed by Code section or by subject matter anywhere in this service, it will be difficult to locate a particular item without an Internal Revenue Bulletin citation.

2. Tax Management Portfolios

BNA issues three series of Tax Management Portfolios: U.S. Income; Foreign Income;[232] and Estates, Gifts, and Trusts. Each series is subdivided into several softbound volumes that cover narrow areas of tax law in great depth.[233] Each Portfolio refers to other Portfolios containing information relevant to a particular problem.

In addition to a Table of Contents, each Portfolio includes a Detailed Analysis section (Section A) with extensive footnoting. A Worksheets section (Section B) includes checklists, forms that can be used as models in drafting documents, and texts of relevant congressional and IRS materials. A Bibliography section (Section C) includes citations to regulations, legislative history, court decisions, and rulings. Books and articles are listed by year of publication.

BNA supplements the Portfolios with Changes & Analysis sheets, or completely revises them, whenever warranted by new developments.

The looseleaf Portfolio Index includes a detailed Master Subject Index for each series. [Illustration 13-13.] A Master Code Section Index covers all series; it indicates the main Portfolio on point with an asterisk (*).

Illustration 13-13. Topic from U.S. Income Master Subject Index

AT-RISK RULES—contd.
Consolidated returns, 756:A-71
Contingent liabilities, 550:A-27
Corporations, 700:A-83, A-84
Credits against taxes, 506:A-22, A-204(2) et
seq.; 550:A-47; 583: A-53; 584:A-75 et seq.
Debt vs. Equity, 550:A-25
Effect of, 504:A-31; 550:A-5
Energy property, 550:A-48
Equipment leasing, 550:A-13, A-18
Estates, 550:A-11
Exceptions, 504:A-32, C&A:A-33; 550:A-14

→Note the reference to Changes & Additions (C&A) in Portfolio 504.

---

[232] See also Chapter 8.

[233] Subdivisions are so narrow that several portfolios may cover one Code section.

Changes will be integrated into Section A when the Portfolio is revised.

Numerical IRS Forms and IRS Publications Finding Tables are cross-referenced to appropriate Portfolios.

The Tax Management Memorandum, a biweekly analysis of current developments, unsettled problems, and other significant items, includes cross-references to discussions in the Portfolios. Tax Management Weekly Report (Chapter 15) includes updating material before it is added to the Portfolios. The Weekly Report also includes Code section indexes.

3. Mertens, Law of Federal Income Taxation

The original Mertens service contained five sets of volumes: treatise; rulings; Code; Code commentary; and regulations. Only the treatise and rulings materials have continued in their original format. Many libraries retain the original materials, which may still be useful for historical research.

a. Treatise. The treatise volumes closely resemble general encyclopedias such as Am. Jur. 2d and C.J.S. in format.[234] Material is presented by subject matter with extensive footnoting. Treatise materials are supplemented monthly; supplements are cumulated semiannually. Supplemental material appears at the beginning of each volume rather than at the beginning of each chapter. Tables and indexes are updated quarterly.

Discussions include extensive historical background information. Because its discussions are so thorough, Mertens is frequently cited in judicial decisions.[235] However, that very thoroughness can be a drawback; using the treatise materials for background knowledge can be very time-consuming.

The **Tables Volume** contains tables indicating where primary source materials are discussed in the treatise volumes. These include the Internal Revenue Code, other United States Code titles, Treasury regulations, other Code of Federal Regulations titles, and IRS materials. IRS materials covered include items printed in the Cumulative Bulletin,

---

[234] These encyclopedias cover a wide variety of topics. Discussions of taxation appear in separate volumes within each service and are thus quite accessible. A tax-oriented looseleaf service or treatise will probably provide more extensive information.

[235] See, e.g., Speltz v. Commissioner, 124 T.C. 165, 178 (2005).

letter rulings, technical advice memoranda, general counsel memoranda, and field service advice. Two other tables provide Cumulative Bulletin citations for revenue rulings and revenue procedures.   There are similar cross-references for judicial decisions in the **Table of Cases Volume.**

The **Index Volume** contains a detailed subject matter index. The monthly Developments & Highlights newsletter in the **Current Materials Volume** includes lists of recent tax articles.

b. Rulings. The Rulings volumes contain the texts of revenue rulings and procedures. Notices, announcements, and other IRS items are excluded. Each volume covers a particular time period and includes rulings in numerical order, followed by procedures in numerical order. Mertens adds current items monthly.

The looseleaf current volume has Code–Rulings and Code–Procedures Tables, which provide chronological listings of every revenue ruling or procedure involving income tax Code sections or subsections.[236] [See Illustration 4-5.] There are separate tables for the current year and for prior years (beginning with 1954).

A Rulings Status Table lists the most recent revenue ruling or procedure affecting the validity of a previously published item. Mertens indicates the effect on the earlier item (e.g., modified, revoked). A separate section of this volume includes Cumulative Bulletin citations for revenue rulings and procedures.

c. Code. Each Code volume contained all income tax provisions enacted or amended during a particular time period (one or more years). Textual notations (diamond shapes and brackets) indicate additions and deletions. A historical note indicates Act, section, and effective date and can be used to reconstruct the prior language. The subject matter index in the looseleaf current volume cross-references each topic to applicable Code sections. This material does not cover the 1986 Code.[237]

d. Code Commentary. Looseleaf volumes of Code Commentary initially provided useful short explanations of statutory provisions as well as cross-references to the discussions in the treatise materials. More recent items are limited to references to statutory changes or to recent cases or rulings for the particular Code section.

---

[236] Although this is an income tax service, these tables do cover estate and gift tax rulings. However, that coverage does not extend back to 1954.

[237] Mertens currently publishes softbound Code volumes, but they are not cross-referenced to the Law of Federal Income Taxation service.

e. Regulations. Regulations materials have undergone change since the mid-1990s. In a separate service, but using the Mertens name, the publisher currently issues a softbound set of regulations in force (volumes 1 through 6) and proposed regulations (volume 7). Regulations appear in Code section order; there is also a subject matter index. New matter issued during the year is filed in a looseleaf Current Developments and Status Table binder. The service also includes looseleaf volumes containing the preambles issued since 1985 to proposed, temporary, and final regulations.

The volumes in the discontinued regulations service included the texts of all income tax regulations issued or amended during a particular time period (two or more years). Publication was in Code section order.

The discontinued volumes have several useful features. Textual notations (diamond shapes and brackets) indicate deletions, additions, and other changes in amended regulations. A historical note, from which you can determine the regulation's prior wording, follows. This facilitates research into early administrative interpretations. Each volume also contains a section reproducing the preamble to the Treasury Decision or Notice of Proposed Rulemaking announcing each proposed and final regulation.

4. Rabkin & Johnson, Federal Income, Gift and Estate Taxation

This service originally had three segments: treatise; Code and Congressional Reports; and Regulations. Only the treatise materials are currently being updated. Supplementation is monthly, with New Matter pages appearing near the beginning of each volume rather than at the beginning of each chapter.

a. Treatise. The treatise materials consist of explanatory materials and two volumes of reference material designed to facilitate research in the remainder of the set. It is arranged in chapters; each chapter is divided into sections that use chapter numbers in their prefixes. Cross-referencing is done by section number.

The first two volumes (1 and 1A) contain tables and other user aids. Volume 1 includes the following indexes and tables, which cross-reference to discussions in the treatise volumes: topical Index; Table of Statutory References (Internal Revenue Code and other parts of United States Code); Table of Cases; and Table of Regulations, Rulings and Releases (publicly available IRS materials in addition to revenue rulings). The Table of Cases indicates discussion in both text and footnotes.

Volume 1A includes a detailed User's Guide to using Rabkin & Johnson. This volume also contains tax calendars and checklists of deductions (arranged by the tax form involved). Tax forms are listed numerically; IRS publications are listed alphabetically. In addition to rates, the Tax Rates section includes imputed interest rates, annuity valuation tables, depreciation tables, and similar helpful tables. Tax Court and IRS Practice Rules also appear in this volume.

Volumes 2 through 5 contain textual discussion of the law. Because this treatise is not arranged in Code section order, it integrates discussions of various aspects of a problem in each section.

While discussions are thorough, they do not purport to cover all types of authority. Letter rulings are rarely discussed or cited as authority "[b]ecause they lack precedential value."[238]

b. Code and Congressional Reports. Volumes 6 through 7B contain the text of the Code in Code section order.[239] You can use the Legislative History notes following each Code subsection to determine how amendments changed prior statutory language. These notes indicate the act, section, and date for amendments, but they do not provide a citation to Statutes at Large.

The legislative history notes refer to congressional committee reports explaining each provision. Relevant excerpts from these reports, including full citations, appear at the end of each Code section. These materials cover only the 1954 Code.

Volume 6 contains a topical index to the Code materials. Volume 7B (Appendix) includes tables cross-referencing 1939 and 1954 Code sections. Because these tables were printed in 1963, they miss section number changes that occurred after 1963. There are no cross-reference tables for the 1986 Code.

c. Regulations. Volumes 8 through 12 include the text of 1954 Code regulations. Regulations are printed in numerical order and are preceded by T.D. numbers and dates for the original version and amendments.[240]

---

[238] 1A RABKIN & JOHNSON, FEDERAL INCOME, GIFT AND ESTATE TAXATION § G 1.03[6], at G-11.

[239] This service omits miscellaneous excise taxes other than those involving registration required obligations, public charities, private foundations, qualified pension plans, real estate investment trusts, and the crude oil windfall profit tax.

[240] Federal Register dates are instead given for IRS procedural rules. These

There is no list of regulations in T.D. number order. Regulations sections are cross- referenced to subject matter discussions in the treatise volumes.

Volume 12A printed selected proposed regulations in numerical order. That volume's Table of Contents contains a numerical list of included provisions. Both the Table of Contents and the heading for each proposed regulation indicate the Federal Register date and a cross-reference to treatise discussion. The volumes do not include preambles.

Table 13-1. Cross-Referencing in Print Looseleaf Services

Service	Method	Location of Updates
SFTR	¶	New Matters; USTC Adv. Sheets
USTR	¶	Compilations; Recent Dev.; AFTR Adv. Sheets; Weekly Alert
Fed. Tax Coordinator	¶	Inserted in chapter
Tax Mgt Portfolios	Page	Beginning of Portfolio; Weekly Report
Mertens	§	Beginning of volume
Rabkin & Johnson	§	Beginning of volume

SECTION C. SUBJECT ARRANGEMENT: LIMITED SCOPE

Various publishers issue textual materials discussing a limited number of Code sections, such as those covering S corporations.[241] These texts are extremely useful for research involving very complex areas of tax law. In recent years the number of texts covering a particular topic, and the number of topics covered, have both grown explosively. You can locate at least one text on almost any topic, from tax problems of the elderly to estate planning for farmers. While these materials are periodically supplemented, their updating is rarely as frequent as that for the services in sections A and B.

The following materials are a representative sample.

• Bittker & Eustice, Federal Income Taxation of Corporations and Shareholders

• Casner & Pennell, Estate Planning

• Fried, Taxation of Securities Transactions

---

materials do not include the text of a regulation's prior versions.

[241] Form books (Chapter 17) may also include extensive textual material.

• Hardesty, Electronic Commerce: Taxation & Planning

• McKee, Nelson & Whitmire, Federal Taxation of Partnerships and Partners

• Schneider, Federal Income Taxation of Inventories

Other potential sources include law school casebooks or textbooks, which may include copious notes. CLE providers such as Practicing Law Institute regularly publish softbound volumes of course materials. Finally, the multivolume Bittker & Lokken, Federal Taxation of Income, Estates and Gifts, provides thorough treatment of difficult issues.

SECTION D. PROBLEMS

1. Using SFTR, locate the paragraph reference in the compilation volumes assigned by your instructor. Then use the New Matters updating materials to find all updating references to the original item. Provide a citation to each new item that includes its location in SFTR and its "official" location (e.g., I.R.B. for a revenue ruling). Your instructor may ask you to use the print SFTR, the online version, or both.

2. Repeat problem 1 using USTR and its Recent Developments feature.

3. Indicate the Tax Management Portfolios concerned with the Code section listed below. Your instructor will tell you whether to indicate the Portfolio titles, numbers, or authors.

a. 25A

b. 72(q)

c. 189

d. 458

e. 864(b)

f. 1504(b)

4. Indicate who authored

a. Tax Management Portfolio: Golden Parachutes

b. Tax Management Portfolio: Partnerships—Conceptual Overview

c. Mertens chapter: Suits for Refund

d. Mertens chapter: Information Returns

5. Indicate if there a Tax Management Portfolio covering

a. Brazil

b. Costa Rica

c. Cuba

d. European Union

Chapter 14. Legal Periodicals and Nongovernmental Reports

Section A. Introduction

This chapter provides information about periodical literature. It covers various methods for locating citations to articles and the articles themselves. It also discusses determining if a judicial opinion has cited an article or if an article has cited a judicial opinion or other authority.

Although periodical literature is a secondary source, and articles cannot be used as authority for avoiding the substantial understatement penalty, they are still important research tools. Because articles often appear more quickly than do treatise supplements, they are valuable tools for learning about new or amended Code sections, regulations, and judicial decisions. In addition, articles may provide citations to primary source materials that you can use as authority.

This chapter also provides information about reports issued by nongovernmental organizations. These include professional groups and think tanks. Reports issued by these groups (or testimony by their representatives at congressional or Treasury Department hearings) may affect legislation or regulations.

Section B. Categorizing Periodicals

Commentary on particular tax problems appears in various legal periodicals. These include general focus, student-edited law reviews, publications that focus on a broad variety of tax-related topics, and publications that specialize in a particular area of taxation.

Although general focus, student-edited law reviews occasionally include tax articles, other sources generally carry a larger number of relevant items.[242] These other sources include law school-based law reviews (student- or faculty-edited[243]) that focus on taxation, tax-oriented

---

[242] See William J. Turnier, *Tax (and Lots of Other) Scholars Need Not Apply: The Changing Venue for Scholarship*, 50 J. LEGAL EDUC. 189 (2000).

[243] Faculty-edited publications may have student editors, who edit work that was by faculty reviewers.

periodicals published by professional groups or commercial entities, and tax-oriented newsletters. Although not technically periodicals, tax institute proceedings contain useful information and can be accessed using several periodical indexes.

Table 14-1. Representative Periodical Titles

Category	Title
Student-edited	Akron Tax Journal
Student-edited	Houston Business & Tax Law Journal
Student-edited	Virginia Tax Review
Faculty-reviewed	Florida Tax Review
Faculty-reviewed	Tax Law Review
Faculty-reviewed	The Tax Lawyer
General tax focus	Journal of Taxation
General tax focus	TAXES–The Tax Magazine
Specialized focus	Real Estate Taxation
Newsletter	Tax Notes
Institute	Heckerling Institute on Estate Planning
Institute	NYU Institute on Federal Taxation

SECTION C. CITATIONS TO PERIODICALS

Your search for relevant publications may begin in a variety of sources. For example, looseleaf services such as Tax Management Portfolios include lists of articles. Citators may also provide citations to articles. Other publications digest articles. These digests may cover a particular topic or a general range of topics; they generally cover fewer articles than do the other tools.

Although the materials mentioned in the preceding paragraph are useful, periodical indexes are the most comprehensive sources for compiling lists of articles. This section divides indexes into three categories—general legal indexes, specialized indexes, and other indexes.

General legal periodical indexes such as Index to Legal Periodicals and Current Law Index cover all areas of law. Two specialized indexes, Federal Tax Articles and Index to Federal Tax Articles, cover only tax-related materials. The third category of indexes covers areas related to law, such as political science, economics, and history and nontax specialized legal topics (such as indexes to articles published in other countries).

The tax-oriented and general indexes differ in their indexing methods, publication frequency, and lists of publications covered. All are available in print versions; the general indexes are also available in electronic formats. Law-related indexes are available in a variety of formats.

This chapter concludes with illustrations of a search for articles in several of the sources discussed in this chapter. Those illustrations cover electronic searches for articles written by Professor Christopher Pietruszkiewicz. I conducted each search on November 3, 2006. I searched in Legal Resource Index (LRI) and Index to Legal Periodicals (ILP) on both Westlaw and on LexisNexis and then expanded my Westlaw and LexisNexis search to their law reviews and journals databases. I also searched in WilsonWeb, HeinOnline, SSRN, Google Scholar, and the author's own web page. As the illustrations indicate, the results were by no means identical.

Publications discussed below are categorized by type—indexes, looseleaf services, citators, miscellaneous, and digests.

1. General Legal Periodicals Indexes

The discussion of general legal periodicals indexes begins with a discussion of Current Law Index, Index to Legal Periodicals (and WilsonWeb), and HeinOnline. Illustrations used in this chapter indicate the risks involved in relying on a single source in compiling a bibliography. Searches in eight electronic databases yielded varying results.

a. Current Law Index; Legal Resource Index; LegalTrac

Current Law Index (CLI) indexes articles by subject, author/title, case name, and statute. Its Table of Statutes includes a heading for Internal Revenue Code. Because that section lists articles in Code section order, CLI is the most convenient print-based general index for researching articles by Code section.

CLI covers more publications than does Index to Legal Periodicals. It includes several tax-oriented publications, including Tax Notes. It began publication in 1980, limiting its usefulness to more recent materials.

An online version, Legal Resource Index (LRI), is available through Westlaw and LexisNexis. The publisher also offers an electronic version, LegalTrac, online through InfoTrac Web. The online versions also cover material indexed since 1980.

CLI is published monthly in print and cumulated quarterly and annually. The online versions are updated more frequently.

b. Index to Legal Periodicals & Books; WilsonWeb; WilsonDisc

Index to Legal Periodicals[244] includes tax articles in its subject matter listings. It indexes articles by subject/author, case name, and act name. Because it indexes by statute, it is not searchable by Code section.

ILP indexes fewer tax-related publications than do the other indexes, and it imposes page minimums for indexed material.[245] Because ILP began publication in 1908, it is useful for historical research.[246]

Both Westlaw and LexisNexis carry ILP. Wilson also offers its own online service, WilsonWeb. WilsonDisc is a CD-ROM product. Because Wilson's electronic offerings cover material indexed since mid-1981, they allow rapid searching for current material but not for earlier items.

ILP is published monthly and cumulated quarterly and annually. The CD-ROM version is cumulated monthly. WilsonWeb is updated daily. The Westlaw and LexisNexis versions of ILP are updated at least weekly.

A recent addition to WilsonWeb's online coverage is the Index to Legal Periodicals Retrospective: 1908-1981. This tool supplements the online information available on LexisNexis and Westlaw.

c. HeinOnline

HeinOnline is discussed in Section D, covering full text.

2. Tax-Oriented Periodicals Indexes

a. Federal Tax Articles

This looseleaf reporter contains summaries of articles on federal taxes appearing in legal, accounting, business, and related periodicals. It also covers proceedings and papers delivered at major tax institutes.

Contents appear in Code section order; each item receives a paragraph cross-reference number. The service is published monthly; contents are cumulated at six-month intervals. The articles receive new paragraph

---

[244] ILP began covering books in 1994.

[245] ILP has steadily reduced its page minimums. The minimum was five pages in volume 38, two pages in volume 39, and one-half page in volume 42.

[246] Renumbering of ILP volumes occurred in 1926. A related series published between 1888 and 1908.

numbers when they are cumulated. There is a cross-reference table linking the old and new numbers. There are topic and author indexes.

Federal Tax Articles is cumulated into multiyear volumes at regular intervals. Those volumes currently cover 1954-67, 1968-72, 1973-78, 1979-84, 1985-89, 1990-96, and 1997-2003. The current looseleaf volume contains the most recent material.

Federal Tax Articles has advantages and disadvantages. It is relatively timely. It covers a wide array of publications, but coverage in recent volumes does not appear as broad as that of other indexes. Its use of Code sections facilitates searching. However, its use is limited to 1954 and later materials. Searching through its multivolume format is more time-consuming than searching electronically, but it is not available in an electronic format.

Illustration 14-1. Excerpt from Federal Tax Articles

---

525   5-2006

¶ 10,183   Imposition of Fraud Penalty (Code Sec. 6663)

2006 Article Summaries

¶ 10,183.02 IRS Clarifies Foreign Bank and Financial Accounts Report Penalty. Lyubomir G Georgiev. 17 Journal of International Taxation 5, May 2006, p. 61.

Refers to a Chief Counsel Advice that explains willful violation in the context of the offshore credit card program and the last chance compliance issues. Notes that counsel's guidance concluded that the IRS could impose a foreign bank and financial accounts report (FBAR) penalty on taxpayers who failed to cooperate. Explains that the FBAR penalty is not a tax or a penalty imposed by Title 31, not Title 26 of the U.S. Code.

→The author index cross-references articles by paragraph number to the Code section listing. The author index does not separately list articles.

b. Index to Federal Tax Articles

This multivolume work covers tax literature contained in legal, specialized tax, accounting, and economics journals, and nonperiodical publications. It includes comprehensive coverage of nontax journals.

Contents appear in topical order. There are separate topical and author indexes but no Code section index. The most recent entry appears first in each listing of articles.

Coverage begins with 1913. Volumes I-III cover through mid-1974. There are cumulation volumes for 1974-81, 1982-83, 1984-87, 1988-92, 1993-96, and 1997-2004. Subsequent material appears in the quarterly cumulative supplement volume. This index is updated less frequently than the other indexes and is available only in a print version.

Because Index to Federal Tax Articles begins coverage with 1913 and covers a wide array of publications, it is an excellent source for locating discussions of early developments in taxation. Although you cannot search by Code section, searching by topic may yield more generalized information. Depending on your familiarity with an area, that can be an advantage or disadvantage. Because it is a multivolume print service, searches take more time than those done with electronic services.

Illustration 14-2. Excerpt from Index to Federal Tax Articles

---

SUMMER 2006 CUMULATIVE SUPPLEMENT

Prizes and Awards—*Cont'd*
Scholarships and Fellowships—*Cont'd*
Extreme Makeover Home Edition, Brian Hirsch, 73 University of Cincinnati Law Review No. 4, 1665 (2005)

The Interaction of Broad-Based State Scholarship Programs with Federal Education Credits, Craig G. White and James R. Hamill, 109 Tax Notes No. 4, 515 (2005)

---

3. Other Periodicals Indexes

Representative titles in this category include Business Periodicals Index, Index to Periodical Articles Related to Law, and Social Sciences Index. If your problem involves another country, indexes such as Index to Foreign Legal Periodicals and European Legal Journals Index may be useful. As Table 14-2 illustrates, many nonlaw publications print articles relevant to taxation.

Table 14-2. Representative List of Nonlaw Articles Related to Tax

Andrew D. Cuccia & Gregory A. Carnes, *A Closer Look at the Relation Between Tax Complexity and Tax Equity Perceptions,* 22 J. ECON. PSYCHOL. 113 (2001)
Thomas W. Hanchett, U.S. *Tax Policy and the Shopping Center Boom of the 1950s and 1960s,* 101 AM HIST. REV. 1082 (1996)
John T. Scholz & Neil Pinney, *Duty, Fear, and Tax Compliance: The Heuristic Basis of Citizenship Behavior,* 39 AM. J. POL. SCI. 490 (1995)
Leo Lawrence Murray, *Bureaucracy and Bi-Partisanship in Taxation: The Mellon Plan Revisited,* 52 BUS. HIST. REV. 201 (1978)
James A. Mirrlees, *An Exploration in the Theory of Optimum Income Taxation,* 38 REV. ECON. STUD. 175 (1971)

You can also compile lists of articles and working papers lists from the Legal Scholarship Network subdivision of Social Science Research Network. Unless an author (or the journal itself) posts to SSRN, the work will not be in its database. As its name implies, SSRN is not limited to law. Thus, you can also use it to locate recent law-related literature relevant to tax.[247]

4. Looseleaf Services

Two of the looseleaf services discussed in Chapter 13 include lists of articles.

a. Tax Management Portfolios

The Bibliography section of each Portfolio includes lists of articles.

b. Mertens, Law of Federal Income Taxation

Mertens lists current articles by topic in the Recent Tax Articles section of its monthly Developments & Highlights newsletter. Although Mertens is an income tax service, the lists include articles on estate planning. The monthly lists are not cumulated.

5. Citators

Citators help you compile lists of articles discussing primary source materials such as statutes and cases. Although you can use the Shepard's print citators for this purpose, you will obtain better results using an online citator. [See Illustrations 14-3 and 14-4.] LexisNexis and Westlaw both provide access to citing material. Citators are discussed in more detail in Chapter 12.

6. Miscellaneous Sources

a. Institutes. The New York University Institute on Federal Taxation has published Consolidated Indexes of its proceedings at irregular intervals. These indexes are arranged by subject, author, title, case name, statute, regulation, and ruling. The second volume of each annual Institute includes current indexes and tables. Other institutes also provide current indexes of their proceedings.

b. Bibliographies. Bibliographies compiled by a librarian or by another researcher may be available in the library's reference section or

---

[247] Berkeley Electronic Press also publishes articles and working papers (www.bepress.com).

in law review symposium issues covering a particular area of law.

Tax Policy in the United States: A Selective Bibliography with Annotations (1960-84) was published by the Vanderbilt University Law Library in cooperation with the ABA Section of Taxation. This looseleaf covers articles, books, and government documents dealing with tax policy. Each item is explained briefly. There are author and subject indexes.

Illustration 14-3. Shepard's Search for Articles Citing a Case

Research or validate citations quickly, easily and reliably. *Shepard's®* - now integrated with LexisNexis® Headnotes.   📇 **Show Me...**

Enter the Citation to be Checked   [?]

| 617 F.2d 14 | Citation Formats

The Report will include:

○ *Shepard's®* for Validation - subsequent history and citing references with analysis (KWIC™)

⊙ *Shepard's®* for Research - prior and subsequent history and all citing references (FULL)

To track future treatment of a case, set up *Shepard's Alert®*
To request multiple citations, use *Get & Print*
                or the new *Shepard's® BriefCheck* ™   ✓ **Check**

→This search involved Ogiony v. Commissioner, 617 F.2d 14 (2d Cir. 1980).

Illustration 14-4. Excerpt from List of Articles Retrieved

☐ 33. ARTICLE: Fog, Fairness, and the Federal Fisc: Tenancy-by-the-Entireties Interests and the Federal Tax Lien, 60 Mo. L. R

☐ 34. NOTE: ONE-MAN PERSONAL SERVICE CORPORATIONS: SINGING A NEW FOGLESONG, 58 Notre Dame L. Rev. 652 (1983)

     58 Notre Dame L. Rev. 652 p.652

☐ 35. ARTICLE: Should Courts Require the Internal Revenue Service to be Consistent?, 40 Tax L. Rev. 411 (1985)

     40 Tax L. Rev. 411 p.425

☐ 36. ARTICLE: DOES THE INTERNAL REVENUE SERVICE HAVE A DUTY TO TREAT SIMILARLY SITUATED TAXPAYERS SIMILARLY?

     74 U. Cin. L. Rev. 531 p.531

→Among the articles citing this decision was one (indicated by the arrow) written by Professor Pietruszkiewicz.

c. Current Index to Legal Periodicals. CILP indexes law review articles on a weekly basis, but it is not cumulated. It is worth consulting because it may cover an article sooner than one or more of the indexes discussed above. Articles are listed both by topic and by law review in each CILP issue.

d. Websites. When you search for articles by a particular author, don't neglect to check the web. Authors often list publications in a resume or publications section. Law and accounting firms and universities are likely to provide this information about their employees. [See Illustration 14-8 for Professor Pietruszkiewicz's web page.] In addition to SSRN, discussed in Subsection 3, Google Scholar [Illustration 14-18] may be useful.

7. Digests

WG & L Tax Journal Digest. Previously published as the Journal of Taxation Digest, this service covers articles published in the Journal of Taxation and several other Warren, Gorham & Lamont publications. Coverage begins with 1977, and the publications covered have varied over time. Digests are arranged by topic. Cross-references are given to relevant articles digested under other topical headings.

SECTION D. TEXTS OF PERIODICALS

1. Print

If your library subscribes to publications printing articles you wish to read, you can easily locate them. Many libraries shelve all periodicals together in alphabetical order; a library with an alcove devoted to a particular subject area may shelve specialized periodicals in the alcove. No matter which shelving method it uses, the library is likely to keep a periodical's most current issues on reserve.

2. Online

If your library does not subscribe to a particular publication, or it is in use by another researcher, try locating it online in LexisNexis or Westlaw. Both online services carry numerous publications in full text. In addition, some periodicals include full-text articles on their own websites. If you search in LexisNexis or Westlaw, you can also find articles on particular topics (e.g., Code sections or cases) by using those topics as search terms.

HeinOnline also provides full-text access. You can search this service by author, title, or words in text and can use Boolean search terms. It allows direct access by citation, and includes an electronic table of contents for each volume. Each page is reproduced as originally published. As of early November 2006, it includes Akron Tax Journal Florida Tax Review, Pittsburgh Tax Review, Tax Law Review, Tax Lawyer, and Virginia Tax Review in its extensive list of journals.

Index to Legal Periodicals Full Text currently provides full-text articles in numerous publications. Retrospective coverage dates vary by periodical. The collection can be searched by topic, case or statute name.

Illustration 14-5. Excerpt from HeinOnline

Marriage, Divorce and Taxes

HARRY J. RUDICK

I. INTRODUCTION

Recently published statistics showing sharp increases in the rates of American marriage and divorce,[1] especially divorce, indicate the desirability of a review of the tax problems that accompany these milestones—the cynics will say millstones. Recent decisions by the Tax Court, interpreting the 1942 amendments which for the first time made alimony taxable to the wife, have also spurred interest in the topic. The present paper, which is concerned only with federal imposts, suggests and attempts to appraise tax problems which may arise for propertied couples (and some who are not propertied) from the meeting to the parting of the twain.

→HeinOnline reproduces actual pages. This page is from Tax Law Review, 1946-47.

3. CD/DVD

LexisNexis provides CD-ROM services that cover the tax institutes held at University of Miami and University of Southern California. These CD-ROMs were previously part of the Matthew Bender Authority service. Some law reviews, such as Harvard Law Review, are available in CD-ROM format. As web-based systems expand their retrospective coverage, the demand for CD-ROM and DVD products is likely to decline.

4. Microform

In addition to HeinOnline, William S. Hein & Co., Inc., provides numerous periodicals in microform. Libraries may purchase microform versions of periodicals if space is at a premium or because the print version is no longer available.

SECTION E. CITATORS FOR ARTICLES

Section C covered using citators to find citations to articles discussing various primary source materials. You can also use a citator to determine if a court has cited a particular article in one of its opinions. Using an online citator, use the article's citation as your search term.]

Illustration 14-6. Shepard's Search for Decisions Citing an Article

Research or validate citations quickly, easily and reliably. *Shepard's*® - now integrated with LexisNexis® Headnotes.

⌐ **Show Me...**

Enter the Citation to be Checked   [?]

`54 syr. l. rev. 1`   Citation Formats

The Report will include:

○ *Shepard's*® for Validation - subsequent history and citing references with analysis (KWIC™)

◉ *Shepard's*® for Research - prior and subsequent history and all citing references (FULL)

To track future treatment of a case, set up *Shepard's Alert*®

To request multiple citations, use *Get & Print*
or the new *Shepard's*® *BriefCheck* ™   ✓ check

→This search involved one of Professor Pietruszkiewicz's articles.

Illustration 14-7. Results of Search for Decisions

CITING DECISIONS (2 citing decisions)

2ND CIRCUIT - COURT OF APPEALS

✔ Select for Delivery
☐   1. **Cited by:**
         Hudson Valley Black Press v. IRS, 409 F.3d 106, 2

         409 F.3d 106 p.113

10TH CIRCUIT - U.S. DISTRICT COURTS

☐   2. **Cited by:**
         Williamson v. Sena, 2006 U.S. Dist. LEXIS 29157 ι

         2006 U.S. Dist. LEXIS 29157

SECTION F. NONGOVERNMENTAL REPORTS

Many groups appear before Congress and the Treasury Department to testify at hearings that may lead to legislation or regulations. These groups may also submit reports to individual legislators and executive branch officials or post them on their websites.

As is true for periodical articles, these reports often include numerous citations to authority to support their policy analysis.

Table 14-3. Examples of Nongovernmental Groups

Group	Website
ABA Section of Taxation	www.abanet.org/tax
AICPA	www.aicpa.org
American Law Institute	www.ali.org
Citizens for Tax Justice	www.ctj.org
The Heritage Foundation	www.heritage.org
National Bureau of Economic Research	www.nber.org
National Taxpayers Union	www.ntu.org/main
Tax Policy Center	www.taxpolicycenter.org
Urban Institute	www.urban.org

SECTION G. ILLUSTRATIONS

Illustration 14-8. Results of Searching Author's Web Page

LAW REVIEW PUBLICATIONS

Discarded Deference: Judicial Independence in Informal Agency Guidance
73 Tennessee Law Review --- (2006)

Does The Intenal Revenue Service Have A Duty To Treat Similarly Situated Taxpayers Similarly?
74 Cincinnati Law Review 531 (2005)

Of Summonses, Required Records And Artificial Entities: Liberating The IRS From Itself
73 Mississippi Law Journal 921 (2004)

A Constitutional Cause Of Action And The Internal Revenue Code: Can You Shoot (Sue) The Messenger?
54 Syracuse Law Review 1 (2004)

The Taming of the Noncontrolled Section 902 Corporation Provisions: A Step Toward Subpart F
15 Journal of Taxation of Investments 257 (1998)

Noncontrolled Section 902 Corporation: Playing Field Leveled by TRA '97
U.S. Taxation of International Operations ¶ 6001 (August 1998)

→This list is available on Professor Pietruszkiewicz's web page, at http://faculty.law.lsu.edu/tax/.

Illustration 14-9. Results from LRI on Westlaw

Edit Search: au(christopher /2 pietruszkiewicz) ▼ **Database:** lri ▼ [SEARCH] Locate in Result

Results: 3 Documents   Add Search to WestClip

SELECT TO PRINT, EMAIL, ETC.

☐ **1.** TITLE: Civil and criminal tax penalties.(Annual Report: Important Developments During the Year). AUTHOR: Abrams, Stuart E.; Rettig, Charles P.; Ungerman, Josh O.; Pietruszkiewicz, Christopher M. YEAR: Publication Date: Summer 2004. Page: 1001-1008. 57 Tax Law. 1001, 2004 WL 3213711 (LRI) <<Full Text Available>>

☐ **2.** TITLE: A constitutional cause of action and the Internal Revenue Code: can you shoot (sue) the messenger? AUTHOR: Pietruszkiewicz, Christopher M. YEAR: Publication Date: February 2004. Page: 1-68. 54 Syracuse L. Rev. 1, 2004 WL 3267658 (LRI) <<Full Text Available>>

☐ **3.** TITLE: Of summonses, required records and artificial entities: liberating the IRS from itself. AUTHOR: Pietruszkiewicz, Christopher M. YEAR: Publication Date: Winter 2004. Page: 921-981. 73 Miss. L.J. 921, 2004 WL 3168548 (LRI) <<Full Text Available>>

→Professor Pietruszkiewicz did not author the first article listed. He served as the editor for an article written by others.

Illustration 14-10. Results from LRI on Lexis Nexis

FOCUS™ Terms AUTHOR (Pietruszkiewicz w/2 Christopher)   Search Within All Documents ▼ [Go ▶] FOCUS Options...

View: Cite | KWIC | Full | Custom   ◀◀◀ 1-2 of 2 ▶▶▶   FAST Print ▼ Print | Download | Fax | Email |
                                                Save As Alert | Hide Hits

Source: Legal > Secondary Legal > Law Reviews & Journals > Legal Resource Index ⓘ
Terms: author (pietruszkiewicz w/2 christopher) (Edit Search | Suggest Terms for My Search)

✔Select for FOCUS™ or Delivery

☐ 1. LGLIND/LEGAL RESOURCE INDEX (TM) Copyright (c) 2005 Information Access Co., Pietruszkiewicz, Christopher M., Of summonses, required records and artificial entities: liberating the IRS from itself., Mississippi Law Journal, 73, 3, 921-981, University of Mississippi, WINTER, 2004, 128152300

☐ 2. LGLIND/LEGAL RESOURCE INDEX (TM) Copyright (c) 2005 Information Access Co., Pietruszkiewicz, Christopher M., A constitutional cause of action and the Internal Revenue Code: can you shoot (sue) the messenger?, Syracuse Law Review, 54, 1, 1-68, Syracuse University, 02/01/2004, 131388946

Source: Legal > Secondary Legal > Law Reviews & Journals > Legal Resource Index ⓘ
Terms: author (pietruszkiewicz w/2 christopher) (Edit Search | Suggest Terms for My Search)
View: Cite
Date/Time: Thursday, November 2, 2006 - 4:14 PM EST

→Note that this search did not find the edited article found in Illustration 14-9 even though both searches were conducted in the Legal Resource Index database.

Illustration 14-11. Results from ILP on Westlaw

Edit Search: au(christopher /2 pietruszkiewicz) ▼   **Database:** ilp ▼   SEARCH   Locate in Result

Results: 3 Documents   Add Search to WestClip

Expand Search: Change Database to Journals and Law Reviews Combined

SELECT TO PRINT, EMAIL, ETC.

☐ **1.** TITLE: A constitutional cause of action and the Internal Revenue Code: can you shoot (sue) the messenger? AUTHOR: Pietruszkiewicz, Christopher M. YEAR:2004. Page: 1-68. 54 Syracuse L. Rev. 1, 2004 WL 2576599 (ILP) <<Full Text Available>>

☐ **2.** TITLE: Of Summonses, Required Records and Artificial Entities: Liberating the IRS from Itself. AUTHOR: Pietruszkiewicz, Christopher M. YEAR:2004. Page: 92-81. 73 Miss. L.J. 921, 2004 WL 2540871 (ILP) <<Full Text Available>>

☐ **3.** TITLE: The taming of the noncontrolled Section 902 corporation provisions: a step toward Subpart F. AUTHOR: Pietruszkiewicz, Christopher M. YEAR:Summe 1998. Page: 267-94. 15 J. Tax'n Inv. 267, 1998 WL 1053331 (ILP)

Illustration 14-12. Results from ILP on LexisNexis

FOCUS™ Terms AUTHOR (Pietruszkiewicz w/2 Christopher)   Search Within All Documents ▼   Go ⊞ FOCUS Options...

View: Cite | KWIC | Full | Custom   ◄◄ 1-2 of 2 ►►   FAST Print ▼ Print | Download | Fax | Email |
Save As Alert | Show Hits

Source: Legal > Secondary Legal > Law Reviews & Journals > Index to Legal Periodicals ⊡
Terms: author (pietruszkiewicz w/2 christopher) (Edit Search | Suggest Terms for My Search)

✔Select for FOCUS™ or Delivery

☐ 1. INDEX TO LEGAL PERIODICALS, Copyright © 2005 H. W. Wilson Co. All Rights Reserved, TITLE: A constitutional cause of action and the Internal Revenue Code: can yo shoot (sue) the messenger?, AUTHOR:Pietruszkiewicz, Christopher M., PUB-CITE: 54 Syracuse Law Rev 1, DATE:2004

☐ 2. INDEX TO LEGAL PERIODICALS, Copyright © 1998 H. W. Wilson Co. All Rights Reserved, TITLE:The taming of the noncontrolled Section 902 corporation provisions: a step toward Subpart F, AUTHOR:Pietruszkiewicz, Christopher M., PUB-CITE:15 J. Tax'n Invest. 267, DATE:Summer 1998

Source: Legal > Secondary Legal > Law Reviews & Journals > Index to Legal Periodicals ⊡

Illustration 14-13. Search Results in HeinOnline

HEIN online

Select Library:
Law Journal Library ▼

• Collection Index • Search • Search History • Help • Feedback • Logout •

There are 2 results.

HeinOnline Law Journal Article Search Results

Searching for "pietruszkiewicz" in AUTHOR

Pietruszkiewicz, Christopher M.
Constitutional Cause of Action and the Internal Revenue Code: Can You Shoot (Sue) the Messenger, A
1. 54 Syracuse L. Rev. 1 (2004)

Pietruszkiewicz, Christopher M.
Of Summonses, Required Records and Artificial Entities: Liberating the IRS from Itself
2. 73 Miss. L.J. 921 (2003-2004)

2 item(s) found

Illustration 14-14. Results from Journals and Law Reviews Combined on Westlaw

Edit Search: au(christopher /2 pietruszkiewicz)   Database: jlr   SEARCH   Locate in Result

Results: 3 Documents   Add Search to WestClip

Expand Search: Change Database to All Texts, Treatises, Law Reviews and Journals

SELECT TO PRINT, EMAIL, ETC.

1. 74 U. Cin. L. Rev. 531
University of Cincinnati Law Review Winter 2005 Article DOES THE INTERNAL REVENUE SERVICE HAVE A DUTY TO TREAT SIMILARLY SITUATED TAXPAYERS SIMILARLY? Christopher M. Pietruszkiewicz [FNa1]

...Article DOES THE INTERNAL REVENUE SERVICE HAVE A DUTY TO TREAT SIMILARLY SITUATED TAXPAYERS SIMILARLY? Christopher M. Pietruszkiewicz [FNa1] Copyright © 2005 University of Cincinnati; Christopher M. Pietruszkiewicz I. Introduction .... 532 II. The IBM Decision ...

2. 73 Miss. L.J. 921
Mississippi Law Journal Winter 2004 Article OF SUMMONSES, REQUIRED RECORDS AND ARTIFICIAL ENTITIES: LIBERATING THE IRS FROM ITSELF Christopher Pietruszkiewicz [FNa1]

...Winter 2004 Article OF SUMMONSES, REQUIRED RECORDS AND ARTIFICIAL ENTITIES: LIBERATING THE IRS FROM ITSELF Christopher M. Pietruszkiewicz [FNa1] Copyright © 2004 Mississippi Law Journal, Inc.; Christopher M. Pietruszkiewicz To most Americans, the term "Boss" conjures ...

3. 54 Syracuse L. Rev. 1
Syracuse Law Review 2004 Articles A CONSTITUTIONAL CAUSE OF ACTION AND THE INTERNAL REVENUE CODE: CAN YOU SHOOT (SUE) THE MESSENGER Christopher M. Pietruszkiewicz [FNd1]

...2004 Articles A CONSTITUTIONAL CAUSE OF ACTION AND THE INTERNAL REVENUE CODE: CAN YOU SHOOT (SUE) THE MESSENGER? Christopher M. Pietruszkiewicz [FNd1] Copyright © 2004 Syracuse Law Review; Christopher M. Pietruszkiewicz Contents Introduction .... 2 I. Supreme Court Precedent ...

Illustration 14-15. Results from Law Reviews and Journals Combined on LexisNexis

FOCUS™ Terms AUTHOR (Pietruszkiewicz w/2 Christopher)   Search Within All Documents   Go → FOCUS Options

View: Cite | KWIC | Full | Custom   ◄◄◄ 1-5 of 5 ►►►   FAST Print ▼ Print | Download | Fax | Email |
                                                      Save As Alert | Show Hits

Source: Legal > Secondary Legal > Law Reviews & Journals > US Law Reviews and Journals, Combined
Terms: author (pietruszkiewicz w/2 christopher) (Edit Search | Suggest Terms for My Search)

↙Select for FOCUS™ or Delivery

1. Copyright (c) 2005 University of Cincinnati Law Review University of Cincinnati Law Review, Winter, 2005, 74 U. Cin. L. Rev. 531, 19914 words, ARTICLE: DOES THE INTERNAL REVENUE SERVICE HAVE A DUTY TO TREAT SIMILARLY SITUATED TAXPAYERS SIMILARLY?, Christopher M. Pietruszkiewicz*

2. Copyright (c) 2003 Georgia Law Review Association Georgia Law Review, Winter, 2003, 37 Ga. L. Rev. 611, 33419 words, ANONYMOUS SPEECH AND SECTION 527 OF THE INTERNAL REVENUE CODE , Donald B. Tobin *

3. Copyright (c) 2004 Mississippi Law Journal Mississippi Law Journal, Winter, 2004, 73 Miss. L.J. 921, 20231 words, ARTICLE: OF SUMMONSES, REQUIRED RECORDS AND ARTIFICIAL ENTITIES: LIBERATING THE IRS FROM ITSELF, Christopher M. Pietruszkiewicz *

4. Copyright (c) 2004 Ohio State Law Journal Ohio State Law Journal, 2004, 65 Ohio St. L.J. 1401, 29296 words, ARTICLE: The Entrepreneurship Effect: An Accidental Externality in the Federal Income Tax , Leandra Lederman*

5. Copyright (c) 2004 Syracuse Law Review Syracuse Law Review, 2004, 54 Syracuse L. Rev. 1, 28789 words, ARTICLE: A CONSTITUTIONAL CAUSE OF ACTION AND THE INTERNAL REVENUE CODE: CAN YOU SHOOT (SUE) THE MESSENGER?, Christopher M. Pietruszkiewicz +

→This search yielded two items for which Professor Pietruszkiewicz was thanked by the authors but was not himself an author.

→The searches in CLI and ILP on LexisNexis did not generate items for which the authors thanked Professor Pietruszkiewicz. None of the searches conducted in Westlaw generated those items.

Illustration 14-16. Search in WilsonWeb

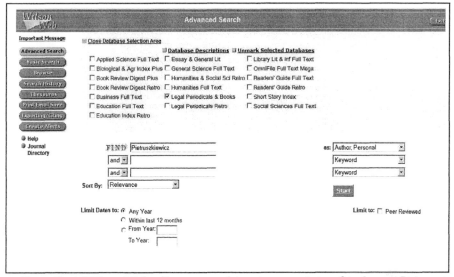

→Note that WilsonWeb allows searching in a variety of indexes. It is not limited to Wilson's Index to Legal Periodicals or even to legal databases.

Illustration 14-17. Search Results in WilsonWeb

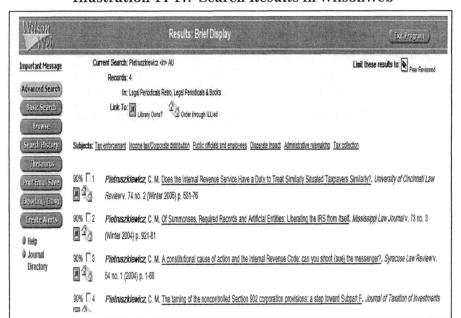

Illustration 14-18. Search in Google Scholar

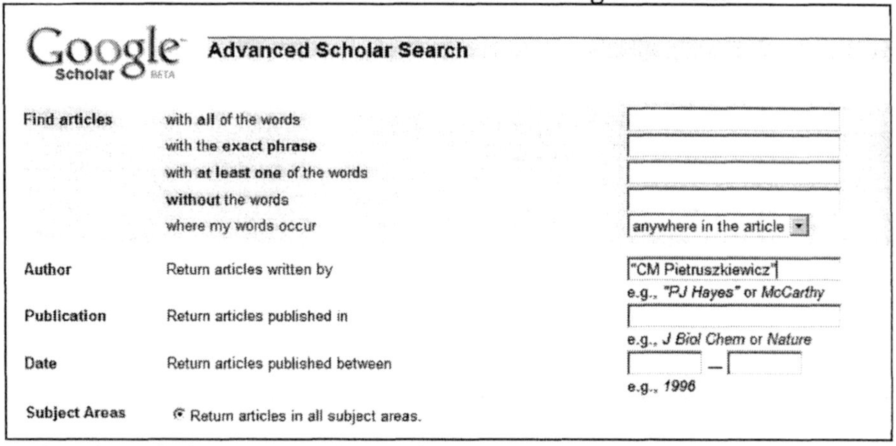

→Google Scholar retrieved the Cincinnati, Syracuse, Mississippi, and Taxation of Investments articles.

Illustration 14-19. Search in Social Science Research Network

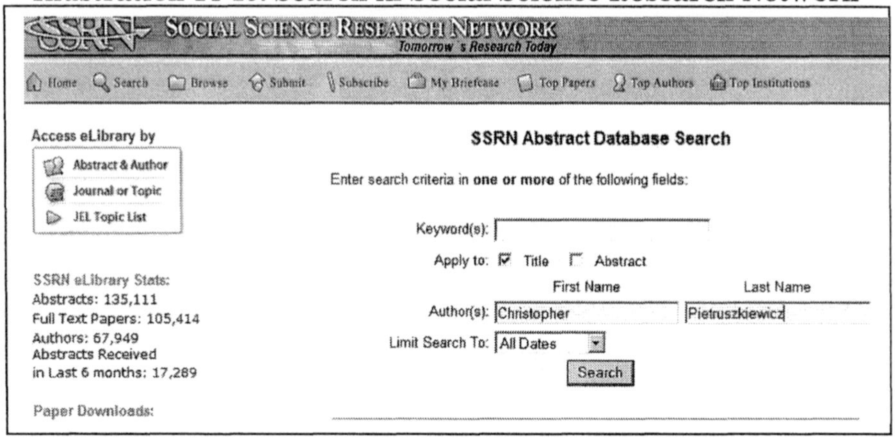

→SSRN's results include the number of downloads and information about when the item was posted or revised.

→SSRN listed the Cincinnati, Mississippi, and Syracuse articles.

Section H. Problems

Your instructor may assign one or more of the sources listed in this chapter for answering the questions below. If you have carte blanche to decide among sources, try using multiple sources so that you can compare their relative value. Unless you receive contrary instructions, your search can include articles in professional journals, newsletters, and institutes in addition to articles in law reviews.

1. Locate the text of the article below online or in its print version. What are the first five words of the article?

a. Mona L. Hymel, *Consumerism, Advertising, and the Role of Tax Policy*, 20 VA. TAX REV. 347 (2000).

b. Edward A. Morse, *Travails of the Entrepreneurial Ant: Reforming Tax-Favored Retirement Saving for Small Business Owners*, 50 DEPAUL L. REV. 49 (2000).

c. C. Garrison Lepow, *The Flimflam Father: Deconstructing Parent-Child Stereotypes in Federal Tax Subsidies*, 5 NYU J. LEGIS. & PUB. POL'Y 129 (2001-2002)..

d. Michael S. Knoll & Thomas D. Griffith, *Taxing Sunny Days: Adjusting Taxes for Regional Living Costs and Amenities*, 116 HARV. L. REV. 987 (2003).

e. Herwig J. Schlunk, *How I Learned to Stop Worrying and Love Double Taxation*, 79 NOTRE DAME L. REV. 127 (2003).

f. Marvin A. Chirelstein & Lawrence A. Zelenak, *Tax Shelters and the Search for a Silver Bullet*, 105 COLUM. L. REV. 1939 (2005).

g. Susan Pace Hamill, *An Evaluation of Federal Tax Policy Based on Judeo-Christian Ethics*, 25 VA. TAX REV. 671 (2006).

2. The articles listed below all appear in at least one online articles index. Add the author name and the law review information to complete the citation.

a. The Entrepreneurship Effect: An Accidental Externality in the Federal Income Tax

b. The Matthew Effect and Federal Taxation

c. Community Property with Right of Survivorship: Uneasy Lies the Head That Wears a Crown of Surviving Spouse for Federal Income Tax Basis Purposes

d. The Marriage Bonus/Penalty in Black and White

e. How the Board of Tax Appeals Changed Hollywood History

f. No More Parking Lots: How the Tax Code Keeps Trees Out of a Tree Museum and Paradise Unpaved

g. What Then to Do with a Non-Cooperative Cooperative?

3. The individual listed below will be speaking at your institution. Using whichever of the sources your instructor assigns from the list below, compile a list of the last five articles he or she has published. Use the year of publication in determining which articles are the last five published.

  Sources:
  (1) Index to Legal Periodicals
  (2) Current Law Index
  (3) Google Scholar
  (4) HeinOnline .
  (5) the author's own web page

 a. Alice Abreu

 b. Paul Caron

 c. Deborah Geier

 d. Steve R. Johnson

 e. Roberta Mann

 f. William Turnier

4. The articles below were published between 1940 and 1979. Add the author name and the law review information to complete the citation. Use Index to Legal Periodicals, CCH Federal Tax Articles, Index to Federal Tax Articles, or HeinOnline.

 a. Deferred Compensation: Conceptual Astigmatism

 b. The Congress and the Tax Lobbyist—How Special Tax Provisions Get Enacted

 c. Quasi-Corporations, Quasi-Employees, and Quasi-Tax Relief for Professional Persons

 d. Common Sense Correlation of the Estate and Gift Taxes

 e. The Criteria of Federal Income Tax Policy

e. The Criteria of Federal Income Tax Policy

f. Federal Tax Policy and the Support of Science

5. The articles below were published before 1940. Add the law review information to complete the citation. Use Index to Legal Periodicals, Index to Federal Tax Articles, or HeinOnline.

a. George Donworth, Federal Taxation of Community Incomes—The Recent History of Pending Questions

b. James E. Fahey, Income Tax Definition of "Reorganization"

c. John M. Maguire, Income Taxes on the Realization of Future Interests

d. Douglas Blount Maggs, Community Property and the Federal Income Tax

e. Randolph E. Paul, A Plea for Better Tax Pleading

f. Roswell F. Magill, The Income Tax Liability of Annuities and Similar Periodical Payments

6. Provide a full citation to an article that includes the act listed below in its title. Unless your instructor tells you otherwise, find the most recent article you can.

a. Foreign Earned Income Act of 1978

b. Revenue Act of 1987

c. Internal Revenue Restructuring and Reform Act of 1998

d. American Jobs Creation Act of 2004

e. Tax Increase Prevention Act of 2005 (TIPRA)

f. Pension Protection Act of 2006

7. Provide a full citation to an article that includes the Code section listed below in its title. Unless your instructor tells you otherwise, find the most recent article you can.

a. 170

c. 513

d. 1031

e. 2036

f. 2053

8. Provide a full citation to an article involving federal taxation that includes the term listed below in its title. Unless your instructor tells you otherwise, find the most recent article you can.

a. collection due process

b. economic substance doctrine

c. family limited partnerships

d. health savings accounts

e. innocent spouse

f. kiddie tax

Chapter 15. Form Books and Model Language

Section A. Using Forms, Checklists, and Model Language

The drafter's choice of language may determine the tax consequences of a contract, law suit settlement, or other legal matter. To avoid adverse consequences, you might consider adapting a form book's model language. The author's comments explain why particular language avoids tax problems. You can also use checklists to guide you in drafting your own form. The IRS occasionally provides model language in revenue procedures and other documents and even in tax return forms. Illustrations at the end of this chapter illustrate both commercially available and IRS forms.

Section B. Form Books Available

The following list illustrates the range of available materials. Forms are most useful if the author includes citations to authority.

• Bittker, Emory & Streng, Federal Income Taxation of Corporations & Shareholders: Forms

• Lowell, Tilton, Sheldrick & Donohue, U.S. International Taxation: Agreements, Checklists & Commentary

• Mancoff & Steinberg, Qualified Deferred Compensation Plans–Forms

• McGaffey, Legal Forms with Tax Analysis

• Murphy's Will Clauses: Annotations and Forms with Tax Effects

• Rabkin & Johnson, Current Legal Forms with Tax Analysis

• Robinson, Real Estate Forms: Tax Analysis & Checklists

In addition to using form books, you can find model language in looseleaf services, articles,[248] and tax institute proceedings. For example,

---

[248] See, e.g., James F. Gulecas, *Old Trusts—New Tricks (With Forms)*, Prac.

several Tax Management Portfolios[249] include model language in their Worksheets section. Section D discusses online sources of forms.

SECTION C. FINDING FORMS AND OTHER DOCUMENTS

You can find drafting language relatively easily using a form book. Relevant forms or checklists will be listed by topic or Code section or will appear along with the topical discussion. You can also use the publication's table of contents or relevant tables of authority to locate forms. The method of publication, print or electronic, should not matter.

If you are interested in IRS model language, you can locate the relevant document through an electronic search. Use such search terms as "model language," "prototype language," or "sample language."

SECTION D. PUBLICATION FORMAT FOR FORMS

Although form books are available in print, materials published in electronic formats have an added advantage. Users can download forms and customize them for their clients' needs. In some instances, a CD/DVD may accompany a print form book.

Westlaw and LexisNexis include form books in their databases (e.g., West's Legal Forms on Westlaw; LEXIS Clause Library – Estates, Gifts and Trusts on LexisNexis). Publishers such as BNA provide form book materials to Westlaw or LexisNexis and also include them in their own subscription databases (e.g., BNATAX Management Library).

Internal Revenue Service forms appear in the Internal Revenue Bulletin, which is available in print, online through commercial services, and online through the IRS website, www.irs.gov. You do not need the actual citation to find IRS forms online. You do need the actual citation to find them in the print version of the I.R.B.[250] Illustrations 15-3 and 15-4 illustrate using the IRS website to search for "model language."

TAX LAW., Winter 2002, at 27.

[249] The Portfolios are described in detail in Chapter 13.

[250] If you have the citation, you can obtain the model language from your library's print version Internal Revenue Bulletin or Cumulative Bulletin. You would use electronic materials if you wanted to download the language.

Illustration 15-1. Contents Section from Murphy's Will Clauses

Murphy's Will Clauses: Annotations and Forms with Tax Effects
  Vol 2: Chapter 3C FEDERAL INCOME TAXATION OF TRUSTS: DRAFTING AND PLANNING CO

§ 3C.01 Introduction
§ 3C.02 Basic Taxable Income Rules for Trusts
§ 3C.03 Underlying Rules for Distribution Deduction by Trusts
§ 3C.04 Trust's Deduction for Distribution to Beneficiaries Under I.R.C. Section 651: Simple Trusts
§ 3C.05 Trust's Deduction for Distributions to Beneficiaries: Complex Trusts
§ 3C.06 Income Tax Imposed on and Payable by Trusts
§ 3C.07 Income Tax Consequences of Property Transactions for Trusts
§ 3C.08 General Income Tax Consequences for Trust Beneficiaries
§ 3C.09 I.R.C. Section 652: Taxing Trust Beneficiaries of Simple Trusts
§ 3C.10 I.R.C. Section 662: Taxing Trust Beneficiaries of Complex Trusts
§ 3C.11 Miscellaneous Tax Consequences to Beneficiaries
§ 3C.12 Controlling Abuses of Trusts
§ 3C.13 Consequences On Termination
§ 3C.14 Planning and Drafting Trusts to Take into Account the Federal Income Taxation of Trusts
§ 3C.15 Forms

→Forms are listed at the end of the chapter's table of contents. Murphy's Wills Clauses is available in print and electronically.

Illustration 15-2. Excerpt from RIA Client Letters on Checkpoint

¶1137 Donating works of art to charity
Client Letters (RIA)

¶1137 Donating works of art to charity

Document Assembly

To the practitioner: For background information on the subject of this letter, see Federal Tax Coordinator ¶ K-3167 et seq.(tangible personal property contributions); Federal Tax Coordinator ¶ T-10081 et seq.(statements of value of art from IRS) United States Tax Reporter ¶ 1704 . .

Dear Client:

You recently asked about what is involved in getting a deduction for a donation to a charity of a work of art.

→The language above is the beginning of a sample client letter discussing tax consequences. Note the cross-references to explanatory material that precedes the letter.

Illustration 15-3. Search for Model Language on IRS Website

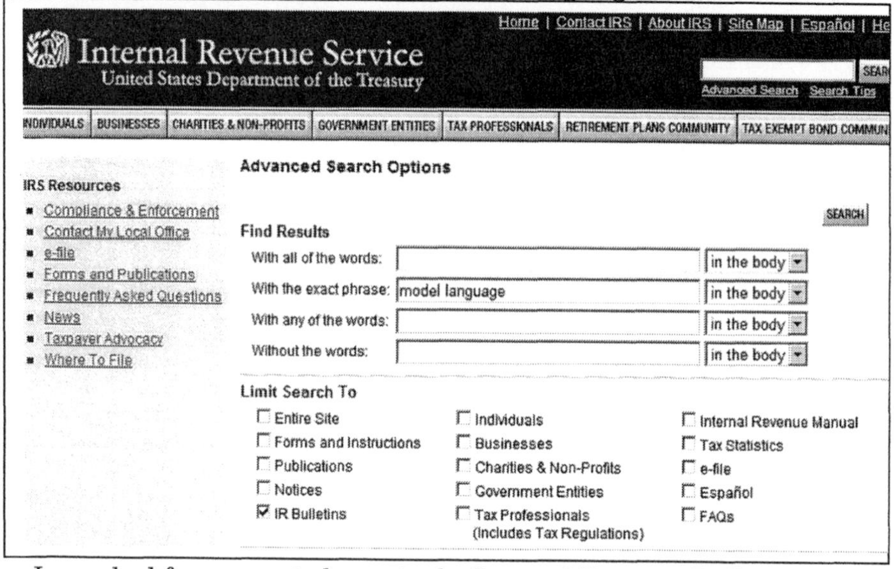

→I searched for an exact phrase in the Internal Revenue Bulletins.

Illustration 15-4. Results of Search on IRS Website

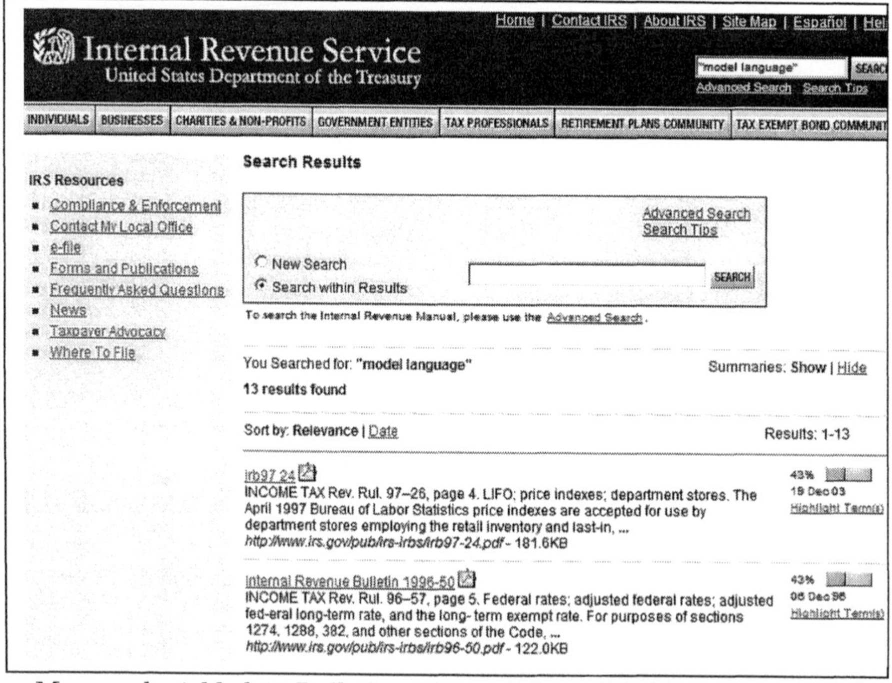

→My search yielded 13 Bulletins. If you click on "Highlight Term(s)," the term will be highlighted when I open the document.

SECTION E. PROBLEMS

1. Locate a form or checklist covering tax consequences of a

   a. shareholder cross-purchase agreement

   b. support agreement for spouses who are separated but not divorced

   c. QTIP trust

   d. stock bonus plan

   e. private annuity

2. Locate the model language described below

   a. declaration of trust for a qualified personal residence trust (2003 Revenue Procedure)

   b. declaration of trust for a testamentary CRUT for a term of years (2005 Revenue Procedure)

   c. enrollment rights in a group health plan (2005 Treasury Decision)

   d. a sample plan amendment providing for designated Roth contributions in a 401(k) plan (2006 IRS Notice)

   e. sample implementing amendment language to be used by a Volume Submitter (2005 IRS Announcement)

3. What is the purpose of IRS Form 5305A-SEP?

Chapter 16. Newsletters

Section A. Introduction

Researchers in any area must update their findings or risk citing obsolete sources. When the research involves taxation, the odds of change are extremely high and the number of sources to consult may appear endless. Although keeping current requires a significant time commitment, it pays off in the long run. Regular self-education ultimately reduces your research time.

Newsletters are convenient tools for keeping up with changes in the law. While they are no substitute for updating with a citator or the new matter section of a looseleaf service, they provide a means for reviewing material issued during a predetermined time period.

Several newsletters print texts or digests of primary source material. The publisher often maintains these materials on electronic databases. If your library has sufficient shelf space for print copies, or you have electronic access, you can also use newsletters to locate and read primary source materials.

Section B. Categorizing Newsletters

Methods for categorizing newsletters include frequency of publication, subject matter, relation to looseleaf services, and publication format.

1. Frequency of Publication

Newsletters may appear daily, weekly, or even monthly. Daily and weekly newsletters either offer longer excerpts from cases and rulings than do their monthly counterparts or cover a wider range of topics. To avoid extraordinary length, monthly newsletters limit their breadth or depth of coverage. The IRS's practice of issuing advance revenue rulings and revenue procedures, notices, and announcements makes daily newsletters particularly attractive. They may carry these items weeks before they appear in the Internal Revenue Bulletin.

Online publication represents the ultimate in frequency. Because electronic databases can update their newsletter files daily, subscribers enjoy instant access while avoiding the library shelving problems associated with daily newsletters. Many newsletters are available online in addition to being published in print versions.

2. Subject Matter

Newsletters may be general in scope, covering all (or at least most) areas of tax. Unless a general purpose newsletter is relatively long, or published very frequently, it gives limited attention to various areas or to particular types of authority. Other newsletters may limit coverage to a particular specialty, such as the estate tax or oil and gas taxation.

3. Relation to Looseleaf Services

Publishers of looseleaf services provide subscribers with pamphlet-type newsletters summarizing major events of the week or other relevant time period. Although their summaries may be short, many of these newsletters include cross-references to discussion in the relevant looseleaf. CCH Taxes on Parade and RIA Weekly Alert are newsletters that are associated with looseleaf services.

In other instances, a looseleaf service subscription may not include a newsletter. Tax Management Weekly Report falls into this category; it is not included in the subscription to Tax Management Portfolios. Even though not included in a subscription, a newsletter may include cross-references to a publisher's looseleaf service. Tax Management Weekly Report includes updating material keyed to the Portfolios.

Finally, some newsletters have no relation to any looseleaf service. Some of these, including Tax Notes, provide cross-references to sources printing full texts of items digested in the newsletter. Others provide no cross-reference service, leaving the choice of full-text reference source to the reader.

4. Publication Format

Most newsletters are available in a variety of formats, but print and online are the most common. CD/DVD or microform publication is useful if shelf space is limited and you want permanent access to the publication.

SECTION C. DESCRIPTIONS OF NEWSLETTERS

It is impossible to provide detailed descriptions of all available newsletters in this short a text. Although I limited this section to a handful of newsletters and publishers, you should not overlook other resources available in print or online. This is particularly important for relatively specialized areas. Many of these newsletters are available on LexisNexis or Westlaw in addition to their publishers' website.

1. Daily Tax Report; Tax Management Weekly Report

a. Daily Tax Report

This newsletter is an invaluable aid in following current developments in the law. Each separately paginated issue includes a section describing congressional activity, including bills passed and introduced, committee hearings, and committee reports.

Daily Tax Report prints full texts or digests of judicial decisions; full texts of most revenue rulings and procedures; summaries of other IRS materials (e.g., private letter rulings); and texts of proposed, temporary, and final regulations.

The indexes follow a subject matter format. Newsletter subscribers can access full text documents online using Tax Management's TaxCore.

Illustration 16-1. Excerpt from Daily Tax Report

TAX, BUDGET & ACCOUNTING   (No. 202) G-7

Notes Disclosure Requirements. On the question of notes disclosures to identify the measurement bases for assets and liabilities, some board members spoke strongly against doing what would amount to recreating a balance sheet in the notes.

The issue, said board member Robert Garnett, is identifying the important information for users.

The notice said the primary types of cases previously handled in the district court CDP cases were those involving employment taxes, the trust fund recovery penalty, and the frivolous return penalty and that these types of cases will now be considered by the Tax Court.

The notice added that taxpayers are only

→Daily Tax Report includes news reports in addition to primary source material. The excerpt above is from the October 19, 2006, print version.

b. Tax Management Weekly Report

The Weekly Report primarily serves as a digest rather than full text service for primary source material. It focuses on news and analysis of current issues. Short articles appear in its Focus section.

The Weekly Report covers court decisions, regulations, revenue rulings and procedures, private letter rulings, and other IRS material. It is particularly useful for subscribers to Tax Management Portfolios, as it includes cross-references and updating information for Portfolio material.

Illustration 16-2. Excerpt from Weekly Report on BNA Website

```
┌─────────────────────────────────────────────────────────────┐
│ ▮▮Tax Management▮▮                                           │
│                                                              │
│      Weekly Report                                           │
│      ─────────────────────────────                           │
│                                                              │
│   Portfolios Affected by Issue Date                          │
│                                                              │
│ ▼2006                                                        │
│   ▼03/20/2006                                                │
│     ▼0630 T.M., Tax Court Litigation                         │
│       ▯ SEC. 7486--REFUND, CREDIT, OR ABATEMENT OF AMOUNTS   │
│         DISALLOWED                                           │
│   ▼03/13/2006                                                │
│     ▼0506 T.M., Tax Credits: Concepts and Calculation        │
│       ▯ SEC. 45--ELECTRICITY PRODUCED FROM CERTAIN RENEWABLE │
│         RESOURCES, ETC.                                       │
│     ▼0627 T.M., Limitations Periods, Interest on Underpayments│
│         and Overpayments, and Mitigation                     │
│       ▯ SEC. 6621--DETERMINATION OF RATE OF INTEREST         │
└─────────────────────────────────────────────────────────────┘
```

→The online version includes links to full-text documents.

2. Tax Notes

This weekly newsletter contains a comprehensive collection of recent tax-oriented material. Tax Notes includes digests or lists of revenue rulings and procedures, other IRS documents, and court opinions. It also includes information about committee reports, testimony at hearings, bills, and statements in Congressional Record. The editors also cover public hearings on regulations and comments received on proposed regulations. Tax Notes publishes one or more articles in each issue.

Full text of documents is available on Tax Notes Today. Tax Notes Today is available on LexisNexis and on Tax Analysts' web-based service.

Illustration 16-3. Excerpt from Tax Notes Print Version

NEWS IN BRIEF

TREASURY AND IRS BALANCING PENSION ACT, 2006 GUIDANCE PLAN. Although Treasury and the IRS have to address many changes in the Pension Protection Act of 2006 (P.L. 109-280) made to pension plan rules, they are "very serious" about "getting guidance out in a timely way," said Joseph Grant, the new director of employee plans in the IRS Tax Exempt and Government Entities Division last week

Corporation to come up with a unified definition of governmental plan, but added that he doesn't expect one to be produced by the end of the year.

Unlocking the Vaults

---

3. Federal Tax Day; Federal Tax Weekly

These newsletters are available online through the Tax Research NetWork. CCH includes links to primary source material discussed in these newsletters. There are also links to discussion in online versions of CCH looseleaf services. Federal Tax Weekly is received by subscribers to the CCH Federal Tax Service.

Illustration 16-4. Excerpt from Federal Tax Weekly

→Online users can access Federal Tax Weekly as a PDF file.

Illustration 16-5. Excerpt from Federal Tax Day

→Note the hyperlinks to primary source materials.

4. Daily Tax Bulletin; Federal Tax Bulletin

The biweekly Federal Tax Bulletin supplements the TaxExpert CD-ROM. It includes reports on major legislative, administrative, and judicial action and brief digests of other items. Each issue has a Code section index; indexes are not cumulated. Subscribers can receive the print newsletter by e-mail. They also can access full-text documents using TaxExpert Online, Kleinrock's online service. The Daily Tax Bulletin is archived online.

Illustration 16-6. Excerpt from Federal Tax Bulletin

Kleinrock's Federal Tax Bulletin • Page 12

IN BRIEF

Bankruptcy

United States v. White, No. 05-15857 (11th Cir. 10/11/06): The Eleventh Circuit, reversing a district court, held that the IRS's assessment against a debtor in bankruptcy after a bankruptcy court's confirmation of a reorganization plan but before the estate assets revested in the debtor did not violate the bankruptcy code's automatic stay provision. *11 U.S.C. Section 362.*

that she is liable for the addition to tax for failure to timely file. *Code Section 183.*

Harrell v. Commissioner, T.C. Summary 2006-165: The Tax Court denied deductions for charitable contributions and excess unreimbursed employee and other miscellaneous expenses for uniforms, supplies and equipment, job search expenses, telephone expenses, and tax preparation fees for lack of substantiation. *Code Section 274.*

errors that a couple claimed entitled them to an interest abatement were ministerial acts and that they were not entitled to the interest abatement. *Code Section 6404.*

In re G-I Holdings, Inc., No. 02-3082 (D.C. N.J. 9/8/06): A district court held that a company did not adequately disclose on its return a transaction which resulted in an omission of more than 25 percent of its gross income. Thus, the six-year statute of limitations applied. *Code Section 6501.*

→The excerpt above is a PDF version of the newsletter and is available on the publisher's website.

Illustration 16-7. Excerpt from Daily Tax Bulletin

Kleinrock Bulletins

Federal Daily Tax Bulletin

Go to Latest Official Tax Documents

Wednesday, November 01 2006

IRS Announces 2007 Standard Mileage Rates

Optional standard mileage rates used to calculate the deductible costs of operating an automobile for business, charitable, medical or moving purposes have been issued for 2007. Rev. Proc. 2006-49, 2006-___ I.R.B. ___.

more >>

End to Taxpayers Nightmare Means an End to Interest Assessments, Court Holds

The IRS could not assess additional interest on the taxpayers after the taxpayers reached stipulated Tax Court decisions with the IRS to "end their nightmare." Larosa's International Fuel co. Inc. v. United States, No. 97-834T (Fed. Cl. 10/27/06).

more >>

PART SIX

COLLECTIONS OF PRIMARY SOURCE MATERIALS

CHAPTER 17. PRINT MATERIALS

The materials described below, and referred to in other chapters, print several types of material used in tax research.[251] Except as indicated below, they contain no textual discussion of the materials presented.

SECTION A. TREASURY AND IRS MATERIALS

1. Internal Revenue Bulletin; Cumulative Bulletin; Bulletin Index-Digest System

These IRS-generated series contain the text of almost every nonjudicial primary authority. As the discussion below indicates, the Bulletin Index-Digest System (Index-Digest) was an excellent aid to using the other two series. Unfortunately, it ceased publication after the 1993/94 edition. As a result, citators and looseleaf services are the best print sources for locating citations to these items.[252]

The primary source materials printed in these volumes are available in microform (Chapter 18), CD/DVD (Chapter 19), and online (Chapter 20) services offered by a variety of vendors. Government-sponsored websites also include many of these materials.

a. Internal Revenue Bulletin

The weekly[253] Internal Revenue Bulletin (I.R.B.) has four parts. Part I prints the text of all revenue rulings, final regulations, and Supreme Court tax decisions issued during the week; publication is in Code section order. Part II covers treaties, including Treasury Department Technical

---

[251] Categories—Treasury and IRS Materials and Legislative and Administrative History Materials—reflect the primary use I make of each service.

[252] You can also search citators and looseleaf services online or simply perform an electronic search through an IRS database looking for a particular topic. For example, you might search for revenue rulings after 2004 dealing with divorce by performing the following Westlaw search: DIVORCE & DA(AFT 12/31/2004) in the FTX-RR database.

[253] Budget constraints occasionally result in a less-frequent publications schedule. See Ann. 93-82, 1993-22 I.R.B. 31, regarding semimonthly publication in June through September 1993. The IRS briefly considered eliminating the Cumulative Bulletin in 1998. See Ann. 99-36, 1999-1 C.B. 925.

Explanations (Subpart A), and tax legislation, including committee reports (Subpart B). Part III contains notices and revenue procedures, while Part IV, "Items of General Interest," is varied in content. Its coverage includes disbarment notices, announcements, and notices of proposed rulemaking. Federal Register dates and comment deadlines are provided in addition to the preambles and text of proposed regulations. The I.R.B. also prints notices of IRS acquiescence or nonacquiescence for judicial decisions against the government.

Each I.R.B. was separately paginated until mid-1999. The I.R.B. is now paginated successively over a six-month period.

Each issue contains a Numerical Finding List for each type of item; a Finding List of Current Action on Previously Published Items indicates IRS, but not judicial, action. These lists lack any tie-in to Code sections and cover no more than six months. The quarterly subject area indexes also lack Code section information.

Because of its index format, the Bulletin is best used to locate material for which you already have a citation[254] or as a tool for staying abreast of recent developments. I.R.B. items are shown in Illustrations 4-6 and 10-1.

b. Cumulative Bulletin

Every six months the material in the I.R.B. is republished in a hardbound Cumulative Bulletin (C.B.). The C.B. began publication in 1919. Volumes initially were given Arabic numerals (1919-1921). Although volume spines may show Arabic numerals, the IRS used Roman numerals for 1922 through 1936 volumes. Since 1937, volumes have been numbered by year (e.g., 1937-1). With the exception of 1943-1945, there have been two volumes annually (with occasional extra volumes for extensive legislative history material)[255] since 1920; the -1, -2 numbering system for each year began in 1922.

The C.B. format has varied over time. Before 1998, it largely followed that of the weekly service with three exceptions. First, major tax legislation and committee reports generally appeared in a third volume rather than in the two semiannual volumes.[256] Second, only disbarment

---

[254] You can locate citations in citators, looseleaf services, periodical articles, and newsletters.

[255] The -3 Cumulative Bulletin may be issued much later. For example, the 1999-3 C.B. was not issued until June 6, 2003.

[256] Committee reports for 1913 through 1938 appear in 1939-1 (pt. 2) C.B.

notices and proposed regulations appeared from Part IV.[257] Finally, rulings appeared in the C.B. in semiannual Code section order; this bore no relation to their numerical order.

In 1998, the IRS ceased recompiling items in the C.B. Instead, C.B.s are simply bound versions of the individual I.R.B.s. If an item appears in the I.R.B., it will also appear in the C.B. Successive pagination for the I.R.B.s began in mid-1999.

At the time it changed format, the C.B. added a Code Sections Affected by Current Actions listing. Although this provides additional assistance in using six-month's worth of material, it does not make searching over longer periods of time any easier. The other C.B. indexes and finding lists are as difficult to use as are their counterparts in the I.R.B.

Table 17-1. Cumulative Bulletin Format Changes

Year	Numbering	Other Major Changes
1919	1, 2, 3	
1922	I-1, I-2, II-1	Rulings divided by type of tax
1937	1937-1, 1937-2	
1939		Committee reports added
1953		End of separate table of contents by type of tax
1974		End of separate sections for 1939 Code
1981		Proposed Regulations added
1993		Acquiescences no longer limited to Tax Court regular decisions
1998		Six-month rearrangement of I.R.B. items ceased

c. Bulletin Index-Digest System

The IRS issued the Index-Digest in four services: Income Tax; Estate and Gift Tax; Employment Tax; and Excise Tax. The Income Tax service, which is the focal point for this discussion, was supplemented quarterly; the other services received semiannual supplementation. New softbound cumulations generally were issued every two years. The last cumulation covered 1954 through 1993 for income tax and 1994 for the other taxes.

Committee reports for the 1954 Code's enactment never appeared in the C.B.

[257] These are printed in Part III or immediately following it through 1997. Proposed regulations, which appear as a separate category, were added in the 1981-1 volume. The C.B.'s format differed from the above description until the 1974-2 volume.

The Index-Digest provided I.R.B. or C.B. citations for revenue rulings and procedures, Supreme Court and adverse Tax Court decisions, Public Laws, Treasury Decisions, and treaties. It also digested the rulings, procedures, and court decisions.

The following paragraphs explain using the final (1954-1993/94) Index-Digest to locate citations and digests.

(1) Statutes and Regulations

Specific Code and regulations sections that were added or amended appear in the Finding Lists for Public Laws and Treasury Decisions. A C.B. citation is given for the first page of each Public Law involved.

Another Finding List, "Public Laws Published in the Bulletin," provides committee report citations and popular names for the various revenue acts. It is in Public Law number order.

(2) Rulings and Procedures

The Finding Lists for Revenue Rulings, Revenue Procedures, and other Items can be used in various ways to locate relevant rulings and procedures. These items appear in Code and regulations section order in the "Internal Revenue Code of 1986" section, and in ruling and procedure number order in the "Revenue Rulings" and "Revenue Procedures" sections. The Index-Digest lists revenue rulings and procedures involving treaties by country in the "Revenue Rulings and Revenue Procedures under Tax Conventions" section. The service covers both 1954 and 1986 Code items.

These Finding Lists do not provide C.B. citations. Instead, citations are given to a digest of each item in the Index-Digest itself; the C.B. citation follows the digest. The two-step format frequently saves time; a glance through the digest may indicate the item is not worth reading in full text.[258] [See Illustration 17-1.]

Because the digests are arranged by subject matter, you can locate pertinent rulings even if you do not know the underlying Code or regulations section. The subject matter divisions are so numerous that the same item may be digested under several different headings.

If a particular ruling or procedure was modified or otherwise affected by subsequent IRS action, the information appears in the "Actions on

---

[258] Unfortunately, the digest may not include a pertinent holding, in which case exclusive use of the digest would yield inadequate results.

Previously Published Revenue Rulings and Revenue Procedures" section of the Finding Lists. Judicial decisions affecting a ruling are not indicated. The IRS provided a C.B. citation for updating material if a subsequent ruling affected.

(3) Judicial Decisions

The Finding Lists for Revenue Rulings, Revenue Procedures, and Other Items listed all Supreme Court decisions and adverse Tax Court decisions in which the IRS acquiesced or nonacquiesced.

Supreme Court decisions appear alphabetically in the "Decisions of the Supreme Court" section of the Finding Lists. They are listed by an IRS-assigned Court Decision (Ct.D.) number in the "Internal Revenue Code of 1986" materials, arranged according to the applicable Code and regulations sections.

Tax Court decisions are listed alphabetically in the "Decisions of the Tax Court" section of the Finding Lists; they are listed by T.C. citation in the "Internal Revenue Code of 1986" materials.

As with rulings and procedures, references to Supreme Court decisions in the Finding Lists give only the digest number.[259] The official and Cumulative Bulletin citations follow the case digest. Because the digests follow a subject matter format, you can locate decisions by digest topic without first consulting the Finding Lists.

Illustration 17-1. Excerpt from Bulletin Index-Digest System

Allowances

they are not ordained, commissioned, or licensed as ministers of the gospel. §1.107-1. (Sec. 22(b), '39 Code; Sec. 107, '86 Code.)
  Rev. Rul. 59-270, 1959-2 C.B. 44 ....

22.47   Rental; minister; traveling evangelist.   An ordained minister, who performs evangelistic services at churches located away from the community in which he maintains his permanent home may exclude ....

nished by the National Guard to officers and enlisted personnel while on active duty is not includible in the gross income of the recipients. §1.61-2 (Sec. 61, '86 Code.)
Rev. Rul. 60-65, 1960-1 C.B. 21.

→The Index-Digest lists digest numbers (e.g., 22.47) after Code and

---

[259] Tax Court citations appear in both the Finding Lists and the digests. The Finding Lists indicate acquiescences; the digests provide citations for them.

regulations sections. The actual digests appear in a separate Index-Digest section.

2. U.S. Code Congressional & Administrative News—Federal Tax Regulations

The annual Federal Tax Regulations volumes contain the text of all income, estate and gift, and employment tax regulations in force on the first day of the year. These materials include references to the T.D. number, date, and Federal Register publication for both original promulgation and all amendments. This service omits T.D. numbers for original promulgation of pre-existing regulations republished in 1960 in T.D. 6498, 6500, or 6516. The final volume for each year includes a subject matter index.

3. Cumulative Changes

See Subsection B.3.

SECTION B. LEGISLATIVE AND ADMINISTRATIVE HISTORY MATERIALS

1. Internal Revenue Acts—Text and Legislative History; U.S. Code Congressional & Administrative News—Internal Revenue Code

You can use these services in researching the texts and histories of 1954 and 1986 Code sections.

Internal Revenue Acts, issued each year in pamphlet form, prints the full text of newly enacted statutes in chronological order. Hardbound volumes cumulate the material in one or more years' pamphlets.

Texts of selected committee reports and Congressional Record statements appear in the second section of each pamphlet. Each pamphlet includes a subject matter index; tables indicate Code sections affected and cross-reference Public Law section numbers to pages in Statutes at Large. The cross-reference table lists acts by name through 1996. Later pamphlets instead include a separate Popular Name table for acts. This series is excerpted from the general U.S. Code Congressional & Administrative News service. It includes cross-references to material printed in USCCAN but omitted here.

The annual Internal Revenue Code volumes contain the text of all Code sections in effect when the most recent congressional session ended.

Dates, Public Law numbers, and Statutes at Large citations appear in the brief history of enactment and amendment following each section. Editorial notes indicate effective dates and provide some information about prior language.[260] The final volume for each year contains a subject matter index.

2. Primary Sources

Primary Sources is an excellent tool for deriving the legislative history of existing Code sections. It also covers the Employee Retirement Income Security Act (ERISA). Unfortunately, its usefulness is limited to the period from 1969 to 2003.

Extensive legislative histories appear for selected Code sections. The sections chosen for inclusion are traced back to their original 1954 Code versions;[261] all changes are presented. [See Illustration 17-2.] Materials presented for each Code section include presidential messages, committee reports, Treasury Department testimony at hearings, and discussion printed in Congressional Record.

The legislative histories are published in several series, each of which covers several years.[262] Within each series, material appears in Code section order. Each series contains a Master Table of Contents in Code section order; these tables cover the current series and all prior series. Primary Sources limits its coverage to Code sections affected by the Tax Reform Act of 1969 or by subsequent legislation.

3. Cumulative Changes

This multivolume looseleaf service tracks changes in the Code and Treasury regulations. There are series for the 1939, 1954, and 1986 Codes and regulations; many libraries lack the 1939 Code series. Cumulative Changes covers employment taxes and provides limited coverage of excise taxes.

The Code and regulations materials appear separately, arranged in

---

[260] Primary Sources provides such information for 1969 and subsequent amendments.

[261] Series I also includes the 1939 Code version for many Code sections.

[262] Series I begins with sections affected by the Tax Reform Act of 1969; Series II begins with the 1976 Tax Reform Act; Series III begins with the Revenue Act of 1978; Series IV begins with the Economic Recovery Tax Act of 1981; Series V begins with the Tax Reform Act of 1986.

Code section order. The 1954 service includes parallel citation tables for the 1939 and 1954 Codes.

a. Internal Revenue Code

A chart for each Code section indicates its original effective date. The chart includes the Public Law number, section, and enactment and effective dates of each amendment and the act section prescribing the effective date. The chart covers Code section subdivisions (subsections, paragraphs, and even smaller subdivisions). It does not include Statutes at Large citations.

The format of Cumulative Changes changed slightly in the mid-1990s. It now prints citations for effective dates rather than the dates themselves. Illustration 17-3 includes both formats for Code section 51.

The pages following each chart reproduce each version (except the current one) since the provision's original introduction in the relevant Code. The current version can be found in any service that includes the current Code.

b. Treasury Regulations

Tables of amendments cover all regulations sections for each tax; individual sections do not have their own charts. Each table indicates the original and all amending T.D. numbers and filing dates and provides a Cumulative Bulletin or Internal Revenue Bulletin citation. The service also includes cross-references to United States Tax Reporter. A numerically ordered Table of Amending TDs indicates the purpose, date and C.B. or I.R.B. citation for each regulation issued.[263]

The tables follow the regulations part designations illustrated in Chapter 9; as a result, they do not follow a strict Code section numerical sequence. The 1954 series includes tables for regulations that have been redesignated or replaced.

Immediately following the tables, the editors print prior versions of each regulation. Older materials note changes in italics and use footnotes

---

[263] Although T.D. 6500, a 1960 republication of existing income tax regulations is not formally included, Cumulative Changes does list the original pre-1960 T.D. A cautionary note warns the user to remember that pre-1960 regulations were republished in T.D. 6500. T.D. 6498 (procedure and administration) and T.D. 6516 (withholding tax) receive similar treatment. None of these T.D.s appears in the Cumulative Bulletin.

to indicate stricken language; recent materials do not use this format. Cumulative Changes includes the T.D. number and the dates of approval and of filing for each version of a regulation.

Illustration 17-2. Excerpt from Primary Sources

IV-26   § 168 [1981] pg.(i)

SEC. 168 – ACCELERATED COST RECOVERY SYSTEM

Table of Contents

Page

→Primary Sources excerpts a wide range of documents.

Illustration 17-3. Excerpt from Cumulative Changes

3-2000   **Section 51. Amount of Credit**   § 51—p. 3

[See definitions preceding chart on page 1 of this section.]

SEC. 51 '86 I.R.C.	SUBSECTIONS					
	(f)—(h)	(i)(1)	(i)(2)	(i)(3)	(j)	(k)
Pub. Law 99-514, 10-22-86				Added by 1701(c) 1701(e)* Note 1		Redesig. 1878(f)(1) 1881* Note 1
AMENDING ACTS						
Pub. Law 103-66 8-10-93		13302(d) 13303* 8-10-93				

Public Law	Law Sec.	IRC Sec.	Eff. Date
P.L. 104-188	1201(a)	51(a)	1201(g)*
	1201(e)(1)	51(a)	1201(g)*
	1201(f)	51(c)(1)	1201(g)*
	1201(d)	51(c)(4)	1201(g)*
	1201(b)	51(d)	1201(g)*
	1201(e)(1)	51(g)	1201(g)*
	1201(c)	51(i)(3)	1201(g)*
	1201(e)(5)	51(j) Heading	1201(g)*
P.L. 105-34	603(b)(2)	51(d)(2)(A)	
	603(c)(2)	51(d)(9)-(11) Redes (10)-(12)	
	603(d)(2)	51(i)(3)	
P.L. 105-277	1002(a)	51(c)(4)(B)	1002(b)
	4006(c)(1)	51(d)(6)(B)(i)	

→As of November 2006, the table for section 51 goes through P.L. 108-311.

4. Barton's Federal Tax Laws Correlated

Five hardbound volumes trace income, estate, and gift tax provisions from the Revenue Act of 1913[264] through the Tax Reform Act of 1969.

a. 1909 through 1952

The five hardbound volumes reproduce in Code or act section order the text of the various tax acts. Because the acts are lined up in several columns on each page, it is possible to read across a page and see every version of a particular section for the period that volume covers.[265] Whenever possible, Barton's uses different typefaces to highlight changes.

The first two volumes provide a citation to Statutes at Large for each act. Volume 1 includes case annotations, and each volume has a subject matter index. The volumes covering the 1939 Code include tables indicating amending acts and effective dates for 1939 Code sections. Volume 5 has a retrospective table cross-referencing sections to pages in the four previous volumes.

b. 1953-1969

The looseleaf sixth volume does not print the text of Code sections. Its Tables instead provide citations to primary sources that print the desired material. Tables A-D are in Code section order; Table E is in Public Law number order.

Table A provides the history of the 1954 Act. It indicates Statutes at Large page; House, Senate, and Conference report page (official and U.S. Code Congressional & Administrative News); 1939 Code counterpart; Revenue Act where the provision originated; and relevant pages in volumes 1-5.

Table B covers amendments to the 1954 Code. For each section it provides Public Law number, section, and enactment date; Statutes at Large citation; House, Senate, and Conference report numbers and location in the Cumulative Bulletin; comment (e.g., revision, amendment); and effective date information.

Table C is similar to Table A, but it covers the 1939 Code. It gives the

---

[264] The original second edition (vol. 1) also contained the text of the income tax laws from 1861 through 1909. The reproduced second edition omits this material.

[265] Volume 1 covers 1913-1924; volume 2 covers 1926-38; volume 3 covers 1939-43; volume 4 covers 1944-49; volume 5 covers 1950-52.

1954 Code section; the origin of the 1939 Code provision; and cross-references to volumes 1-5.

Table D is the same as Table B, but it covers post-1953 changes to the 1939 Code.

Table E provides citations to legislative history for all acts from 1953 through 1969. It also provides the following information for each act: Public Law number; date of enactment; congressional session; Statutes at Large, Cumulative Bulletin, and USCCAN citations for the act; congressional sessions, dates, and Cumulative Bulletin and USCCAN citations for House, Senate, and Conference report numbers; and Congressional Record citations for floor debate. Acts are not cited by popular name.

5. Seidman's Legislative History of Federal Income and Excess Profits Tax Laws[266]

Seidman's stops in 1953, but it remains useful for determining the legislative history of provisions that originated in the 1939 Code or even earlier.[267] This series follows each act, beginning with the most recent, presenting the text of Code sections, followed by relevant committee reports and citations to hearings[268] and the Congressional Record.[269] In some cases, Seidman's excerpts these documents. [See Illustration 17-4.] Because Seidman's uses different type styles, you can easily ascertain where in Congress a provision originated or was deleted. [See Illustration 17-5.[270]]

Seidman's prints proposed sections that were not enacted along with relevant history explaining their omission. This information can aid you in interpreting provisions Congress did enact.

---

[266] The two volumes covering 1939 through 1953 include both taxes. Separate volumes for the income tax and the excess profits tax were used for the earlier materials, covering 1861 through 1938 and 1917 through 1946, respectively.

[267] I.R.C. § 263, for example, contains language taken almost verbatim from § 117 of the 1864 Act. See Act of June 30, 1864, ch. 173, 13 Stat. 223, 281-82.

[268] Seidman's cites relevant page numbers in the hearings and indicates appearances by Treasury representatives.

[269] Seidman's cites to relevant pages and reproduces the text itself in some instances.

[270] Illustration 17-7 covers the report excerpted in Illustration 17-5.

Although its coverage has great breadth, Seidman's does not print every Code section. It omits provisions with no legislative history, items lacking substantial interpretive significance, and provisions the editor considered long outmoded. Seidman's does not cover gift, estate, or excise taxes.

Seidman's has three indexes. The Code section index lists each section by act and assigns it a key number. The same key number is assigned to corresponding sections in subsequent acts. The key number index indicates every act, by section number and page in the text, where the item involved appears. A subject index lists key numbers by topic.

Volume II of the 1953-1939 set contains a table cross-referencing 1953 and 1954 Code sections covered in Seidman's. [See Illustration 7-9.]

Seidman's is no longer in print, and thus may not be on the shelf in every library. It has been added to the HeinOnline database in both the Legal Classics Library and the U.S. Federal Legislative History Library. Both of the illustrations below are from HeinOnline.

Illustration 17-4. Congressional Discussion in Seidman's

1861 ACT   1043

I presume it means the net income; and, if so, it seems to me it ought to be more guarded.

* * *

MR. SIMMONS. * * * Now, to avoid all question about the deterioration of property, I think we had better not put that word in. A man will say his house lost five or ten per cent. by the wear of it; that the tenants have destroyed the wood-work, and all those kind of evasions; but nobody can mistake the word "income." It is the net profits of a man for the year, and the Secretary of the Treasury will provide all the ways and means to ascertain it. If you undertake to do it in the bill, you will only make it more confused than it is now; and that is my objection to the amendment.

MR. CLARK. It does not seem so, because it would be very easy to insert in the third line before the word "income"

the word "net." That is the meaning, and why should it not be done?

MR. SIMMONS. That is the very thing that would cause trouble. Suppose a person owed a dozen stores on one of the wharves in Boston, from which he got $10,000 a year rent. I mean to tax $9,-000 of that amount by this bill. If I put in the word "net" income, he would try to have all the repairs, and so on, deducted, and would make them amount to as much as the income. That would be the trouble. When a man repairs his buildings, he will have less income that year, because he spends it in repairing. I thought of putting this word "net" in; but I could see so many ways of evading it that I thought it better to let the Secretary of the Treasury prescribe his rules, and let the bill cover all incomes. (p. 315)

Illustration 17-5. Statutory Language and History in Seidman's

for key to statute type]   **1934 ACT**   **381**

SEC. 164. DIFFERENT TAXABLE YEARS.   Sec.
                                                                            164

If the taxable year of a beneficiary is different from that of the estate
or trust, the amount which he is required, under section 162 (b), to include
in computing his net income, shall be based upon the income of the estate
or trust for any taxable year of the estate or trust (whether beginning on,
before, or after January 1, 1934) ending within his taxable year.

Committee Reports

Report—Ways and Means Commit-   adopted in section 1 to add additional
tee (73d Cong., 2d Sess., H. Rept.   language to provide for cases where the
704).—Section 164. Different taxable   estate or trust has a taxable year begin-
years: The present law requires a bene-   ning in 1933 and ending in 1934. (p.32)
ficiary of an estate or trust to include in   Report—Senate Finance Committee
his income amounts allowed as a deduc-   (73d Cong., 2d Sess., S. Rept. 558).—
tion to the estate or trust under section   Same as Ways and Means Committee
162 (b). In order to continue this pol-   Report. (p.40)
icy, it is necessary in view of the policy

SEC. 166. REVOCABLE TRUSTS.   Sec.
                                                                            166

Where at any time **(96)** <during the taxable year> the power to
revest in the grantor title to any part of the corpus of the trust is vested—
     (1)   in the grantor, either alone or in conjunction with any person

→The 1934 Act predated the first Internal Revenue Code. Section
numbers do not correspond to the numbering system used for the 1954
and 1986 Codes.

→Note how Seidman's indicates language stricken on the Senate floor in
Sec. 166.

6. The Internal Revenue Acts of the United States: 1909-1950; 1950-1972; 1973-

a. Original Series

This set, edited by Bernard D. Reams, Jr., provides the most comprehensive legislative histories of all the services discussed in this chapter.
In addition to each congressional version of revenue bills, the 144 original
volumes (1909-1950) contain the full texts of hearings, committee reports,
Treasury studies, and regulations. Official pagination is retained for
relevant documents. In addition to income and excise taxes, this set
includes estate and gift, social security, railroad retirement, and
unemployment taxes. This set is available in print and microfiche.

An Index volume contains several indexes for locating relevant materials. A chronological index lists each act and every item comprising its legislative history. That index indicates the volume, but not the page, where each item is located.[271] Other indexes cover miscellaneous subjects, such as hearings on items that did not result in legislation; Treasury studies; Joint Committee reports; regulations; congressional reports; congressional documents; bill numbers; and hearings. Unfortunately, there is neither a Code section nor a subject matter index.

Full text materials appear by type of document rather than by the act involved. All hearings are printed together, as are all bills, laws, studies, and regulations. You will need to use several volumes to assemble all materials for a particular law or provision. This is by no means a substantial drawback to using this set; assembling the same materials from elsewhere in the collection (assuming they are all available) would be far more difficult.

b. Subsequent Series[272]

Professor Reams subsequently compiled materials to extend this set's coverage to later years. The later volumes are similar in coverage and format to the 1909-50 materials, although hearings receive less attention.

The 1954 volumes include committee reports, hearings, debates, and the final act. Revenue bills and Treasury studies do not appear. Because the IRS Cumulative Bulletins do not cover the 1954 Act, these materials are particularly valuable. A two-volume update published in 1993 includes fifty House and Senate bills missing from the original volumes. The 11 volumes of the original 1954 series are also available in the HeinOnline service.

Additional sets cover 1950-51, 1953-72, 1969, 1971, 1975, 1976, 1978, 1980, 1984, 1985 (Balanced Budget), 1986, 1987 (Balanced Budget), 1988, 1990, and 1993. Two other sets, covering the Taxpayer Relief Act of 1997 and the Economic Growth and Tax Relief Reconciliation Act of 2001, were edited by William Manz.

---

[271] These volumes are not consecutively paginated, so neither a detailed table of contents nor an index will lead you to the correct page. Although you will have to page through the particular volume to reach the material you seek, that is a minor inconvenience.

[272] I have used libraries that shelve other legislative history materials between sets of the Reams materials. Check the library catalog to determine which sets your library has.

7. Eldridge, The United States Internal Revenue System

This reprint of early legislative materials is a useful complement to The Internal Revenue Acts of the United States, discussed in Subsection B.6. It includes texts of revenue acts passed through 1894. There is extensive textual material as well as annotations for the various acts. It also contains a descriptive history of the various acts.

Illustration 17-6. Excerpt from The Internal Revenue Acts of the United States Index Volume

REVENUE ACT OF 1934

Volume

BILL IN ITS VARIOUS FORMS
Compiler's note 74

Introduced: 73d Cong.. 2d session.
H.R. 7835. In the House of Representatives
February 9, 1934. Mr. Doughton of North
Carolina introduced the following bill,
which was referred to the Committee on Ways
and Means and ordered to be printed 74

House committee print No. 1. (Confidential
committee print No. 1). 73d Cong.,
2d session H.R. (7835). In the House of
Representatives February (2), 1934. Mr.
introduced the following bill, which
was referred to the Committee on Ways and
Means and ordered to be printed 74

Reported to the House: 73d Cong.,
2d session. H.R. 7835 (Report No. 704).
....
of the Union and ordered to be printed 74

→The report excerpted in Illustration 17-5 (Seidman's) appears in full text in volume 100 of The Internal Revenue Acts of the United States. [See Illustration 17-7.]

→The text missing from the third entry ("Mr. introduced") is also omitted in the original Index volume.

Illustration 17-7. Excerpt from The Internal Revenue Acts of the United States Volume 100

Section 148(b). Profits of taxable year declared: This subsection is entirely rewritten, not with any view to a change in policy, but with the intent to set forth in more definite language the present policy.

Section 164. Different taxable years: The present law requires a beneficiary of an estate or trust to include in his income amounts allowed as a deduction to the estate or trust under section 162(b). In order to continue this policy, it is necessary in view of the policy adopted in section 1 to add additional language to provide for cases where the estate or trust has a taxable year beginning in 1933 and ending in 1934.

Section 168 (Revenue Act of 1932). Capital net gains and losses: This section is omitted from the bill in view of the change of policy in taxing capital gains.

Section 182. Tax on partners: this section represents a change in section 182 of existing law in two respects: First, because of the change in the policy of treating fiscal-year returns, a new section (sec. 188) is carried in

→The Internal Revenue Acts reprints reports in the format used by Congress; all sections for each act appear in order. Compare the treatment in Seidman's [Illustration 16-4], which groups reports by act or Code section.

→Because there was no Internal Revenue Code in 1934, some act sections merely repeat sections enacted in previous years. Other act sections change earlier language or add entirely new provisions.

8. Legislative History of the Internal Revenue Code of 1954

Prepared for the Joint Committee on Internal Revenue Taxation in 1967, this volume tracks all changes to the 1954 Code through October 23, 1965. It is arranged in Code section order and provides full text of the original 1954 language and all changes. It also includes ancillary provisions (both in other parts of U.S.C. and not in U.S.C.) and citations to Statutes at Large. There are four tables: 1939 Code sources of each 1954 provision; corresponding sections of the two Codes; post 1954 amendments to the 1939 Code; and amendatory statutes. The last table includes the Public Law number; date enacted; bill number; congressional report numbers; Act name; and Statutes at Large citation.

9. Cumulative Bulletin

See Subsection A.1.

CHAPTER 18. MICROFORMS

SECTION A. ADVANTAGES AND DISADVANTAGES

Microforms have three important advantages. The first relates to space. As primary and secondary source materials proliferate, libraries can use microforms to reduce their space needs. A second advantage relates to availability. Your library may be able to buy non-electronic versions of some historical materials only in microform. A third advantage relates to cost. Once the library has purchased materials in microform, it has no obligation to make further outlays to ensure its access to those materials.

There are several reasons why other formats may be preferable to microforms. These relate to availability, ease of searching, mobility, space, and security.

Availability may be the most critical factor. Many publishers are eliminating microform products and switching to CD/DVD and online services. Even if a publisher no longer updates a microform service, these materials remain valuable for historical research.

Navigation and mobility are also important. Electronic sources are easier to navigate and permit word and phrase searching. Microforms are effectively used only if the compiler has indexed them well. In addition, electronic materials do not tie you to a fixed place. Microforms require a reader or reader-printer. If you have the appropriate computer configuration, you can use electronic materials anywhere.

Space and security are relevant factors for many libraries. Web-based systems require no library storage space; CD/DVDs require relatively little space. Although microforms require less space than their print counterparts, they do require more than the electronic versions. Finally, microforms share a problem with looseleaf services; the individual forms can be misfiled or pilfered from the library.

SECTION B. FORMAT

Microforms are available in a variety of formats, including microfilm, microprint, microcard, microfiche, and ultrafiche. You can use a reader-printer to produce a copy of materials you locate.

SECTION C. AVAILABLE MATERIALS

Government publications available in microform include Congressional Record, Statutes at Large, Federal Register, Code of Federal Regulations, and the Cumulative Bulletin. Other materials include Tax Court and Supreme Court case reporter services. Many libraries include briefs filed with the United States Supreme Court in their microform collections.

You are also likely to find legislative history materials available in microform. Publishers using this format include Congressional Information Service (part of LexisNexis) and William S. Hein & Co., Inc.

The CIS/Microfiche Library includes committee hearings, reports, and prints and public laws since 1970. Libraries can customize their purchases to include only certain types of documents. The CIS/Index, available in print or online, provides abstracts of publications and a separate index.[273]

Several series of Hein's Internal Revenue Acts of the United States (Chapter 17) are available in microform. These include the sets for 1909-1950, 1950-51, 1954, 1953-72, 1978, and 1984.

Some libraries may own ultrafiche copies of Tax Management Primary Sources–Series I (Chapter 17).

Law reviews and other periodicals may also be available in microform. Representative publications available from Hein include Akron Tax Journal, American Journal of Tax Policy, Tax Law Review, Tax Lawyer, and several tax institutes.[274]

Because the number of materials and the microform format used varies, always consult a librarian about microform access before concluding that your library lacks a particular resource.

---

[273] See http://www.lexisnexis.com/academic/3cis/cisl/cis-index.asp for a listing of CIS publications. Many of the CIS publications are now available online.

[274] HeinOnline, a web-based source for both primary and secondary authority materials, is discussed in Chapters 14 and 20.

CHAPTER 19. CD/DVD

SECTION A. ADVANTAGES AND DISADVANTAGES

Disc-based services store significant amounts of information yet require little storage space. In many areas of research, CD/DVD and online services have supplanted microform as an alternative to print materials.

Although CD/DVD materials may be updated less frequently than looseleaf services or other research tools are,[275] they have offsetting advantages. The CD/DVD format lets you perform more efficient searches than can be accomplished using print services. Some publishers even provide a direct link to their online services. This option reduces your online time, an important factor if you are billed based on that time.

Most looseleaf services print recent developments in separate subdivisions, sometimes even in separate volumes. Update discs integrate new material directly into the original text. Because all material is on the same CD/DVD,[276] you don't have to worry about filing errors or damaged pages.

Discs are not a perfect substitute for print versions of primary source materials. A disc may not use the citation form you need for a brief or article; even if it does, it may not show page numbers for individual sections of text. In some instances, the citation provided is erroneous.

There are two reasons to make sure you have the most recent version of a disc. First, some discs have expiration dates; you won't be able to access their contents after that date. Second, a disc is only as current as the underlying material it includes. A publisher that updates a particular print treatise quarterly is unlikely to update it more frequently in CD/DVD.

A major disadvantage of disc-based services relates to access. Unless the service is networked, only one researcher can use it at a time. In

---

[275] Several CD/DVD services offer updating options. Check the option in use (for example, monthly or quarterly) so that you don't erroneously assume your disc reflects the most recent changes in the law.

[276] Some services require multiple CD-ROMs. In that case, you will be prompted to insert the appropriate CD if your computer is not attached to a CD changer.

contrast, several researchers can simultaneously use different volumes of a print reporter service. If they use an online service, they can search the same volumes simultaneously.

Section B. Search Strategies

1. Similarity to Searching Print Materials

You can use CD/DVD materials much as you would print items. In the case of treatises, for example, you can locate a topic in the table of contents and then review that text segment or download it for later reading.

As is true for other types of research, you must consider synonyms if your concept can be expressed in different ways.[277] In addition, just as print publishers use different cross-referencing methods, CD/DVD publishers may use different search commands. Table 19-1 lists common search commands.

2. Search Strategies Unique to Electronic Materials

A major difference between print and electronic services relates to the latter's use of hypertext links. When you click on a link, you are transported to other text sections or to primary source materials such as the Code or Treasury regulations. To return to the original text, you merely click on the appropriate command. Although it appears similar to conducting a search using multiple print volumes, using links is not the same. Be careful to backtrack rather than exit the service if you want to retrace your steps.

Another difference relates to your initial search strategy. Rather than using indexes or tables to find material, you can use electronic services to find primary source material directly. As shown in Illustration 19-9, these services offer several search fields and also let you specify words that must appear in the document.

Electronic services also allow more sophisticated searching. You can specify Boolean connectors (e.g., and, or, and not). You can also take advantage of wild card symbols (e.g., deduct* for deduct, deducting, deduction, deducted, deductions, and deductible) to expand your search

---

[277] Check to see if the CD/DVD includes a thesaurus feature. If you insert a $ sign at the end of a word on some services, your results will include synonyms. [See Illustration 19-7.]

results.

Because search commands vary, you should read the user's guide for each service. If you regularly use CD/DVDs from different publishers, you might benefit from compiling a short command list for each service you use. Remember also to check the contents; electronic services often expand or contract their coverage based on market demand.

3. Differences Between CD/DVD and Online Services

Online services are likely to include more primary and secondary sources than a single CD/DVD, thus avoiding the need to change discs.[278] Online services are more likely to let you narrow searches by year or by dates within a year. Online services also use their own search command structure. If you use a particular service's disc version, don't be surprised if you must use different commands online. You are most likely to encounter different search commands if you use a general online service rather than one offered by the CD/DVD's publisher.[279]

Section C. Representative Materials

The sources discussed below are a sampling of the materials available. Some are disc-based versions of the publisher's print materials. Others are available only electronically.

1. Tax Analysts

a. OneDisc

Tax Analysts offers two versions of its OneDisc product. The basic OneDisc is a CD-ROM product; the OneDisc Premium is a DVD product. Both versions are available with monthly or quarterly updates.

Both products include the Code, regulations, Internal Revenue Bulletin items, and other IRS publications (including private letter rulings and chief counsel documents). Both provide information about new legislation. Both provide explanatory material (the Tax Analysts Baedeker) and helpful tables of IRS information, including inflation adjustments and

---

[278] Government-sponsored and other nonsubscription online services may use hyperlinks both within their websites and to other sites.

[279] For example, if you search Federal Tax Coordinator 2d using OnPoint, you can add letters at the end of a word using an asterisk (*). If you use Westlaw, the comparable command is an exclamation point (!).

interest rates.

The major difference relates to coverage of judicial decisions and tax treaties. The basic OneDisc doesn't include treaties and publishes full text only of current judicial decisions. It includes summaries of older decisions. The OneDisc Premium does include treaties and publishes full text of older decisions. It also includes the Internal Revenue Manual. The illustrations in this section are for the OneDisc Premium DVD.

Illustration 19-1. Excerpt from OneDisc Premium Contents

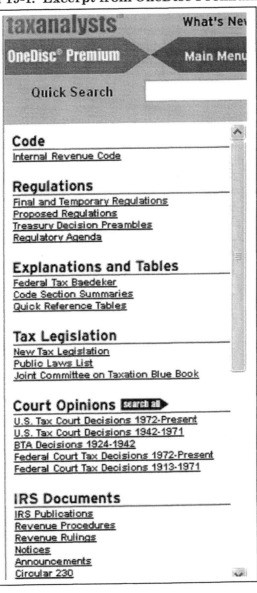

Illustration 19-2. Search Using OneDisc

Tax Court Decisions 1972-Present | Advanced Word Search

Search for word or phrase:

| cosmetic surgery | **HELP with this search**

○ all the words
◉ exact phrase
○ within [10] words of each other

◉ And   ○ Or   ○ Not   ○ within [10] words of each other

Search for word or phrase:

| deduction |

◉ all the words
○ exact phrase
○ within [10] words of each other

[Search] [Clear] [Cancel]

Thesaurus is: ○ On ◉ Off

→I decided to search in the U.S. Tax Court 1972-Present Opinions file using words (cosmetic surgery AND deductible) as the search terms. I could instead have used criteria such as Code section, case name, citation, or jurisdiction (assuming I knew them). I did not turn on the Thesaurus function.

Illustration 19-3. Excerpt from Items Found Using OneDisc

	Document	Heading
1	Al-Murshidi, Cynthia S. v. Comm. (December 13, 2001)	RECONSTRUCTIVE SURGERY AFTER WEIGHT LOSS IS DEDUCTIBLE.
2	Baker, Thomas J., et ux. v. Comm. (May 30, 1990)	TAX COURT SPLITS THE BABY AND DETERMINES VALUE OF CORPORATE STOCK CONTRIBUTED TO F
3	Mattes, William W., Jr. v. Comm. (September 21, 1981)	COST OF HAIR TRANSPLANT WAS DEDUCTIBLE; COURT EMPHASIZED LACK OF EFFECTIVE DRUGS.
4	Maxwell, Peter E., et ux. v. Comm. (July 31, 1990)	PAYMENT TO EMPLOYEE/SHAREHOLDER FOR JOB-RELATED INJURY IS EXCLUDABLE FROM GROSS IN
5	Wilkinson, Tolbert S., et ux. v. Comm. (February 1, 1996)	COURT SUSTAINS DISALLOWANCE OF SURGEON'S CLAIMED LOSSES FROM RANCH.

→The search located five opinions. I could then click for full text of those I wanted to read.

Illustration 19-4. Excerpt from Tax Analysts Baedeker

3.2-02 Deductible medical expenses.

Deductible medical expenses are amounts paid for the diagnosis, mitigation, treatment, or prevention of disease, or for the purpose 213(d)(1)) They also include amounts paid for qualified long-term services provided to a taxpayer or to the taxpayer's spouse or depen

On the other hand, expenses merely beneficial to the individual's general health aren't deductible. (Reg. section 1.213-1(e)(1)(ii))

Transportation. The expenses of transportation primarily for and essential to medical care qualify as medical expenses. (IRC secti automobile expenses, including gas, oil, tolls, and parking fees, but not depreciation, repair, insurance, or maintenance. In lieu of claimin specified amount for each mile the car is used for qualified medical transportation (15 cents per mile for 2005 before September 1 and 898, Announcement 2005-71; 18 cents per mile for 2006, Rev. Proc. 2005-78, 2005-51 IRB 1177). The cost of parking and tolls ma

Meals and lodging. Taxpayers may take medical expense deductions for lodging, but not meals, while away from home, when the The deduction for lodging is limited to amounts that are not lavish or extravagant; it cannot be more than $50 per night for each individu the individual seeking medical care also may claim the deduction.

Deductible and nondeductible expenses. What expenses are deductible? And what claimed deductions will be denied? Here ar

Unnecessary cosmetic surgery -- not deductible. Cosmetic surgery includes any procedure directed at improving the patient's a function of the body, or prevent or treat illness or disease. (IRC section 213(d)(9))

→I could have read an explanation of the medical expense deduction before doing the search conducted above. The Baedeker includes annotations that are hyperlinked to the primary sources.

b. Other Tax Analysts CD-ROM Products

Tax Analysts publishes the Internal Revenue Manual and The Tax Directory. The latter provides information about government officials and corporate tax managers. Both services are updated quarterly.

2. Research Institute of America

a. OnPoint

RIA offers two products that include a variety of research tools, OnPoint and Public Domain Library. Both are updated monthly.

The OnPoint service offers several combinations of sources on CD-ROM. Materials available include primary source, citator, looseleaf service, and treatise materials. In addition to the sources normally included in each service, subscribers can add selected other RIA services. Optional state tax modules that can be combined with the OnPoint federal materials. Two examples of OnPoint services are described in this section.

System 1 includes Federal Tax Coordinator 2d, Federal Tax Handbook, various practice aids, the Internal Revenue Code, Treasury regulations, revenue rulings and revenue procedures, IRS publications, and legislation.

System 5 includes United States Tax Reporter explanations and annotations, Federal Tax Handbook, the Internal Revenue Code, Treasury regulations, revenue rulings and revenue procedures, IRS publications, legislation, court decisions, and RIA Citator 2d.

The Public Domain Library is similar to OnPoint System 5, but it is more extensive. This CD includes IRS documents (such as private letter rulings) that do not appear in the Internal Revenue Bulletin. Its coverage of case materials begins in 1860, and it includes preambles to regulations.

The illustrations in this section are from OnPoint System 1.

Illustration 19-5. Excerpt from OnPoint Contents

```
📂 Federal Editorial Materials, Newsletters
     📄 Analysis: Federal Tax Coordinator
     📄 Federal Tax Handbook
     📄 Weekly Alert, Tax Planning Practice Guides
📂 Code, Regs, Treaties
     📄 Internal Revenue Code
     📄 Internal Revenue Code History
     📄 Regulations, Circular 230, Procedural Rules
     📄 Circular 230
     📄 Tax Treaties
📂 IRS Rulings, Releases, Publications, Tables
     📄 IRS Revenue Rulings, Procedures, Releases
     📄 Tables, Rates
     📄 IRS Taxpayer Information Publications
📂 Practice Aids, Compliance, Rules
     📄 Tax Practice Development
     📄 Elections and Compliance Statements
📄 Indexes
📂 New Law Analysis
     📄 Analysis of the Pension Protection Act of 2006
```

→The contents list reflects subject matter rather than Code section arrangement. This service is arranged by paragraph rather than by page or section.

→When the folders are open, as above, they display a list of contents.

Illustration 19-6. Search for IRS Documents in OnPoint

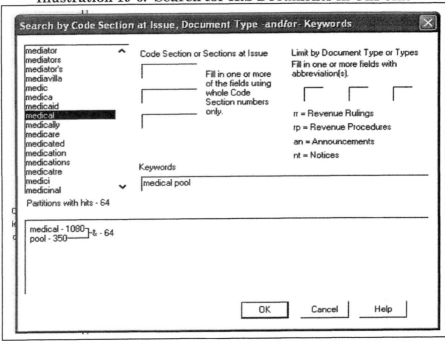

→I found 64 IRS documents that included both "medical" and "pool."

Illustration 19-7. Search in OnPoint Using Synonyms

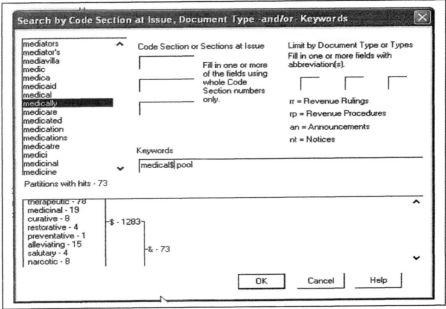

→Using medical$ yields several synonyms and 73 "hits."

Illustration 19-8. Available Search Options in OnPoint

→Search options include searching by phrase or proximity and using word variants.. You can also change how results are displayed.

Illustration 19-9. Partial Results from Illustration 19-6 Search

Rev. Proc. 2006-3, 2006-1 IRB 122, 01/03/2006 -- IRC Secs. 61, 79, 83, 101, 103, 104, 115, 117...
Rev. Proc. 2005-3, 2005-1 IRB 118, 01/06/2005 -- IRC Secs. 61, 79, 83, 101, 103, 104, 115, 117...
Ann. 2005-65, 2005-38 IRB 587, 09/15/2005 -- IRC Sec. 509
Rev. Proc. 2004-3, 2004-1 IRB 114, 01/07/2004 -- IRC Secs. 61, 79, 83, 101, 103, 104, 115, 117...
Rev. Proc. 2004-12, 2004-9 IRB, 02/12/2004 -- IRC Secs. 35(e), 35
Rev. Proc. 2004-43, 2004-31 IRB, 07/14/2004 -- IRC Secs. 6041, 6041A, 3406
Notice 2004-50, 2004-33 IRB, 07/23/2004 -- IRC Sec. 223
Ann. 2004-76, 2004-40 IRB 588, 09/30/2004 -- IRC Sec. 509
Rev. Proc. 2003-3, 2003-1 IRB 113, 01/09/2003 -- IRC Secs. 61, 79, 83, 101, 103, 104, 115, 117...
Notice 2003-37, 2003-26 IRB 1121, 06/27/2003 -- IRC Secs. 6041, 6041A
Rev. Proc. 2002-3, 2002-1 IRB 117, 01/16/2002 -- IRC Secs. 29, 61, 79, 83, 101, 103, 104, 115, ...
Rev. Proc. 2002-9, 2002-3 IRB 327, 01/08/2002 -- IRC Sec. 446
Rev. Proc. 2001-3, 2001-1 IRB 111, 01/08/2001 -- IRC Secs. 29, 61, 79, 83, 101, 103, 104, 115, ...
Ann. 2001-68, 2001-26 IRB 1357, 06/25/2001 -- IRC Secs. 170, 509

→An adjacent screen shows the text of each item as you select it. You can also link to Federal Tax Coordinator analysis for the items found.

b. Legislative History

RIA offers a Pending and Enacted Legislation CD-ROM. It covers laws, bills, and committee reports and begins with 1995. Updating is monthly.

c. IRS Material and Judicial Opinions

RIA offers an IRS Letter Rulings & Memoranda CD-ROM, which is updated monthly. This service covers private letter rulings, technical advice memoranda, actions on decisions, and general counsel memoranda. It also includes the Internal Revenue Code and Code history, regulations and preambles, and the Weekly Alert newsletter.

An IRS Practice CD-ROM covers the Internal Revenue Manual, the Market Specialization Program, Market Segment Understandings, Industry Specialization Program Papers, Circular 230, and the AICPA Statements of Responsibilities in Tax Practice. This service is updated quarterly.

RIA offers three CD-ROM services covering judicial opinions: American Federal Tax Reports (monthly updating); Tax Court Reported & Memorandum Decisions (monthly updating); and Tax Cases 1860-1953.

The RIA Citator 2nd, covering cases and rulings since 1954, is also available as a monthly subscription.

d. Other RIA Products

RIA offers two CD-ROMS, Elections & Compliance Statements and Tax Advisors Planning System, that provide language for completing IRS election forms or assist in drafting documents. Each is updated monthly.

3. LexisNexis

LexisNexis offers several Matthew Bender titles in various LexisNexis CD services. These include Murphy's Will Clauses; Rabkin & Johnson, Current Legal Forms with Tax Analysis; Rhoades & Langer, U.S. International Taxation and Tax Treaties; and various tax institutes (New York University, University of Miami, and University of Southern California).

4. Kleinrock

The Federal TaxExpert CD-ROM includes analysis and primary sources. The CD also has a link to Kleinrock's online service (Chapter 20). Illustrations 19-11 through 19-14 use TaxExpert to search for IRS notices or announcements for the tax treaty with Denmark illustrated in Chapter 8.

Illustration 19-10. Database Choices on TaxExpert

Search   Results

Databases

Select a database or multiple databases

☐ Kleinrock's Analysis
☐ Kleinrock's Federal Tax Bulletin
☐ Kleinrock's Tax Planning and Practice
☐ Kleinrock's Quick Reference Library
☐ Internal Revenue Code
☐ Treasury Regulations
☐ Proposed Regulations
☐ Treasury Decision Preambles
☐ IRS Letter Rulings and TAMs
☐ IRS Publications
☐ IRS Revenue Rulings
☐ IRS Revenue Procedures
☑ IRS Announcements
☑ IRS Notices
☐ Tax Court Reported
☐ Tax Court Memorandums
☐ Federal Tax Cases

→I selected the IRS Notices and IRS Announcements databases.

→The IRS Letter Rulings and TAMs selection includes many of the other non-I.R.B. items discussed in Chapter 10.

Illustration 19-11. Word Search on TaxExpert

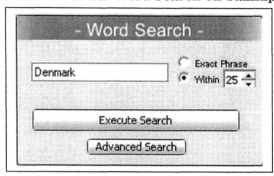

- Word Search -

Denmark
  ○ Exact Phrase
  ◉ Within 25

Execute Search

Advanced Search

→Instead of a single word, I could have searched on an exact phrase or for two terms within a set distance from each other.

Illustration 19-12. Results Obtained with TaxExpert

Search Results

Words Searched: Denmark
Document 6 of 6

[   ] (Find Term)
(Back) (Next)

Announcement 2000-59, 2000-29 I.R.B. 120(Changes to Publications 515 and 901)
Announcement 99-88, 1999-36 I.R.B. 407(Foundations Status of Certain Organizations)
Notice 2003-69, 2003-42 I.R.B. 851(United States Income Tax Treaties That Meet the Requirements ...
Notice 87-56, 1987-2 C.B. 367(Effect of Income Tax Treaties on Section 884)
Notice 87-52, 1987-2 C.B. 362(Certification of Exchange of Information Programs of Treaty ...
Notice 84-15, 1984-2 C.B. 474(Certification of Exchange of Information Programs of Treaty ...

→TaxExpert located six items. I started with Notice 2003-69, which is the most recent item.

Illustration 19-13. Excerpt from Notice 2003-69 on TaxExpert

Notice 2003-69, 2003-42 I.R.B. 851(United State...

(Prev Hit) (Next Hit)

test.

  The notice is effective for taxable years beginning after December 31, 2002.

APPENDIX

U.S. INCOME TAX TREATIES SATISFYING THE REQUIREMENTS OF SECTION 1(h)(11)(C)(i)(II)

Australia	Greece	Lithuania	Slovak Republic
Austria	Hungary	Luxembourg	Slovenia
Belgium	Iceland	Mexico	South Africa
Canada	India	Morocco	Spain
China	Indonesia	Netherlands	Sweden
Cyprus	Ireland	New Zealand	Switzerland
Czech Republic	Israel	Norway	Thailand
Denmark	Italy	Pakistan	Trinidad and Tobago
Egypt	Jamaica	Philippines	Tunisia
Estonia	Japan	Poland	Turkey
Finland	Kazakhstan	Portugal	Ukraine
France	Korea	Romania	United Kingdom
Germany	Latvia	Russian Federation	Venezuela

→This notice related to treaties satisfying the requirements of Code section 1(h)(11)(C)(i)(II). Dividends paid by Danish corporations will qualify for that provision's reduced tax rate on dividends.

Illustration 19-14. Using Connectors in TaxExpert

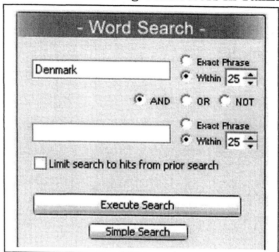

→If I had wanted to use two search terms, I could have used both connector and proximity options. TaxExpert also recognizes the wildcards * and ?.

5. Warren, Gorham & Lamont

Warren, Gorham & Lamont offers several treatises on CD-ROM. Representative titles include Bittker & Lokken, Federal Taxation of Income, Estates & Gifts; Saltzman, IRS Practice & Procedure; and Bishop & Kleinberger, Limited Liability Companies: Tax & Business Law.

Table 19-1. Common CD-ROM Search Connectors and Wildcards

Term	Meaning
And	Both terms must appear
Or	Either term must appear (both terms may appear)
Not	Only the first term may appear
Xor	Only the first or only the second term may appear
/N	Second term must follow first by no more than N words
@N	First and second terms must be within N words of each other
?	Replaces a single character (used anywhere in word)
*	Replaces one or more characters (used at end of word)
%	Finds variations of word endings (used at end of word)
$	Finds synonyms for word (used at end of word)

→Check the CD-ROM service you are using to ascertain the search connectors and wildcard symbols.

Chapter 20. Online Legal Research

Section A. Introduction

This chapter continues the discussion of electronic research begun in Chapter 3 and continued in several other chapters. In addition to discussing advantages and disadvantages of online research, it describes three types of service: general focus subscription services; tax-oriented subscription services; and other online services.

Section B. Advantages and Disadvantages

Online legal research systems have many useful features. First, they bring research materials together in one readily accessible location. Libraries with tax alcoves require several shelf ranges to house the relevant information; libraries without alcoves may shelve these items on several floors. An online system requires only a computer, a modem or other online access tool, and a printer. If you have wireless access and a good battery, you can conduct online research from virtually any location.

The Internet provides a quick means for transmitting and accessing both text and graphics. More important than the time saved in gathering the material is the ability to do searches that are virtually impossible to accomplish using print materials. Because the service responds to queries based on words appearing or not appearing in its database, you could easily use an online system to locate all opinions by a particular judge[280] or all decisions rendered in 2006, at every court level, involving the medical expense deduction. Although CD/DVD searches can yield similar results, online services often include more material and are updated more frequently.

Given these advantages, why isn't research conducted solely online? That question was raised in Chapter 3, Section C, in comparing print and electronic services. As noted there, online services may be less suited than print materials for certain research tasks, such as using looseleaf services to familiarize yourself with a topic. Some older material may not be available online, and tax-oriented articles indexes are not available in any online service. Publisher consolidation, discussed in Chapter 1, is also a factor. If you have access only to Westlaw, for example, you currently lack

---

[280] See the example for Judge Marvel in Chapter 3.

access to Shepard's and Tax Analysts publications. Even if an online service carries a particular source, your subscription option may not cover it.

Cost constraints may limit the time you can spend online. If your final product requires accurate page numbers, a final check of print sources may be necessary to assure yourself that you have made no citation errors. As the discussion in Chapter 3 indicates, there is no "best source" for tax research.

Keep two important rules in mind. First, you must check the time period covered for materials made available online. Don't assume a source included in an online service begins its coverage with the first print volume of that service. Coverage for many sources begins at a later date online than it does in print. This is true for both subscription and free services.

Second, remember that different systems use different search commands, rules for wildcard searches, or methods for indicating you want to use a Boolean search. You will not achieve the desired results unless you tailor your search to the rules imposed by the service you are using.[281]

SECTION C. AVAILABLE MATERIALS

Some subscription-based services include tax materials in a general database. Others focus exclusively on taxation. Nonsubscription services vary in their coverage; they may include data from a variety of sources or may focus on a single type of information. They may provide links to relevant materials rather than including text in their databases.

Materials available online may also be available in print or on CD/DVD, often from the same publisher. Several publishers offer their own online services and also include their materials on services such as Westlaw or LexisNexis.

D. SUBSCRIPTION SERVICES—GENERAL FOCUS

Although they do not focus on tax, two commercial services, LexisNexis and Westlaw, have extensive tax databases. Two others, Loislaw and

---

[281] We encountered a print service analogy in Chapter 13, dealing with looseleaf services. Those services vary in using page, paragraph, and section numbers for categorizing and cross-referencing information.

VersusLaw, currently include fewer tax materials. Services frequently expand the number of sources and time periods covered.[282] They also add and delete sources. Such changes on LexisNexis and Westlaw often occur when their parent companies acquire other publishers.

Each of these services differs slightly in its coverage and search commands. All allow you to specify particular words that must appear or be absent in a document; if the words must be in a desired proximity, you can include that limitation. You can use these systems to locate decisions involving damages within five words of the term personal injury, or for decisions involving damages but not personal injury. You can limit your search to particular types of authority (e.g., only Tax Court) or to particular dates.

Before formulating a search query, you should become familiar with the search term symbols used on the system being accessed. In addition to each service's explanatory texts, other guides are available.

The discussion in this section relates to each service's web-based service. Because LexisNexis includes Tax Notes, my newsletter of choice, I often use it instead of Westlaw even though I find Westlaw's organization more user-friendly. Unless Loislaw significantly expands its tax materials, it will be of limited use for many tax research projects.[283]

Subsections 1 through 3 compare LexisNexis, Westlaw, and Loislaw. The discussion includes database contents, proximity connectors, wildcard characters, synonyms, and citators. I searched for the same items in each service—Tax Court decisions in 2006 that mention *Chevron* (Chapter 9).

1. LexisNexis

a. Database Contents

The LexisNexis tax library, FEDTAX, is divided into files.[284] There are also files for state taxes and for various publishers. FEDTAX materials

---

[282] For some tools (e.g., articles indexes), you may need to extend LexisNexis and Westlaw searches to their nontax libraries.

[283] VersusLaw, another general service, also is relatively limited in its coverage of tax sources. For example, in mid-November 2006, its retrospective Tax Court coverage went back only to 1999 and Court of Federal Claims to 1997.

[284] Although I mention them, you do not need to know library or file names to use LexisNexis.

are accessed through individual files (e.g., CASREL for judicial decisions and IRS material; TXLAWS for statutes and regulations); an OMNI file combines most primary source material.

Within each database, you can click on an icon to see dates of coverage. LexisNexis's coverage of the Supreme Court begins in 1790; its Tax Court coverage begins in 1924 with the Board of Tax Appeals.

Secondary source files cover tax-oriented law reviews, Shepard's Citations, and services published by Matthew Bender, Kleinrock, and Tax Analysts.

b. Proximity Connectors, Wildcard Characters, and Synonyms

LexisNexis uses several connectors in searches:

Table 20-1. LexisNexis Connectors

Term	Meaning
AND	Both terms must appear
OR	At least one of the terms must appear
AND NOT	Only the first term may appear
W/n	Terms must appear within n words of each other; either can appear first (n can be any number up to 255)
W/s	Terms must appear within the same sentence
W/p	Terms must appear within the same paragraph
W/seg	Terms must appear in the same segment (e.g., case caption, text)
PRE/n	First term must precede second by no more than n words

If you use multiple words without a connector, LexisNexis treats them as a phrase.

LexisNexis also lets you state proximity connectors in the negative (e.g., NOT W/s). You can exclude documents unless the term appears AT LEAST a stated number of times, and you can specify that the term must appear in all capital letters or only as a plural.

LexisNexis allows you to use an exclamation point (!) as a wild card symbol to expand words by any number of letters following the !. You can use an asterisk (*) to add missing letters anywhere except at the beginning of the word. Each * represents a single missing letter.

LexisNexis does not automatically add synonyms to your search. If you use the Select Words and Concepts option, it suggests possible search terms based on those you have already selected. LexisNexis also allows you to use natural language searching instead of using Boolean connectors.

c. Citator

LexisNexis includes the Shepard's Citator. Symbols to the left of cases indicate that you will find updating material using the citator; click on these symbols to go directly to the citator results. [See Illustration 20-4.]

Illustration 20-1. LexisNexis Partial List of Sources

→LexisNexis lets you customize your opening page by area of law. This is a partial source list for the Taxation tab.

→Click on the link next to the folder icon to obtain a contents list. For this search, I will select <u>View more sources</u> in the Cases and Court Rules option. I will then select Federal.

Illustration 20-2. LexisNexis Federal Court List

Taxation > Cases and Court Rules > Federal (Remove "Taxation" tab)

Use checkboxes to select sources for searching across categories, pages, and tabs. Show Me...   [Combine Sources]

☐	Tax Cases, Federal and State	☐	US Tax Court Cases	
☐	Federal Courts Tax Cases	☐	US Tax Court Memorandum Decisions	
☐	US Ct. of Federal Claims, Claims Ct., & Ct. of Claims - Tax Cases	☐	US Tax Court Summary Opinions	
☑	US Tax Court Cases, Memorandum Decs. & Board of Tax Appeals Decisions	☐	US Board of Tax Appeals Cases	
☐	U.S. Supreme Court Cases, Lawyers' Edition - Selected Federal Tax Material	☐	US Court of International Trade Tax Cases	
☐	US Courts of Appeal Tax Cases	☐	US Customs Court Tax Cases	
☐	US Court of Appeals Federal Circuit Tax Cases	☐	USCS - Rules of Practice and Procedure of the United States Tax Court	
☐	US District Court Tax Cases	☐	Tax Analysts Tax Court Filings	

→I selected the US Tax Court Cases, Memorandum Decs., & Board of Tax Appeals Decisions file because it includes Regular, Memorandum, and Summary decisions. I could instead have searched only for one of these opinion types.

Illustration 20-3. LexisNexis Search

Enter Search Terms   [?]

⦿ Terms and Connectors   ○ Natural Language   ○ Easy Search

Chevron   Suggest Terms   [🔍 Search]
                                                 for My Search
                                                 Check Spelling

Restrict by Segment:

Select a segment, enter search terms for the segment, then click Add.

[Select a Segment ▾] [   ] [Add ↑]

Note: Segment availability differs between sources. Segments may not be applied consistently across sources.

Restrict by Date:

○ [No Date Restrictions ▾] ⦿ From [/1/2006] To [18/2006] Date Formats...

→The Restrict by Date option is part of the search screen. Use the Restrict by Segment option to limit the search by court, judge, attorney, and several other items. Compare this Date Restriction format to the format used for Westlaw in Illustration 20-7.

Illustration 20-4. Partial List of LexisNexis Results

✔Select for FOCUS™ or Delivery

☐ 1. <u>Estate of Gerson v. Comm'r</u>, No. 13534-04 , UNITED STATES TAX COURT , 2006 U.S. Tax Ct. LEXIS 31; 127 T.C. No.

OVERVIEW: United States Tax Court held that 26 C.F.R. § 26.2601-1(b)(1)(i) was reasonable and valid. Testamenta appointment over trust property in favor of decedent's grandchildren were subject to generation-skipping transfer ta> skip.

CORE TERMS: regulation, generation-skipping, general power of appointment, decedent, irrevocable, lapse, grandchilc appointment ...

☐ ◆ 2. <u>Swallows Holding, Ltd. v. Comm'r</u>, No. 8045-02 , UNITED STATES TAX COURT , 126 T.C. 96; 2006 U.S. Tax Ct. LEXIS

OVERVIEW: Foreign corporation was not precluded from deducting its expenses because it failed to file timely return: reading of 26 U.S.C.S. § 882(c)(2), and 26 C.F.R. § 1.882-4(a)(2) and (3)(i) were invalid to the extent they imposed

CORE TERMS: regulation, timely filing, Revenue Act, disputed, taxable year, tax return, filing deadline, income tax, de

☐ ❶ 3. <u>Arnett v. Comm'r</u>, No. 8866-03 , UNITED STATES TAX COURT , 126 T.C. 89; 2006 U.S. Tax Ct. LEXIS 5; 126 T.C. No.

OVERVIEW: In the light of the Antarctic Treaty, Dec. 1, 1959, 12 U.S.T. 794, Antarctica was a sovereignless region meaning of 26 U.S.C.S. § 911. Accordingly, a taxpayer's income earned in Antarctica was subject to tax in the Unitec exclusion under 26 U.S.C.S. § 911.

→LexisNexis located four cases, of which three are illustrated above. I can use the hyperlinks to go directly to those cases. LexisNexis cites to the official and LexisNexis citation and to the CCH and RIA Tax Court Memorandum decisions services. It uses symbols to indicate I can find additional information by Shepardizing two of the cases.

→LexisNexis did not find the Stringham decision located by Westlaw. After reading the decision in Westlaw, I found that the taxpayer worked for Chevron; the case did not involve the *Chevron* doctrine.

→When I search within the cases found, LexisNexis lets me navigate directly to the place where the term is used.

→A Show Hits option (not illustrated above) lets me display the term sought in context.

2. Westlaw

a. Database Contents

The Westlaw tax database, FTX-ALL, gives access to virtually every type of primary source material.[285] These materials can also be accessed separately through individual databases (e.g., FTX-CSRELS for judicial decisions and IRS material; FTX-CODREG for statutes and regulations).

Within each database, you can click on an icon to see dates of coverage.

---

[285] Although I mention the database names, you do not need to know them to use Westlaw.

Westlaw's coverage of the Supreme Court begins in 1790; its Tax Court coverage begins in 1924 with the Board of Tax Appeals.

Secondary source files cover tax-oriented law reviews, RIA Citator 2nd and West's KeyCite, and services published by Bureau of National Affairs/Tax Management, Research Institute of America, Warren, Gorham & Lamont, and other West Group entities (e.g., the Mertens service discussed in Chapter 13).

b. Proximity Connectors, Wildcard Characters, and Synonyms

Westlaw uses several search connectors:

Table 20-2. Westlaw Proximity Connectors

Term	Meaning
&	both terms must appear
space	at least one of the terms must appear
%	only the first term may appear
/n	terms must appear within n words of each other
/s	terms must appear within the same sentence
/p	terms must appear within the same paragraph
+n	first term must precede the second by no more than n words
+s	first term must precede the second in same sentence
+p	first term must precede the second in same paragraph
""	terms must appear in order (a phrase)

You can use a single exclamation point (!) as a wild card symbol (root expander) to expand words by any number of letters following the !. An asterisk (*) adds missing letters anywhere but at the beginning of the word. Each * represents a single missing letter. Westlaw also allows searches based on West topics and key numbers.

Westlaw does not automatically add synonyms. If you use the Thesaurus option, it suggests search terms based on those you selected. Westlaw offers both Natural Language and Boolean search options.

c. Citator

Westlaw offers two citators, RIA 2nd Citator and KeyCite. KeyCite is the default option in the court database. You can instead enter the RIA Citator 2nd directly and type the case or other item you want to check (by party or by citation).

Illustration 20-5. Westlaw Directory

Resources

Search Combined Sources
Click here to search across topics

Federal Tax Primary Sources ⓘ
All Federal Tax Primary Materials
Internal Revenue Code (USCA version)
Historical Codes
Regulations - Final, Temporary & Proposed
IRS Administrative Materials Combined
Federal Tax Cases Combined
More...

Legislative History Sources ⓘ
Tax Public Laws
Committee Reports
Blue Books
More...

Tax Practice & Procedure ⓘ
Internal Revenue Manual
WGL-Tax Practice Treatises Combined
Saltzman: IRS Practice and Procedure
More...

Journals & Newsletters
BNA Daily Tax Report
RIA Federal Taxes Weekly Alert
Journal of Taxation
Journal of Corporate Taxation
Journal of Business Entities
Journal of Taxation of Exempt Organiza
More...

Estate & Gift
WG&L Estate Planning Treatises
Estate Planning Journal
Estate Planners Alert
Thomson-West Estate Planning Treatis
RIA Estate Planning Collection Complet
BNA Portfolios - Estate, Gifts & Trusts
More...

International
RIA Tax Treaties and Explanations
RIA International Taxes Weekly
WG&L International Treatises Combine
Journal of International Taxation

→Westlaw lets you customize your opening page by area of law. This is a partial source list for the Tax tab.

→I clicked on the <u>More...</u> option for Federal Tax Primary Sources because I did not to search in any court other than Tax Court.

Illustration 20-6. Westlaw Court List

Tax Cases
- ☐ Cases - All Courts (FTX-CS) ⓘ
- ☐ Supreme Court (FTX-SCT) ⓘ
- ☐ Courts of Appeals (FTX-CTA) ⓘ
- ☐ District Courts (FTX-DCT) ⓘ
- ☐ Court of Federal Claims (FTX-FEDCL) ⓘ
- ☑ Tax Court (FTX-TCT) ⓘ
- ☐ Federal Taxation - Headnotes (FTX-HN) ⓘ

Tax Court Materials by Type
- ☐ Tax Court Regular Decisions (FTX-TC) ⓘ
- ☐ Tax Court Summary Opinions (FTX-TCSO) ⓘ
- ☐ Tax Court Memorandum Decisions (FTX-TCM) ⓘ
- ☐ Tax Court Rules (FTX-RULES) ⓘ

→I selected the Tax Court file because it includes Regular, Memorandum, and Summary decisions.

Illustration 20-7. Westlaw Search

Terms and Connectors	Natural Language

Search: Chevron & YE(2006)

Recent Searches & Locates

Fields: Select an Option

→I used the Fields option to limit the date. That option also allows me to limit my search by court, judge, attorney, and other items.

Illustration 20-8. Westlaw Results

SELECT TO PRINT, EMAIL, ETC.

☐ **1. Estate of Gerson v. C.I.R.,**
127 T.C. No. 11, 2006 WL 3019177, Tax Ct. Rep. (CCH) 56,654, Tax Ct. Rep. Dec. (RIA

☐ C **2. Dallas v. C.I.R.,**
T.C. Memo. 2006-212, 2006 WL 2792684, 92 T.C.M. (CCH) 313, T.C.M. (RIA) 2006-212,

☐ **3. Stringham v. C.I.R.,**
T.C. Summ.Op. 2006-44, 2006 WL 800753, Pens. Plan Guide (CCH) P 23995I, U.S.Tax (

☐ C **4. Swallows Holding, Ltd. v. C.I.R.,**
126 T.C. No. 6, 126 T.C. 96, Tax Ct. Rep. (CCH) 56,417, Tax Ct. Rep. Dec. (RIA) 126.6,

☐ C **5. Arnett v. C.I.R.,**
126 T.C. No. 5, 126 T.C. 89, Tax Ct. Rep. (CCH) 56,415, Tax Ct. Rep. Dec. (RIA) 126.6,

→I can use the hyperlinks to go directly to those cases. Westlaw lists official, Westlaw, CCH, and RIA citations. I can KeyCite for additional information about three of the cases. Although LexisNexis didn't indicate any information for *Dallas*, all Westlaw references to *Dallas* were to secondary authorities.

→A Show Terms in List option (not illustrated above) displays the term sought in context.

3. Loislaw

a. Database Contents

Loislaw does not have a separate tax database. Its coverage of federal taxation is currently limited to primary source materials (although it offers access to several nontax treatises[286] published by Aspen). Judicial decisions covered include those from the Tax Court, District Courts, Bankruptcy Court, Courts of Appeals, and the Supreme Court. Loislaw also offers access to the United States Code, slip laws since the 105th Congress,, the Constitution, Code of Federal Regulations, and the Federal Register.

Within each database, you can click a currency button for information about how up-to-date the materials are. Retrospective coverage varies by database. As of November 2006, Tax Court coverage begins in 1942, thus omitting cases from the Board of Tax Appeals.

Although Loislaw is a lower-cost alternative to LexisNexis and Westlaw, its utility is limited by its lack of IRS documents, legislative history materials, and secondary source materials.

When searching for judicial decisions, you can search all of the federal court options at once or you can narrow your search to particular courts.

b. Proximity Connectors, Wildcard Characters, and Synonyms

Loislaw uses several connectors in searches. You can express them as words or symbols:

Table 20-3. Proximity Connectors in Loislaw

Term	Symbol	Meaning
And	&	both terms must appear
Or	|	at least one of the terms must appear
Not	%	only the first term may appear
Near	/	terms must appear within 20 words of each other
Nearx	/x	terms must appear within x words of each other
	" "	terms in exact order (phrase)

You can use an asterisk (*) as a wild card symbol to find variations of

---

[286] Several of these treatises are in areas related to tax, such as elder law, estate planning, family law, and business entities.

search terms. A question mark (?) can be used to substitute for a letter anywhere in the word.

Loislaw does not add synonyms for you, and it does not have a thesaurus you can use to find similar terms.

c. Citator

The Loislaw citator is GlobalCite. You activate it within the item you are viewing and it provides a link to the later items. GlobalCite does not currently use symbols to indicate if the later item agrees with the earlier one. It does place the cited item in context on the GlobalCite screen.

Illustration 20-9. Loislaw Directory Page

Primary Law	Secondary Law
Type of Law:	
• Case Law	• Treatise Libraries
• Statutes & Acts	• Bar Publications
• Admin. Rules & Regulations	
• Court Rules	**Public Records**
	• Personal Public Records
Jurisdiction:	• Corporate Public Records
	• UCC Filings & Corporate Public Records
• Federal	
• State	**Legal News & Business Information**

→You enter Loislaw through this contents page.

Illustration 20-10. Portion of Loislaw Case Law Page

Search All Federal (Circuits Only)

☐ U.S. Supreme Court
☑ U.S. Tax Court
☐ First Circuit
☐ Second Circuit
☐ Third Circuit
☐ Fourth Circuit
☐ Fifth Circuit
☐ Sixth Circuit
☐ Seventh Circuit
☐ Eighth Circuit

Illustration 20-11. Search in Loislaw

Search United States Tax Court

SelectCite

Search Entire Document

Chevron

Date Range: between ▾ mm **01** dd **01** yyyy **2006**   **AND**   mm **11** dd **18** yyyy **2006**

Case Cite   *for example: 115 T.C. 589*

Case Name   *for example: smith and jones   or   smith v state*

Docket Number

Appellate Court

Judge & Court Appealed

→Although the Loislaw has many field search options, our search involved a single term, *Chevron*.

Illustration 20-12. Search Results in Loislaw

#1
United States Tax Court
ESTATE OF GERSON v. COMMR. OF INTERNAL REVENUE, 127 T.C. No. 11 (T.C. 2006)
No. 13534-04.
Filed October 24, 2006.

#2
United States Tax Court
SWALLOWS HOLDING, LTD. v. COMMISSIONER, 126 T.C. 96 (2006)
Docket No. 8045-02.
Filed January 26, 2006.

#3
United States Tax Court
ARNETT v. COMMISSIONER, 126 T.C. 89 (2006)
Docket No. 8866-03.
Filed January 25, 2006.

→Loislaw found only three decisions because it does not cover Memorandum or Summary Opinions. That is a weakness of Loislaw.

SECTION E. SUBSCRIPTION SERVICES—TAX FOCUS

The services discussed in this section provide access to a variety of primary and secondary source materials. I used three of them—Tax Research NetWork, Checkpoint, and TaxExpert Online—to replicate the search from Section D (finding Tax Court decisions in 2006 that mentioned *Chevron*).

1. Tax Research NetWork

Commerce Clearing House offers a web-based service, Tax Research NetWork. The materials below discuss using this service.

a. Database Contents

Tax Research NetWork includes the Internal Revenue Code, committee reports, regulations, treaties, IRS materials (including items such as revenue rulings, letter rulings, field service advice, and the Internal Revenue Manual), and judicial decisions. The service includes Standard Federal Tax Reporter, CCH newsletters and journals, a citator, and various practice aids. It does not include Federal Tax Articles, which is available only in print.

Supreme Court coverage begins in 1913; Tax Court coverage begins in 1924 with the Board of Tax Appeals.

b. Proximity Connectors, Wildcard Characters, and Synonyms

Tax Research NetWork uses prescribed search methods. You select the method in the Search Options Screen. Boolean searching is allowed.

Table 20-4. Proximity Connectors in Tax Research NetWork

Term	Meaning
ALL TERMS	all of the terms must appear
ANY TERM	at least one of the terms must appear
NEAR	terms must be within 20 words of each other
EXACT PHRASE	terms must appear in order exactly as typed
AND	both terms must appear
OR	either term must appear
NOT	only the first term may appear
W/n	the first term must appear within n words of the second (n cannot exceed 127)
F/n	the first term must follow within n words of the second (n cannot exceed 127)
P/n	the first term must precede the second within n words of the second (n cannot exceed 127)
W/sen	the first term must appear within 20 words of the second
W/par	the first term must appear within 80 words of the second

Tax Research NetWork lets you use a single exclamation point (!) as a wild card symbol to expand words by any number of letters at the end of a word. You can use an asterisk (*) to add missing letters anywhere except the beginning of the word. Each * represents a single missing letter.

Tax Research NetWork has a Thesaurus function. It will search on synonyms if you enable that option.

Before beginning searching, go to the Search Tools page to specify options such as date range, number of items to retrieve, and whether you want the item you searched highlighted within the results.

c. Citator

Tax Research NetWork includes the CCH Citator. The looseleaf version of this citator (Chapter 12) is divided into three services, one for each of CCH's Code-based looseleaf services. The online version is not divided in this manner. For example, you can find both income and gift tax cases that cite to a particular tax case with a single search.

Illustration 20-13. Excerpt from Tax Research NetWork Directory

CCH Explanations and Analysis — Select All ☐	
☐ CCH Tax Research Consultant	☐ Federal Estate and Gift Tax Reporter
☐ Standard Federal Income Tax Reporter	☐ Fed Excise Tax Reporter
☐ Standard Federal Income Tax Reporter-- Explanations	☐ Tax Treaties Reporter
Primary Sources — Select All ☐	
☐ Current Internal Revenue Code	☐ Federal Tax Regulations
☐ Last 1954 Code	☐ Cases
☐ Last 1939 Code	☐ Letter Rulings & IRS Positions (including TAMs and FSAs)
Practice Aids — Select All ☐	

→Click on Cases to reach the listing of courts.

Illustration 20-14. Cases Page in Tax Research Network

Cases— Select All ☐
☐ United States Tax Cases
☑ Tax Court Regulars
☑ Tax Court Memoranda
☑ Tax Court Small Tax Cases
☐ Board of Tax Appeals Regulars and Memoranda

→Remember United States Tax Cases doesn't include Tax Court.

Illustration 20-15. Search in Tax Research NetWork

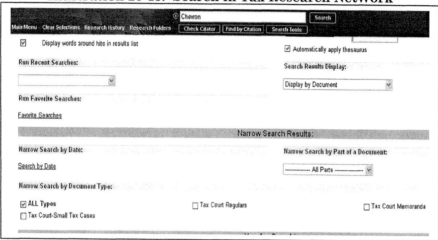

→After selecting a database, I typed Chevron in the Search box.

Illustration 20-16. Search Results in Tax Research NetWork

1. 🖨 TC-SMALL-TAX-CASE, [T.C. Summary Opinion 2006-44], **Marilyn Stringham, a.k.** Innocent spouse relief: Actual knowledge: Equitable relief: Abuse of discretion. -- (M an early retirement option in 1999 when Chevron was

2. 🖨 TCM, [CCH Dec. 56,638(M)], **Robert Dallas v. Commissioner.**, Gift tax: Valuation: made no argument about it on brief. See Chevron Corp. v. Commissioner [Dec. 50,7

3. 🖨 TC, [CCH Dec. 56,417], , Foreign corporation: Effectively connected income: Deduct National Muffler and Chevron --"reasonableness" using the National Muffler factors i

4. 🖨 TC, [CCH Dec. 56,417], , Foreign corporation: Effectively connected income: Deduct supra, the Supreme Court decided Chevron U.S.A., Inc. v. Natural Res. Def. Counc

5. 🖨 TC, [CCH Dec. 56,654], , Generation-skipping transfer tax: Effective date: Exempt s! trumps an agency construction otherwise entitled to Chevron deference only if the p

6. 🖨 TC, [CCH Dec. 56,415], , Gross income: Foreign country exclusion: Antarctica. -- (J binding on the courts unless procedurally defective, arbitrary or

→Although Tax Research NetWork reports six decisions, two of them are the same. Tax Research NetWork and Westlaw found the same cases.

2. Checkpoint

RIA offers a web-based service, Checkpoint. The materials below discuss using this service.

a. Database Contents

Checkpoint includes the Internal Revenue Code, committee reports, regulations, treaties, IRS materials (including items such as revenue rulings, letter rulings, and field service advice), and judicial decisions. The service includes United States Tax Reporter, Federal Tax Coordinator 2d, newsletters and journals, a citator, and various practice aids.

Supreme Court coverage begins in 1796; Tax Court coverage begins in 1924 with the Board of Tax Appeals.

b. Proximity Connectors, Wildcard Characters, and Synonyms

Checkpoint uses prescribed search methods. You select the method in the Search Options Screen. Boolean searching is allowed.

Table 20-5. Proximity Connectors in Checkpoint

Term	Symbol	Meaning
AND	&; space	both terms must appear
OR	|	either term must appear
NOT	^	only the first term may appear
/#		the first term must appear within # words of the second
P/#		the first term must precede the second within # words of the second
/s		the first term must appear within 20 words of the second
Pre/s		the first term must precede the second within 20 words
/p		the first term must appear within 50 words of the second
Pre/p		The first term must precede the second within 50 words
	" "	terms must appear together in order (phrase)

Checkpoint uses an asterisk (*) as a placeholder for one or more characters; a question mark (?) is a placeholder for a single character.

Checkpoint has a Thesaurus function. It will search on synonyms if you enable that option.

Before beginning searching, go to the Search Tools page to specify options such as date range, number of items to retrieve, and whether you want the item you searched highlighted within the results.

c. Citator

Checkpoint includes the RIA Citator 2d. It does not include the earlier RIA (and Prentice-Hall) citator service.

Illustration 20-17. Excerpt from Checkpoint Contents Page

2 Choose Sources from: [All Federal ▾] <u>Save</u>

☐ **Editorial Materials**
  ✚ ☐ Citator 2nd (RIA)
     ☐ Federal Tax Handbook (RIA)
  ✚ ☐ Federal Tax Coordinator (RIA)
  ✚ ☐ Return Guides (RIA)
     ☐ Tables & Rates (RIA)
  ✚ ☐ Tax Alerts (RIA)
     ☐ Tax Planning and Practice Guides (Special Studies) (RIA)
  ✚ ☐ United States Tax Reporter - Annotations (RIA)
  ✚ ☐ United States Tax Reporter - Explanations (RIA)
☐ **News/Current Awareness**
     ☐ Cummings' Corporate Tax Insights

☐ **Primary Source Materials**
  ✚ ☐ Code, Regulations, Committee Reports
  ✚ ☐ Current Pending/Enacted Legislation
  ✚ ☐ Federal Tax Cases
     ☐ IRS Publications
  ✚ ☐ IRS Rulings and Releases
     ☐ U.S. Tax Treaties in Force
☐ **Legislation (Editorial Analysis and Sourc**
     ☐ Complete Analysis of the Pension Prote
  ✚ ☐ Complete Analysis of the Tax Increase
        Act of 2005
  ✚ ☐ Complete Analysis of the Gulf Opportur
        Emergency Tax Relief
     ☐ Complete Analysis of the Tax Provision

Illustration 20-18. Tax Court Cases on Checkpoint

– ☐ Federal Tax Cases

   ☐ American Federal Tax Reports (1860 - 2005)

   ☐ American Federal Tax Reports (Current Year)

   ☐ Tax Court & Board of Tax Appeals Memorandum Decisions (1928 - 2005)

   ☐ Tax Court & Board of Tax Appeals Reported Decisions (1924 - 2005)

   ☐ Tax Court, Federal Procedural & Federal Claims Court Rules

   ☑ Tax Court Memorandum Decisions (Current Year)

   ☑ Tax Court Reported Decisions (Current Year)

   ☑ Tax Court Summary Opinions

→ Summary Opinions did not have a current year option.

Illustration 20-19. Search Results in Checkpoint

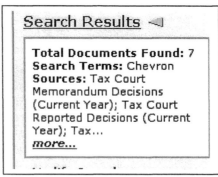

Search Results ◁

Total Documents Found: 7
Search Terms: Chevron
Sources: Tax Court
Memorandum Decisions
(Current Year); Tax Court
Reported Decisions (Current
Year); Tax...
more...

→There were three Summary Opinions (two from before 2006), one Memorandum Opinion, and three Regular Opinions.

Illustration 20-20. Modified Search in Checkpoint

Search Federal Cases by Date

☐ All Federal Cases
    ☐ American Federal Tax Reports (1860 - Present)
    ☑ Tax Court & Board of Tax Appeals Reported Decisions (1924 - Present)
    ☑ Tax Court & Board of Tax Appeals Memorandum Decisions (1928 - Present)
    ☑ Tax Court Summary Opinions

Select Date Range:
From `1/1/2006` To `11/18/2006`

Enter Keywords: **Thesaurus/Query Tool**
`Chevron`   [Search]

→This search yielded the five decisions I expected to find based on the previous searches.

3. Federal TaxExpert

LexisNexis includes Kleinrock's newsletters and analytical materials in its database. Kleinrock also offers its own web-based service, Federal TaxExpert. The materials below discuss this service.

a. Database Contents

TaxExpert includes the Internal Revenue Code, committee reports, regulations, preambles (since 1995), treaties, IRS materials (including items such as letter rulings, field service advice, and the penalties handbook from the Internal Revenue Manual), and judicial decisions. The service includes back issues of Daily Tax Bulletin and practice aids.

Supreme Court coverage begins in 1984; the service covers "key cases" from 1917. TaxExpert Online begins Tax Court coverage in 1954 and does not include the Board of Tax Appeals. Coverage dates for IRS materials vary widely. For example revenue rulings begin in 1954; revenue procedures, in 1955; notices, in 1980; and announcements, in 1993. Coverage for publicly released items begins as early as 1990 for letter rulings and as late as 1999 for documents such as field service advice.

b. Proximity Connectors, Wildcard Characters, and Synonyms

Tax Expert Online has three search method options: treat words as a phrase; find words within 25 words of each other; or enter your own syntax. If you choose to enter your own syntax, you can select from four connector commands and can use words or symbols for three of them:

Illustration 20-6. Proximity Connectors in Federal TaxExpert

Term	Symbol	Meaning
AND	&	both terms must appear
OR	|	either term must appear
NOT	^	only the first term may appear

To search for terms within N words of each other, you must structure your command as follows: NEAR((term1, term2, ...), N). Make sure that all terms subject to this command are in a single parenthetical phrase *and* that the proximity number (N) follows a comma and shares a second parentheses with the desired terms.

TaxExpert Online lets you use a percentage sign (%) to add all possible endings to a word. You use one or more underlines (_) to add as many additional characters as you specify anywhere in the word.

TaxExpert Online does not have a thesaurus feature.

c. Citator

TaxExpert does not have a citator. You can simulate citator results by using a case or other item as a search term. You must read the later items to determine if they agree with the earlier one.

Illustration 20-21. TaxExpert Directory and Search

→I inserted 2006 as a search term, using Enter own syntax. TaxExpert has no date search function. Use Advanced Search for this purpose.

Illustration 20-22. TaxExpert Search Results

Search found 5 documents from 31513 searched. Search Query is " Chevron & 2006"

1. Estate of Eleanor R. Gerson v. Commissioner, 127 T.C. No. 11

2. Swallows Holding, Ltd. v. Commissioner, 126 T.C. No. 6

3. Arnett v. Commissioner, 126 T.C. No. 5

4. Dallas v. Commissioner, T.C. Memo. 2006-212

5. Exxon Corporation v. Commissioner, T.C. Memo 1992-92

→TaxExpert found five cases. One was from 1992 but used the term 2006 in the case. TaxExpert currently omits Summary Opinions from its database.

4. TaxCore

Tax Management's web-based service is called TaxCore. Tax Management provides links from the web-based Daily Tax Report (Chapter 16) to the full text materials available in TaxCore. Available sources include the Code, committee reports, testimony at hearings, regulations and their preambles, IRS materials, and judicial decisions. Its retrospective coverage is not as extensive as that of the other services discussed here, but it is an excellent source for current primary source material.

Illustration 20-23. Links to Primary Sources on TaxCore

BNA, Inc.

TaxCore®

About TaxCore® Document Types

By Agency Date

▼2006
   ▼03/30/2006
      ▼Federal Courts
         United States v. Davis
      ▼Notices
         IRS Notice of 2006 Renewable Energy Inflation Adjustment,
      ▼U.S. Tax Court
         Christensen v. Commissioner

5. Complete Federal Research Library; Tax Notes Today

LexisNexis includes materials from Tax Analysts. Tax Analysts also offers a separate web-based option, Federal Research Library, in two versions: Basic and Complete. The Complete version includes the Code, regulations and plans for regulations, IRS materials, judicial decisions, and Tax Practice newsletter. It also offers web-based subscriptions to Tax Notes Today; it also includes full text of the primary sources it covers. (Tax Notes is discussed briefly in Chapter 16.)

Tax Analysts does not have its own citator service. Its extensive database permits you to conduct citator-like searches using case names or other words as search terms. [See Illustrations 19-1 through 19-4 illustrating its OneDisc DVD.]

SECTION F. OTHER ONLINE SERVICES

There are a variety of useful websites available. Some provide primary source material directly; some provide hypertext links to other websites; some perform both functions. Unfortunately, websites often change address or cease to exist altogether. You are likely to find that many of your searches lead you to at least a few nonexistent sites.

The following list includes both subscription-based and free sites. If the site has been discussed in one or more other chapters, that information appears in this section.

1. Government Sites[287]

a. Government Printing Office

This site provides text of, or links to, documents generated by all branches of the federal government. It offers PDF format for many documents, thus allowing you to cite original pagination. It is particularly useful for statutes and legislative history (Chapters 6 and 7).

This site allows limited searching by terms; you do not need an exact citation to find many of the covered documents.

---

[287] Many government sites link to each other. Online access to government documents is attributable to the Government Printing Office Electronic Information Access Enhancement Act of 1993, Pub. L. No. 103-40, 107 Stat. 112.

Illustration 20-24. Excerpt from Resource Listing on GPO Access

GPO Access Resources by Branch

Legislative Resources
- View All
- Congressional Bills
- Congressional Record
- Public and Private Laws
- United States Code

Executive Resources
- View All
- Code of Federal Regulations
- Federal Register
- Presidential Materials

Judicial Resources
- View All
- Supreme Court Web Site

→GPO Access has directories for legislative, executive, other administrative, and judicial documents. It also links to other government sites.

b. Library of Congress THOMAS

Users can find texts of bills, note the progress of bills in Congress, and gain access to the Congressional Record, committee reports, and hearings.[288] You can use THOMAS to find various versions of a bill, trace its history, and read it as a public law. Using THOMAS is discussed and illustrated in Chapters 6 and 7.

c. Treasury Department

The most useful parts of this site are pages for the Office of Tax Policy page, which provides text for recent tax treaties and Treasury testimony at congressional hearings, and for the Office of Tax Analysis, which includes analytical reports on tax policy issues. See Chapters 7 (Legislative Histories) and 9 (Treasury Regulations) for additional information about Treasury materials.

d. Internal Revenue Service

The IRS site includes text of tax forms and publications, Internal

---

[288] Chapter 7 provides additional information about websites providing legislative history material.

Revenue Bulletins, the Internal Revenue Manual, IRS releases that are not included in the I.R.B., and income tax treaties. The site also includes links to the United States Code, Code of Federal Regulations, and Federal Register. Chapter 10 includes illustrations from the IRS website.

e. White House Home Page

This site provides text of presidential speeches, including bill-signing messages. It also provides links to such support functions as the Office of Management and Budget.

f. Federal Judiciary Home Page

This site provides links to individual courts. The Opinions page of the Supreme Court site (www.supremecourtus.gov) includes a Case Citation Finder. This service provides the preferred citation, as determined by the Reporter of Decisions, for all Supreme Court decisions scheduled for publication in a bound volume since 1790.

g. United States Tax Court Home Page

This site provides text of Regular, Memorandum, and Summary Opinions. You can search the site by judge, date, taxpayer name, and opinion type. It currently includes Regular and Memorandum decisions since 1999 and Summary decisions since 2001. You cannot search by topic or Code section. The Tax Court site is illustrated in Chapter 3.

2. HeinOnline

HeinOnline was initially known as a site for finding old law review issues. It has since evolved into a significant source for finding full text of articles, legislative history materials, and other services. HeinOnline is illustrated in Chapter 14 with respect to finding articles and in Chapter 17 with respect to legislative histories in Seidman's.

3. Tax-Oriented Blogs

Several attorneys and academics maintain blogs focusing on taxation. In addition to commentary on current statutes, judicial decisions, or other matters, the blogs include a variety of links to primary sources, to professional and research organizations, and to other blogs. The sites below are a sample of those available.

A Taxing Matter (http://ataxingmatter.blogs.com/tax/)

Mauled Again (http://mauledagain.blogspot.com/)

TaxProf
(http://taxprof.typepad.com/taxprof_blog/about_this_blog/index.html)

4. Other Sites

The sites below are a sample of those available. Each provides access to a variety of primary and secondary source materials. In addition to primary source material, these sites provide links to other relevant sites.[289]

• Cornell Law School Legal Information Institute
(http://www.law.cornell.edu)

• FindLaw (http://lp.findlaw.com) (legal professionals page)

• Hieros Gamos (http://www.hg.org/; www.hg.org/tax.html for tax)

• Villanova University School of Law Tax Master
(http://vls.law.vill.edu/prof/maule/taxmaster/taxhome.htm)

• Washburn University School of Law (http://www.washlaw.edu)

SECTION G. USING SEARCH ENGINES

1. Overview

Online sites have Uniform Resource Locator (URL) addresses, most of which begin with http://www. This text provides URL locations for several government, commercial, nonprofit, and academic sites. Those sites represent only a small portion of what is available online.

Navigating online can be a daunting task if you lack a site's URL or if you don't know if a site exists. Fortunately, you can use search engines and related services to locate information based on key words.

---

[289] A list of tax and accounting industry (both professional and government) websites appears at http://ria.thomson.com/tax_accounting/taxsites.asp.

Search engines are unlikely to lead you to as much primary source material as you can locate using the subscription services discussed in Sections D and E. But they frequently find articles and other analysis that don't appear on those sites. If information is posted to a site in PDF format, your search engine may not locate it.[290]

No matter how you locate your material, remember to determine the last time it was updated. Materials posted to websites may be current, but there is no requirement that they be. Indeed, unlike government or subscription services, there is no guarantee that items posted to a particular website were ever accurate.

Now that Google has become part of everyday vocabulary, many researchers use it or other search engines to find articles, reports, and even primary source material. In this section, I use several search engines for the search I illustrated in Sections D and E. I did, however, make one change. Because I am not interested in articles about Chevron as a company, I searched instead (as I should have in Sections D and E) on the term Chevron deference.

2. Sample Search

On November 19, 2006, I submitted the search words **Chevron deference** to four services: AltaVista; Excite; Google; and HotBot. I entered it as a phrase if the service allowed that option.

I specified 2006 as the year, and English as a language, but did not impose any other limitation. I did not enclose the search terms in quotation marks. My results (first two "hits" reproduced) appear below.

AltaVista

AltaVista found 3,098 results

SSRN-Chevron Deference and Foreign Affairs by Curtis Bradley
... Download Rank: 20714. **Chevron Deference** and Foreign Affairs ... Bradley, Curti Vol ...
papers.ssrn.com/sol3/papers.cfm?cfid=341678&cftoken=128029128abstract_id=1908
More pages from papers.ssrn.com

EMLF: Supreme Court Substantially Limits **Chevron Deference**
EMLF is a non-profit educational organization providing information on legal issues publications and electronic information. ... They stated that **Chevron deference** migh
www.emlf.org/lastowka.aspx
More pages from emlf.org

---

[290] See Thomas R. Keefe, *The Invisible Web: What You Can't See Might Hurt You*, RES. ADVISOR, May 2002, at 1.

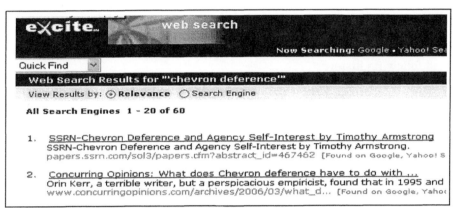

SECTION H. PROBLEMS

You can solve many of the problems in earlier chapters using online services. For some of them, online or CD/DVD searches are your only viable option. Those problems lack sufficient identifying information to allow searches using print materials. To practice your online research skills, try the following additional tasks.

1. Find recently introduced legislation on a topic your instructor selects and follow its history.

2. Track the progress of a regulations project your instructor selects.

3. Find all IRS documents released this year that mention a Code section your instructor selects.

4. Download a presidential tax return.

5. Find articles posted on the web on a topic your instructor selects. Concentrate on websites for law and accounting firms.

6. Using a search engine, search for a phrase of your instructor's choice. First, conduct your search without treating the words as a phrase. Then redo the search using the search engine's advanced search options. What refinements did you need to produce more relevant results?

PART SEVEN

APPENDIXES

APPENDIX A. COMMONLY USED ABBREVIATIONS

NOTE: Abbreviations may appear with or without periods, depending on
the service you use. The list below presents some items in both formats.

A	Acquiescence
Acq.	Acquiescence
AF; AF2d	American Federal Tax Reports
A.F.T.R.; A.F.T.R.2d	American Federal Tax Reports
ALI	American Law Institute
Am. Jur.	American Jurisprudence
Ann.	Announcement
ANPRM	Advance Notice of Proposed Rulemaking
AOD	Action on Decision
APA	Advance Pricing Agreement; Administrative Procedure Act
App.	Appeals
A.R.M.	Committee on Appeals and Review Memorandum
A.R.R.	Committee on Appeals and Review Recommendation
Art.	Article
A.T.	Alcohol Tax Unit; Alcohol and Tobacco Tax Division
Bankr.	Bankruptcy
BAP	Bankruptcy Appellate Panel
BATF	Bureau of Alcohol, Tobacco, and Firearms
BNA	Bureau of National Affairs
B.R.	Bankruptcy Reporter
BTA	Board of Tax Appeals
Bull.	Bulletin
CA	Court of Appeals
CB; C.B.	Cumulative Bulletin
CBO	Congressional Budget Office
CBS	Collection, Bankruptcy and Summons Bulletin
CC	Chief Counsel
CCA	Chief Counsel Advice or Advisory
CCDM	Chief Counsel Directives Manual
CCH	Commerce Clearing House
CCM	Chief Counsel Memorandum
CCN	Chief Counsel Notice
CEA	Council of Economic Advisers
C.F.R.	Code of Federal Regulations
Ch.	Chapter

CIR	Commissioner of Internal Revenue
Cir.	Circuit; Circular
CIS	Congressional Information Service
CIT	Court of International Trade
C.J.S.	Corpus Juris Secundum
Cl.	Clause
Cl. Ct.	Claims Court Reporter
CLI	Current Law Index
C.L.T.	Child-Labor Tax Division
CO	IRS Corporate Division
Comm.	Commissioner; Commission; Committee
Comm'r	Commissioner
Comp.	Compilation; Compliance
Con.	Concurrent
Conf.	Conference
Cong.	Congress
Const.	Constitution
CPE	Continuing Professional Education
CRS	Congressional Research Service
C.S.T.	Capital-Stock Tax Division
C.T.	Carriers Taxing Act of 1937; Taxes on Employment by Carriers
Ct.	Court
CTB	Criminal Tax Bulletin
Ct. Cl.	Court of Claims
Cum. Bull.	Cumulative Bulletin
D.	Decision; District
D.C.	Treasury Department Circular
Dec.	Decision
Del. Order	Delegation Order
Deleg. Order	Delegation Order
Dept. Cir.	Treasury Department Circular
Dist.	District
Dkt.	Docket
DLB	Disclosure Litigation Bulletin
D.O.	Delegation Order
Doc.	Document
E.A.S.	Executive Agreement Series
EE	IRS Employee Plans and Exempt Organization Division
Em. T.	Employment Taxes
E.O.	Executive Orders
EO	Exempt Organizations

E.P.C.	Excess Profits Tax Council Ruling or Memorandum
E.T.	Estate and Gift Tax Division or Ruling
Ex.	Executive
Exec. Order	Executive Order
F.; F.2d; F.3d	Federal Reporter
Fed.	Federal; Federal Reporter
Fed. Cl.	Court of Federal Claims
Fed. Reg.	Federal Register
Fed. Supp.; Fed. Supp. 2d	Federal Supplement
FI	IRS Financial Institutions and Products Division
FOIA	Freedom of Information Act
FR	Federal Register
FSA	Field Service Advice
F. Supp.; F. Supp.2d	Federal Supplement
FTC; FTC2d	Federal Tax Coordinator
GAO	General Accounting Office; Government Accountability Office
GATT	General Agreement on Tariffs and Trade
GCM	General Counsel Memorandum
G.C.M.	Chief Counsel's Memorandum; General Counsel's Memorandum; Assistant General Counsel's Memorandum
Gen. Couns. Mem.	General Counsel Memorandum
GL	IRS General Litigation Division
GPO	Government Printing Office
GSA	General Services Administration
H	House of Representatives
H.R.	House of Representatives
HRG	Hearing
IA	IRS Income Tax and Accounting Division
ICM	IRS Compliance Officer Memorandum
IIL	IRS Information Letter
IL	IRS International Division
ILM	IRS Legal Memoranda
ILP	Index to Legal Periodicals
INTL	IRS International Division
Int'l	International
IR	Information Release

IRB	Internal Revenue Bulletin
IRC	Internal Revenue Code
IRM	Internal Revenue Manual
IR-Mim.	Published Internal Revenue Mimeograph
IRS	Internal Revenue Service
ISP	Industry Specialization Program
I.T.	Income Tax Unit or Division
ITA	IRS Technical Assistance
ITC	International Tax Counsel
JEC	Joint Economic Committee
JCT	Joint Committee on Taxation
Jt.	Joint
KC	KeyCite
L.	Law; Legal; Letter
L. Ed.	United States Supreme Court Reports, Lawyers' Edition
LGM	Litigation Guideline Memorandum
L.M.	Legal Memorandum
LMSB	IRS Large & Mid-Size Business Operating Division
L.O.	Solicitor's Law Opinion
LR; L & R	IRS Legislation and Regulations Division
LRI	Legal Resource Index
LTR	Private Letter Ruling
Ltr. Rul.	Private Letter Ruling
M.A.	Miscellaneous Announcements
Mem.	Memorandum
Memo.	Memorandum
Mim.	Mimeographed Letter; Mimeograph
MS.	Miscellaneous Unit or Division or Branch
MSSP	Market Segment Specialization Paper
M.S.U.	Market Segment Understanding
M.T.	Miscellaneous Division or Branch
NA	Nonacquiescence
NARA	National Archives and Records Administration
Nonacq.	Nonacquiescence
NPRM	Notice of Proposed Rulemaking
NSAR	Non Docketed Service Advice Review
O.	Solicitor's Law Opinion
O.D.	Office Decision

OECD	Organisation for Economic Co-operation and Development
Off. Mem.	Office Memorandum
OMB	Office of Management and Budget
Op.	Opinion
Op. A.G.	Opinion of Attorney General
OTA	Treasury Department Office of Tax Analysis
OTP	Treasury Department Office of Tax Policy
Para.	Paragraph
PDF	Portable Document Format
PH; P-H	Prentice-Hall
PLR	Private Letter Ruling
Priv. Ltr. Rul.	Private Letter Ruling
Prop.	Proposed
PS	IRS Passthroughs and Special Industries Division
P.T.	Processing Tax Decision or Division
Pt.	Part
P.T.E.	Prohibited Transaction Exemption
PTO	United States Patent and Trade Office
Pub.	Public; Published
Rec.	Record
Reg.	Register; Registration; Regular; Regulation
Rep.	Report; Reports; Representatives; Reporter
Res.	Resolution
Rev. Proc.	Revenue Procedure
Rev. Rul.	Revenue Ruling
RIA	Research Institute of America
RIN	Regulation Identifier Number
RISC	Regulatory Information Service Center
RP	Revenue Procedure
RR	Revenue Ruling
S.	Senate; Solicitor's Memorandum
SAM	Strategic Advice Memorandum
SB/SE	IRS Small Business/Self-Employed Operating Division
SCA	Service Center Advice
S. Ct.	Supreme Court
Sec.	Section
Sess.	Session
SFTR	Standard Federal Tax Reporter
Sil.	Silver Tax Division
S.M.	Solicitor's Memorandum

Sol. Op.	Solicitor's Opinion
S.P.R.	Statement of Procedural Rules
S.R.	Solicitor's Recommendation
S.S.T.	Social Security Tax and Carriers' Tax; Social Security Tax; Taxes on Employment by Other than Carriers
S.T.	Sales Tax Unit or Division or Branch
Stat.	United States Statutes at Large
T.	Temporary; Tobacco Division; Treaty
TAM	Technical Advice Memorandum
T.B.M.	Advisory Tax Board Memorandum
T.B.R.	Advisory Tax Board Recommendation
T.C.	Tax Court Reports
TCM	Tax Court Memorandum Opinion
TC Memo	Tax Court Memorandum Opinion
T. Ct.	Tax Court
T.D.	Treasury Decision
TEAM	Technical Expedited Advice Memorandum
TECH	Assistant Commissioner, Technical
Tech. Adv. Mem.	Technical Advice Memorandum
Tech. Info. Rel.	Technical Information Release
Tech. Mem.	Technical Memorandum
TE/GE	IRS Tax Exempt/Government Entities Operating Division
Temp.	Temporary
T.I.A.S.	Treaties and International Acts Series
TIGTA	Treasury Inspector General for Tax Administration
T.I.R.	Technical Information Release
TLB	Tax Litigation Bulletin
TLC	Tax Legislative Counsel
TM	Technical Memorandum
Tob.	Tobacco Branch
TRAC	Tip Reporting Alternative Commitment
Treas.	Treasury Department
Treas. Dep't Order	Treasury Department Order
Treas. Reg.	Treasury Regulation
T.S.	Treaty Series
UIL	Uniform Issue List
UNTS	United Nations Treaty Series
U.S.	United States Reports
U.S.C.	United States Code
U.S.C.A.	United States Code Annotated

USCCAN	United States Code Congressional & Administrative News
U.S.C.S.	United States Code Service
USPTO	United States Patent and Trade Office
U.S.T.	United States Treaties and Other International Agreements
U.S. Tax Cas.	U.S. Tax Cases
USTC	U.S. Tax Cases
USTR	United States Tax Reporter
UTC	U.S. Tax Cases
WG & L	Warren Gorham & Lamont
W & I	IRS Wage and Investment Operating Division
WL	Westlaw
WTO	World Trade Organization

APPENDIX B. ALTERNATE CITATION FORMS

This appendix does not cover all possible citation forms. It reflects formats I found in citation manuals and in several tax-oriented periodicals. Chapter 10 provides several abbreviation formats for IRS items.

1. Sources Used
ALWD Citation Manual (3d ed. 2006)
The Bluebook: A Uniform System of Citation (18th ed. 2005)
TaxCite (1995 edition)
Various periodical articles

2. Citations for Internal Revenue Code section 61
I.R.C. § 61 (year of U.S.C.)
I.R.C. § 61
Section 61
Code Sec. 61

3. Citations for Treasury Regulation section 1.61-1
Treas. Reg. § 1.61-1 (promulgation/amendment year)
Reg. § 1.61-1 (promulgation/amendment year)
Reg. § 1.61-1
Reg. §1.61-1
Reg. section 1.61-1
Teas. reg. section 1.61-1
Treasury reg. section 1.61-1
Reg. 1.61-1

4. Citations for Temporary Treasury Regulation section 1.71-1T
Temp. Treas. Reg. § 1.71-1T (promulgation/amendment year)
Temp. Reg. § 1.71-1T (promulgation/amendment year)
Temp. Reg. § 1.71-1T
Temporary Reg. §1.71-1T
Treas. reg. section 1.71-1T
Temp. Reg. 1.71-1T

5. Citations for Cumulative Bulletin
C.B.
CB

6. Citations for Private Letter Ruling 199929039
Priv. Ltr. Rul. 1999-29-039 (Apr. 12, 1999)
P.L.R. 1999-29-039 (Apr. 12, 1999)
LTR 199929039 (Apr. 12, 1999)
Ltr. Rul. 199929039
PLR 199929039

APPENDIX C. POTENTIAL RESEARCH ERRORS

Statements in this section reflect comments made elsewhere in this text.

Don't assume that a library lacks a source because it is not available in its general print collection or online. Check the CD/DVD, microform, and government documents collections.

Check a service's coverage dates before you begin your research. An electronic service may omit a source's initial years. A print service may not have been updated recently enough to catch a very recent item.

Before using a service, determine how it treats revoked items. Some services delete these items; others include them but indicate they have been revoked.

If you check research results in a second publication, try to select a source from a different publishing group. Although corporate parents offer several imprints (Appendix E), there is no guarantee they will always use separate editors.

If you find a Code section on point, don't forget to check effective dates and special rules that may not be codified.

Never assume a definition in one section of the Code or regulations applies to all other sections.

Don't ignore potentially related Code provisions merely because they don't refer to each other.

Don't confuse an act section number with a Code section number.

Don't assume every relevant provision is actually codified.

Don't assume section numbers in a bill remain unchanged through the enactment process.

Don't confuse enactment date, effective date, and sunset date for statutes (or the comparable date limitations for treaties and regulations).

If you use cross-reference tables to trace a statute's history, remember that these tables may not reflect changes in a section's numbering.

Don't forget to compare the issue date of regulations and the decision date for cases against the revision date for relevant statutory amendments. Otherwise you risk citing sources whose authority has been weakened or overruled altogether. Online citators may indicate this information.

Remember to use the designation required by the source you are searching. For example, don't insert hyphens in IRS documents when searching online unless the service allows hyphens; remember that Tax Analysts frequently gives its own names to chief counsel advice documents.

Don't forget to check for pending items (legislation, regulations, appeals from judicial decisions) that may be relevant to your project.

Don't overestimate the degree of deference a court will accord legislative history and Treasury or IRS documents.

Don't assume the government conceded an issue merely because it didn't appeal after losing a case. Check to see if there is an AOD or other announcement regarding the case.

If you find a notice of acquiescence or nonacquiescence, check to make sure the IRS didn't reverse itself in a later AOD or Internal Revenue Bulletin.

When searching for cases using the taxpayer's name, remember that early cases are not captioned Taxpayer v. Commissioner or Taxpayer v. United States. Eisner and Helvering are government officials, not taxpayers. Likewise, remember that different services use different caption formats for bankruptcy cases.

Remember that U.S.T.C. is an abbreviation for U.S. Tax Cases; that case reporter service does not include United States Tax Court cases.

Don't confuse page and paragraph numbers. Make sure you know if a service cross-references by page, by paragraph, or by section number. Make sure you know whether new material is located in the same volume or a different volume (and where in the relevant volume it appears). Although online services avoid this problem, you must still use the appropriate format in any memorandum or brief you prepare.

Don't rely on a service's editor for a holding. Read the document yourself.

Remember that Index to Legal Periodicals only recently began indexing short articles.

When using electronic materials (CD/DVD or online), make sure you understand the particular service's Boolean search rules and rules for limiting searches to a particular range of dates. From date 1 to date 2 is not the same as after date 1 and before date 2.

Make sure that s means sentence (and p means paragraph) in an electronic service. Some services define sentence and paragraph by a maximum number of words rather than by grammatical rules.

If a URL no longer yields the desired website, assume the site changed its URL but still exists. Try using your service provider's search function (or a search engine) to search for the new URL.

Appendix D. Bibliography

Chapter 1. Overview

Roy M. Mersky & Donald J. Dunn, Fundamentals of Legal Research (9th ed. 2007).

ALWD Citation Manual: A Professional System of Citation (3d ed. 2006).

The Bluebook: A Uniform System of Citation (18th ed. 2005).

Gail Levin Richmond, *Federal Tax Locator: Basic Tax Library*, Community Tax L. Rep., Fall/Winter 2001, at 11.

Robert C. Berring, *Legal Information and the Search for Cognitive Authority*, 88 Cal. L. Rev. 1673 (2000).

Katherine T. Pratt, *Federal Tax Sources Recommended for Law School Libraries*, 87 Law Libr. J. 387 (1995).

TaxCite: A Federal Tax Citation and Reference Manual (1995).

Carol A. Roehrenbeck & Gail Levin Richmond, *Three Researchers in Search of an Alcove: A Play in Six Acts*, 84 Law Libr. J. 13 (1992).

Louis F. Lobenhofer, *Tax Law Libraries for Small and Medium-Sized Firms*, Prac. Tax Law., Fall 1988, at 17, and Winter 1989, at 31.

Gail Levin Richmond, *Research Tools for Federal Taxation*, 2 Legal Reference Services Q., Spring 1982, at 25.

Chapter 2. Sources of Law

Bernard Wolfman, James P. Holden, and Kenneth L. Harris, Standards of Tax Practice (6th ed. 2004).

Franklin L. Green, *Exercising Judgment in the Wonderland Gymnasium*, Tax Notes, Mar. 19, 2001, at 1691.

Kip Dellinger, *The Substantial Understatement, Negligence and Tax-*

Return Preparers' Penalties—An Overview, TAXES, Nov. 1999, at 41.

Office of Tax Policy, Department of the Treasury, REPORT TO THE CONGRESS ON PENALTY AND INTEREST PROVISIONS OF THE INTERNAL REVENUE CODE (1999).

Shop Talk, *IRS FSA Gives Guidance on Substantial Authority in Penalty Situation*, 91 J. TAX'N 61 (1999).

Staff of the Joint Committee on Taxation, STUDY OF PRESENT-LAW PENALTY AND INTEREST PROVISIONS AS REQUIRED BY SECTION 3801 OF THE INTERNAL REVENUE SERVICE RESTRUCTURING AND REFORM ACT OF 1998 (INCLUDING PROVISIONS RELATING TO CORPORATE TAX SHELTERS), JCS 3-99 (106th Cong., 1st Sess.) (Jt. Comm. Print 1999).

George R. Goodman, *Tax Return Compliance*, TAX NOTES, Sept. 1, 1997, at 1201.

Shop Talk, *Courts Disagree on Substantial Authority*, 82 J. TAX'N 380 (1995).

CHAPTER 3. RESEARCH PROCESS

Jasper L. Cummings, Jr., *Legal Research in Federal Taxation*, TAX NOTES, Oct. 17, 2005, at 335.

Michelle M. Wu, *Why Print and Electronic Resources Are Essential to the Academic Law Library*, 97 LAW LIBR. J. 233 (2005).

John A. Barrick, *The Effect of Code Section Knowledge on Tax Research Performance*, J. AM. TAX. ASS'N, Fall 2001, at 20.

Gitelle Seer, *10 Things You Hate to Hear: Tips from Your Librarian*, LAW PRAC. Q., Aug. 2001, at 20.

CHAPTER 5. CONSTITUTION

Michael W. Evans, *'A Source of Frequent and Obstinate Altercations': The History and Application of the Origination Clause*, TAX NOTES, Nov. 29, 2004, at 1215.

Calvin H. Johnson, *Purging Out Pollock: The Constitutionality of Federal Wealth or Sales Taxes*, TAX NOTES, Dec. 30, 2002, at 1723.

Erik M. Jensen, *The Taxing Power, The Sixteenth Amendment, and the Meaning of Incomes*, TAX NOTES, Oct. 7, 2002, at 99.

Bruce Ackerman, *Taxation and the Constitution*, 99 COLUM. L. REV. 1 (1999).

Boris I. Bittker & Lawrence Lokken, FEDERAL TAXATION OF INCOME, ESTATES AND GIFTS ch. 1 (3d ed. 1999 & Cum. Supp.).

Calvin H. Johnson, *The Constitutional Meaning of 'Apportionment of Direct Taxes,'* TAX NOTES, Aug. 3, 1998, at 591.

Erik M. Jensen, *The Apportionment of "Direct Taxes": Are Consumption Taxes Constitutional?*, 97 COLUM. L. REV. 2334 (1997).

John O. McGinnis & Michael B. Rappaport, *The Rights of Legislators and the Wrongs of Interpretation: A Further Defense of the Constitutionality of Legislative Supermajority Rules*, 47 DUKE L.J. 327 (1997).

Richard Belas, *The Post-Carlton World: Just When Is a Retroactive Tax Unconstitutional?*, TAX NOTES, Oct. 30, 1995, at 633.

CHAPTER 6. STATUTES

Christopher H. Hanna, *The Magic in the Tax Legislative Process*, 59 SMU L. REV. 649 (2006).

William D. Popkin, STATUTES IN COURT: THE HISTORY AND THEORY OF STATUTORY INTERPRETATION (1999).

John F. Coverdale, *Text as Limit: A Plea for a Decent Respect for the Tax Code*, 71 TUL. L. REV. 1501 (1997).

Edward A. Zelinsky, *Text, Purpose, Capacity and* Albertson's*: A Response to Professor Geier*, 2 FLA. TAX REV. 717 (1996).

Jasper L. Cummings, Jr., *Statutory Interpretation and* Albertson's, TAX NOTES, Jan. 23, 1995, at 559.

Myron Grauer, *A Case for Congressional Facilitation of a Collaborative Model of Statutory Interpretation in the Tax Area: Lessons to be Learned from the* Corn Products *and* Arkansas Best *Cases and the Historical Development of the Statutory Definition of "Capital Asset(s),"* 84 KY. L.J. 1 (1995).

Deborah A. Geier, *Commentary: Textualism and Tax Cases*, 66 TEMP. L. REV. 445 (1993).

CHAPTER 7. LEGISLATIVE HISTORIES

See also separate section on deference following Chapter 11.

Tax History Project (http://www.taxhistory.org) (Tax Analysts website for historical research, including such documents as policy papers from presidential libraries, posters, presidential tax returns, The Federalist Papers, and a "Tax History Museum").

Michael Livingston, *What's Blue and White and Not Quite As Good As a Committee Report: General Explanations and the Role of "Subsequent" Tax Legislative History*, 11 AM J. TAX POL'Y 91 (1994).

CHAPTER 8. TREATIES

William P. Streng, *U.S. Tax Treaties: Trends, Issues, & Policies in 2006 and Beyond*, 59 SMU L. REV. 853 (2006)

Anthony C. Infanti, *The Proposed Domestic Reverse Hybrid Entity Regulations: Can the Treasury Department Override Treaties?*, 30 TAX MGMT. INT'L J. 307 (2001).

John A. Townsend, *Tax Treaty Interpretation*, 55 TAX LAW. 221 (2001).

John F. Avery Jones, *The David R. Tillinghast Lecture: Are Tax Treaties Necessary?*, 53 TAX L. REV. 1 (1999).

Philip F. Postlewaite & David S. Makarski, *The A.L.I. Tax Treaty Study—A Critique and a Proposal*, 49 TAX LAW. 731 (1999).

Ernest R. Larkins, *U.S. Income Tax Treaties in Research and Planning: A Primer*, 18 VA. TAX REV. 133 (1998).

Robert Thornton Smith, *Tax Treaty Interpretation by the Judiciary*, 49 TAX LAW. 845 (1996).

CHAPTER 9. REGULATIONS

See also separate section on deference following Chapter 11.

Philip Gall, *Phantom Regulations: The Curse of Spurned Delegation*, 56 TAX LAW. 413 (2003).

Naftali Z. Dembitzer, *Beyond the IRS Restructuring and Reform Act of 1998: Perceived Abuses of the Treasury Department's Rulemaking Authority*, 52 TAX LAW. 501 (1999).

CHAPTER 10. INTERNAL REVENUE SERVICE DOCUMENTS

See also separate section on deference following Chapter 11.

Marion Marshall, Sheryl Stratton, and Christopher Bergin, *The Changing Landscape of IRS Guidance: A Downward Slope*, TAX NOTES, Jan. 29, 2001, at 673.

Inventory of IRS Guidance Documents—A Draft, TAX NOTES, July 17, 2000, at 305.

CHAPTER 11. JUDICIAL

See also separate section on deference following Chapter 11.

Daniel M. Schneider, *Assessing and Predicting Who Wins Federal Tax Trial Decisions*, 37 WAKE FOREST L. REV. 473 (2002).

Mark P. Altieri, Jerome E. Apple, Penny Marquette & Charles K. Moore, *Political Affiliation of Appointing President and Outcome of Tax Court Cases*, 84 JUDICATURE 310 (May/June 2001).

Cornish F. Hitchcock, *Public Access to Special Trial Judge Reports*, TAX NOTES, Oct. 15, 2001, at 403.

Robert A. Mead, *"Unpublished" Opinions as the Bulk of the Iceberg: Publication Patterns in the Eighth and Tenth Circuit United States Courts of Appeals*, 93 LAW LIBR. J. 589 (2001).

Daniel M. Schneider, *Empirical Research on Judicial Reasoning: Statutory Interpretation in Federal Tax Cases*, 31 N.M. L. REV. 325 (2001).

Kirk J. Stark, *The Unfulfilled Tax Legacy of Justice Robert H. Jackson*, 54 TAX L. REV. 171 (2001).

Paul E. Treusch, *What to Consider in Choosing a Forum to Resolve an Ordinary Tax Dispute*, 55 TAX LAW. 83 (2001).

James Edward Maule, *Instant Replay, Weak Teams, and Disputed Calls: An Empirical Study of Alleged Tax Court Bias*, 66 TENN. L. REV. 351 (1999).

Mark F. Sommer & Anne D. Waters, *Tax Court Memorandum Opinions—What Are They Worth?*, TAX NOTES, July 20, 1998, at 384.

CHAPTERS 7-11. DEFERENCE

Irving Salem, *Supreme Court Should Clarify Its Deference Standard*, TAX NOTES, Sept. 18, 2006, at 1063.

Andre L. Smith, *Deferential Review of Tax Court Decisions of Law: Promoting Expertise, Uniformity, and Impartiality*, 58 TAX LAW. 361 (2005).

Gregg D. Polsky, *Can Treasury Overrule the Supreme Court?*, 84 B.U. L. REV. 185 (2004).

Peter A. Lowy & Juan F. Vasquez, Jr., *How Revenue Rulings Are Made and the Implications of That Process for Judicial Deference*, J. TAX'N, Oct. 2004, at 230.

ABA Section of Taxation, *Report of the Task Force on Deference*, TAX NOTES, Sept. 13, 2004, at 1231 (reprinted from 57 TAX LAW. 717 (2004)).

Mitchell M. Gans, *Deference and the End of Tax Practice*, 36 REAL PROP., PROB. & TR. J. 731 (2002).

Edward J. Schnee & W. Eugene Seago, *Deference Issues in the Tax Law:* Mead *Clarifies the* Chevron *Rule—Or Does It?*, 96 J. TAX'N 366 (2002).

David F. Shores, *Deferential Review of Tax Court Decisions: Taking Institutional Choice Seriously*, 55 TAX LAW. 667 (2002).

Irving Salem & Richard Bress, *Agency Deference Under the Judicial Microscope of the Supreme Court*, TAX NOTES, Sept. 4, 2000, at 1257.

David F. Shores, *Rethinking Deferential Review of Tax Court Decisions*, 53 TAX LAW. 35 (1999).

Benjamin J. Cohen & Catherine A. Harrington, *Is the Internal Revenue Service Bound by Its Own Regulations and Rulings?*, 51 TAX LAW. 675

(1998).

Steve R. Johnson, *The Phoenix and the Perils of the Second Best: Why Heightened Appellate Deference to Tax Court Decisions Is Undesirable*, 77 OR. L. REV. 235 (1998).

David A. Brennen, *Treasury Regulations and Judicial Deference in the Post*-Chevron *Era*, 13 GA. ST. U. L. REV. 387 (1997).

Ellen P. Aprill, *Muffled* Chevron: *Judicial Review of Tax Regulations*, 3 FLA. TAX REV. 51 (1996).

Paul L. Caron, *Tax Myopia Meets Tax Hyperopia: The Unproven Case of Increased Judicial Deference to Revenue Rulings*, 57 OHIO ST. L.J. 637 (1996).

Beverly I. Moran & Daniel M. Schneider, *The Elephant and the Four Blind Men: The Burger Court and Its Federal Tax Decisions*, 39 HOW. L.J. 841 (1996).

John F. Coverdale, *Court Review of Tax Regulations and Revenue Rulings in the Chevron Era*, 64 GEO. WASH. L. REV. 35 (1995).

Linda Galler, *Judicial Deference to Revenue Rulings: Reconciling Divergent Standards*, 56 OHIO ST. L.J. 1037 (1995).

Paul L. Caron, *Tax Myopia, or Mamas Don't Let Your Babies Grow Up to be Tax Lawyers*, 13 VA. TAX REV. 517 (1994).

CHAPTER 14. LEGAL PERIODICALS AND NONGOVERNMENTAL REPORTS

Mary Rumsey, *Runaway Train: Problems of Permanence, Accessibility, and Stability in the Use of Web Sources in Law Review Citations*, 94 LAW LIBR. J. 27 (2002).

Richard A. Danner, *Electronic Publication of Legal Scholarship: New Issues and New Models*, 52 J. LEGAL EDUC. 347 (2002).

William J. Turnier, *Tax (and Lots of Other) Scholars Need Not Apply: The Changing Venue for Scholarship*, 50 J. LEGAL EDUC. 189 (2000).

CHAPTER 20. ONLINE LEGAL RESEARCH

Thomas R. Keefe, *The Invisible Web: What You Can't See Might Hurt You*, RES. ADVISOR, May 2002, at 1.

Mary Rumsey, *Runaway Train: Problems of Permanence, Accessibility, and Stability in the Use of Web Sources in Law Review Citations*, 94 LAW LIBR. J. 27 (2002).

Diana Botluk, *Search Engines Comparison 2001*, at http://www.llrx.com/features/engine2001.htm (Aug. 1, 2001).

Gary W. White, *Internet Resources for Taxation: A Selective, Annotated Guide*, LEGAL REFERENCE SERVICES Q., vol. 18(4), at 49 (2001).

Lisa Smith-Butler, *Cost Effective Legal Research*, LEGAL REFERENCE SERVICES Q., vol. 18(2), at 61 (2000).

APPENDIX E. COMMONLY OWNED PUBLISHERS

Aspen	WoltersKluwer
Bureau of National Affairs	Bureau of National Affairs
Butterworths	Reed Elsevier
Clark Boardman Callahan	Thomson
Commerce Clearing House	WoltersKluwer
Congressional Information Service	Reed Elsevier
Dialog	Thomson
FindLaw	Thomson
Foundation Press	Thomson
Gale Group	Thomson
Hein	William S. Hein & Co., Inc.
Kleinrock	WoltersKluwer
Kluwer	WoltersKluwer
Lawyers Cooperative	Thomson
Lexis Publishing	Reed Elsevier
LexisNexis	Reed Elsevier
Little, Brown	[291]
Loislaw	WoltersKluwer
Matthew Bender	Reed Elsevier
Michie	Reed Elsevier
Oceana	Oceana
Prentice-Hall	[292]
Research Institute of America	Thomson
Rothman	William S. Hein & Co., Inc.
Shepard's	Reed Elsevier
Tax Analysts	Tax Analysts
Tax Management	Bureau of National Affairs
Warren Gorham & Lamont	Thomson
West Group	Thomson
Westlaw	Thomson

→The information above reflects ownership groups in November 2006.

---

[291] Aspen purchased several publications that formerly appeared under the Little, Brown imprint.

[292] Research Institute of America and Warren Gorham & Lamont purchased several publications that formerly appeared under the Prentice-Hall imprint.

INDEX (REFERENCES TO PAGE NUMBERS)